Taking Juvenile Justice Seriously

CHRISTOPHER J. SULLIVAN

Taking Juvenile Justice Seriously

Developmental Insights and System Challenges

TEMPLE UNIVERSITY PRESS
Philadelphia • Rome • Tokyo

TEMPLE UNIVERSITY PRESS
Philadelphia, Pennsylvania 19122
tupress.temple.edu

Library of Congress Cataloging-in-Publication Data

Names: Sullivan, Christopher J., author.
Title: Taking juvenile justice seriously : developmental insights and system challenges /
    Christopher J. Sullivan.
Description: Philadelphia : Temple University Press, 2019. | Includes bibliographical
    references and index. |
Identifiers: LCCN 2019003671 (print) | LCCN 2019003976 (ebook) | ISBN 9781439915806
    (E-book) | ISBN 9781439915783 (cloth : alk. paper) | ISBN 9781439915790
    (pbk. : alk. paper)
Subjects: LCSH: Juvenile justice, Administration of—United States. | Juvenile
    delinquency—United States.
Classification: LCC KF9779 (ebook) | LCC KF9779 .S85 2019 (print) |
    DDC 364.360973—dc23
LC record available at https://lccn.loc.gov/2019003671

Printed in the United States of America

9 8 7 6 5 4 3 2 1

Contents

Preface

Youth who come into contact with the juvenile justice system demand a great deal of concern because of the circumstances and needs that brought them there as well as their later pathways predicted by that contact. The increased formalization of handling misbehavior means that a sizable proportion of youths will have an encounter with the juvenile justice system at some point as they grow up. Experts and advocates have discussed juvenile justice reform extensively in the first two decades of the 2000s. Much of this discussion implicitly or explicitly draws on the literature about youth and adolescent development. Still, advocates have focused comparatively less attention on the practicalities involved in taking this research and translating it into the structure, process, and decisions of juvenile justice systems. In fact, how these pieces fit together to define the future of juvenile justice is not necessarily clear. This book is an attempt to address that gap by identifying the relevant ideas, integrating and synthesizing pertinent research, and offering suggestions about how to translate those ideas and research into policy and practice. This book critically and comprehensively looks at prospects for their implementation in the contemporary juvenile justice system.

There are many useful solutions to pursue, and insights from corners of the world of research, practice, and general thought about youth and adolescent development can contribute to the discussion. At the same time, rather than have this conversation primarily at two poles, with youths as pure innocents at one end and "super predators" at the other, the book acknowledges the full range of cases in juvenile justice systems and presents ways of thinking and reacting to those cases in a developmentally informed fashion.

Acknowledgments

Although this is a single-authored work, numerous people contributed to its development in a variety of ways. I gratefully acknowledge that help and support.

I appreciate Ryan Mulligan and Aaron Javsicas's work in moving the book through the publication process at Temple University Press. Ryan was instrumental in sharpening important aspects of the book and helping me better articulate its key themes. He also commissioned reviews that helped strengthen the book; I am appreciative to those anonymous reviewers. The marketing, artwork, and production editing staff at Temple were extremely helpful in polishing the text and making the final product look as good as possible.

The content of the book is in part the by-product of several sponsored research studies for which I have been lead investigator over the last twelve years. I am grateful to the agencies that funded that work, including the Office of Juvenile Justice and Delinquency Prevention, the National Institute of Justice, and the Ohio Department of Youth Services. I also appreciate the insight of staff at those organizations, including Benjamin Adams, Jennifer Tyson, Kristi Oden, Bruce Sowards, Jeff Spears, and Ryan Gies, who have made formal and informal comments that continue to shape my thoughts about how research intersects (or does not intersect) with juvenile justice policy and practice.

University of Cincinnati research staff and I have spent a considerable amount of time interacting with juvenile and criminal justice agencies in the field. I am grateful to all the agency administrators and staff who helped us obtain data and/or lent their time and insight as research participants during the course of our studies. At times in the book, when assessing research evidence and its implementation in the field, I try to channel the perspective of the healthy skeptic working in a juvenile justice agency. I am thankful for the perspectives and candor of those participants who do that work.

In addition, I am grateful for the many University of Cincinnati graduate students and research staff who contributed to those studies by collecting, managing, and analyzing data. I also appreciate the formal and informal discussions that we had about these topics during the course of our studies. They offer invaluable input into the various points made in this book.

I am grateful for my colleagues and students who have also contributed to this book in a variety of ways. With my colleagues at the University of Cincinnati and elsewhere, that contribution often came from informal conversations about the topics covered here. I am very thankful to work in an environment where those discussions are commonplace and constructive but also challenging. Much of the formal content for this book was generated and refined during the course of the graduate seminars in life-course criminology and juvenile justice that I have led since 2010. I appreciate the discussions that I have had with graduate students in those courses, which helped in the evolution of many of the points at the core of the book.

I am extremely grateful to Brandon Welsh, of Northeastern University, who gave me especially helpful comments on an early draft of the book proposal and offered constructive support throughout the writing process.

Early writing on this book was completed while I was a visiting scholar in the School of Criminology and Criminal Justice at Griffith University in Brisbane, Australia. I am grateful to Tara McGee, Paul Mazerolle, and Anna Stewart, who helped facilitate my visit there in the spring of 2016.

Finally, Carrie Coen Sullivan's contributions, through her substantive critiques, careful reading and editing, and general encouragement over a long writing and rewriting process, have been most valuable. I certainly could not have completed this (or any other) project without her constant feedback and support.

Taking Juvenile Justice Seriously

PART I

Delinquency, Juvenile Justice, and Youth Development

Introduction

Juvenile Justice and Twenty-First-Century Calls for Reform

The juvenile court handles an expansive caseload of offense types, degrees of seriousness, situational circumstances, youth risk profiles, and needs and barriers to effective intervention. This variability defines the space in which juvenile justice must identify appropriate treatment and sanction options to meet its long-held goals of promoting change for youths and preventing harm to both youths and their communities.

Case hearings often tell the story of this variability, providing insight about the nature of the cases and youths who encounter the juvenile justice system, their interaction with its personnel, and the prescriptive orders meant to stop further delinquency and improve their prospects for the future. A few dockets from one large- and one medium-sized juvenile court reflect the wide span of cases.[1] Two cases called in disposition hearings observed in one of these courts illustrate this point. The first involved a truancy case, which is somewhat anomalous for this court given its policy of handling minor offenses more informally. Only a few other people were in the court at that point besides the youth, his mother, a probation officer supervising the case, and the judge. The probation officer assigned to the case described the charge against the youth, the continued nature of his truancy, and his school performance in detail before making a recommendation. The judge talked directly with the youth, explaining the charges and court process and repeatedly inquiring whether he understood the details of the proceeding. He also asked the youth's mother for her input and explanation of the situation before eventually asking the youth what should or could be done about his truancy. Ultimately, the case was disposed of informally with the youth being ordered to go to school or else face more serious sanctions, a directive also aimed at ensuring that his mother exerted greater control in pushing his school attendance.

The second case on this docket shifted the tone because it involved a concealed weapons charge for a youth with a prior history of delinquency. A parent and a court-appointed public defender accompanied him. The probation officer first described the offense and the accused youth before suggesting a resolution: continued custody, a drug and alcohol treatment program, and eventual release to his mother with electronic monitoring. The defense attorney then gave an explanation on behalf of the youth, touching on him as an individual and the offense of which he was accused. As the hearing progressed, the judge sought input from probation, the mother, lawyer, and the youth. The judge then contemplated aloud about some potential placement options on the basis of concerns about the youth's living situation before deciding to have probation investigate whether the home of a family friend might be a good eventual point of release for the youth. The judge ordered a continuance during which the probation officer gathered information and the youth was held in the detention center.

These two cases represent different poles of the juvenile court process in terms of seriousness of the offenses and the youths' prior records, and the rest of the cases on the judges' and court magistrates' dockets demonstrate the variation in between. The circumstances of the delinquent events and case histories illustrate that youths come before the juvenile court for different types of offenses; with more or less extensive prior histories; with individual risks, strengths, and needs; and with seemingly different prospects for the future.

A smaller court in the same state had other layers of variability of juvenile delinquency cases while also reinforcing the array of tasks and challenges faced by the juvenile justice system. Its morning docket consisted of sixteen cases. Several of these were for misdemeanors involving property, drugs, and violent offenses, and one case was a felony drug possession. The majority of the session involved continuing review of cases already under court supervision, but an early adjudication hearing for a youth who was in court for violation of prior court orders illustrates the complexity of such cases and the difficulty of finding the right disposition and placement. The youth was already in detention pending the hearing. The public defender gave the judge a written statement from the youth in which she admitted to the offense. The prosecutor had agreed to dismiss the violation of supervision conditions if she did so. The judge read rights to the accused juvenile and made her aware of the possible consequences of a delinquency adjudication, such as remand to a residential facility. The violation was then dismissed, but a psychological evaluation was to be conducted before the disposition and weighed alongside previous such evaluations. The public defender asked if the youth could stay with her father for a trial period before the final disposition. The judge continued the case and ordered that she remain in detention until a new hearing in ten days. During that time, child services staff would evaluate whether placement with her father was appropriate and potentially beneficial. Other cases on the docket varied in type, seriousness, and situational circumstances. The observation in this court, such as for the hearings just considered, demonstrates the different responses of the juvenile justice system in the immediate juvenile court hearing and over time. Specifically, judges' and magistrates' decision making includes a range of dispositions that would ultimately draw in other parts of the juvenile justice system and community agencies: electronic monitoring, substance use treatment, detention, and community service.

These brief case summaries from observation of juvenile courts illustrate the high degree of variation in youth risk and needs, patterns of delinquency, system responses, and resources employed that the system regularly encounters. Many other cases in these counties had already been diverted from the formal court process through dismissal or informal disposition, reflecting even more variation than directly described here. Notably, these cases also involved possible developmental risk factors (e.g., school engagement, family management), patterns of delinquency over time, and juvenile justice decisions that might affect later developmental pathways (e.g., wait-and-see approach on truancy, time in detention for a weapons charge). Through such crucial considerations by the court, the juvenile justice process is intrinsically developmental in its information gathering, decision making, and potential impact. The degree of difference in these cases of delinquency impels the juvenile court to react to a wide range of youth and adolescent problems and consider the possible developmental consequences to their reaction, which also have consequences for their family and community.

This book systematically analyzes key facets of juvenile justice populations, parsing cases like these (and others) to better understand core developmental influences on delinquency, including those aspects of the life course affected by juvenile justice contact. In parallel, the book takes a comprehensive look at the juvenile justice system's operations and its multifaceted mission of delivering both treatment and sanctions to a population of youths. Analysis of the juvenile justice system has frequently looked at similar questions about what works to promote change without doing harm, but contemporary juvenile justice has unique features that factor into reform efforts. Pulling these threads together, I consider the implications for juvenile justice responses to delinquent youths, focusing specifically on twenty-first-century calls for a more developmental approach, without avoiding the inevitable challenges of altering routine practice and implementing new ideas.

The Intervention Imperative in Juvenile Justice

An overview of official delinquency trends by Howard Snyder (2012) found that the annual rate of delinquency cases disposed by juvenile courts increased from the mid-1980s to the mid-1990s. Using Federal Bureau of Investigation Uniform Crime Report data, Charles Puzzanchera (2014) reported that, across the United States, juvenile arrests were 37 percent lower in 2003 than in 2012; in fact, 2003 saw juvenile violent crime arrests at their lowest rates since 1980, but numbers were fairly low in the 2010s as well. With this effective reduction in youth referrals, juvenile court caseloads have diminished, but it is not a one-to-one match. Looking back at Snyder's analysis, while the juvenile arrest rate in 2005 was 10 percent of its 1985 level, the juvenile court case rate in 2005 was 22 percent of its 1985 level (Snyder 2012). Likewise, Nina Hyland (2018) found that juvenile court caseloads declined from their peak of about 1.9 million in 1997 to under 1 million (975,000) in 2014 for the first time in forty years. Controlling for arrests, 2010s referral levels are still higher than in the 1960s (more than 125 percent in 2012) (Hockenberry and Puzzanchera 2014), outpacing the estimated 17 percent increase in the population subject to juvenile justice jurisdiction during that period.[2] Even as juvenile arrest rates have declined over the last twenty-five years, formal processing of youths in the juvenile justice system has not changed very much and may have increased slightly, which means that the juvenile justice system casts a wide net. Those increases in formally processed youths likewise expand the variation in youths and case types that must be resolved.

Juvenile court cases can be categorized in several ways, starting with the seriousness and situational circumstances of an offense, such as the number of youths involved, use of drugs or alcohol, and the presence or type of victim. Policy and practice also must factor in the characteristics of individual youths who reach the court. A delinquent youth may be a first-time offender or have an extensive record and may have risk factors across multiple domains. His or her needs might range from basics like food and clothing to intensive treatment and medication for mental illness. Youths also differ in their affect during the juvenile justice process, which can influence perceptions about their attitudes or character (Emerson 1969). While considerations of individuals' circumstances and reasons for behavior are not entirely foreign in adult courts, juvenile justice decision making is especially dependent on court actors' perceptions of whether an otherwise good kid was unduly affected by his or her environment and swept up in the moment or is a contemptuous, recalcitrant delinquent who will grow into a serious adult offender.

Most juvenile courts must both consider previous patterns of behavior and develop expectations about what might happen to a youth in the future.

Juvenile court intake officers, juvenile court hearings, and the research on delinquency and other risky behavior reveal the varied patterns and distinct narratives the court must respond to. The many contexts and individuals considered by the court is a defining aspect of the juvenile justice system and one that can strain its individualized focus. Still, some discernable facts about delinquency, delinquents, and the system itself indicate that the court does not need to operate exclusively on a case-by-case basis and can devise general strategies for processing, treating, and sanctioning delinquency cases. Systematically describing and extracting lessons from that variation is a necessary precursor to effective policy and practice.

End Point or Long-Term Turning Point?

The diversity of cases in the juvenile court and its partner agencies is the most obvious variability. Lurking behind that are the different paths by which youths may be involved in delinquency and subsequently come into contact with juvenile justice. Current research on the nature of delinquency suggests that a host of influences, from stable personality traits and recurring cognitive-behavioral scripts to youths' immediate and distal social environment, can directly or indirectly affect youth development. Certain youths may have behavioral problems from early ages that manifest in the home, school, and community environment. Other behavioral problems can emerge in transitional periods, such as the move from an elementary school to a secondary school. Some youths face the juvenile court for the first time after abrupt exposure to social situations favorable to delinquency.

All these pathways to court involvement mean that a youth standing in front of a juvenile court judge may be at an end point on an early life pathway that has led to that undesirable outcome. Considered in that way, juvenile justice contact is the result of a set of events, decisions, and influences. Alternatively, it may also prove to be a reinforcing experience that leads to recidivism; even as contact with the justice system can be an end point on an early trajectory, it can also become a launching point for further delinquency and criminal behavior. Once involved in the juvenile justice system, youths may have very different experiences according to case characteristics, their individual risks and strengths, and the orientation and resources of the court in which they are processed. Thus, the path from the juvenile justice system to later aspects of a youth's life is as variable as the path that led the youth to it in the first place. It could be a fleeting brush with formal authority followed by an immediate redirection to some informal sanction or intervention. Alternatively, a youth's adolescence could involve a series of repeated contacts with the juvenile court that end with the equivalent of imprisonment in a secure juvenile facility or transfer to the adult system. These paths have implications for continued engagement in delinquency and then adult crime, completion of developmental milestones on the way to adulthood, and possible opportunities for further entrenchment in antisocial behavior.

The Juvenile Court: Past and Present

The juvenile justice system originated with the view that patterns of delinquent or analogous behavior could be redirected to prevent its continuance and push youths away from related problem outcomes—which would ultimately prove harmful to them, their families, and their communities—toward more conventional pathways (Tanenhaus 2004; Zimring 2005a). From this perspective, the encounter with the juvenile court is an initial step on a more prosocial trajectory, a way to help youths turn toward alternative ways of thinking and behaving and offer them social support. The juvenile justice system is a powerful institution in the lives of many youths, families, and communities because an encounter with it is an outcome of earlier developmental influences, and the system is a potential influence, or turning point, in its own right.

The juvenile justice system occupies a unique position as an institution that takes responsibility for both helping youths and holding them accountable. The court has multiple, sometimes competing, goals as it attempts to tailor appropriate responses to cases and youths (Caldwell 1961). Its personnel therefore walk a delicate line in pursuing their day-to-day tasks. Modern court officials must make a series of vital decisions about how best to process, treat, and sanction youths. Early screening and detention decisions in addition to later adjudicatory and dispositional judgments can also stress collective system efficiency and effectiveness. For example, juvenile court actors may wish to err toward caution and intervene with youths or provide intensive treatment, but that invariably exposes more youths to the system and also may lead to their deeper penetration of the system. Likewise, sanction and treatment referral decisions may increase the likelihood that youths will recidivate, affecting their long-term prospects and community safety.

The juvenile justice system's day-to-day tasks also must compete—or at least coexist—with the social awareness that causes it to confront larger societal trends underlying delinquency trends. Disproportionate minority youth contact with justice or the special treatment needs of youths with mental health problems provide examples of this tension; courts and referral agencies may offer services or court dockets in addition to the usual complement of functions. While the original philosophy of the juvenile court definitely still holds today, it is not fully intact, and the public's, policy makers', and even court officials' belief in that philosophy has waxed and waned over time (Bernard and Kurlychek 2010). Certainly, the reality today has not fully met the rhetoric of the late 1800s, when the juvenile court was conceived, but it also has not faltered as significantly as its most vocal critics suggest (Sullivan, Piquero, and Cullen 2012). Its proponents were perhaps overly optimistic about the prospects for redirecting the lives of delinquent youths, but the juvenile court's critics are arguably overly pessimistic and do not necessarily provide viable alternatives (Crippen 1999).

Activists', researchers', and policy makers' suggestions for making the juvenile justice system more developmental echo the beliefs of the early founders of the court in some ways. Consequently, policy and practice proposals must be tied to modern developmental research but also coupled with awareness of the juvenile delinquent population, the juvenile justice system as it currently stands, and the success or failure of previous initiatives during the 120-year lifespan of the juvenile court.

Contemporary Juvenile Justice Meets Adolescent Development

The juvenile court's centennial period in the 1990s and first decade of the 2000s saw an accounting of what the court had or had not done to live up to its ideals, an accounting that became a question of whether the court should be abolished (Crippen 1999; Dawson 1990; Feld 1997). This was due to experts' and activists' perceived shortcomings of the court and a related belief that it had become less distinct from the criminal court in its processes and the results for youths. The question of the juvenile court's continued existence has been settled, and the discussion among critics has moved on to consider what its future should be (Crippen 1999; Edwards 1996).

The beginning of the second century of the juvenile court has seen a lot of research and commentary on the prospects of a developmental approach to juvenile justice, which introduced developmental principles that were implicit in forming the court but that have been revisited more explicitly in this century. These include the general ideas that social conditions—rather than individual character—drive the decisions of young people, and punishment and treatment should take those conditions into account. Biological and neurological research with implications for delinquency has bolstered the status of the developmental perspective (Cauffman and Steinberg 2012). Elizabeth S. Scott and Laurence D. Steinberg's *Rethinking Juvenile Justice* (2008) synthesized emerging insights on youth development and linked them to public policy toward adolescents. The authors suggest that the key objectives of the juvenile justice system should be fair punishment and cost-effective crime reduction, arguing that a scheme based on developmental knowledge is more apt to realize these goals than get-tough, control-oriented strategies. Responding in part to the calls for abolition of the juvenile justice system, their recommendations focus first on a separate juvenile system being necessary and its boundary with the adult court being relaxed only in very serious cases. Second, they suggest expanding the dispositional jurisdiction of the juvenile court to age twenty-five to reflect new developmental research. Third, the developmental stages of youths should inform juvenile justice programming.

A National Research Council (NRC 2013) report on a more developmental juvenile justice system adds a great deal to this discussion. An expert panel made several structural recommendations, such as creating statewide task forces consisting of stakeholder groups to recommend legislative changes and to introduce and monitor evidence-based shifts in agency policy and practice. The NRC also identified the desirability of funding, technical assistance, and data infrastructure from the federal government.

Operationally, the focus of these efforts is to "align laws, policies, and practices at every stage of the process with evolving knowledge regarding adolescent development and the effects of specific juvenile justice interventions and programs" (NRC 2013, 327). Reform should focus on promoting accountability, reducing recidivism, and ensuring fairness (NRC 2013). In the view of the panel, accountability requires sanctions, like restitution and community service, which make youths take responsibility for their actions and involves families and guardians to reinforce their acceptance of responsibility. They also suggest limits on the use of secure confinement and on youths' exposure to potential collateral consequences like unsealing juvenile records. The panel notes that the prevention of reoffending begins with a structured risk and needs assessment to match youths to appropriate treatment. The assessment and decision-making process must be coupled with effective programs that draw on developmental research and each youth's risks and needs. Fairness is promoted by how youths are processed and their perceptions of how they have been treated by those in the system.

Several aspects of these 2013 proposals for policy reform are novel, but others contain ideas that have lain dormant in the juvenile justice system. The integration of a developmental perspective on sanctions, for example, in the NRC report serves as a starting point for discussion of how to rightsize punishment for juvenile delinquents. Similarly, the report's focus on perceptions of fairness and legal socialization raise concerns that police, courts, and corrections might be losing opportunities to redirect trajectories of antisocial behavior because of their approach. The suggestion that the modern juvenile justice system use structured risk and needs assessments alongside a developmental approach to juvenile justice policy and practice is reminiscent of William Healy's (1912, 1913) diagnostic approach in the court clinic in Chicago. Thus, the most prominent recommendations for developmental juvenile justice are probably best thought of as a blend of old and new.

From a legal and policy standpoint, the U.S. Supreme Court offers a prominent window on the reach of developmental research into judicial reasoning. A string of three decisions, in *Roper v. Simmons* (2005), *Graham v. Florida* (2010), and *Miller v. Alabama* (2012), rolled back the use of the most severe adult sanctions for youths, with the majority opinions relying in part on principles and research about adolescent development.[3] In the first of these, *Roper v. Simmons* (2005), the court ruled against imposition of the death penalty for crimes that occurred before youths turned eighteen. Justice Anthony Kennedy cited immaturity, susceptibility to negative influences, and the still-forming character of juveniles that precludes them being characterized as the "worst offenders," which is a natural criterion for use of capital punishment. Kennedy again wrote the majority opinion in *Graham v. Florida* (2010), in which the court ruled that juveniles cannot be sentenced to life without parole for offenses other than homicide. In that opinion, he considered justifications for such a sentence (e.g., deterrence, incapacitation, retribution) and found them wanting. This likewise points to youths' perceived malleability and the developmental circumstances that affect culpability in making decisions about the most severe sanctions available to U.S. courts. While these legal opinions do not directly influence the imposition of juvenile court sanctions, the three cases beginning with *Roper*, as well a string of major Supreme Court decisions in the 1960s, signaled a shift in the legal understanding of young offenders and reinforced the arguments of those who wished to introduce modern developmental science to the courts.

In the 2010s, state legislatures began taking action to raise the age for adult court jurisdiction. The NRC report (2013) gives the example of Connecticut, which raised the age of juvenile court jurisdiction to eighteen in July 2012. The efforts of advocates and political leaders to make the case for that action, which proceeded as a multiphase increase of the boundary age— the age separating juvenile and adult court jurisdiction—required extensive policy projection, planning, and community and legislative outreach. According to the Justice Policy Institute (2013), this legislative change kept thousands of sixteen-year-olds in juvenile court who otherwise would have been assigned to adult court. Even the International Association of Chiefs of Police (2014) has discussed how police fit into juvenile justice reforms driven by developmental principles, suggesting that this strand of policy and practice has transcended courts and corrections agencies that are more closely aligned with juvenile justice.

Despite these cases of legal reform and shifts in policy and practice, the political pushes to increase the purview of juvenile court in accordance with research on human development have not totally rolled back existing legislation that lowered the age of criminal court jurisdiction. Additionally, while some have called for a full-scale expansion of the literature on brain development into responses toward young adult offenders (e.g., Farrington, Loeber, and Howell 2012), broader political limitations and implementation challenges face those who wish to extend that research to policy and practice with late adolescents and young adults (Cauffman 2012). Indeed, some policy makers in Connecticut have sought to push the boundary age to twenty-one but have met with early resistance (De Avila 2015). While significant achievements in changing the response to delinquency have been made, the resistance to change in even those systems most open-minded toward embracing it signals possible challenges to fully altering juvenile justice policy and practice. In turn, this suggests the need for further examination of the underlying philosophy and practicalities of a more developmental juvenile justice system.

Though NRC (2013), Franklin E. Zimring and David S. Tanenhaus (2014), and Nancy E. Dowd (2015) tackle questions about youth processing, sanctions, and treatment, much of the research and related reforms of the twenty-first century tend to focus on the appropriate venue for trying youths (e.g., Scott and Steinberg 2008) and the possible effects of incarceration on adolescent development (e.g., Mulvey and Schubert 2012). The success of the juvenile justice system requires increased and more precise integration of developmental and life-course principles to maximize the use of appropriate treatment and sanctions across the full scope of cases and youths that it encounters. Identifying the best approaches and the appropriate processes for successfully implementing calls for change requires careful consideration of the complex, developmental interaction between youths and the juvenile justice system. While the research that informed broad distinctions about jurisdiction and incarceration effects is a good starting point for juvenile justice reform, there is room for the addition of other principles and findings into the discussion.

Implementing Juvenile Justice Reform

Research and legislative and judicial initiatives have certainly set the stage for improvements in juvenile justice policy and practice, especially because they provide connections between developmental and life-course insights and the juvenile justice system. To this point, the implications of this research for treatment have largely centered on primary prevention and early intervention with at-risk youths, which are essential in responding to juvenile delinquency and transforming the lives of at-risk children (Howell 2003; Farrington and Welsh 2007; Greenwood 2006). Evaluation research in juvenile justice since the 1990s has identified some effective treatment and sanction strategies that help reduce recidivism even for serious juvenile offenders (Lipsey 1999), underscoring these strategies' potential impact on youths and public safety outcomes by reducing the likelihood that problem behavior will continue into adulthood. The NRC report notes, however, that most recommendations for reform have been adopted at just a few model sites and that the knowledge base has limitations for enacting the proposed changes. A deeper dive into the research on implementation will help identify how juvenile justice agencies might change their rehabilitative and sanction strategies and point toward some potential obstacles—such as that the best method for transferring these ideas to the field likely varies across states and locales (Paina and Peters 2012).

Juvenile justice policy and practice currently seem to be open to new ideas or refinement of existing ones; agencies, researchers, and policy makers are taking steps to implement evidence-based policy and practice and promote change in delinquent youths. The juvenile court's history and an evaluation of program implementation in juvenile justice suggests that, although it may seemingly be in a mind-set favorable to change (Scott and Steinberg 2008), there are inevitable barriers (Bernard and Kurlychek 2010; Howell 2003). Consequently, sustainable change and adherence to best practices will require more than the introduction of new research, ideas, and model programs and policies. Work in implementation science that blends research, practice, and their integration (e.g., Backer 2000; Fixsen, Blase, Naoom, et al. 2009; Fixsen, Blase, Metz, et al. 2013; Laub 2016; Welsh et al. 2010) is therefore useful in understanding the possibilities and limits of initiatives to improve the juvenile justice system.

The ideas and research in implementation science focus squarely on the complex process of moving research findings into policy and practice. Differing target populations, fidelity to evidence-based models, and implementation context all affect taking ideas to the field and then translating initial successes to other places and settings. Moving research to practice in juvenile justice requires enumeration and attention to challenges. Those formulating new policies and practices must also consider the pressures on juvenile justice systems and their stakeholders—both existing pressures and those brought by change—and how those pressures affect implementing and sustaining proposed reforms.

Toward a More Developmental Juvenile Justice System?

When considering research on delinquency and the juvenile court or talking to those in the system, it is clear that the court encounters a wide range of cases and youths—even with recent drops in juvenile arrests. An interview with a juvenile court special programs coordinator in a medium-sized county was a reminder that, along with volume and variety, the system does not have all that much choice about which cases reach its doors and thus its dockets contain "all kinds of kids."[4] This includes offense types; previous histories; sociodemographic profiles; and risks, strengths, and needs. Invariably this means that the juvenile justice system will see numerous complex cases with different seriousness, circumstances, youth and family risk and needs patterns, prior histories, and future prospects. It will continue to process roughly a million youths each year, especially those who come from disadvantaged individual, family, or community circumstances.

Bigger than juvenile justice involvement and a youth's life course is the question of what is the best approach to realizing positive outcomes in light of the difficulties faced by justice-involved youths and pressures exerted on the system. Using response to heterogeneous populations as a jumping-off point and calls for reform to make the system more developmental in policy and practice, this book considers what is known about the youths who come before juvenile courts in the United States, describes how the court functions with respect to their risks and needs and what that might mean in the long term, and identifies how the court might better sanction and treat these youths.

Since its founding, the juvenile justice system has been a frequent topic of analysis and writing, but beginning in the late 1990s, a great deal of emphasis has been placed on reform and the introduction of evidence-based practice into juvenile justice practice. Much discussion implicitly or explicitly draws on research about youth and adolescent development and subsequent or concurrent actions by courts, legislatures, private philanthropists, and system personnel. The practicalities involved in translating research and ideas into the structure, process, and decisions of contemporary juvenile justice systems garner less attention. Given that, there is room for greater clarity about how the pieces of research and perspectives on youth development and delinquency might fit together in a way that will improve system operations and youth outcomes.

This book addresses those open questions by considering the ideas intrinsic to the juvenile justice system, integrating and synthesizing relevant contemporary research, and offering suggestions about its translation to practice. With the push toward formal risk and needs assessment, data collection and research to better understand the youths and adolescents who reach the court has been considerably expanded, and attempts to identify behavioral, situational, and contextual influences that promote onset, continuance, and desistance in delinquent behavior have increased. This has led to specific and general principles that are valuable in working with delinquent youths—albeit perhaps just more technologically refined versions of ideas from the early court (Laub 2000).

In some ways, the juvenile court is at a point much like where it stood at its inception. Like reform advocates of today, the court's founders believed that greater scientific understanding could lead to treatment of and response to delinquent behavior that would redirect individual developmental pathways, improving the lives of those youths and benefiting the community in the process. Since the late 1800s and through the 1900s, however, there are numerous examples of the juvenile court's limitations in realizing those ideals despite its best intentions (Caldwell 1961; Platt 1969; Rothman 1980; Ryerson 1978). A thorough understanding of the reasons for delinquency and knowledge of the juvenile court's contemporary status improves the prospects of doing better with justice-involved youths in the twenty-first century.

As the optimistic child savers had to do in the past, contemporary juvenile justice reform advocates must take a clear-eyed look at what can and cannot be done for delinquent youths to determine the best ways to make the system more developmental. This necessitates an expanded view of and greater synthesis of the developmental and life-course evidence across various fields. The juvenile justice system is not a blank canvas for implementation, so analysis of possible refinements requires a thorough understanding of the system itself and best practices for intervention and sanction. Suggestions for reform must respond to the contexts of both offenses and offenders across several key areas: general developmental factors and life-course characteristics that affect behavior; risks emanating from the individual or family, peers, or community; and needs that may (or may not) be addressed through juvenile justice interventions.

Any changes must further account for the full scope of the court's mission: rehabilitation and redirection of a diverse pool of delinquent youths *and* doing justice by providing appropriate sanctions on behalf of communities whose beliefs about youthfulness and delinquency differ. The day-to-day tasks of the court and its pursuit of other initiatives aimed at social problems and specialized populations are counterweights to full implementation of alternative practices. The growing research on implementation science can explicate the potential obstacles and suggest how to overcome them.

This book considers each of these themes in more depth, starting with an overview of the youths who encounter the system and then describing the system's present operations, synthesizing relevant developmental insights, and reviewing current practices in treatment and sanction. It then draws on research regarding implementation of innovative policy and practice. The chapters that follow discuss many of the central ideas that drive contemporary juvenile justice and integrate and synthesize the relevant research and practical examples of where that research is already present in the system to generate a series of well-grounded recommendations.

Part I describes delinquent youth populations and juvenile justice practice. It synthesizes important foundations for that practice with detailed coverage of theory and research on youth development. This Introduction briefly considers the range of cases encountered by the court on the basis of direct observation and existing research, summarizes its history and current obligations, introduces aspects of its developmental mission, and identifies questions for current policy and practice. The historical arc and status of the juvenile justice system is multifaceted, and this book considers its present and possible future across several dimensions. The chapters that follow cover these topics in depth and integrate the relevant elements: youths, their offenses, and their risks and needs (Chapter 1); the juvenile justice operations and the sanctions and treatment that it delivers to youths whom it encounters (Chapter 2); and the developmental space within which these different influences and outcomes emerge (Chapters 3 and 4).

Part II of this book examines the scope of the considerations undertaken by the court, identifies some reasons for the variation, and makes suggestions about how the system might respond to the different types of cases using developmental insights and existing best practices as a guide. By following these recommendations, juvenile justice can serve as both an effective provider (and broker) of suitable services for delinquent youths and as a respected institution that works on behalf of the community to appropriately sanction youths in order to foster moral development (Chapter 5). The research on effective practices offers a starting point, and a growing body of work on implementation provides useful advice for ensuring that this evidence reaches the broader juvenile justice system (Chapter 6). Several recommendations for a more developmental and effective juvenile justice system emerge from this review of research and existing practice and complementary new research and analysis (Conclusion). The chapters in Part II build on the background and theory from Part I to consider what is likely to be effective in a more developmental juvenile justice system and assess its implementation potential.

1

Characterizing Contemporary Delinquency

I nformed analysis of changes to juvenile justice requires a baseline description of who is coming into the system, the circumstances of that contact, and possible reasons for it. Without both precision and comprehensiveness, suggestions risk ignoring the challenges faced by the system and presenting solutions that are not fully mindful of the current caseload and of processing and making decisions about those cases. This is especially true now because juvenile crime, and therefore juvenile justice, looks different in some respects from the latter part of the twentieth century when the enactment or expansion of much of the law and policy counter to a developmentally informed juvenile justice occurred.

Although there has been discussion of certain crime rates' rebound from historical declines (e.g., Rosenfeld 2016), government statistics suggest that juvenile crime remains in decline overall. Using case referral data from about 2,400 courts in the United States, Nina Hyland (2018) reports that total delinquency was down 5 percent between 2013 and 2014. This was part of a decline between the late 1990s and 2014 (roughly 42 percent from 2005 and about 49 percent from the peak in 1996) and placed juvenile court caseloads at levels near where they were before a sharp rise in the mid-1980s. With this background on case levels, the context of juvenile justice policy and practice reviews shifts from a perceived crisis mode (Cook and Laub 2002) to one more conducive to sober analysis and judgment (NRC 2013; Scott and Steinberg 2008). Still, these trends do not precisely describe the juvenile justice system as it stands in the second decade of the twenty-first century or fully characterize the potential effects of its reform on youths. A close look at existing case processing and disposition is therefore essential in setting the foundation for new practice and policy. This chapter focuses on what youths come into the system, what they have done to get there, and why they committed the delinquent act that got them there.

A great deal of the discussion about general policy and practice decisions in the juvenile court has focused on the two ends of the distribution of its cases, which are in-versus-out decisions because they concern whether youths should fall under its jurisdiction or not. There has been consternation about processing cases that are relatively nonserious but nevertheless swept into the system via increased formalization and unintended net widening in official diversion programs (e.g., Polk 1984; Schur 1973). These concerns led in part to reform of the response to status offenses via formal deinstitutionalization that took place owing to the Juvenile Justice and Delinquency Prevention Act in 1974 (see OJJDP 2019), but how cases are processed varies tremendously across states and localities along with their effectiveness in addressing the problem (see, e.g., Feld 2009; Steinhart 1996). This creates difficulty in determining the best response for youths whose offenses fall into less serious categories or who have no or limited previous contacts with the system and are therefore at relatively low risk but high need. The 1990s and first decade of the 2000s discussion at the other extreme—regarding juveniles processed in the adult system—has perhaps been more conspicuous because of its central role in twenty-first-century policy. In fact, the concern for that group tends to be a key impetus in calls for a more developmentally informed response to juvenile offenders as demonstrated, for example, in advocates' use of developmental evidence in initiatives to raise the age of adult court jurisdiction.

This chapter deals with youths and delinquency that fall into these categories, but it expands the scope of analysis to include cases that encounter the contemporary juvenile court in order to provide a comprehensive overview of its caseload. Understanding this range then informs further assessment of juvenile justice policy and practice. A defining feature—which is identifiable in the descriptive research and the impressions of those working in the system—is the sheer amount of diversity handled in the juvenile justice system. To be most informative, this analysis must move beyond the general descriptions that often appear in statistical summaries of official court caseloads to delve into the nature of cases encountered—especially with developmental insights in mind. Figure 1.1 identifies delinquent acts and justice-involved youths and portrays the many linkages among them, which point to the complexity of resolving individual cases and setting broader policies. These elements include:

- Type and seriousness of offense
- Whether the youth reaches the system
- Situational and social circumstances of offense

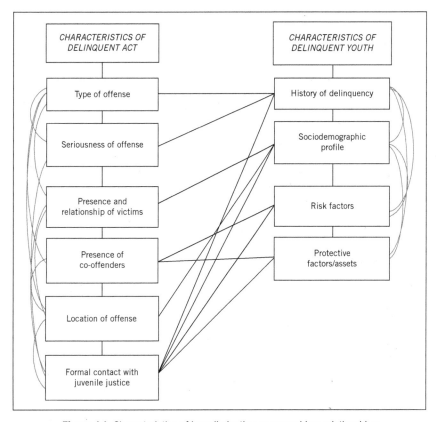

Figure 1.1 Characteristics of juvenile justice cases and key relationships

- Sociodemographic profile
- Individual, familial, peer, and community risk factors
- Protective factors, strengths, and possible resilience
- Delinquency history (serious, violent, or chronic offender)

Trends and discrepancies in these dimensions are relevant in characterizing the caseloads in the juvenile justice system and setting a context for changes to the current system.

Risky Behavior and Delinquent Offenses

Only a portion of the youths and delinquent acts that are committed come to the attention of the juvenile justice system. Farrington and colleagues (2007) compared self-reports with official court contacts and found a ratio of approximately eighty self-reported offenses for every one that came to the attention of the court. This differential results from some behaviors having lesser probability of detection or involving greater discretionary decision making among police officers and those making early juvenile court intake decisions—especially at young ages and for minor offenses. Other scholars have documented the distinction between self-reported behavior and official records as well, recognizing the filtering process that drives official responses to youth behavior (Williams and Gold 1972, 210). Thus, self-reporting behavior by juveniles may offer a different view of youth delinquency and its relationship to other, related risk-taking behaviors (Childs and Sullivan 2013; Jessor and Jessor 1997), but what the system sees from its vantage point is most pertinent to its policies and practices.

Officially Reported Delinquency

The commonality and seriousness of delinquency are the most instructive characteristics in getting a basic sense of the types of cases that come into the juvenile justice system. Juveniles make up a relatively small proportion of overall arrest rates of those eighteen or over. In 2012, they accounted for roughly 1.3 million arrests of a total of 12.2 million recorded by the Uniform Crime Reporting system. This means that roughly 11 percent of total arrests involved those below the traditional youth-adult boundary.[1] Translated to arrests per 1,000 population in 2012, this represents an arrest rate of 39.7 for ages ten to seventeen and 45.3 for ages eighteen and older.

Statistical reports from the federal government and states reveal shifts in the patterns of offense types since the 1990s. The report authored by Julie Furdella and Charles Puzzanchera (2015) for the Office of Juvenile Justice and Delinquency Prevention (OJJDP) of the U.S. Department of Justice on the most serious offenses referred to U.S. juvenile courts in 2013 indicates that the most typical serious offense for juveniles was property related (see Table 1.1). Those cases accounted for about 35 percent of the total. Person and public order offenses each make up roughly one-fourth of the cases in U.S. juvenile courts. Drug law violations make up the smallest proportion of cases. Each of these categories saw a substantial reduction in referrals from 2004 to 2013. Except for drug law violations, this generally conforms to trends over the two decades since the late 1990s (see Snyder 2012). The public order offense category reported by Furdella and Puzzanchera comprises several subtypes. Obstruction of justice charges made up a substantial percentage of the cases in that category (48.6 percent). Disorderly conduct was also relatively frequent at roughly 27 percent. Public order offenses include approximately 21,000 weapons offenses referred to juvenile courts as well (8.0 percent). That summary of court cases did not include reported status offenses, but Melissa Sickmund and Charles Puzzanchera (2014) estimated that approximately 137,000 such cases (e.g., runaway, truancy, ungovernable, liquor law violations) appeared in juvenile courts in 2010. This was about 16 percent of the total cases.

TABLE 1.1 JUVENILE COURT REFERRALS BY TYPE IN 2013 AND DECENNIAL CHANGE

Offense category	Number of referrals	Percentage of total	Percent change in count, 2004–2013
Person offenses	278,300	26.3	−34.0
Property offenses	366,600	34.6	−42.0
Drug law violations	141,700	13.4	−23.0
Public order offenses	271,800	25.7	−38.0
Total	1,058,400	100.0	−37.0

Source: Adapted from Furdella and Puzzanchera 2015.

The relative prevalence of offenses within these broader categories shows that the clear majority of the person offenses were simple assaults (67.0 percent), with aggravated assaults (9.7 percent) and robberies (7.9 percent) making up smaller proportions of that total. Rapes (2.7 percent) and homicide (0.3 percent) make up the smallest proportion of person offenses. Except for robbery, which saw an increase of roughly 4 percent, each of these saw a decline from 2004 to 2013. The most frequently occurring property offense, which made up roughly half of that total, was larceny-theft. Burglary accounted for 17.8 percent of property offense cases. Each of those offenses declined over the ten-year window. The reported figures aggregate drug law violations, but Uniform Crime Reporting arrest statistics disaggregate drug abuse violations into possession or sales and manufacturing (see Snyder and Mulako-Wangota 2017). The majority of the 140,000 recorded arrests for those under age eighteen in 2012 were for drug possession (86.8 percent).

Juvenile court cases span the same range and diversity of those in criminal courts but differ in concentrations of offenses and subtypes. Comparatively, for the juvenile age range, the least serious offenses (e.g., simple assault, larceny-theft) predominated in each type. Most of these offenses had double-digit declines within five- and ten-year reference points. In addition to its impact on broader perceptions, the nature of the offense plays an objective and subjective role in characterizing a given youth within the system and, in turn, the disposition of his or her case. That characterization is then linked to pathways through the juvenile justice system and beyond.

Circumstances of Delinquent Acts

Situational elements of delinquent acts have descriptive and explanatory value from the standpoint of understanding delinquency and the processes that drive it and of fashioning an appropriate response to it. Multiple dimensions are pertinent, but the social nature of delinquency and pattern of places and situations where it tends to occur are two key areas of focus, because they can generate delinquency and are related to youth development.

Co-offending. The presence or absence of others is a recurring characteristic of delinquency events. The distinction between individual offending and co-offending is instructive because many offenses at the juvenile level are committed with peers, and therefore it matters in thinking generally about juvenile justice policy and practice (Zimring and Laqueur 2015; cf. Stolzenberg and D'Alessio 2008). This is also quite clearly linked to developmentally normative behavior in contrast to offending that occurs for reasons more ingrained in the youth (Moffitt 1993; Scott and Steinberg 2008). The collective nature of delinquency is a focal point in understanding why adolescents behave in certain ways (Warr 2002; Weerman 2003).

Albert J. Reiss and David P. Farrington (1991) studied co-offending in the Cambridge Study on Delinquent Development in the United Kingdom. They used conviction records to identify patterns of co-offending among those who had official contact with the justice system. They found that, between ages ten and thirty-two, co-offenses made up slightly more than half of all offenses; however, most of the offenses committed between ages ten and twenty involved other individuals. For instance, 61 percent of offenses committed by youths ages fourteen to sixteen were co-offenses. They also found that others' involvement varied by crime type, such that burglaries, thefts, and robberies often involved co-offending, but acts like threatening behavior or assault were less likely to be committed with others.

Sarah B. van Mastrigt and David P. Farrington (2009) likewise studied co-offending in a sample from the United Kingdom, but they used a much larger database of official police records in their assessment. While their findings tend to show a lesser overall prevalence of co-offending, the relationship with age remained consistent, being most prominent during adolescence. In a random sample of four hundred juvenile offenders in Philadelphia, 84 percent had at least one offense committed with others during the years in which they were under juvenile court jurisdiction (Conway and McCord 2002; McGloin et al. 2008). A mere 16 percent were "stable solo offenders" throughout adolescence (McGloin et al. 2008, 162). The other youths generally fit into groups that had low officially recorded counts (co-offending or solo) that were fairly stable or slightly increasing from age ten to seventeen. Two small groups (approximately 2.0 percent and 3.8 percent, respectively) showed broad peaks in co-offending at different points in adolescence. In the first group, a peak in co-offending preceded a decline, and in the second it was part of broader inconsistency from age fourteen through seventeen. While there tended to be a good deal of co-offending in the sample, the co-offender affiliated with an individual youth changed. This signals that, although the presence of co-offenders was consistent, the exact duo or group changed at times. Several factors could explain this co-offending pattern, but the immediate presence of explicit or implicit reinforcement from peers certainly has a strong effect (Warr 2002).

Gangs. Gangs are an extreme manifestation of the association between peers and co-offenders and are also related to lifestyle and routines conducive to chronic and serious delinquency. When considered from a general population standpoint (e.g., high school youths), relatively few youths report gang involvement. A study by Erika Gebo and Christopher J. Sullivan (2014) compared youths who self-reported gang membership in the prior year to those who did not on indicators of risky behaviors, victimization, and alcohol and drug use. The study, which used approximately 2,700 respondents from the 2009 Massachusetts Youth Risk Behavior Survey, which is a study conducted as a part of the Youth Risk Behavior Surveillance System of the Centers for Disease Control, found that 7 percent reported gang membership in the year prior. Not surprisingly, those who reported gang involvement also tended to fall into higher-risk groups identified in classification analysis. Those groups tended to report substantially elevated levels of weapon carrying, physical fighting, and alcohol and drug use. Only 17 percent of participants in the Pathways to Desistance study, of exclusively adjudicated youths, reported gang involvement in the six-month period immediately preceding their adjudication. Data from the Rochester Youth Development Study, in which researchers purposely selected a higher-risk sample, show that roughly 30 percent were involved in a gang at some time between ages fourteen and eighteen (Thornberry, Huizinga, and Loeber 2004). This is like the self-reported gang affiliation observed across the four waves of the Rural Substance Abuse and Violence Project (RSVP) in Kentucky in which 15 percent of youths reported gang affiliation at some point during the study period.

These studies suggest that, although the prevalence of gang membership is relatively low in all youth populations, at-risk and justice-involved youths have risk factors and engage in individual and collective acts that are both more frequent and more serious than other youth populations. Other research suggests that involvement in and commitment to street gangs and delinquency networks can be especially influential in serious delinquent behavior (Huff 1998; Gordon et al. 2004) and that youths in gangs commit more delinquent acts—especially serious and violent acts—than those who are not in gangs (Esbensen and Huizinga 1993; Thornberry et al. 1993; Huff 1998). These findings suggest a potential intensifying effect of delinquent behavior or, at the very least, indicate that a gang might accentuate individual tendencies toward delinquency (Thornberry et al. 1993). Terence P. Thornberry, David Huizinga, and Rolf Loeber (2004) reported that the 30 percent of Rochester youths involved with gangs were responsible for more than 80 percent of the serious delinquency committed by the entire sample and more than half its arrests. Clearly, gang-involved youths are a minority portion of the population but one requiring expansive attention by juvenile justice given their elevated risk, the possible intensification of their delinquent behavior, and its effects on development.

Delinquency and Place. A place-based analysis of delinquency identifies additional properties of offenses. Unfortunately, relatively few studies or perspectives touch on this question of delinquency and place in great depth. David Weisburd, Nancy A. Morris, and Elizabeth R. Groff (2009) studied juvenile arrests at street segments in Seattle for fourteen years (1989 to 2002). They consider the role of place in juveniles' lives to assert its relationship with delinquency events. Their study included areas generally recognized as youth hangouts, like malls, as well as those where they spent a considerable amount of time, like school. As is commonly the case in geospatial studies of crime, they found a concentration of juvenile arrests at particular street segments. For instance, all the incidents recorded in a given year were attributed to no more than 5 percent of street segments. These trends were generally stable over the study's time period.

The study identified eight juvenile arrest trajectories.[2] Some street segments with high rates of arrests had properties relevant to adolescent activity patterns. Notably, the street segments with the lowest juvenile arrest rate, which covered a large proportion of the sample of street segments (89 percent) demonstrating the highly concentrated nature of arrests at places, tended to have the greatest proportion of arrest incidents at "street, alley, and public spaces" or "private dwellings." Conversely, the three highest-rate groups, which made up less than 1 percent of the street segments but one-third of all arrest incidents, had more arrests at segments with "schools and youth centers," "shops, malls, and restaurants," or "street, alley, and public spaces." When activities at these locations involve unsupervised groups, they may be more apt to generate delinquency (Agnew and Peterson 1989; Haynie and Osgood 2005; Osgood et al. 1996; Osgood and Anderson 2004). The social and situational circumstances of delinquency can affect patterns of arrest and inform evaluation of the individual cases that come before juvenile courts.

School-Based Offenses. Within this larger set of high-delinquency places, school-based delinquent acts and arrests are a common source of referrals to the juvenile justice system. This appears to have started in the 1980s and accelerated after the introduction of zero-tolerance policies in the 1990s (Deal et al. 2014; Kupchik 2010). School-based offenses are an increasingly central point in research, broader public concern about a possible school-to-prison pipeline (Hirschfield 2009), and discussions about the increase in school resource officer programs and presence of juvenile probation officers in schools (Griffin 1999b; Kupchik 2010; Theriot 2009). This is especially palpable in trends in disproportionate school discipline and juvenile justice contact for minority youths (Nicholson-Crotty, Birchmeier, and Valentine 2009).

The actual prevalence of delinquency on school grounds is subject to some debate and is likely affected by the increased formalization that seems to be the norm in handling offenses. The Youth Risk Behavior Survey contains questions on physical violence at school and on property victimization. Sickmund and Puzzanchera (2014) found that roughly one-third of respondents in 2011 reported being in a physical fight in the previous year, but only 12 percent occurred on school grounds. In 2015, the relative prevalence values for physical fighting and its occurrence on school property were 23 percent and 8 percent, respectively (CDC 2018). According to Sickmund and Puzzanchera's analysis, approximately one in four respondents stated that they had property (such as cars, clothing, or books) stolen or damaged on school grounds in the previous year. Roughly 20 percent reported being bullied at school in 2011, which was similar to 2013 but a decline from 28 percent in 2009 (CDC 2018). This may be related to the increasing role of cyberspace in adolescent interactions, because 16 percent reported some type of online bullying compared to 6 percent in 2009.

The Sickmund and Puzzanchera (2014) report, which uses National Incident-Based Reporting System data, on juvenile offenders and victims also suggests that the likelihood of delinquent events involving multiple juveniles varies depending on whether it is a school or nonschool day. A situational influence, in which much juvenile robbery and aggravated assault victimizations occur during the hours just after school—with a notable increase around three o'clock—is evident. On days when there was no school (e.g., weekends), the peak occurred later at night. These data suggest that the school setting plays a multifaceted role in adolescent delinquency and victimization. They also suggest that the school environment can have either a corrective or a deleterious impact on youths' developmental pathways.

Delinquency in the Home. Family involvement in delinquency is equally informative in understanding its situational nature and acquiring a firm sense of risk factors, developmental pathways, and prospects for change. Incidents that occur in the home or involve family members can complicate juvenile justice decision making. Howard N. Snyder and Carl McCurley (2008) studied National Incident-Based Reporting System data from 2004 to identify key features of domestic assault incidents involving juvenile offenders (those under age eighteen). The authors defined these cases as involving parents, children, siblings, and boyfriends or girlfriends. Eighty-eight percent of these incidents occurred in a residence. Adults made up the clear majority of the domestic violence incidents studied (roughly 9 percent were

juveniles), and about one-fourth of the assaults committed by juveniles involved domestic relationships. A parent was a victim of juvenile domestic
violence about half the time, a sibling or other family member about 34 percent of the time, and an intimate partner 11 percent of the time. A small
percentage of cases involved assault of the juvenile offender's child. Prevalence estimates vary with the age of the offender, including within childhood
and adolescence. Not surprisingly, domestic offenses tended to engender less
co-offender prevalence than comparable assaults with acquaintance or
stranger victims (16 versus 37 percent).

The victims of these assaults are predominantly females (60 percent),
with only one-third of the offenders being girls (Snyder and McCurley 2008).
Despite their relatively low overall prevalence, Barry C. Feld (2009) argues
that these cases have a pronounced impact on young females' contact and
penetration of the juvenile justice system. Consequently, these assault cases
are a useful example of how situational circumstances can offer insight about
youths as well as their broader circumstances and risks. In turn, sorting out
the nature of the delinquent event can illuminate the reasons for the act, the
youths involved, and his or her family dynamics. Specifically, does the youth
act this way across different settings as is often the case for more serious
delinquents, what Terrie E. Moffitt has called "cross-situational consistency"
(1993, 679), or is the trigger in family dynamics? The answer may prove helpful in understanding the extent to which youths will reoffend or commit
delinquency in other circumstances and also provides clues about whether
the family will help the youth to an alternative pathway.

A Sketch of Justice-Involved Youths

Delinquent acts drive the case-level decision making of system actors and
have broader implications for reform efforts. Given that individuals commit
the acts and encounter the system, it is necessary to understand them, their
race/ethnicity and gender, risk and protective factors, juvenile justice histories, and other dimensions. The sociodemographic makeup of the delinquency population has implications for explaining the reasons for justice
contact and the system response. It is especially relevant in disentangling
structural factors and resource availability, which are linked to the success
of the juvenile justice system (e.g., Mulvey and Reppuci 1988; Woolard, Fondacaro, and Slobogin 2001).

Race. Race in juvenile justice contact and outcome has been an issue of concern for decades (Bishop and Leiber 2012). It has implications for reform efforts because race can be associated with some aspects of case assessment
(Bishop and Leiber 2012; Bridges and Steen 1998), which can differentially
affect minority youths. Among 2013 delinquency cases in juvenile courts, 62

TABLE 1.2 OVERVIEW OF COURT OUTCOMES ACROSS SAMPLE AND
RACE GROUPS

	Percentage nonwhite (n)	Percentage white (n)	χ^2 (df) (Φ)
Diversion			
No	96.7 (33,673)	95.7 (22,967)	45.0 (1)*
Yes	3.3 (1,136)	4.3 (1,039)	0.03
Dismissal			
No	76.7 (33,229)	79.7 (22,996)	90.8 (1)*
Yes	23.3 (10,144)	20.3 (5,868)	0.04
Detention			
No	79.2 (31,737)	87.3 (22,356)	699.8 (1)*
Yes	20.8 (8,336)	12.7 (3,262)	0.10
Adjudication			
No	32.0 (12,240)	28.3 (7,666)	101.9 (1)*
Yes	68.0 (26,039)	71.7 (19,434)	0.04
Secure placement			
No	95.0 (39,053)	97.0 (26,083)	161.4 (1)*
Yes	5.0 (2,070)	3.0 (814)	0.05
Transfer to adult court			
No	99.2 (42,982)	99.8 (28,817)	134.7 (1)*
Yes	0.9 (369)	0.2 (52)	0.04

*$p < .05$

percent involved white youths, 35 percent were black, and 3 percent were of another race (Furdella and Puzzanchera 2015). These numbers, particularly for black youths, are out of proportion to their relative prevalence in the population (35 percent of delinquency cases versus 16 percent in the population).

A 2016 study showed the disadvantage faced by minority youths in the juvenile justice system and its complex manifestations (Sullivan, Latessa, et al. 2016; see Table 1.2). Of 75,536 cases heard in 2010 and 2011 in thirteen juvenile courts in Ohio, 60 percent were for nonwhite youths and 40 percent were for white youths. According to the 2010 census, however, these groups accounted for 22 percent and 78 percent, respectively, of the juvenile population in Ohio. On the surface, then, the cases coming into the juvenile courts during the study period evince a substantial level of disproportionate minority contact. The juvenile court diverted just 3.7 percent of the cases in the sample.[3] In addition, 22.2 percent of the youths had their cases dismissed, 17.6 percent were detained before adjudication, 69.4 percent were adjudicated, and 4.2 percent were placed in secure confinement. Less than 1 percent of the sample was bound over to the adult court. In the statistical models,

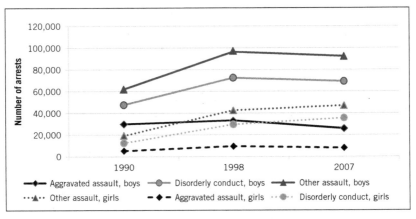

Figure 1.2 Comparison of juvenile arrest counts and trends by sex
Source: Data from Kempf-Leonard 2012.

youth race was significant—to varying degrees—in each of the six outcomes. In particular, nonwhite youths were significantly more likely than white youths to be detained, have their case dismissed, be placed in a secure confinement facility, or be waived to criminal court. Conversely, nonwhite youths were less likely to be diverted from official court processing and slightly more likely to be adjudicated delinquent. These differentials are relevant to the discussion of juvenile justice reform because they are likely to be correlated with developmental factors and have implications for potential differences in long-term outcomes for youths of different races.

Sex. As with the race differential, delinquency studies find recurring evidence of disproportionate prevalence of boys' delinquency. The split was 75–25 percent male to female in Furdella and Puzzanchera's (2015) sample of 2013 juvenile court cases. Both groups were subject to similar declines in different types of offenses over the ten-year window in that report, but the trends were not totally static. Boys are certainly more delinquent overall, but trends have seemingly moved in different directions on some offenses since the 1990s (Sickmund and Puzzanchera 2014; Snyder 2012), suggesting that differences in offenses led to changes in level of system contact (Feld 2009; Kempf-Leonard 2012). Using data from Kimberly Kempf-Leonard (2012), Figure 1.2 shows a difference in the overall scale of offending among boys and girls and on some offenses that involve discretion of police or those making referrals (e.g., disorderly conduct), those offenses having increased for girls and declined for boys.

Researchers suggest these trends are due more to a change in system practices than in behavior. Feld (2009), for example, argues that the observed trends are a product of differences in interrelated system practices regarding status offenses and domestic violence, which, paradoxically, affect more girls, and not a reduction in the gender gap in violence or delinquency. Jennifer Schwartz, Darrell J. Steffensmeier, and Ben Feldmeyer (2009) studied this issue using multiple data sources (e.g., official records, victimization surveys) and found that the trends in official arrests for violent offenses by women were more illusory than real manifestations of societal-level changes in behavior (see also Steffensmeier and Schwartz 2009).

Risk Factors for Delinquency

Sociodemographic factors can serve as effective lead indicators to focus concerted attention but are generally only as good as the underlying processes with which they are correlated. To better understand the development of delinquent behavior, researchers identified several risk factors present before the onset of delinquency that are informative for understanding trends in delinquency and the juvenile justice system response. Much of this work occurred in the 1990s. Multiple longitudinal studies, including the OJJDP's Causes and Correlates of Delinquency initiative, evaluated the knowledge base on risk and protective factors for delinquency (see OJJDP, n.d.). This knowledge base has grown considerably as researchers sought a starting point for causal explanations for antisocial behavior and to identify potential intervention targets for delinquent and at-risk youths.

Risk and protective factors are characteristics or experiences that suggest a greater likelihood of later delinquency (Jessor et al. 1995). They are often categorized as those emerging from the individual, family, peers, and community (U.S. Surgeon General 2001). Thomas Dishion, Deborah Capaldi, and Karen Yoerger (1999) found that individual, family, and peer factors predicted the onset of youth substance use. Likewise, J. David Hawkins and colleagues (1998) summarize risk factors for serious (repeated) and violent juvenile offending from a comprehensive review of the research literature. These risk factors include low cognitive development, male sex, difficult temperament, parental antisocial behavior, poverty, marital discord, harsh and erratic discipline, aggressive or disruptive behavior, poor parental supervision, delinquent peers, and residence in poor neighborhoods.

Individual Factors

As is evident in some case descriptions in the Introduction, the investigation by a probation or intake officer and later decisions by a judge or magistrate start with a youth and then extend outward to the circumstances of the event and the factors that motivated the youth's delinquent behavior or indirectly influenced it. Consequently, factors at the center of the developmental pattern offer a place to begin. Several constitutional characteristics are risk factors for delinquent behavior (e.g., Loeber et al. 1998) and are defined in terms of behavioral propensity or potential. They are usually aspects of a youth's personality and temperament that condition the person's actions in some way (Lahey and Waldman 2005; Wikström 2005; Farrington 2005a). Examples of such factors include self-control (Gottfredson and Hirschi 1990; Pratt and Cullen 2000), morality (Wikström 2005), cognitive ability (Catalano and Hawkins 1996; Catalano et al. 2005; Lahey and Waldman 2005), maladaptive aggression (Farrington 1991; Loeber and Hay 1997), and emotionality (Lahey and Waldman 2005). Other research has pointed to individual biological or genetic factors that may predispose youths to delinquency in particular environments (Brennan and Raine 1997; Moffitt 2005).

A youth's personality and makeup can predict later delinquent behavior. The social environment in which a youth develops and interacts over time also has an effect (McCord, Widom, and Crowell 2003). Robert J. Sampson and John H. Laub noted, "It appears that knowledge of [individual] childhood propensities is not a sufficient condition for explaining delinquency" (1993, 94). This is evident in talking to those in the juvenile justice system. Even as they focus on the individual case, they frequently discuss families and communities in explaining a youth's delinquent behavior.

Family Factors

The youth's family and parents have frequently been seen as risk and protective factors for delinquent behavior (Cantelon 1994; Patterson and Yoerger 1993; Shader 2001; Simons, Simons, and Wallace 2004; Sullivan 2006; Yoshikawa 1994). Familial influences are relevant in the early onset of delinquent behavior (Lahey, Waldman, and McBurnett 1999; Moffitt 1993). Rolf Loeber (1982) suggests that antisocial behavior results from an interruption in appropriate family and child interactions, which can encompass multiple dimensions. Rolf Loeber and Magda Stouthamer-Loeber (1986) reviewed longitudinal studies and found that a lack of parental supervision, along with parental rejection and less parent-child involvement, was related to conduct problems and delinquency.

In a later review of the research, Hirokazu Yoshikawa (1994) found that parental hostility and monitoring have direct effects on delinquency. Family structure (e.g., single- versus two-parent family) has indirect effects. Poor parental discipline is a factor in the development of problem behavior in adolescence as well (Dishion, Capaldi, and Yoerger 1999; Mayer 2001). Inconsistent parenting and permissiveness also put youth at risk for drug use during early adolescence as well (Block, Block, and Keyes 1988; Dishion, Capaldi, and Yoerger 1999).

Exemplifying these findings, Terence P. Thornberry and colleagues (1999) found that increased family transition, such as changes in residence, finances, or family roles and relationships, was related to higher levels of delinquency and drug use. Conversely, a longitudinal study of male adolescents by David B. Henry, Patrick H. Tolan, and Deborah Gorman-Smith (2001) found that youths from families marked by closeness and strong parenting engaged in less delinquency. Clearly, the family factors into youth development, particularly at early stages of life, but additional influences emerge in moving outward from that immediate context. Different classes of risk factors are likely to take on salience throughout development, often interacting with enduring propensity and dispositions that result from earlier experiences (Ayers et al. 1999; Childs, Sullivan, and Gulledge 2010).

Peers

As noted earlier, peers play a significant role in adolescents' choices. Most delinquency occurs with codelinquents, and peer delinquency is one of the most robust predictors of individual delinquency (Warr 2002). One of the few regularities around delinquency that garner substantial agreement is that it is often group based. Mark Warr's (2002) review of the extensive research on juvenile delinquency indicates that its most consistent and strongest correlate is a count of delinquent associates. While this correlation may be the product of several different mechanisms, the peer social environment is a facilitator of delinquent behavior during adolescence (Haynie and Osgood 2005; Smetana, Campione-Barr, and Metzger 2005; Steinberg and Morris 2001). Dishion, Capaldi, and Yoerger (1999) found that early contact with delinquent youths was related to adolescent substance use. Henry, Tolan, and Gorman-Smith (2001) found that increased interaction with violent peers predicted youths' greater likelihood of violence, but having peers who engaged in nonviolent delinquency did not predict the same behavior in a youth. Peer associations partially mediated the effects of family influences on delinquent behavior, meaning that peer relationships may be a later developmental conduit for such early risk.

This influence is age graded. By early adolescence (ages eleven to twelve), a large portion of youths' social activity happens with other similar-age peers, so it is natural that peers will start to play a prominent role in choices about risky and delinquent behavior. Looking just a couple of years beyond that, adolescents report spending significantly more time with their peers than with their parents (Csikzentmihalyi, Larson, and Prescott 1977; Collins and Laursen 2004). This corresponds with patterns in the age and crime relationship (Warr 2002). While parents undoubtedly maintain some direct and residual influence during adolescence—especially when compared to young adulthood—the relative weight of peer versus parental approval seeking may depend on a youth's relationship with his or her family or other adults (Scott, Reppucci, and Woolard 1995). During this period, time spent with peers increases dramatically, priming the social environment for mutual influence based on factors also linked to delinquent behavior, like elevated reward sensitivity and attenuated self-control (Sullivan, Childs, and Gann, 2019).

Overall, the research suggests that individuals often consciously or subconsciously select peer groups on the basis of predispositions to certain behavior and attitudes, but these peers influence later behavior as well. This is vital both in understanding contributors to delinquency and in determining how peer influence fits into developmental patterns of delinquency. In his review, Warr (2002) found that the idea of peer pressure was too simplistic an explanation for the peer-delinquency relationship (see also Steinberg and Morris 2001). Discerning among selection, socialization, and situation as elements of peer risk has implications for understanding behavioral patterns and the response to delinquency.

Community

The larger environmental context affects youth development and exposure to prosocial and antisocial opportunities. It also affects youths' risk for delinquency (Shader 2001; Wikström and Sampson 2003). Environment has garnered increased attention in understanding the impact of communities on youth development in general and antisocial behavior specifically (Leventhal and Brooks-Gunn 2000; Leventhal, Dupéré, and Brooks-Gunn 2009; Sampson 2006; Wikström and Sampson 2003). Among other problems, children growing up in disadvantaged neighborhoods are more likely to use drugs and become involved with delinquency in adolescence (Hawkins, Catalano, and Miller 1992; Loeber and Wikström 1993; Wikström and Loeber 2000). Historically, antisocial behavior has been studied through community-level social (dis)organization and structural and cultural perspectives (see review in Bursik and Grasmick 1993). A multisite study of adolescent development shows that informal social control mediates the effects of disadvantaged neighborhoods on problem behavior (Elliott et al. 1996). Informal social control is reduced in disadvantaged neighborhoods, which leads to higher rates of delinquency and drug use. Consequently, that lack of broader social control is a risk mechanism for community effects on youth behavior.

Among the community influences on youth development are "institutional resources," "norms and collective efficacy," and "relationships and ties" (Leventhal et al. 2009, 422), which implies that structural and indirect and direct social relationships within communities can affect youth development. Robert J. Sampson (2006) focuses on the role that neighborhood collective efficacy can play in development and antisocial behavior. Basically, whether neighborhood residents can come together around shared concerns and collectively govern the community affects the lives of those who reside there, including children and adolescents. The broader social environment may influence youths' options for acting in a delinquent or prosocial manner as well, making it a risk factor through its role in exposing youths to criminogenic situations (Wikström and Sampson 2003). Community effects on delinquency are less clear in some studies, however. Per-Olof H. Wikström and Rolf Loeber (2000), for instance, found that community context had little effect on early onset of offending but had a direct impact on late onset of delinquency for youths with high levels of protective factors. This indicates that the relationship between communities and delinquency may manifest itself in complex ways at different stages of development.

Multiproblem Youths, Juvenile Delinquency, and Juvenile Justice

This enumeration of risk factors suggests that several different and overlapping individual and social factors may manifest themselves in youths' lives such that they co-occur in distinct but related ways. This, in turn, presents some challenges for the juvenile justice system if it is the only service-providing agency that the youth encounters or the only one that can offer needed intervention. The profile of risks and needs of delinquent youths therefore offers insight on what is necessary to effectively respond.

Multiproblem delinquents are youths who might need or who concurrently encounter systems such as child welfare, juvenile court, and mental health. Youths who come to the attention of the juvenile justice system are known to be more frequently involved in one or more of the following: the child welfare system, children's hospitals, mental health facilities, and alternative schools. Broader theoretical work has focused on the linkages between different types of problem behaviors. Problem behavior theory, for instance, created a conceptual structure consisting of distal social structural background and socialization variables, social-psychological variables, and problem behaviors (Jessor and Jessor 1997). The idea of a problem behavior syndrome reflects the linkages between different risk factors and consequent behaviors (Childs and Sullivan 2013). Similarly, Michael R. Gottfredson and Travis Hirschi's (1990) general theory of crime tied delinquency to analogous behaviors (e.g., substance use) that are affected by self-control (see also Hirschi and Gottfredson 1994).

David Huizinga and Cynthia Jakob-Chien (1998) use self-report data from the Denver Youth Study to determine overlap of common problems and risks with delinquency and violence in its participants—some of whom encounter the juvenile justice system. The authors focused on drug use, school problems, mental health issues, and victimization. Phyllis Ellickson,

Hilary Saner, and Kimberly. A. McGuigan (1997) carried out a similar study on violent youths and associated public health problems with a longitudinal sample of about 4,500 youths from California and Oregon. These, and some related studies, identify potential correlates of delinquency and highlight further layers of variability in delinquent youths and cases that reach the juvenile justice system.

Substance Use. Although substance use varies by type and seems to have declined recently, it is a relatively common risky behavior for adolescents. Researchers have typically found a robust relationship between drug use and delinquency (Bennett, Holloway, and Farrington 2008; Chaiken and Chaiken 1990) and across developmental periods (D'Amico et al. 2008; Sullivan and Hamilton 2007). In the Denver data, Huizinga and Jakob-Chien found a relationship between self-reported delinquency and substance use. Roughly three-fourths of the drug users in their sample were also serious delinquents. Similarly, Ellickson, Saner, and McGuigan (1997) found that individuals who engaged in multiple instances of violence were significantly more likely to have elevated levels of drinking, cigarette use, problem substance use, and polydrug use. Similarly, a study of Youth Risk Behavior Survey data from Delaware found that youths in statistically identified subgroups in which delinquency was relatively more prevalent were also likely to use alcohol and marijuana at high levels (Sullivan, Childs, and O'Connell 2009).

Edward P. Mulvey, Carol A. Schubert, and Laurie Chassin (2010) use data from the Pathways to Desistance study to assess the relationship between delinquent behavior and substance use in a sample of adolescent offenders. The authors found that the majority of adolescents in their sample used alcohol (80 percent) and marijuana (85 percent) at some point in their lives. In addition, 23 percent of these youths had used cocaine, 15 percent reported stimulant use, and 7 percent used opiates. Most youths (81 percent) also reported some type of substance use, most often marijuana or alcohol, during a two-year follow-up period. Mulvey and colleagues found that the relationship between substance use and delinquency was stable across their longitudinal measurement window and that it held within and across time periods—though substance use tended to be a more robust influence on delinquency than the reverse. Perhaps most pertinent with respect to justice intervention, roughly 36 percent of the Pathways youths met criteria for a substance dependence disorder (alcohol or drug).

Mental Health Problems. Huizinga and Jakob-Chien (1998) also measured mental health problems among subgroups of delinquents. While not all youths who engage in delinquency have mental health issues, those who do often require additional services or treatments. Although courts and treatment agencies should assess youths individually rather than assuming all youths have those needs, they must give careful consideration to mental illness that might affect court outcomes (Vieira, Skilling, and Peterson-Badali 2009). Youths' mental health problems may influence the system's response as it considers these problems and specialized needs (Skowyra and Cocozza 2006). Youths with mental health problems have complex needs and sometimes cycle through juvenile courts, treatment agencies, and other social service agencies (Armstrong 1998; Cocozza 1992; U.S. Surgeon General 2000).

In a study of more than 1,800 detained youths in Illinois using a valid and reliable instrument for measuring emotional disorder (the Diagnostic Interview Schedule for Children), Teplin and colleagues (2002) found that 66 percent of males and 74 percent of females met criteria for at least one psychiatric disorder. Excluding conduct disorder diagnoses, prevalence rates for mental disorder were 61 percent for males and 70 percent for females.[4] Jennie L. Shufelt and Joseph J. Cocozza (2006) studied 1,400 youths in detention centers, community programs, and residential facilities in three states and found that 70 percent met criteria for a mental health diagnosis (e.g., disruptive disorder, substance use disorder, anxiety disorder) and more than half had multiple diagnoses. When substance use disorder is left out, rates of mental health problems remain fairly high, at about 46 percent.

Although Huizinga and Jakob-Chien (1998) did not find clear trends relating violent delinquency to mental health, they do show that delinquent youths who committed any type of offense have a higher prevalence of psychological problems (both internalizing and externalizing) than nondelinquents. Ellickson, Saner, and McGuigan (1997) report that the youths in their sample who engaged in some violence or had a pattern of violence were 1.3 and 1.5 times, respectively, more likely to exhibit poor mental health on a validated assessment than youths who reported no violence. These problems appear to be a correlate of delinquency, and their impact on development might confer additional risk (e.g., Hoagwood et al. 1996).

Academic Problems. As mentioned earlier, school-based offenses have become more conspicuous in juvenile justice referrals since school safety initiatives were implemented with greater frequency starting in the 1990s. Evidence also suggests that school problems and low academic achievement may be correlates of delinquency and related behavioral problems (see Hinshaw 1992; Maguin and Loeber 1996). Bonding to school is in turn related to key markers of positive youth development, such as engagement in prosocial activities and school achievement, and avoidance of risky behaviors like delinquency and early substance use (Catalano et al. 2004). Huizinga and Jakob-Chien found that academic success and delinquency were related, albeit not perfectly. A high proportion of serious offenders were also truant, not surprisingly, and the authors report similar trends for suspension from school. The authors also created an any-school-problem measure that incorporated academic problems, truancy, suspension, and dropout. In all categories of offenders (serious, violent, minor) the proportion of delinquent youths with school problems was greater than for nondelinquents, increasing from less to more serious offenders. For example, 87 percent of serious violent delinquents included in the study had a school problem compared to 65 percent of minor offenders and 41 percent of nondelinquents.

Ellickson, Saner, and McGuigan's (1997) study likewise found that youths who reported violent behavior were about twice as likely to drop out of school or have low academic orientation, a measure that combined their grades and future intentions. David M. Fergusson and L. John Horwood (1995) studied the interlinkages among early conduct problems, school achievement, and delinquency while also accounting for IQ. They used data from 1,265 participants in the Christchurch (New Zealand) Health and Development Study and self-, parental, and teacher reports. The authors found relationships between behavioral problems, IQ, and school outcomes that suggest academic problems and delinquency have common causes.

Victimization and Trauma. Like substance use, mental health, and academic problems, victimization and trauma present difficulties in effectively treating justice-involved youths. Prior or ongoing victimization and related involvement in child protective service agencies is prevalent among justice-involved youths, and those youths tend to have worse outcomes (Sickmund and Puzzanchera 2014). Juvenile victimization rates developed from the National Crime Victimization Survey on the basis of responses for youths ages twelve and older show that violent victimization (simple assault and serious violence) has declined substantially (by 60 percent) among those ages twelve to seventeen since the mid-1990s. Still, that analysis shows that youths are more than twice as likely as adults to be victims of serious violent offenses and simple assaults. Julian Ford and colleagues (2013) studied direct experiences of victimization and trauma in a sample of two thousand youths in detention in Connecticut. They found that 28 percent reported at least one prior traumatic victimization experience.

Dean G. Kilpatrick, Benjamin E. Saunders, and Daniel W. Smith (2003) report findings from the National Survey of Adolescents, which included approximately four thousand youths between the ages of twelve and seventeen in 1995. Nearly 40 percent had witnessed violence at some point in their lives, and 17 percent had experienced a physical assault. Some had been victims of physically abusive punishment (9.4 percent) or sexual assault (8.1 percent); many of those who experienced victimization had some type of post-traumatic stress. Another piece of Kilpatrick and colleagues' analysis considered the relationship between victimization and delinquent behavior, finding elevated prevalence of delinquent behavior in youths who reported experiencing some victimization. Twelve percent of their sample reported engaging in at least one Uniform Crime Reporting index offense (e.g., aggravated assault, theft over fifty dollars). This was considerably higher for boys (46.7 percent) and girls (29.4 percent) who had been physically assaulted or physically abused (44.6 percent and 20.0 percent, respectively).

In their study of the community-based, albeit high-risk, Denver sample, Huizinga and Jakob-Chien (1998) also identify some overlap between delinquency and victimization. For violent victimization, those who reported no delinquency had a prevalence level of about 11 percent, compared with 28 percent for minor delinquents, 31 percent for serious nonviolent delinquency, and 42 percent for serious violent delinquency. There was greater parity and prevalence for nondelinquents but still similar patterns for nonviolent victimization as well. Adverse childhood experiences—especially victimization and trauma—have formative effects on development and can affect delinquency (Fox et al. 2015; Ireland, Smith, and Thornberry 2002). Therefore, juvenile justice settings must consider how these influences from earlier in the life course affect current behavior and how to respond to them to promote prosocial development.

Risks, Needs, and Delinquent Youths

Youths frequently have co-occurring needs and thus could have contact with several agencies. The juvenile court could become the last resort for processing youths or a default service provider for other agencies. Some co-occurring problems can inhibit provision of effective treatment by the juvenile court. For instance, substance abuse is a factor that can prolong involvement in delinquency and hinder its desistance at the end of adolescence (Hussong et al. 2004). Likewise, unmet mental health or educational needs may adversely affect treatment (Chitsabesan et al. 2006).

Problems that are *more likely* to occur in delinquent youths should not, however, be perceived to characterize *all* such cases. A study based on the Rochester and Pittsburgh sites of the Causes and Correlates of Delinquency studies and that followed up the Huizinga and Jakob-Chien (1998) analyses reviewed earlier found similar ties between substance use and delinquency but also some differences in the pattern of relationships for school problems and mental health with delinquency (Huizinga et al. 2000). These findings suggest multiple unique configurations in the youth population.

This emphasis on understanding justice-involved youths naturally requires means for characterizing risk markers, ancillary needs, or their behavioral patterns or histories so that appropriate decisions are made in individual cases or for similar groups of cases. Assessment data are increasingly prevalent in juvenile justice, and the results of those information-gathering processes offer another dimension to consider in understanding youths who reach the juvenile justice system. At this point, juvenile justice systems have—at least nominally—moved from individualistic, clinical characterizations of delinquent youths to standardized screening and assessment tools that use empirical evidence to find risk and protective factors and their relationship with recidivism (Schwalbe 2007).

Figure 1.3 shows level of risk at two phases of the juvenile justice process—detention and disposition. This sample of cases from 2010 and 2011 is from a juvenile court serving a large county in Ohio and collected in the Ohio Youth Assessment System as part of the Disproportionate Minority Contact Assessment Study.[5] The risk characterizations are relative, depending on the features of the county's juvenile justice system and local practices (McCafferty 2016), but provide a general sense of the risks of youths as they encounter the juvenile justice system and progress through it. For the detention phase roughly ten thousand cases were assessed. The preadjudication detention decision included items on prior juvenile justice contact record, current-offense level, anger control, and negative attitudes toward the juvenile justice system.[6] Thirty-seven percent of assessed cases were low risk, roughly half were moderate risk, and 13 percent were high risk.

The prior juvenile justice history indicators and score have a significant impact on the levels of risk observed in Figure 1.3. Indicators are prior offenses and age at first contact.[7] More than three-fourths of youths had a prior offense (77.5 percent), and nearly nine of ten (87.4 percent) had their first contact at age fifteen or younger. Many of the nondiverted cases had prior offenses.

For the disposition phase, roughly 2,400 cases were assessed. The prevalence of high-risk youths was relatively low at 10.6 percent. More fell into the moderate-risk group (37.8 percent), and roughly half were in the low-risk

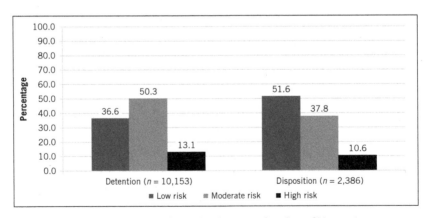

Figure 1.3 Risk levels for 2010–2011 cases for a large Ohio county
Source: Data from the Ohio Youth Assessment System.

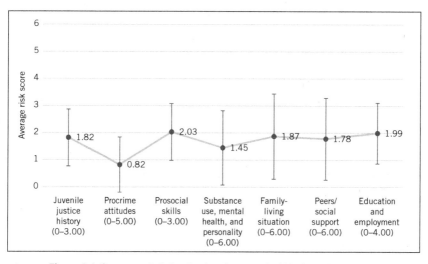

Figure 1.4 Summary statistics for domain scores in Ohio Youth Assessment System disposition tool

group (51.6 percent). Figure 1.4 shows average risk scores in domains of risk for the OYAS disposition tool, which gathers information about each youth to inform the juvenile court about appropriate sanctions or treatment for a youth for the disposition cases.

The value of 1.82 for juvenile justice history indicates that, on average, youths who reached the disposition phase tended to have a previous history of involvement with juvenile justice, but there was a fair degree of variation around that value. Only 16 percent of youths had no prior history. The value of 0.82 (SD = 1.02) for the procrime attitude suggests a relatively low internalization of future orientation toward crime, supportive attitudes toward gangs, externalizing blame, and procriminal sentiments. The mean risk score of about 2 for prosocial skills on a scale with a maximum of 3 shows a pattern of risk in that domain, however. This domain includes items tapping into whether a youth can identify his or her triggers for antisocial or risky behavior and can weigh the pros and cons of different decisions. The substance use, mental health, and personality domain captures whether a youth used alcohol and drugs and when he or she started, whether the youth displays any significant mental health issue, and whether the youth has inflated self-esteem. The average score was 1.45 on a scale to 6, which suggests just moderate risk on this domain. There was a good deal of variation, however, because the standard deviation (SD = 1.37) is quite close to the mean. Fifty-eight percent of cases had a score of just 0 or 1 on this domain.

The final three domains touch on families, peers, and education and employment. The means for the family and living situation (1.87) and the peer risk (1.78) measures are comparable and indicate moderate problems in each of those areas. They both show substantial variation relative to their averages (standard deviations of approximately 1.5). Employment and educational deficits, which include school suspension and expulsion and the youth's relationship to his or her school or employer, tended to be moderate in this sample, with a mean of almost 2 and a standard deviation of 1. This domain had the lowest prevalence of cases with scores of 0, or an absence of risk, at 10 percent.

Strengths in Delinquent Youths

The orientation of courts and allied agencies means that assessment tools are predominantly developed to find risk of further delinquency and needs that might hinder effective treatment. Some assessments do emphasize skills and strengths to a greater degree, however. The Youth Assessment and Screening Instrument measures risks, but it also has measures for several strengths (Jones et al. 2015, 2016). These include youths' compliance with their parents, school attendance, recent improvements in school conduct or grades, positive peer associations, and their acceptance of responsibility (Jones et al. 2016).

Analysis of 464 probation youths in Alberta, Canada, found that the strength score had significant predictive validity, suggesting a protective effect whereby youths with higher scores had a lower likelihood of recidivism during an eighteen-month follow-up period (Jones et al. 2016). Specifically, and controlling for other relevant factors, the odds of recidivism decreased 5 percent for each unit increase on the strength score. Jones and colleagues also identified an interaction effect in which high-risk youths saw a greater buffer effect of strengths. Recidivism rates were 43 percent for high-risk, low-strength youths and less than half that (19.7 percent) for youths who were high risk, high strength. This was still higher than the recidivism rates for low-risk youths, but the presence of more strengths significantly attenuated the risk. In a similar study of adults, Natalie Jones and colleagues concluded that "risk and strength factors co-exist in relative combinations within an individual, collectively influencing criminal outcome" (2015, 332). This is true for youths too. In fact, establishing the presence of protective factors or strengths is even more essential because of youths' lack of autonomy, relative to adults, in certain decisions (e.g., limited choice in residence or school; see, e.g., Sharkey and Sampson 2010).

The presence of strengths and some level of protective factors are also apparent in analyzing data on youthful offenders from the Pathways to Desistance study. These youths, all of whom were adjudicated delinquent, possessed strengths or assets alongside their risk factors and delinquency. For example, when study participants were asked in their initial interview about the support of caring adults, more than two-thirds mentioned multiple caring adults at least three times. About two-thirds of the Pathways sample chose "somewhat true" or a higher level on a measure tapping the perceived value of religion and spirituality. On average, the youths in the sample were also beyond the midpoint of the scale, which ranges from 1 to 5, on aspirations for work, family, and law (4.43, SD = 0.57) and motivation to succeed (3.25, SD = 0.64). Similarly, a review of the social support domain for the delinquent youths from the Ohio Youth Assessment System sample discussed previously showed that less than 5 percent were at the top two scores in their respective distributions. This means that most youths have some degree of social support to build on in intervention programs and to serve as a basis for a prosocial pathway from juvenile justice. Although delinquent youths frequently carry multiple risk factors, many clearly also possess some foundation for positive change.

Delinquency Histories

Historical patterns of delinquency vary considerably across youths as well. This is evident when looking retrospectively at the risks underlying youths' involvement in delinquency, the situational circumstances of the delinquent referral, and at the continuity or desistance of delinquency that follows contact with the juvenile court. The elements reviewed to this point interact and accumulate to generate delinquency histories. These, of course, play a role in determining the response to individual cases and allocation of resources across juvenile court caseloads.

Age and Delinquency Patterns. The study of the relationship between age and criminal behavior stretches back to the work of Adolphe Quetelet in the 1800s (Loeber 2012; Quetelet [1831] 1984). As the concept of adolescence developed, it appeared there as well. G. Stanley Hall argued that many children struggled as they moved toward "complete maturity, so that every step of the upward way is strewn with wreckage of body, mind, and morals. There is not only arrest, but perversion, at every stage, and hoodlumism, juvenile crime and secret vice" (1904, xiv). Although exaggerated, this reflects an innate sense of the relationship between age and crime, but later statistical analysis bolstered the notion of the age-crime curve, which is one of just a few recurring findings about crime (Farrington 1986). While some argued that this trend was invariant and therefore did not require much investigation (e.g., Hirschi and Gottfredson 1983), others saw enough variation to consider possible distinctions between overall crime rates and the contributions of individuals to those broader trends (e.g., Farrington 1986; Greenberg 1985; Loeber 2012; Sweeten, Piquero, and Steinberg 2013) to further dissect

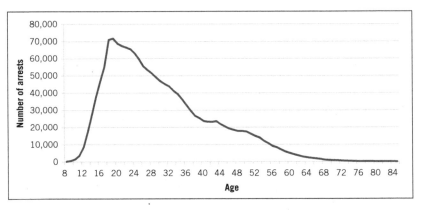

Figure 1.5 Age and reported arrests
Source: Data from 2014 National Incident-Based Reporting System.

distinctions within that general relationship (Moffitt 1993). For the purposes of juvenile justice, one can simply note that the peak of the aggregate age-crime curve is in the late teens (see Figure 1.5).

Assessment of the overall crime problem requires the separation of prevalence and incidence. "Prevalence" refers to the proportion of the population who have committed any delinquency, and "incidence" is the actual level of delinquency among those who engage in it (Farrington 1986). David P. Farrington (1986) concluded that the age-crime curve heavily depends on increased prevalence during adolescence and early adulthood, but varying incidence rates mean that individual youths do not uniformly follow that pattern (see also Blumstein and Cohen 1979). The juvenile justice system therefore encounters cases of fleeting delinquency as well as those that are more enduring and damaging in nature. It must discern between them to be effective and efficient in its interventions.

The youth's age upon encountering the justice system is a key demarcation point in how the case is handled. Likewise, age is relevant to thinking about how to reposition a more developmental juvenile justice system. Age considerations are directly affected by statutes, and other considerations affect case-level decisions. Age is a statutory guideline in juvenile and adult court jurisdiction in all fifty states (see Griffin et al. 2011), and the age guideline is "the most obvious way in which the criminal [or juvenile] justice system influences the age-crime curve [and the relationship between age and crime]" (Farrington 1986, 233). The understanding of the timing of offenses, particularly early delinquency, is useful in comprehending the etiology of delinquency and developing a response to it. For example, decision makers might make a distinction between early onset delinquency and delinquency by youths who first come to the system later in adolescence, which might lead the former to be seen as riskier than the latter.

TABLE 1.3 AGE AT REFERRAL, 2010–2011, DELINQUENCY CASES IN SAMPLE
OF THIRTEEN OHIO JUVENILE COURTS

Age at referral	Number of cases	Percentage	Cumulative percentage
9	32	0.1	0.1
10	233	0.4	0.4
11	799	1.2	1.7
12	1,787	2.8	4.4
13	4,127	6.4	10.8
14	7,661	11.9	22.7
15	12,412	19.3	42.0
16	16,862	26.2	68.2
17	20,473	31.8	100.0
Total	64,386	100.0	

Furdella and Puzzanchera's (2015) review of delinquency cases in juvenile courts for 2013 showed a roughly even split between those younger than sixteen (53 percent) and those age sixteen or older (47 percent). The group of those younger than sixteen was a majority in all offense categories except for drug law violations, which tended to involve youths who were sixteen or older. These proportions are similar to those from a sample of youths from Ohio referred to one of thirteen juvenile courts between 2010 and 2011. This sample excludes some diversion cases, but 42 percent of the 64,000 cases were fifteen or younger at the time of involvement with the juvenile court (see Table 1.3). It is possible that some older youths charged with delinquent or criminal offenses were waived directly to adult court—leading to underestimates of their relative presence—but youths who have not yet hit middle adolescence make up a large proportion of those in juvenile court.

The age question is inherently conditioned by whether a youth has encountered the system before or not. The age of first official system contact was known for approximately 27,000 of the cases described in Table 1.3. Roughly two-thirds had a prior contact with the juvenile court, suggesting that there is some degree of repetitive contact among those who made it past the case filing or diversion stages of the process. First-time offenders were a majority at only one age group (twelve years old). The data presented in Figure 1.6 suggest some interesting age and first-contact patterns. At the very earliest ages with data (ten and younger), most delinquent youths were not encountering the system for the first time. This is a very small group (about 0.67 percent), which suggests that precocious delinquent youths encountered the system before late childhood. First contacts were relatively more frequent at ages eleven through thirteen, after which at least 60 percent of cases had a prior contact when they encountered these juvenile courts. In line with the

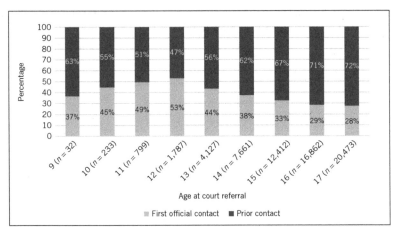

Figure 1.6 Age of youth at referral and first or prior contact, thirteen Ohio juvenile courts

juvenile justice history data presented earlier, Figure 1.6 shows a decline in the percentage of first-contact youths after age twelve.

Chronic and Serious Offenders. Juvenile offenders can also be characterized by the consistency and seriousness of their delinquency. These characteristics are behind calls for more severe juvenile penalties and transfer to adult court (Fagan 2008), as well as more stringent individual case judgments in juvenile courts (Salekin, Rogers, and Ustad 2001). Youths who have repetitively or chronically engaged in delinquency and those who have serious offenses are treated as distinct. Many youths are "one and done" in the system, but repetitive contacts may indicate a more serious delinquency issue. This question of repeat offending came up in interviews with juvenile court personnel and in focus groups with police officers from the Ohio Disproportionate Minority Contact Assessment discussed in this book—both in terms of processing individual cases and in more general resource allocation decisions (i.e., toward chronic delinquents or high-crime places).

Howard N. Snyder (1998) conducted a major study on the isolation, recurrence, and type of youth contact with the juvenile justice system. It was set against the backdrop of disagreements about significant increases in youth violence in the 1990s and the related question of whether there was a group of especially recalcitrant and dangerous juvenile offenders (see Cook and Laub 1998; Dilulio 1995; Moore and Tonry 1998). Snyder describes "juvenile court careers" for about 150,000 youths in Maricopa County, Arizona, from 1980 to 1995, and he developed an aggregate case profile of juveniles with serious, chronic, or violent offenses, or some combination (1998, 429). He excluded cases with only status offenses (e.g., running away, truancy) or traffic offenses. Nearly two-thirds (63.9 percent) of youths were nonchronic (fewer than four referrals) with no serious or violent offense—meaning they did not have extensive contact with the system or any serious or violent offenses. About 18 percent had at least one serious nonviolent offense—that is, they were the portion of the serious offender group that did not include violent offenders.

Chronic, serious offenders made up about 8 percent of the total sample. Roughly 3 percent of cases were chronic, serious, and violent offenders. As in Marvin E. Wolfgang, Robert M. Figlio, and Thorsten Sellin's (1972) famous cohort study, Snyder (1998) found that a small group of youths was responsible for a disproportionate number of referrals. About 15 percent of youths were responsible for 45 percent of all referrals, 39 percent of all nonserious referrals, 58 percent of serious nonviolent referrals, and 60 percent of violent referrals. In general, most delinquents are not so entrenched in their behaviors that the response of the system is unlikely to have an impact. Snyder's findings also indicate that policy and practice aimed primarily at extreme cases may not be beneficial for the majority of justice-involved youths, raising the question of how to effectively respond to the many youths who are nonserious offenders.

Data from four hundred randomly selected juvenile offenders in Philadelphia were used to attempt to replicate those findings and expand the discussion (Conway and McCord 2002). This sample was selected in 1987, which falls roughly in the midpoint of Snyder's (1998) fifteen-year window. The data are an evenly split selection of co-offense cases and solo-offense cases. The authors collected official record data on all juvenile arrests for the sample cases. Using Snyder's definition of four or more offenses, roughly half the sample (48.5 percent) qualified as chronic offenders, which is about 10 percentage points higher than in Snyder's study. Approximately 60 percent of youths had at least one violent offense, defined as rape, robbery, aggravated assault, or attempted murder, in their juvenile record. This was like the definition used in the Arizona study, but the prevalence of youths who engaged in a violent offense was greater. Snyder also identifies serious, but nonviolent, offenses (e.g., burglary, serious larceny). Although the offenses are not identical, the sample used by Kevin Conway and Joan McCord (2002) includes an indicator for "burglary, theft, vehicle theft, and arson," which comes close to Snyder's definition. Approximately 70 percent of cases were charged with at least one offense from those categories. All in all, about one-third of cases qualified as serious, chronic, or violent when using Snyder's definitions. That group accounts for 57 percent of the total arrests from this sample.[8]

The relatively small groups of serious, chronic, or violent delinquents exist alongside a larger, diverse population of youths who also require juvenile justice attention. The analysis from the Philadelphia group suggests that these career patterns may vary across place and that the composition of the juvenile offender population contains multiple permutations. The most serious offenders are but one part of that population with the rest perhaps best described as nonserious offenders who engage in delinquency for a relatively short time. This confirms assertions about adolescence-limited offenders from the developmental and life-course research. Still, beyond the risk and needs principles in effective intervention (see Lipsey 2009), from a broader reform perspective nonserious-offender cases can disproportionately draw down resources if the full composition of caseloads is absent from agency and case-level decisions. They therefore require concerted attention in discussions of reform.

Layers of Variation and Contemporary Juvenile Justice

The preceding survey of delinquency and delinquents offers insight across several dimensions, including trends in court- or police-recorded delinquency, relative prevalence in seriousness and type of delinquent offense, associated problems and assets that occur simultaneously with or before delinquency, and the chronicity and seriousness of delinquency. The juvenile court must pull these pieces together to deal with the many types of case and offense profiles in fashioning its sanctions and treatments. The characteristics of justice-involved youths and their delinquent acts frequently show developmental traces that reflect long- and short-term interactions between youths and their environments. Something as seemingly mundane as age and arrest location can reveal familial or peer leverage, based on supervision and attachment, on youth behavior and attitudes. The family or peer context for the delinquency might also show whether a youth faces an elevated likelihood of arrest and therefore may be subject to an arrest's downstream developmental implications. Given the delinquency population's individuality and the court's multifaceted mission, the juvenile justice system must respond in multiple distinct ways.

This creates challenges and potential obstacles to a reform agenda for juvenile justice. Simply stated, cases before the typical juvenile court—with their offenses, individual delinquency history, risks and needs, and youth and family responses to the process—are tremendously varied. Appropriately handling cases that have different levels of severity (of offenses and youth risks and needs) requires that the system not underreact to cases involving more serious offenses or prior records and not overreact and expend resources on low-risk, first-time cases. The service component of the system's mission means that it may be inclined to respond to cases that are low risk but high need, which has implications if done improperly because those youths may wind up worse off developmentally after their contact with the system.

Age can strongly influence the narrative that emerges around a given case (or set of them). A youth who offends at age ten or eleven, which is a small group according to the data presented earlier, could be perceived simply as a victim of familial circumstances, peer associations, or school environment *or* as a precocious offender making an initial foray into delinquency and crime that could continue into adulthood. This has implications for sanction and treatment regimens, which may be consequential in later offending and developmental pathways. Just as setting overly restrictive distinctions in adult and juvenile court jurisdictions can hinder solving individual delinquency cases (Scott and Steinberg 2008), so too simply including developmental principles in responding to justice-involved youths will not be the solution to the complex problems in individuals, communities, and society at large that often contribute to delinquency. All this means that it is necessary to consider the full scope of cases treated and sanctioned by juvenile courts when implementing juvenile justice reform and deciding on appropriate sanctions and plausible interventions.

The information presented here suggests that the easy narrative of "wayward youths" or "hostile predators" (Morse 1997, 15) works when considering the culpability of delinquents or how to best respond to their risks and needs. Instead, the system must respond to a complicated mix of cases and incomplete information about past behavior and future prospects. That variation affects both day-to-day processes (e.g., risk and needs assessment, diversion or intake decisions, effective referral and treatment) and large-scale initiatives (e.g., developing specialized caseloads, deinstitutionalization). Within this context the juvenile justice system must respond effectively and efficiently to protect the safety of the community and uphold its values while promoting developmental change and minimizing harm for youths. This chapter has considered important who, why, and what questions pertaining to the current landscape of the juvenile court. A full accounting of the juvenile justice system for contemporary analysis and adjustment of policy and practice also requires some attention to the question of how it processes and disposes delinquency cases. That is the focus of Chapter 2.

2

Characterizing Contemporary Juvenile Justice

This chapter is a companion to Chapter 1. It provides an overview of current juvenile justice policy and practice to characterize the system encountered by youths just described. It describes the origins and evolution of the juvenile justice system to set a historical foundation before moving on to the system's current operations and objectives. Although frequently proactive in seeking solutions, the juvenile justice system carries out institutionalized tasks and missions. It is not unusual to find juvenile courts dealing with service gaps for girls and minority youths, implementing evidence-based treatment and specialized courts, and making efforts to reduce detention while simultaneously imposing sanctions and facilitating treatment for the juvenile court's general caseload and missions. After discussing the court's day-to-day objectives and ongoing initiatives, I describe the broader climate of the juvenile justice system to set the stage for further analysis in later chapters.

Foundation and Evolution of the Juvenile Justice System

Any talk of reform must draw on theory, research, and views of youthfulness as well as the pragmatic question of how those pieces fit in the current juvenile justice system. The early developers of the court were responding to at least two, related, problems. One was the perceived risks and needs of youths in urban environments who were getting into trouble and seemed to have little or no adult oversight (Caldwell 1961). The general stance of the juvenile court is characterized in prior analysis as either mostly benevolent or nefarious (see Platt 1969; Schultz 1973). The operating assumption was that—without intervention—these youths would continue to get into progressively more serious trouble, hurting themselves and society. With this came a desire to reroute youths who were on potentially problematic pathways. A second objective was to ensure that youths were not treated the same as adults (Mack 1909). Together, these goals confer on the juvenile justice system a presumption of intervention but also a desire to avoid the most restrictive placements for delinquent youths. These early objectives manifested themselves in a system that sought not only to provide services to youths with needs but also to be a court that would dispatch sanctions for wrongdoing. As there is today, there was variation in points of emphasis, but both sanction and treatment were a part of the court's initial mission (Mack 1909; Tanenhaus 2004).

Parens patriae was a foundation for intervention in the lives of youths perceived to need it (Fader et al. 2001; Pisciotta 1982) as was the problem resolution practiced by equity courts in British common law as opposed to adversarial fact-finding (Crippen 1999). For this to work, separate case processing and disposition in a self-contained court system was essential. The juvenile court embodied those ideals, and many of the early child savers who helped lead its development, such as Jane Addams, Lucy Flower, and Julie Lathrop, were social workers or members of women's groups concerned with treatment (Tanenhaus 2004). The court's creators hoped to use social and behavioral science, just emerging at the time, to treat youths in a separate system that fit that philosophy (Sullivan et al. 2012). The work of William Healy (1912, 1933) and others, like Augustus Bronner (1925), provided a scientific basis for many of the court's ideas. Youths, it was thought, could be saved from a life of crime by limiting their warehousing in institutions and instead treating them (Rothman 1980).

The early juvenile court judges, whose personalities and philosophies about youth and delinquency played an outsized role in juvenile justice, informed the direction of the court (Fox 1996; Mack 1909; Tanenhaus 2004). The court was interventionist and treatment focused, but early officials differed in how they operationalized that mission. Julian Mack described the early mission of the juvenile court as reducing possible stigma on "mischievous" juveniles to prevent later adult criminality. He also noted the value of sanctions for delinquent acts, writing that "the object of the juvenile court and of the intervention of the state is, of course, in no case to lessen or to weaken the sense of responsibility either of the child or of the parent. On the contrary, the aim is to develop and to enforce it" (1909, 120). Analyzing the court's history, David S. Tanenhaus wrote that "through vesting state responsibility for both dependent and delinquent children in a juvenile court, they [the court founders] had merged the goals of promoting child welfare and controlling crime" (2004, 22). Of course, this was an idealized framework, and differing philosophies and practicalities over time would affect the relative balance of those goals (Bernard and Kurlychek 2010; Howell 2003).

Given this orientation to both youths and the community, the juvenile justice system continually experiences debate about philosophy and tactics, a pendulum alternately swinging toward treatment or control (Bernard and Kurlychek 2010). To an extent, the argument is irresolvable because it inevitably draws on empirical evidence and value judgments—and value judgments about that empirical evidence. This is evident in the disagreements that have emerged over time and the periodic debates about the nature of the system and the way it operates. For example, debates about the effectiveness and appropriateness of juvenile diversion programs blended analysis of philosophical positions with empirical evidence (see, e.g., Binder and Geis 1984; Polk 1984). Those programs are still frequently used in juvenile justice systems.

A string of developments beginning in the 1960s introduced some shocks to the system. U.S. Supreme Court decisions, like *In Re Gault* and *Kent v. United States*, restricted the informality of the U.S. juvenile justice system by adding procedural protections that were more in line with those available to defendants in the criminal court. These changes came both from this case law that questioned the credibility and effectiveness of aspects of the juvenile court process and from broader societal dissatisfaction with the status quo. Those inside and outside the system raised concerns about whether the juvenile justice system was delivering on its promise and providing protections for juveniles in terms of due process and effective treatment options while also being mindful of public safety. A shifting landscape at the societal, legislative, and executive levels affected the juvenile justice system during the 1960s and 1970s as well. Geoff Ward and Aaron Kupchik (2009, 87) characterize this shift toward "system accountability" as frequently leading to efforts in diversion and deinstitutionalization (Klein 1979; Ohlin, Coates, and Miller 1975). The later toughening up of delinquency response at the end of twentieth century was driven in part by conclusions reached through research that, in hindsight, appear to have been interpreted without a full accounting of the influences on youth violence and delinquency (Cook and Laub 1998).

The court is sometimes faulted in political arguments as either being an insufficient guardian of youth rights or falling short in effective intervention. Conversely, others argue that it treats delinquent youths too leniently and fails to provide preemptive restraint on future criminal behavior (Bernard and Kurlychek 2010). The latter position had more leverage late in the twentieth century, when tougher sanctions for the juvenile justice system were instituted. Although this was not all-consuming and elements of the juvenile court's early philosophy and practice remain (see Mears 2002; Mulvey and

Iselin 2008), the net effect was a more formalized system that emphasized punishment more than it previously had (Bazemore and Umbreit 1995). Simon I. Singer (1997), for example, describes the recriminalization of delinquency through New York's 1978 Juvenile Offender law, which was ahead of its time in reducing the age of adult eligibility for certain categories of offenses (especially violent ones). This, in effect, created legislative waiver or automatic transfer of cases to adult court (Griffin et al. 2011) in response to political concerns about a series of prominent violent acts committed by juveniles. Numerous states eventually adopted this stance as political figures led the charge for harsher sanctions (Haberman 2014). Among the most prominent was Alfred Regnery (1985), who, drawing on Marvin E. Wolfgang, Robert M. Figlio, and Thorsten Sellin's (1972) research on a Philadelphia birth cohort, argued for a move away from treating youths and toward deterrence, unsealing of juvenile records, and a dropping of age distinctions in how cases were processed. This represents the individual accountability phase of juvenile justice (Ward and Kupchik 2009).

While these shifts certainly had a large effect in many systems across the United States and shaped the response to juvenile delinquency in consequential ways, the system nevertheless retained its fundamental characteristics. As it moved toward its one-hundredth anniversary, some critics argued that the uneasy tension of the newer due process and punishment influences coupled with a social service orientation were failing and that states and localities should abolish the juvenile court in favor of a single age-graded justice system with repatriation of service functions to other public agencies (Ainsworth 1990; Feld 1997).

The historical accounts make one point abundantly clear: like many institutions that have lasted over decades, the juvenile court has changed in some ways since its inception while also remaining quite stable in others. Some changes have clearly come from within, such as recent efforts to partner with researchers, communities, and philanthropic organizations to reduce detention rates. Other catalysts come from outside, such as a string of U.S. Supreme Court decisions in the 1960s. But as with any institution, tradition and inertia have held certain initiatives in check or caused a rebalancing before significant changes start to take hold (Bernard and Kurlychek 2010). This historical account is relevant to today's reform efforts because it identifies boundaries for change and identifies obstacles to moving in a new direction. It also sets the basis for what the juvenile justice system regularly does, which is vital since current policy and practice must be analyzed to find what will be effective in the future. Juvenile courts' structure and process differ across the United States and the world. The implementation context for any newly proposed policy or practice is set by these institutionalized tasks and each system's individual method in carrying them out.

What the Juvenile Justice System Does Today

Juvenile courts in the United States are responsible for handling more than a million delinquency cases in any given year (Furdella and Puzzanchera 2015), most of which were formally petitioned to the juvenile courts (55 percent in 2013). After being formally petitioned to juvenile courts, youths proceed down several paths. Figure 2.1 shows the processing options, which generate complex contingencies in formal and informal processes, sanctions, and monitoring.[1] Each of the juvenile justice decision points in the figure is relevant in considering the actions taken by the juvenile justice system as it responds to cases. The juvenile court process makes use of both official and unofficial discretionary decisions with varying degrees of structure and supervision. The figure highlights that the juvenile justice system bends toward intervention. The patterns shown in case outcomes also reflect interrelated steps in juvenile justice case processing and decisions made by various system personnel.

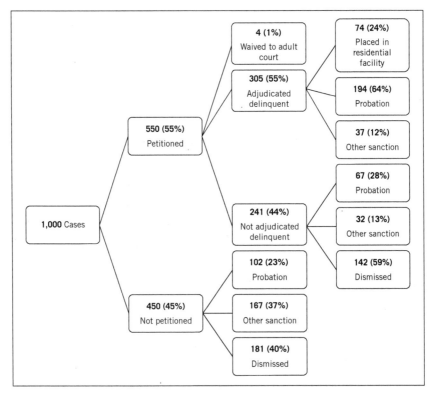

Figure 2.1 Overview of juvenile justice processing, 2013
Source: Furdella and Puzzanchera 2015, 4.

Intake and Screening. The process of resolving delinquency cases starts at juvenile court intake. The decisions made at initial stages of processing significantly affect the operations of the juvenile justice system and other related agencies, have potential impacts on community safety, and, of course, hold possibilities for positive or negative effects for youths. The decision-making process is somewhat different and, arguably, more complex in juvenile justice than that in the adult system. The decision maker and sources and weighting of information used in reaching decisions can vary considerably across juvenile justice agencies (Mears and Kelly 1999). Screening occurs either inside or outside the court (Hockenberry and Puzzanchera 2015). In some localities, such as Florida, the process begins at a designated assessment center (see, e.g., Dembo and Brown 1994; McReynolds et al. 2008). These how and who questions have effects on the progression of cases through the system. This is due, at least in part, to there possibly being distinct groups of decision makers who handle these cases. In some cases, probation officers or another intake official might handle that initial-decision stage, whereas a prosecutor's office might take the lead in some jurisdictions or for certain types of cases (Mears 2012).

During the intake process, cases may be dismissed for insufficient legal evidence or diverted because of the low severity of the offense. These decisions combine offense seriousness and a youth's past record (Mears and Kelly 1999). There will inherently be some subjectivity in the decisions made by different actors and in different places. This variability may also reflect whether the intake decision is tied to detention or not. Available resources and other focal concerns are likely to vary across place, leading to differences in intake policies and decisions (see, e.g., Mears and Kelly 1999). Individuals in different roles in the system, such as prosecutors, may also have different perspectives on juvenile offender culpability and accountability compared to other juvenile justice professionals. Ward and Kupchik (2009) found, for instance, that prosecutors were significantly more likely than probation officers to prioritize just deserts and victims' rights over rehabilitation in delinquency cases.[2]

As Figure 2.1 shows, a youth has roughly fifty-fifty odds of being formally petitioned in court (55 percent in 2013). The early intake and screening process ripples out to other stages as well. This ancillary processing means that nonpetitioned cases frequently receive probation supervision or continue other system involvement (e.g., formal diversion program) or have some further contact with or supervision by the court or its affiliates.

Detention. If a youth is formally processed, the juvenile court faces a decision of whether to hold or release the youth while the case is in progress. "Detention serves as a gateway to the rest of the juvenile justice system" and therefore plays a significant role in case and youth outcomes (Barton 2012,

637). Roughly 22 percent of delinquency cases were detained in 2014 (OJJDP 2017). This is a larger relative prevalence than in 1985 but represents a drop of roughly 6 percent in the absolute number of youths held in detention facilities. This followed a period between the mid-1980s and 2005 with a steady climb in the number of youths detained by the juvenile justice system (Barton 2012).

David W. Roush (1996) identifies two functions of detention. The first relates to the notion of the restrictive environment. This is the preventive function and is meant to give the juvenile justice system security that a youth will appear at court hearings; it is also meant to preserve the safety of the youth and the community and to prevent further delinquency. The decision in *Schall v. Martin* (1984) upheld the preventive use of juvenile detention, in accordance with the protective aspect of the juvenile court's mission (Feld 1984). The second function is therapeutic detention, in which the youth is held while going through the court process and the system addresses his or her risks or needs during that time (Roush 1996). This starts with assessment and diagnosis, which presumably can then carry over into appropriate intervention that continues during the court process and following adjudication.

Courts might try to limit the use of preadjudication detention for several reasons (Holman and Ziedenberg 2006; Stanfield 1999; Wordes and Jones 1998). All things equal, detaining youths is a more expensive alternative than keeping them in the community while moving through the juvenile justice process. Keeping them in the community also affords them the opportunity to maintain their family relationships and school routines and—especially for lower-risk youths—limits even greater contact with other youths who may exacerbate their delinquency or related attitudes (Dodge et al. 2007). Even short-term stays in preadjudication detention may have a negative developmental influence (Holman and Ziedenberg 2006). More research has investigated the effects of longer stays in secure placement (e.g., Loughran et al. 2009) than has been done for shorter ones. There is also the potential for overuse of detention with minority youths because race affects those decisions (e.g., perceived dangerousness, assumptions about family supervision) (Bridges and Steen 1998; Rodriguez 2010).

Diversion. Diversion programming is one way of limiting detention (Krisberg and Austin 1993; Shelden 1999), but it has potential functions in addition to that. Decisions to redirect youths away from the juvenile justice system often happen soon after court referral at intake but can come up as options later in the process as well. This is a key aspect of juvenile justice because it is both an organizing philosophy that drives response to (some) delinquency and an umbrella label for practical intervention or prevention programs. The goal is to remove kids from the system who—on the basis of some criteria—are deemed inappropriate for formal processing. Its underlying logic is based in part on labeling theory, which suggests that how adults respond to youth misbehavior has implications for its repetition (Lemert 1951). The theory recommends that the system should maintain a hands-off approach to youths in as many cases as possible (Schur 1973).

The reality of juvenile diversion in action is somewhat different than that implied by the philosophy. Juvenile justice policy and practice invoke the idea of diversion in a multitude of ways, meaning that the term has a lack of precision. Diversion is often determined during the intake process and, as described earlier, multiple court actors make these decisions depending on the jurisdiction and offense seriousness (e.g., prosecutors, intake staff, and magistrates). Charles Whitebread and John Heilman (1988) identify several criteria used in making these decisions: a youth's admission or denial of the delinquency, parental supervision of the youth, the youth's status in school or work, the willingness of the youth and family to commit to mandatory programming, the youth's age, and the nature of the offense. In some cases, there are also specialized diversion programs for youths with particular risks or needs, such as mental health problems or for school-based offenses.

Diversionary decision making is evident in multiple parts of Figure 2.1. First, roughly 45 percent of cases were not petitioned and took a path away from formal court processing. A minority of the diverted cases were dismissed outright (40 percent). The other 60 percent split between informal probation and another sanction (community service, restitution, treatment). Even when youths were not adjudicated delinquent, which was 44 percent of those petitioned, about 40 percent were on probation or received an alternative sanction. This was 10 percent of the overall cases processed during that year, which means that diversion plus some type of supervision or intervention is quite common in the juvenile justice system. It also illustrates the complex configurations of formal and informal youth involvement with the juvenile court. Even those youths seemingly passed over for processing are not totally exempt from sanctions or treatment as a result.

Many types of individual programs fall under the label of diversion, and they often correspond to different dispositional options. The research to this point is somewhat equivocal about the effectiveness of formal diversion programs. Unfortunately, a preponderance of weak evaluation designs for diversion programs raises concerns about making inferences from these findings (McGrath 2008). Given its widespread influence as an operating philosophy and vehicle for delivering services to delinquent youths, diversion should be a well-established method for handling delinquent youths, but the reality is more complicated. Craig S. Schwalbe and his colleagues (2012) conducted a meta-analysis of juvenile justice diversion programs, including case management, individual treatment, family-based treatment, youth courts, and restorative-justice-type programs. Their meta-analysis resulted in an odds ratio of 0.83, which means that, on average, the twenty-eight diversion programs in their study reduced recidivism by 17 percent compared with other groups (either justice referral or minimal service diversion). This effect is not statistically significant.

Despite the proliferation of formal diversion programs in juvenile justice systems there is little reliable evidence that they are working as intended, and their effects greatly vary. Several factors may be at work. First, the nature and quality of diversion programs substantially differ, as do their selection criteria (Schwalbe et al. 2012). Programs range from all-encompassing family or school-based treatment interventions to minor sanctions like civil citation or community service, or they attempt to provide services to specific subgroups (see Sullivan et al. 2007; Sullivan et al. 2010). Additionally, youth assessment and matching differ across courts as do eligibility criteria of strategies and programs, which focus on specialized offenses, risks, or needs to varying degrees.

The well-intended notion of diversion can interact with the underlying parens patriae orientation of the system to some unintended ends. Figure 2.1 illustrates this potential for net widening: a majority of not-formally-petitioned youths have some type of probation contact or other sanction. In a study of 1,200 cases in a multisite diversion program, Charles E. Frazier and John K. Cochran (1986) found that diverted youths were often subject to the same amount and length of system contact as nondiverted youths. On the basis of the authors' interviews and field observation, the explanation lies in a mix of preservation of previous ways of doing things (i.e., an inclination to intervention) and the treatment orientation of the program personnel. They often equated doing good with intervention and therefore maintained connection with and supervision of diversion cases.

Diversion may be a vehicle for needed treatment and is the result of some delinquent act or status offense by youths (Binder and Geis 1984), but the treatment that youths receive and the way noncompliance with diversion is handled affects the balance between helpful intervention with lesser penetration of the system and greater system penetration and related collateral consequences such as a more serious juvenile record (Pogrebin, Poole, and Regoli 1984). If youths receive necessary treatment that limits their further penetration or later contact with the system, then diversion may be appropriate, but if they face more punishment for noncompliance for problems that emerge during diversion programming, this may create a negative downstream effect rather than a benefit. The notion of diversion is essential to considering prospects for a more developmental juvenile justice because in-versus-out and depth-of-penetration questions have consequences for the impact of developmental juvenile justice. A developmental perspective suggests that these are opportunities for intervention with youths at risk—

regardless of the seriousness of their offense—but the nature of that response requires a good deal of thought because it affects a youth's pathway.

Adjudication and Disposition. Adjudication involves the convergence of several aspects of the court process. Youths are found delinquent if the facts presented before the court support that she or he committed the offense beyond a reasonable doubt (Kaufman 1980) or if the youth admits to the offense in court (Sanborn 1992). A judge leads this process. The court's decision is based on evidence brought by a court official, such as a prosecutor or probation officer. It typically involves a two-pronged focus on the youth's situation and the facts of the case (see Emerson 1969; Kupchik 2006). Figure 2.1 shows that roughly 55 percent of formally petitioned cases are later adjudicated delinquent.

Possible dispositions for youths who are adjudicated delinquent are quite varied and may involve juvenile justice system resources as well as referral to other affiliated facilities or agencies (e.g., day reporting centers, treatment facilities, community service agencies). Decisions often involve multiple parts. For example, a youth may be placed on formal supervision but also must complete mandatory treatment, perform community service, or pay back victims (Furdella and Puzzanchera 2015). These disposition options can be categorized in a few ways, pointing to clear differences in how cases are handled following adjudication. The nature and effectiveness of these dispositions determine whether youths are positively or detrimentally affected by contact with the juvenile justice system. Figure 2.2 categorizes possible dispositions used for 1,000 randomly selected cases over the course of two years at a juvenile court in Ohio.[3] This is a court in a jurisdiction of about five hundred thousand residents (U.S. Census Bureau 2018).

Between-court variation in the availability and use of different disposition options is substantial and has implications both for individual case outcomes and uniformity in implementation of policy and practice. As shown in Figure 2.2, there are fourteen distinct possibilities for this court. They are roughly ordered by seriousness. Notably, custodial placements make up a small proportion of the total (3.6 percent), and most of the sanctions and dispositions are seemingly nonserious. Dismissal (20.6 percent) and diversion and unofficial resolutions (16.3 percent) make up 37 percent of the case dispositions. In other cases, the court admonished the youth (10 percent) or told her or him to attend school (7.7 percent) and then monitored its orders through further probation and court contact. The juvenile court required other youths to engage in reparative acts such as writing an apology letter to the victim (7.2 percent), performing community service (12.9 percent), or making restitution (4.4 percent). Orders for some type of counseling or treatment—frequently related to substance use—were also prevalent in this set of cases (17.7 percent). This reflects the variety of case outcomes—from

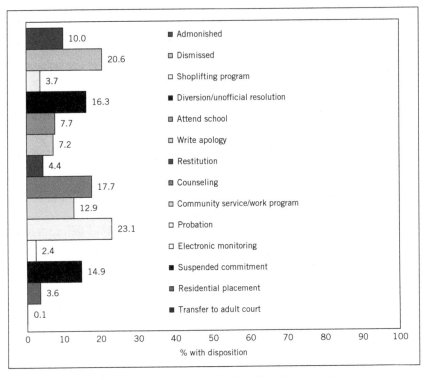

Figure 2.2 The many possible dispositions in one court

the most serious, which are rare, to those that seek to minimize youths' penetration into the system but require something of them.

About 23 percent of the case dispositions involved probation; just over 2 percent of cases were placed on electronic monitoring. Fewer than 4 percent of youths were placed in residential facilities, but nearly 15 percent had dispositions involving a suspended commitment, offering the contingency of placement should a youth not comply with the court's orders and probation supervision. The judge waived less than 1 percent of these cases to adult court. Of those with disposition information, 57 percent had just 1 case disposition; 43 percent had more than 1 disposition. The average was 2.04, with a maximum of 9, dispositions among these categories. Probation supervision was frequently coupled with other sanctions or treatment (78 percent).

Probation. There are several permutations of community-based dispositions for youths, but probation is clearly the most prominent of them. While probation is a community corrections sanction in the adult system and is therefore quite common, making up about 56 percent of those under correctional control or supervision (Kaeble and Glaze 2016), it plays an even more expansive role in the juvenile justice system (Matthews and Hubbard 2007) and has throughout the juvenile court's history. One of the court's early judges called it the "keynote of juvenile-court legislation" (Mack 1909, 116), and it was later described as the "workhorse" of the juvenile justice system (Torbet 1996).

The central role of probation in handling juvenile justice cases is evident in Figure 2.1. Probation is the disposition in 64 percent of cases that were adjudicated delinquent. Of the 1,000 cases depicted in the figure, 36 percent were involved with probation as the most restrictive or severe sanction (Furdella and Puzzanchera 2015). Strikingly, while 194 out of 305 youths received a probation disposition as part of their formal case, resulting in a delinquency adjudication, almost as many (169) were either never petitioned or went through the court process but not adjudicated delinquent. Probation departments therefore serve a supervisory or support function for youths at all depths of the juvenile justice system, giving them a varied and essential role in case management and supervision.

Juvenile probation agencies are also involved in intake screening, information gathering, and disposition recommendations, such that they lie at the core of most juvenile justice cases (Mears 2012; Schwalbe and Maschi 2009). Probation officers frequently work in an investigative and advisory capacity, doing much of the early assessment to develop a sense of the delinquent event, the youth, and his or her social circumstances, before delivering the information to the juvenile court. They then must supervise and mentor the youths and broker services for them while also monitoring compliance and enforcing court orders (Ward and Kupchik 2010). This array of roles means that probation does it all for the juvenile justice system, and the way it operates can have a profound impact on decisions made in juvenile courts and its potential developmental impact.

Research on juvenile probation illustrates its essential function in several aspects of the court process. Probation processes routinely operationalize the juvenile justice system's two broad objectives: sanction and treatment (Schwalbe and Maschi 2009; Ward and Kupchik 2010). Craig S. Schwalbe and Tina Maschi (2009) developed the Probation Practices Assessment Survey to take stock of juvenile probation officers' routines. With a specific index case in mind as a benchmark, 308 juvenile probation officers answered questions about their approaches to managing and supervising youths (deterrence, treatment, restorative justice) and tactics for gaining and maintaining compliance (confrontation, counseling, behavioral) from juvenile probationers. Juvenile probation officers tended to use a balanced approach calibrated to some aspects of the case (e.g., juvenile risk or needs, age) but not others (e.g., past frequency of offending, current offense severity). Their supervisory approaches reflected individual attitudes (e.g., punitiveness, beliefs about probation effectiveness) as well.

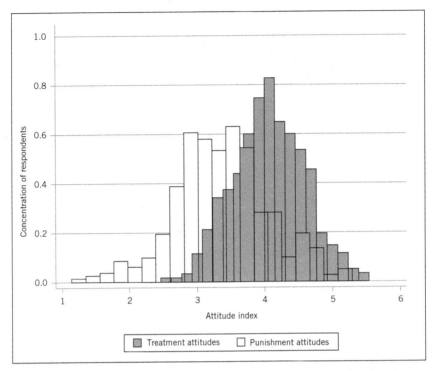

Figure 2.3 Overlap in probation officers' orientation to punishment and treatment
Source: Data from Ward and Kupchik 2010.
Note: Higher scores on the index indicate a stronger tendency toward treatment or punishment.

Ward and Kupchik (2010) analyzed data from a survey of 399 probation officers and found some comparability between their orientations toward treatment (mean = 4.1, SD = 0.5 on an index of relevant items) and punishment (mean = 3.4, SD = 0.7 on an index). Figure 2.3 shows a simulated set of data that is projected out to three standard deviations from the mean using Ward and Kupchik's data and an assumed normal distribution. At that sample size, there is considerable expected overlap in the distribution of treatment and punishment. The overlap in the figure represented by the covering of clear bars with the gray ones is from about 2.6 to 5.2, which is not the entire distribution but is substantial. This reflects the duality and tension in individual probation officers' attitudes and tasks, which must be balanced in routine practice as well as in a prospective developmental juvenile justice system.

Through the history of the juvenile court, probation has been a constant even as other changes have occurred. Today, probation officers serve a range of valuable roles in juvenile court processes and have much of the direct interaction that occurs with delinquent youths, families, and other community agencies. They also must balance the different objectives of the juvenile justice system in a way that is responsive to individual cases, which is evident in recent studies of probation personnel.

Juvenile Corrections. Like its adult counterpart, the juvenile justice system has an extensive set of community and institutional corrections facilities for delinquent youths. The case flow in Figure 2.1 shows that 24 percent of adjudicated delinquents receive residential facility placements (Furdella and Puzzanchera 2015). This amounts to about seven cases per 1,000 youths who enter the system. The number of facilities in both public and private sectors has declined significantly since the 1990s (Hockenberry 2016). Generally, public facilities house more youths and the declines largely reflect changes in the frequency of those placements. In 2013, estimates based on the Census of Juveniles in Residential Facilities were that 54,000 youths were in juvenile corrections facilities in the United States (Hockenberry 2016). This is a drop of nearly 50 percent since 1997.

Given the profiles of youths in custody, juvenile correction facilities frequently must sustain and deliver an array of treatment and educational options targeted to the needs and risks of the youths in them—just as courts and community-based agencies do for youths with noncustodial or community-based dispositions. An analysis of a sample of 22,603 treatment entry logs for about 150 youths committed to secure placement facilities in Ohio over the course of three and a half years found several distinct types of treatments on offer. These included cognitive behavioral therapy, substance abuse treatment, sex offender therapy, anger management, mental health treatment, general-skills training, mentoring, family therapy, mediation, and gang interventions.

Many of these broad categories are shown in Figure 2.4. Mental health and counseling interventions made up about a fourth of the treatment sessions for the sample and ranged from psychotherapy groups to grief counseling and crisis intervention. Addiction treatment covered different substances as well as more general topics like relapse prevention and identification of high-risk situations.[4] The "other" category captures a range of different interactions between youths and intervention staff—including domestic violence programs, hate and bias programs, and planning for reentry (e.g., "Getting Close to Getting Out" curriculum). When added to other aspects of youths' experiences in the facility, like schooling and facilitating family visits, the range of tasks managed in residential placements increases further. All this, of course, comes on top of ensuring security for youths and staff.

Aftercare. A final task for juvenile justice agencies along the continuum of youth involvement is helping those who are transitioning back into the community from residential placements. Although trends from the early years

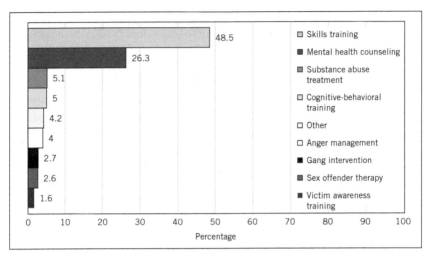

Figure 2.4 Summary of treatment and programming in state residential facilities in Ohio, 2011–2014

of the twenty-first century have produced lower prevalence of commitments to correctional facilities, juvenile justice officials still must consider the needs of those youths who will be returning to the community from residential placements. Given that the overall prevalence of youths placed in secure facilities is lower than in the past, those sent to state-level corrections now will have more extensive and serious records—and likely more risks and needs—than those who have left those facilities previously. The risks and needs of youths returning to communities can present considerable challenges for the justice infrastructure and local agencies that provide relevant services (Mears and Travis 2004). Youths with the greatest needs often return to the most disadvantaged communities, which compounds those challenges (Sullivan 2004). Studies of youth experiences during reentry find several key issues in this process, including difficulties that stem from reconnecting to school and work and from returns to old neighborhoods and friendships (Abrams 2006; Inderbitzin 2009). Youths may also struggle to maintain gains made in treatment without continuity in care in the community (Henderson et al. 2007), increasing the likelihood that they will recidivate upon release (James et al. 2013).

The prospect of reentry for youths and young adults has developmental considerations because those who have been incarcerated face unique obstacles upon release and, while there are many successes, often recidivate (Council of State Governments 2015). The obstacles to success in staying out of the system range from the potential expansion of access to juvenile proceedings and records that weakens the ability of youths to overcome their delinquency history (Dalton 1997; Henning 2004) to loss of opportunity for educational growth and skill development necessary for workforce engagement, to the prospect of missing developmental milestones or going through them in a stressful social context (Mulvey and Schubert 2012; Uggen and Wakefield 2005).

Howard Snyder and Melissa Sickmund (2006) summarize recidivism rates from roughly fifteen states and found average twelve-month recidivism ranged from 25 percent for reincarceration to 55 percent for rearrest as a juvenile or adult. These rates may have shifted somewhat over time but still require consideration in assessing the effectiveness of juvenile justice. Two of the states included in that earlier report, Virginia and Ohio, have updated their recidivism rates. The Virginia Department of Juvenile Justice (2015) reports a 2014 rearrest rate of 52 percent and the Ohio Department of Youth Services (2016) reported a 2014 reincarceration rate of 20 percent.

Several aspects of the reentry process require attention, which, when added to the court-level dispositional options mentioned previously, illustrates the considerable number of decisions that must be made and programming offered in order to match the variation inherent in the justice-involved youth population. This is true at lower levels of risk, such as in diversion programming, as well as with higher-risk and higher-needs cases, as in residential placements and reentry. Together these many cases and stages of processing ensure that the juvenile justice system must respond to a range of offense types and youth risk and needs profiles in its case-level decision making, supervision, and treatment functions. This is true in shifting to more developmental approaches as well.

Far-Reaching Challenges and Juvenile Justice Initiatives

Despite clear changes in juvenile crime rates and reductions in the prevalence of detained or placed youths, it is evident that the juvenile justice system still faces the daunting task of processing a lot of youths and that even routine or low-risk cases come with needs that require attention. The juvenile justice system must address complex challenges on a day-to-day basis. These challenges concern several subareas that relate to the youths encountered, available resources and operational factors, and external pressures on the system. This forms an outer context for juvenile justice that can be influential, and even determinative, in the system's efforts to implement new ideas (Aarons, Hurlburt, and Horwitz 2011).

Child-Saving Disposition and the System's Significant Undertakings

The juvenile justice system faces internal and external pressures to respond to apparently intractable problems, which alternately recede and recur over time. In keeping with its origins in social action, the juvenile justice system has a strong tendency to take on larger initiatives that affect youths, families, and communities but that do not totally fall under its routine operations. It is not unusual, for example, to find a special programs coordinator position within larger juvenile justice agencies. There is a forward-leaning aspect of juvenile justice, although it certainly varies across agencies and individuals, which means that many of its key stakeholders identify problems faced by youths, and in turn the system, and take steps toward solutions.

The problems of disproportionate minority contact (DMC) with the juvenile justice system and need for detention reform are good places to start in looking at these types of initiatives. DMC has been an issue of concern for some time and continues to generate thought and planning about how the juvenile justice system might best respond. In some ways, these concerns trace back to the origins of juvenile courts during the industrial era when they frequently encountered ethnic and racial minorities or children of immigrants. Racial disparities are also among the most challenging problems for an agency to tackle because of the multifaceted causes and the need to look outside the system for at least part of the solution (Piquero 2008). This has greater salience with recognition of the relationships between system practices and disadvantage that can accrue for minority youths (Bishop and Leiber 2012), particularly from a developmental perspective in which early disparities affect later life chances (Mcloyd and Lozoff 2001). Racial disparities and the school-to-prison pipeline are prominent examples of system contact having later developmental repercussions (Hirschfield 2008; Nicholson-Crotty et al. 2009).

At the court level this has led to both broad and focused efforts to identify and respond to DMC. A recent study of DMC in thirteen counties in Ohio identified an array of approaches to the problem that were both internal to the court and external (Sullivan et al. 2016). These included:

- Development of steering committees composed of juvenile justice officials, concerned community members, school administrators, elected officials, religious leaders, and local social service agencies
- Partnerships with state agencies for funding and technical assistance
- Partnerships with private foundations, such as the W. Haywood Burns Institute and Annie E. Casey Foundation
- Reviewing data and mapping key decision points
- Reviews of policies and practices on key decisions like intake and detention
- Seeking and obtaining grants from state and federal sources
- Developing strategies to deal with associated financial and family needs, such as family resource centers

- Changing assessment practices to limit racial disparities
- Implementing practical initiatives to reduce detention usage like reminder calls before court dates
- Increasing resources for alternatives to formal processing
- Developing general and focused diversion strategies to reduce DMC

In interviews, several court officials—especially those linked to the court's planning and policies—named several of these strategies when asked about their county's approach to the DMC problem. This inventory of potential strategies suggests that juvenile courts are not only working to process and supervise their dockets and caseloads but are also engaging in activities aimed at specific problems they believe to be related to the system's broader goals. This involves a good deal of court staff time and resources.

A second major initiative that has affected recent juvenile justice policy and practice, which is inherently related to other undertakings aimed at larger problems faced by justice-involved youths (e.g., limiting disproportionate minority contact, fostering positive youth development), is curtailing use of juvenile incarceration and detention to whatever extent possible (Austin, Dedel, and Weitzer 2005). In that DMC study in thirteen Ohio counties, an interviewee identified detention reduction efforts as the court's major initiative for dealing with DMC, arguing that reducing those placements would substantially benefit minority youths owing to their high referral rates (see also Zimring 2005b). This has implications for the effectiveness of the system at an aggregate level, outcomes for youths, and resource allocation.

One example of these efforts, the Juvenile Detention Alternatives Initiative (JDAI) is a set of related practices implemented in locales across the United States to reduce the use of detention and increase focus on community-based alternatives (Austin et al. 2005). It has been in operation for about twenty-five years, first beginning in Florida and now including 250 counties spread across thirty-nine U.S. states and Washington, D.C. (Mendel 2014). Its core components include data collection and review, development of alternatives to detention, objective screening and assessment for detention decisions, changes in case processing practices, and attention to certain special populations of youths (e.g., mental health needs, probation violations). It requires a commitment from juvenile court sites and key stakeholders for the full, system-spanning package of recommended changes.

General trends in the effectiveness of JDAI sites are positive (Mendel 2014). Systematic evaluation has been somewhat limited, but two independent studies report some positive results. The Chief Justice Earl Warren Institute on Law and Social Policy (2012) at the University of California, Berkeley, carried out an aggregate-level analysis of JDAI states and sites. The study found larger reductions in detention at JDAI sites relative to the states in which they were located (and non-JDAI sites). In thirteen of the twenty-three states studied, the change in commitments over time was more favorable in JDAI sites compared to the state as a whole. The average daily population comparison showed that JDAI sites were better than the states in eighteen of twenty-three cases. Scott R. Maggard (2015) made before- and after-JDAI comparisons in one juvenile court in Virginia. The JDAI comparison indicator was not statistically significant in a model predicting likelihood of detention commitment but it was in the length-of-stay analysis. He also found some evidence that JDAI moderated the impact of legally relevant factors in those decisions such that those influences were stronger after its introduction. The analysis did not find a difference between pre- and post-JDAI periods for the relationship between race and those outcomes. The JDAI initiative demonstrates one approach taken to tackling a big issue that has met with some success while also illustrating potential practical preconditions for carrying that out in a sustainable way.

The Impact of These Initiatives

While addressing these challenges, the juvenile justice system has generally pushed to become more evidence based since the 1990s. This is consistent with professionalization of its staff and the significant growth in research, technical assistance, and training relevant to its goals. Consequently, initiatives to reduce juvenile incarceration or DMC have both operational and moral components, but they also illustrate a related desire to implement practices to address youths' risks and needs more effectively. Risk assessment, for example, has implications for making better detention decisions and, potentially, may aid in reducing the implicit and explicit biases in decision making that contribute to DMC problems (Steinhart 2006).[5] In this sense, states and local agencies have also become involved in platform-establishing initiatives, like risk and needs assessment, that attempt to help them better do their work across multiple dimensions.

The impact of these efforts goes largely unconsidered because potential benefits often carry greater weight and the impetus to do something is quite strong. The desire to make things better for youths, families, and communities is directly in line with juvenile courts' core missions. Some of these efforts certainly lead to diversion programs, processing strategies, sanctions, and interventions that are demonstrably more effective than alternatives. They may even be more cost effective. Still, addressing these concerns, which may be long standing (like DMC) or emerging (e.g., greater focus on early trauma in youth) at any given point in time, can take away from time and resources needed for the system to meet basic objectives in processing youths. In the 2012 multistate study (Chief Justice Earl Warren Institute on Law and Social Policy 2012) of implementation of a big initiative toward a systematic risk and needs assessment, some of those interviewed and surveyed expressed concern about receiving training on multiple tools, each adopted to meet a state-level initiative, and not clearly understanding why these new initiatives were implemented seemingly every few years. One interviewee said her agency had used several different assessments and needed to stop making changes and instead let its personnel become proficient with it.

The Developmental Status of Juvenile Justice

Initiatives in addressing DMC and reducing youth incarceration and detention illustrate that many—though certainly not all—juvenile justice systems are open to some form of change. The history of the juvenile court highlights direct and indirect effects from the broader context in which the court resides as well. The juvenile court emerged in part out of a progressive response to industrialization and urban expansion and has shifted with societal and political tides since—while still retaining core aspects of its original mission. The one-hundredth anniversary of the juvenile court brought with it some analysis of how the juvenile justice system currently operates and how consistent those operations are with its original principles and practices. The conclusions are mixed, but that contrast likely helped in reconsidering the degree to which policy changes made to strengthen the responses to delinquent offenses countermanded those goals. That meant that some efforts to raise the age of adult court jurisdiction or reduce the use of secure state facilities for youths are linked to both the evidence on youth development emerging since the 1990s and the early belief system of the juvenile court about responding to delinquency.

Just as individual youths are characterized in terms of their developmental status and research identifies factors that may affect that process for good or bad, the juvenile justice system can be viewed within a similar framework when considering its prospects for change. U.S. juvenile courts deal with upwards of a million cases a year, formally processing roughly half those and taking on responsibilities in them regardless of whether the youth is petitioned to the court or adjudicated delinquent. This includes front-end intake and screening, possible predisposition detention, community supervision, community-based treatment and alternatives to justice processing that occur in diversion programming, court hearings and disposition, correctional custody and treatment, and aftercare. A majority of those in the other half of that group (nonpetitioned) receive some attention from the juvenile court and affiliated agencies. This has resulted in a complex network of interrelated, but still independent, personnel and agencies that must advance the court's multifaceted mission. As the court has evolved, it also responded to bigger-picture issues that affect youths, families, and communities because of its child-saving reflex.

Juvenile justice scholars have spent a good deal of time analyzing and discussing the early philosophy of the juvenile court and whether it has changed for better or worse over time. Still, what drives the court today in its general operations and attention to larger issues is more significant in setting a context for the implementation of developmentally informed changes in the coming years. The court performs several categories of routine tasks. It must make initial determinations via threshold decisions at intake. Many youths are not expected to offend for an extensive period but may still have risks and needs that raise uncertainty about their future pathways and that call for intervention when considering the court's wider mission to respond to children in need of services. This creates a tension; developmental and life-course research evidence suggests that most youths will grow out of their delinquent behavior. It also means that there is inherently some net widening lying in wait if the juvenile court addresses those needs.

Even in diversion cases the court must offer effective and resource-efficient alternatives for those who remain under its authority. Some youths require preadjudication detention, which requires an early decision with often limited information and a safe and constructive environment for them. While the length of stay depends on the time that it takes to process a youth's case, this may be a developmentally salient experience. From the system's perspective it also expands the number of youths in custody, which can increase costs and resource needs for personnel, programming, and facilities. Deeper in the system, the court must make adjudication and disposition decisions. The relevant determining factors include, among others, the facts of the case, which may include developmentally relevant factors like peer involvement and appreciation for the wrongfulness of the act. Those decisions inherently involve some projection of probable short- and long-term outcomes.

Available options for sanctioning and treating youths also have developmental implications. Youths may receive a community-based sanction when they need treatment, but this can be accomplished in a nonrestrictive setting. On the other hand, those who have committed more serious offenses or who have a more extensive delinquency record often end up in more restrictive locked facilities or state-level residential placement but also require treatment. The juvenile justice system must provide placement and intervention options that address youth risk and needs while also trying to balance long-term developmental considerations. Invariably some of the responsibility for meeting these benchmarks will move from the courts to probation and institutional corrections as well as community providers, which have varying degrees of affiliation and goal overlap with the court.

The sheer number of current functions and initiatives carried out by the juvenile court raise questions about the juvenile justice system's readiness for change at both the individual and organizational level (Backer 1995). The processes detailed in this chapter reveal the range of tasks that these agencies must perform—both in routine practice and in thinking about bigger-picture problems that affect youths, families, and communities. The stages highlighted in Figures 2.1 and 2.2 illustrate the range of possible outcomes and the numerous discretionary decisions that lead to them. At other points, the expansive treatment needs of juvenile justice cases were on display. Consequently, the current configuration and way its personnel work within that infrastructure will inevitably affect the success of changes in its mission, policies, and practices. Like many of the youths processed within it, the juvenile justice system is well meaning and favorably predisposed, but its situational circumstances can make wholesale changes difficult.

With these contemporary characterizations in mind, Chapter 3 synthesizes and reviews the evidence base underlying calls for change in the juvenile justice system. These proposed changes seem mainly to have emerged from the perception that the court became more adultlike late in the twentieth century. It is equally—if not more—important to consider those propositions against the juvenile justice system's current practices and challenges, especially since a full embrace of the principles and methods would permeate all aspects of the juvenile justice system. As all the processing, sanction, and treatment options identified in this chapter suggest, the juvenile justice system is generally disposed toward problem solving. Whether it has the right mix of those elements to be fully successful has been questioned in the past (Caldwell 1961; Feld 1997), leading to concerns about whether the juvenile court can assimilate developmental evidence and effectively use it.

Changes to policy and practice necessarily must involve consideration of existing cases and responses of the juvenile justice system to identify prospects and challenges of proposed changes. This is likewise needed when thinking about how basic theory and research around development and life-course influences will fit when considered next to real-world sanctions and treatment. Of course, the court itself is only one part of the equation because individual outcomes stemming from juvenile justice involvement, sanctions, and treatment will invariably be coproductions of the system and the youths (and other developmental influences). Developmental and life-course factors are important in understanding that interactive process and responding to justice-involved youths.

3

Development, Decision Making, and Identity

Traditional psychosocial research and newer neurobiological findings are at the center of calls and action for a more developmental juvenile justice system. This chapter reviews the main scientific basis for developmental juvenile justice, focusing on two key dimensions that inform the court's view of adolescent behavior: *choice* and *character*. It starts with some discussion of the broad presumptions of development and youthfulness in juvenile justice.

Developmental Presumptions about Youths in Juvenile Justice

Early twenty-first-century calls for broad reform of juvenile justice have drawn largely on a developmental perspective grounded in empirical evidence of distinctions between childhood, adolescence, and adulthood (Sullivan, Piquero, and Cullen 2012). The starting point for arguments about remaking the juvenile justice system can be as simple as an appeal to people's innate sense of the fundamental differences between youths and adults, a "faith in childhood" (Tanenhaus 2004, xxiv)—which was a driving force behind creating the juvenile court. Elizabeth Scott and Laurence Steinberg note, "Although teenagers are not childlike, they are less competent decision makers than adults" (2008, 14) and state that this distinction is largely "self-evident" (29). Their invocation of that point before reviewing the research illustrates that—though empirical evidence supports elements of the proposals for juvenile justice reform—there are subjective elements at work as well.

The general spirit of the reform discussion is about reaffirming the notion that delinquent youths are distinct and often have some growing up to do before they are treated the same as adult offenders. The current push for a more developmental system partly is a reaction to the perception that youths are too readily being transferred to the adult system (Benekos and Merlo 2008; Bishop and Frazier 2000; Fagan 2008; McGowan et al. 2007) or that the juvenile justice system had begun to approximate the adult court in its processing and handling of youths (Bazemore and Umbreit 1995; Feld 1997). Frequently, both problems were emerging simultaneously (Feld 1998; Singer 1996).

In that sense, the starting point for more developmental juvenile justice is a philosophical one: kids are different from adults, and therefore to be fair in responding to their undesirable behaviors, the reaction must differ from that for adults. The juvenile justice system draws on scientific insight to maximize its effectiveness in responding to delinquent youths (see Bronner 1925; NRC 2013). These arguments about fairness and effectiveness have origins in the early history of the juvenile court as well. Writing about the juvenile court when it emerged and its future potential, Samuel J. Barrows noted that the court's founders were not just establishing an alternative legal institution. Instead, the most monumental development was the "introduction of a new spirit and a new aim" that more clearly recognized distinctions between youths and adults (1904, ix).

More recently, Franklin E. Zimring framed adolescence as a time for learning, when youths should have latitude to take some risks and make mistakes within reason:

> Growing up in modern Western nations is a process of learning to choose freely the path of our own lives. But the only way to learn free choice is to experience firsthand making choices and living with the consequences of those choices. . . . It is inevitable that young people with less experience in making decisions will make more mistakes as a result. These are the necessary hazards of growing up in a free society. (2005a, 21)

This is an intuitive argument that fits with conceptions of adolescence as a transitory period between childhood and adulthood and reflects the spirit and aim of the juvenile court that Barrows described. It also calls on some philosophical and moral imperatives in making arguments about how to best respond to delinquent behavior (see Scott, Reppucci, and Woolard 1995).

This perspective on delinquent youths is widely held by the public—even when more serious delinquency is considered. Daniel S. Nagin and colleagues (2006) studied public opinion around the toughening of sanctions for juvenile offenders using a willingness-to-pay framework, in which agreement or disagreement is based on the respondent's views of investment in hypothetical policy alternatives. They surveyed a politically moderate state, Pennsylvania. The questions were the same for all except that the researchers randomly and systematically varied one item to ask respondents if they would be willing to vote for a crime control policy proposal requiring each household to pay additional taxes. Even when interpreted conservatively, the study suggests that the public is at least as willing to pay for rehabilitative costs as punitive ones. On that point, the authors found a fair amount of agreement across the political spectrum and among those with differing general attitudes about criminal justice and punishment. A later study by Alex R. Piquero and Laurence Steinberg (2010) expands the survey to three additional states (Illinois, Louisiana, and Washington) and largely replicated the earlier findings: respondents were less willing to pay for additional incarceration for juvenile offenders than for rehabilitative programs. These findings reflect a recognition on the part of the general public that child and adolescent antisocial behavior does not have quite the same etiology as that of adults and that there are some distinctions between the two groups.

The research generally supports the differential nature of adolescent and adult behavior. Despite being a time of peak health and settling into grown-up levels of cognition and physical prowess, adolescence offers several challenges for self-regulation of emotions and behaviors relevant to understanding and contextualizing that time in a person's life (Dahl 2004). Adolescents are attempting to meet physical, psychological, and social benchmarks (Ernst, Pine, and Hardin 2006) and trying to coordinate affect, thought, and behavior in often stressful contexts (Steinberg 2005). This is essential subtext for understanding and responding to attitudes and behaviors during this period. Despite public support, the views of some political leaders, and the vision of the court's original developers, the question of how to respond to delinquency is more complex than asserting the intuitive differences between youths and adults—especially after factoring in the variation within the delinquent population and the agencies that respond to it described in previous chapters. These observations about delinquent youths and juvenile justice practices require attention to the evidence for differences between adults and youths as well as discussion of the developmental factors that may affect delinquency in juvenile justice cases. A more expansive focus on these points allows a move beyond a nebulous appreciation of the differences between juveniles and adults and toward an improved understanding of delinquency and identifying leverage points for system response.

How Delinquents Are Different

The first couple of decades of the twenty-first century have seen a renewed interest in understanding the distinctions between youths and adults. New ways to research structural aspects of human development that were previously out of reach have emerged (Casey et al. 2005; Forbes and Dahl 2010; Sisk and Zehr 2005; Smith, Chein, and Steinberg 2013; Spear 2000; Steinberg 2008). These studies and the ideas they generate have implications for the viability of the juvenile court's foundation, its current practices, and broader crime control policy (Cauffman and Steinberg 2012; Scott and Steinberg 2008). While the presumption of youths as distinct is certainly the embodied ideal of the juvenile court, and many contemporary reformers would like to see that approach return, how well it takes hold depends on several other factors. Given the inevitable counterweight of community safety that tempers the desire to always defer to this distinction between youths and adults, the tangible ways in which delinquent youths—even those who commit adult crimes—stand out and therefore require distinct sanctions and treatment must be identified precisely and linked to behavior. Modern advocates of a developmental approach to handling juvenile delinquency have amassed more evidence than was present in earlier cycles of policy and practice (Bernard and Kurlychek 2010; Tanenhaus 2004).

The distinctions are also supported by a multidimensional body of research and more than merely self-evident. Choice and character, articulated by Scott and Steinberg (2008) in *Rethinking Juvenile Justice*, are good orientation points in the discussion of development and juvenile court policy and practice. Juvenile justice decisions are based on the offense at hand (i.e., choice), the prior behavioral and risk history of the individual youth, a projection of the reasons for delinquency, and future potential for similar behavior (i.e., character).

Choice, Delinquency, and Adolescent Development

Some risky behavior in adolescence is "statistically normative and psychologically adaptive" (Parsons, Siegel, and Cousins 1997, 382; see also Moffitt 1993). Adolescents are stereotypically perceived as irrational and risk prone. The complex processes contributing to their choices are determined by multiple distinct developmental and situational inputs, however (Fischhoff 2008; Reyna and Farley 2006; Reyna and Rivers 2008). Some of those inputs may be perfectly rational within the youths' decision-making space. Regardless of whether delinquency is normative or socially beneficial, the potential consequences for individuals and society raise the stakes in understanding and responding to those behaviors—especially when they recur (Fischhoff 2008).

Adolescent behavior and decision making are particularly relevant in understanding adolescence in a free society, because this is when individuals come to rely less on the constraints and supports offered by parents and other adults and start a process of separation (Byrnes 2002), which places oversight of their behavior outside the home and forces them to self-regulate.

Understanding these facets of social interaction is essential for the juvenile court because doing justice is inherently about making assessments about choices and then deciding how to best respond. Therefore, understanding adolescent decision making in a developmental context is a prerequisite for evidence-based juvenile justice.[1]

The relationship between adolescent behavior and development sheds light on the choice component of delinquency. That relationship is central to how justice-involved youths will be assessed and treated; "behavioral patterns are built up decision by decision" (Beyth-Maron et al. 1993, 561), and habits that prolong those patterns can emerge from those decisions (Reyna and Farley 2006). Several strands of related research on the situational nature of delinquency indirectly explain decisions to engage in both prosocial and antisocial acts. These range from the potential effect of pubertal hormonal shifts to the impact of the macrosocial environment on individual choice (Reyna and Rivers 2008).

Adolescent propensities emerge from "predetermined ontogenic changes" that affect risk-seeking and reward-seeking behavior (Ernst, Pine, and Hardin 2006, 308; see also Spear 2000). Misconceptions about development and decision making have made achieving clarity on these points more challenging, however:

> Among the widely-held beliefs about adolescent risk-taking that have not been supported empirically are (a) that adolescents are irrational or deficient in their information processing, or that they reason about risk in fundamentally different ways than adults; (b) that adolescents do not perceive risks where adults do or are more likely to believe that they are invulnerable; and (c) that adolescents are less risk-averse than adults. None of these assertions is correct. (Steinberg 2008, 79)

These misconceptions naturally raise questions about the categorization of adolescent development and behavior and its implications for understanding and responding to delinquency.

Comparative studies illustrate these complexities. To determine whether risky behaviors reflect a sense of invincibility and sensation seeking or an inability to grasp the true stakes involved, Lawrence D. Cohn and colleagues (1995) studied how adolescents and adults perceive information. The researchers surveyed teenagers and parents about the risks of different behaviors, like using drugs, drinking alcohol, or driving drunk, and found that adolescents had significantly less optimism about their ability to avoid problem outcomes than the parents had about their children's ability to avoid problems. When asked about the potential harm in these activities (e.g., experimentally, habitually), the parents, however, saw teens' involvement in such activities as significantly more harmful than the group of teens did. These findings suggest that while adolescents did not perceive their behavior as all that harmful in a relative sense, they also did not view themselves as especially invulnerable compared to adults.

In a survey in which teenage and adult respondents (199 in each group) identified possible outcomes for themselves of different courses of action (e.g., drink and drive, smoke pot, have sex), adolescent subjects were generally more likely to mention social reactions than adults; the teens mentioned the social reaction of peers as a possible negative consequence of not engaging in risky behavior (Beyth-Marom et al. 1993). Teens also identified a higher proportion of short-term positive outcomes from one-time risky behavior than adults did, suggesting that the time perspective mattered in decision making. Otherwise, there was a good deal of comparability in the value and nature of the identified consequences, suggesting potential overlap in decision-making processes between the two groups.

Mechanisms of Choice in Adolescence

Choice occurs when a person, who carries certain proclivities or preferences into a situation, meets an environmental stimulus and must react in some way. The individual must process information about potential outcomes and merge it with preferences to reach a conclusion about how he or she should act in a given situation or type of situation. The classic model of rational decision making suggests that individuals will take the action that leads to a desirable result or "subjective expected utility" (Manktelow 2012, 188; Byrnes 2002; Reyna and Farley 2006). Ruth Beyth-Marom and colleagues (1993) summarize the steps as follows: (1) identify the possible options, (2) enumerate the potential consequences or outcomes of each of them, (3) attach a degree of desirability to each, (4) assess their relative likelihood of occurrence, and (5) make a decision based on some rules.

This framework can play an implicit role in thinking about decisions about delinquent behavior as well. A youth invited to a party where he knows there will be drinking will have to consider the potential positive and negative outcomes and assimilate them with his disposition and preferences on those possible outcomes. These proximal individual (e.g., intensity of individual goals) and environmental (e.g., peer approval) elements affect decision making directly and indirectly. Still, viewing these choices as clear-cut is inaccurate when considering how youth development affects delinquency in an immediate sense and in turn factors into longer-term behavioral patterns. This is so because of the general bounded nature of rational decision making, with distinctions between "normative" and actual choices (Kahneman 2003; Simon 1972) and because of characteristics of adolescent judgment (Furby and Beyth-Marom 1992). The adolescent behavior at the heart of discussion of development and delinquency is less deliberate and more "spontaneous, reactive, and impulsive" than in rational choice models (Reyna and Farley 2006, 6).

Adolescents usually reach a fairly sophisticated cognitive level by the midteens, which raises questions about how developmental differences can be used as pretext for justice response or setting boundaries between youths and adults. Elevated risk-taking in adolescence does not seem to be affected by the introduction of additional data about a risk into the decision-making process, either. This offers an additional puzzle, reinforcing the complexity of how cognitive factors affect underlying adolescent risk-taking. Developments in theory and research since the 1990s provide some insight on how to better understand these relationships.

With pubertal development and the neural restructuring that follows it in adolescence, influences on decisions and actions bifurcate, leading the socioemotional system to become more salient than the cognitive control in regulating impulse toward reward (Steinberg et al. 2008). From a neurobiological perspective, these socioemotional reactors, which are in the limbic and paralimbic centers of the brain (e.g., amygdala, ventral striatum), unify toward dopamine-based reward sensitivity at a time when other neural areas that provide constraint, including the lateral prefrontal and parietal cortex, are less developed. Adriana Galvan and colleagues (2007) studied this reward sensitivity using functional magnetic resonance imaging (fMRI) with thirty-seven children, adolescents, and adults, finding that relevant brain centers (e.g., the nucleus accumbens) were more active for those who anticipated positive consequences of risky behavior. This brain activity was especially pronounced among the adolescent group, leading the researchers to infer a developmental influence on these processes. Monique Ernst, Daniel Pine, and Michael Hardin state that "the activity of the reward system prevails over that of the avoidant system while the still immature regulatory system fails to adaptively balance these two behavioral controllers" (2006, 303).

They point out that this is due to the relative progress in development of the amygdala (related to avoidant behavior), ventral striatum (serves a reward-related function), and the ventromedial prefrontal cortex (which is inhibitive and regulatory). Other researchers have identified similar neurobehavioral processes and describe the mediated effects of hormonal processes in slightly more depth. Cheryl Sisk and Julia Zehr (2005, 164) argue that puberty, which overlaps but is not synonymous with adolescence, is a "brain event" because hormonal and nervous system activation are intertwined. These organizational and activational effects on the brain are driven in part by increased hormonal releases that come with adrenarche and gonardarche in puberty (Spear 2000), which in turn affect neural and social processes (Sisk and Zehr 2005; Steinberg 2008).

B. J. Casey, Rebecca M. Jones, and Todd A. Hare (2008) apply modern brain science to assess the physical adjustments and vulnerabilities that occur during adolescence—and their implications for behavior. They first note the frequently observed linear relationship between age and cognitive development from childhood through adolescence to adulthood juxtaposed with a curvilinear pattern of risky behavior across that same basic time frame. Reviewing evidence from diffusion tensor imaging, which measures connections in brain white matter, and structural and functional magnetic resonance imaging, which maps size, shape, and activation of certain neural structures, the authors found that earlier maturation in the limbic system, which governs emotional arousal, in juxtaposition with more elongated development of the prefrontal region, creates a mismatch, or a "dys-synchrony" (Dahl 2004, 16), between reward salience and regulatory control that might rein in risky behaviors. This relative immaturity in control may lead adolescents to prioritize shorter-term rewards (e.g., peer approval) over those that will accrue only in the future (e.g., lack of an arrest record). Adriana Galvan and colleagues (2006) also used fMRI to study neural and behavioral responses to rewards by thirty-seven subjects. They found that the changes in incentive-centered brain activity were greater for adolescents than for children or adults after introduction of a reward. The effect of this heightened attraction to reward on behavior is likely to be stronger in adolescence (Galvan 2010).

Tying this process to a specific type of risky behavior, R. Andrew Chambers, Jane R. Taylor, and Marc N. Potenza (2003) reviewed relevant research to determine whether adolescents might be especially vulnerable to addiction, which is partly neurodevelopmental. Experimental substance use is somewhat common in teens, but the degree to which adolescents are primed for dependency is less clear. Like other researchers, the authors suggest that adolescents' motivational and reward proclivities, impulsivity, and novelty seeking, which tend to emerge earlier in adolescence, are ahead of their regulatory control, which takes longer and is subject to progressive enhancement from childhood to mid-to-late adolescence. Youths may become ensnared in addictive substance use (see also Spear 2000)—especially since drug use can pharmacologically affect dopamine receptors implicated in how youths experience rewards.

From the Body and Brain to Behavior: Layering in the Adolescent Environment

The preceding discussion is not the entire story of adolescent risky behavior, because these neurobiological processes are unlikely to have a direct relationship with individual actions without the presence of environmental influence (Spear 2000). Research suggests that cognitive systems are reasonably well developed by middle adolescence, but another potential disconnect comes in here. The implication from Casey and colleagues' work (2005, 2008) is that adolescents are cognitively situated to make decisions that rival those of adults, but their socioemotional development has not necessarily caught up, which means that they may make reasonably good decisions in the abstract but falter in situations in which other pressures come into play. Essentially, this suggests that the anomaly described by Ronald E. Dahl (2004) may simply be a matter of bad timing and out-of-sync development of key subsystems that affect behavior.

Margo Gardner and Laurence Steinberg's (2005) experimental research with adolescents highlights the social environment's influence on youths' decisions about risk-taking, which is primed by the processes just described. Their study of three age groups, 306 individuals ranging in age from adolescence to adult, combined survey measures and a simulated laboratory task involving risky decisions. The risk-taking task was a driving scenario in which the participant had to make a rapid decision about whether to stop or drive through a yellow light. The experimental conditions involved the presence or absence of peers, who sometimes would advise the subject on what to do. The researchers found significant differences across age groups. Younger participants tended to wait longer to stop the car after the appearance of the yellow light. Gardner and Steinberg also identified peer influence effects on both survey responses and the simulated risk-taking task. Subjects in the yellow-light game tended to take more risks when peers were present. Interaction analysis also showed that the peer influence effects were more pronounced among younger study subjects, suggesting an age-graded response in adolescence. This study provides insight into the possible situational effects of peers on decision making in a lab environment.

Building on this dual-system integration of incentive processing and cognitive control, Jason Chein and colleagues (2011) extended this study with forty adolescent and adult subjects. Their key enhancement was that neural scanning monitored brain activity while subjects completed the task. Using fMRI, the researchers again found age-graded effects in reward processing. Adolescents seemed motivated to take greater risks when peers were present, while adults did not. The adolescent's reward centers in the brain were more active when peers were present. This was not the case for adults. Results from this study support key findings from Gardner and Steinberg's work while also linking neural processes to social rewards in a way that more thoroughly specifies the mechanisms that affect risky decisions. These studies suggest that the decision to engage in risk-taking is quick and reflects reasoning that is often rational for the short-term context (peer approval) but faulty over the long-term (prolonged justice involvement).

As a complement to their work in lab settings, Laurence Steinberg and colleagues (2008) and Steinberg (2010) studied differences in self-report and behavioral tasks across different age groups to elaborate on the developmental distinctions between adolescents and adults that contribute to observed behavioral differences. Both studies relied on a multisite, community-based study of 935 volunteers ages ten to thirty. They found curvilinear age effects on levels of sensation seeking but a linear relationship between age and impulsivity (see also Casey, Jones, and Hare 2008). Individuals who were older tended to be less impulsive than those who were younger, but sensation seeking followed a pattern that was higher for adolescents relative to those at the younger and older ends of the age distribution. These findings are consistent with the neurobiological findings regarding heightened reward sensitivity in adolescence coupled with slower development in self-regulation from childhood to adulthood, which lends them more coherence in explaining development and behavior (Steinberg 2008).

Developmental features such as reward sensitivity and attenuated capacity for self-regulation may not be solely responsible for adolescent choices, but they do help structure them (Cauffman and Steinberg 2012; Scott and Steinberg 2008; Scott, Reppucci, and Woolard 1995). Behaviorally, these processes mean that youths appreciate the risks of potential choices in circumstances in which there is not much tension or anxiety but behave differently in real-world situations in which emotions run hotter and immediate rewards are perceived to be greater (Dahl 2004; Reyna and Farley 2006). Thus, adolescents' ability to make appropriate choices in the abstract tends to diverge from the actions that they take in situ and is affected by tension between executive control over thoughts and behaviors and socioemotional decision making (Steinberg 2005, 2007). This influence on their ability to make abstract choices is especially challenging for them because the neural systems often implicated in decision making are sensitive to the social and emotional stressors of that developmental stage (Spear 2000).

The social situations in which adolescents find themselves frequently value short-term outcomes like status maintenance and solidarity in behavior and attitudes (Warr 2002). James Coleman pointed this out in one of the early studies of the teenage social environment, stating, "Parents and parental desires are of great importance to children in a long-range sense, but it is their peers whose approval, admiration, and respect they attempt to win in their everyday activities" (1961, 11). This highlights the distinctions between short- and long-term preferences in the routine choices of adolescents. It also illustrates that, while these choices are poor from the perspective of parents and juvenile justice actors, they may be a rational adaptation to the imperatives of their social environment that confer attractive benefits at that time (Furby and Beyth-Marom 1992; Reyna and Farley 2006). A study of adolescent peer networks by Derek A. Kreager, Kelly Rulison, and James Moody (2011), for instance, found that members of groups with higher, on average, levels of drinking were also more popular and had greater centrality in social networks.

Developmental factors work in interaction with the adolescent social environment to increase the likelihood of delinquent behavior. The ability to comprehend and integrate potential consequences in making decisions is a necessary component of choice (Furby and Beyth-Marom 1992; Manktelow 2012; Reyna and Farley 2006). Although there are likely to be significant individual differences within the youth population (see Moffitt 1990), adolescents tend to be able to appreciate the potential outcomes of their actions by their midteens (Scott and Steinberg 2008). Decision making is frequently moderated by factors such as impulsivity and emotionality, and competent decision making may be differentially affected in certain situations and across certain individuals. Thus, risk-taking can be a by-product of the fast thinking that might occur in these situations (Chandler and Pronin 2012). This is especially true when socioemotional processes surpass individuals' capacity to mitigate sensitivities that prioritize immediate or short-term rewards (Steinberg 2005) and make it difficult to check the effect of affect and emotion in decision making (Dahl 2004). Terrie E. Moffitt (1990, 1993) identifies neuropsychological deficits that can affect the thought, control, and behavioral link in adolescent delinquency.

Studies suggest that aspects of cognitive development applied to the social environment tend to lag ability to appreciate the different elements that go into decisions. Consequently, decision making is still compromised in adolescence (Cauffman and Steinberg 2012; Steinberg 2007). Linda P. Spear attributes this to a relatively stronger "excitatory" push coupled with a more limited "inhibitory" restraint (2000, 436). When linked to the priority given to other elements of adolescence, like weighting of peer influences, shorter-term orientation to reward and risk, and ability to exercise self-control, this elevates the likelihood that many youths will take greater risks and engage in delinquent behavior.

Character, Delinquency, and Adolescent Development

In addition to adolescent choices, the rigidity or malleability of character is another principal distinction made in the juvenile justice system. Adolescents are unformed with respect to their identity, meaning their character is still a work in progress and they will be more responsive to treatment efforts than harsh punishment (Tyler and Rankin 2012; Woolard, Fondacaro, and Slobogin 2001). Deservedness also affects the interpretation of criminal history with respect to offender age (see Bushway and Piehl 2007), which raises different considerations for juveniles and adults. If judges and other juvenile court decision makers develop sanctions on the basis of what an offense implies about a youth's enduring makeup, they may be mistaken. This is a central premise of the "irreparable corruption" designation in the U.S. Supreme Court decision in *Miller v. Alabama* (Grisso and Kavanaugh 2016). Bringing the full weight of sanctions on a youth is often problematic because adolescents have not yet reached the point at which their character can be evaluated to provide a valid sense of who they are and will be well into the future.

Character and Adolescent Development

Character is a vague concept (Blasi 2005) but nevertheless points to actions and beliefs that define an individual in a relatively stable sense, an identity. In addition to its dispositional qualities, identity has a functional purpose in understanding oneself, providing direction for attitudes and actions, and facilitating coherence in beliefs, values, and action. It simultaneously takes on moral connotations and can affect behavior across a variety of social relationships and interactions (Adams and Marshall 1996)—including delinquent behavior.

In framing the idea of character in juvenile justice decisions, Scott and Steinberg note that adolescents become adults through processes of "individuation," in which there is a separation from the family of origin so that a young man or woman becomes his or her own person (2008, 50). The development of a sense of self influences ability to exercise willpower for moral action with great consistency (Blasi 2005). The process of individuation is cognitive in that people consider how their traits and attitudes differ from or resemble their parents' (see Koepke and Denissen 2012; Mazor and Enright 1988) but is also behavioral because an adolescent may desire to engage in behaviors perceived as adultlike. Moffitt (1993) has pointed to this phenomenon as a maturity gap that creates a misfit between biological status and environmental opportunities for expressing that status (see also Eccles et al. 1993; Ge, Conger, and Elder 2001).

Youths can take on adult roles because of maturational changes and puberty, but desirable opportunities remain closed to them (e.g., work, smoking and drinking, sex), and consequently they may push the boundaries. David F. Greenberg (1977) asserts that the teen labor market and school environment are central factors in adolescent behavioral expression that tend to subside in adulthood. Schools constrain autonomy sought by teens by compelling them to continue the socialization and learning process even as they begin to hold some biological and cognitive similarities to adults. Regardless of the precise mechanisms, which inevitably include interdependent effects of individuals and their environments (Coleman 1994), elevated levels of risk-taking in adolescence imply that something other than bad character drives a good deal of delinquency.

Individuation and Development

Figure 3.1 shows individuation across three adjacent developmental periods (late childhood, adolescence, and early adulthood) to illustrate the relative salience of self-identity and social influences (see Hart 2005). In late childhood, a youth's identity is still forming and is tied up in that of his or her family. The large overlap between the individual and the family depicts such a scenario. Peer influences are less salient at that stage as well. In adolescence, peers generally have greater effect on identity and behavior, and a strong self-identity has yet to emerge, but there is increasing separation from the family. Some overlap between family and peer influence owes to the enduring effects of socialization and parental management and monitoring that may affect the peers to which the youth is exposed and their frequency of unstructured socializing with those friends (Thornberry 1987).

In accordance with the research on individuation and emergence of self-identity, the third diagram shows an individual more differentiated from both the peer group and the family of origin in attitudes and behavior. Some overlap in identity and influence remains because individuals tend to seek both a "sense of uniqueness and a sense of belonging" (Adams and Marshall 1996, 430). Adolescent moral development is also still in flux during the period when youths fall under juvenile justice jurisdiction. Erik Erikson (1968) identifies the resolution and sense of identity as a core aspect of human development (see also Berman et al. 2001). Taking more individual responsibility is part of this process and involves a move toward a more prosocial identity at the close of adolescence. Several characteristics of the individuation process require that a youth have reached a minimum threshold of cognitive development, and therefore this is particularly relevant in considering the juvenile justice response to delinquent behavior. The status

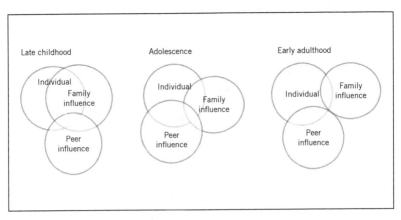

Figure 3.1 Individuation, development, and the salience of self-identity

of individuation and cognitive development may be pertinent to considerations of choice and character.

Exploration plays a role in individuation (Berman et al. 2001), which adds another dimension to the neurobehavioral perspectives on adolescent decision making covered earlier. Youths may test limits as they separate from the family of origin to establish a distinct self. An implicit information-gathering process occurs before committing to an established identity. The style used to gather that information (e.g., diffuse, or avoidant; normative, or obedient) and cognitive competence (e.g., problem solving, critical evaluation) necessary for its processing affect identity development (Berman et al. 2001). James E. Côté (1996) identifies several other factors central to individuation, including self-monitoring, self-efficacy, and an effective and situationally varied behavioral repertoire. These elements help youths understand and navigate developmental challenges, like establishing adult relationships and moving into the workforce, and establish a separate identity.

Development and Moral Identity

Identity development is multifaceted and draws on processes of the person, situation, and society (Côté 1996). Like those governing choice, these processes may be indirectly affected by neurocognitive development (Blair et al. 2006). Identity drives actions and is also forged by them such that it carries forward to later life. It captures the things that matter to a person, such as goals and values, and will "form a basis for perceiving, judging, and acting" (Hart 2005, 168). Much of the work on development and morality starts with the work of Lawrence Kohlberg (1969). His perspective suggests that, as the capacity for moral reasoning grows, those principles affect decision making to a greater degree, and individuals will act more consistently with their moral views. Dan P. McAdams (2009) enumerates personal narratives associated with prosocial identity in which the individual's moral virtue becomes integrated into his or her view of self (see also Habermas and Bluck 2000).

Establishing an identity is a formative task in late adolescence and early adulthood (McAdams 2009), when youths are also learning from experience via positive or negative reinforcement in facets of their life influenced by previous choices (Turiel 2006). Daniel K. Lapsley and Patrick L. Hill (2009) suggest that disposition and socialization coalesce to form something more coherent during that period of the life course. With this comes a clear sense of responsibility for behavior and drive toward self-consistency in beliefs and actions (Blasi 2005). This is binding in that actions that fit with the self-image maintain and build the coherence of that narrative (Hart 2005). A coherent moral identity, or character, fosters a kind of compelled action in given situations, and individuals may feel guilt or shame when they do not act in accordance with it (Eisenberg 2000; Malti and Ongley 2014).

As with many behaviors that emerge from both state and trait factors, the search for a better understanding of the why of moral identity and action starts with a discussion of seemingly stable traits, like conscientiousness and agreeableness, or is situationally dependent (Lapsley and Hill 2009; Walker 2014). The consensus is that moral identity is multifaceted in its expression, influences, and development and that both pieces are necessary (Carlo 2014; Hardy 2006; McAdams 2009; Turiel 2006, 2014). It begins with children developing understanding of social rules and expectations (Smetana, Jambon, and Ball 2014). Although morality and identity are individual traits, they are inherently affected by social relationships and group processes (Carlo 2014; Hart 2005). In addition to stable interpersonal differences, identity is developed through interactions with situations and social institutions like family and peers. Contact with the juvenile justice system as an adolescent certainly can have such a developmental impact as well.

The expression of identity through behavior occurs in an interactive, socially situated fashion in everyday circumstances in which both emotion and reason interdependently resolve preferences that are sometimes at odds with one another (Decety and Howard 2014; Smetana, Jambon, and Ball 2014; Turiel 2006, 2014). Lapsley and Hill assert that this moral personality "unfolds in the dynamic transaction between dispositional tendencies and context" (2009, 195; see also Carlo 2014). A youth, or adult for that matter, may face a challenging moral dilemma when trying to behave honestly but not hurt the feelings of a friend or family member. In those circumstances, the individual may be predisposed to follow a personal script, not another youth's script, but will likely adapt it to the situation (McAdams 2009). At that stage, youths recognize moral considerations that are relevant in a given situation but do not necessarily feel compelled by them as they might later (Blasi 2005).

Social and cultural expectations influence the development of identity. Moffitt (1993) frames the desistance of adolescence-limited delinquents in terms of the closing of a biological maturity gap but also mentions the relevance of a transition to adult roles. The same processes that help those youths wind down their offending are at work in their broader transition to adult responsibility and self-concept. The social aspect of moral development comes into play as perspective taking and empathy begin to set the stage for greater awareness of the potential outcomes of decisions relative to moral norms (Arsenio and Lemerise 2004; Malti and Ongley 2014). McAdams (2009) argues that these views and societal expectations arrive in late adolescence, necessitating a move from the experimentation and identity tryouts that come at that stage to the figuring-things-out stage in adulthood. Greater self-definition of moral identity is a by-product of that process.

The need for reasoning in this process suggests that the coherence of identity and its situational expression are at least partly age graded and therefore should inform the broader understanding of adolescent behaviors and underlying motivational forces. Like choice more generally, this character emerges situationally, so it is not surprising that it would be somewhat fluid into adulthood and that individuals would find greater coherence in their moral identity and express it more consistently after adolescence. Augusto Blasi (2005) argues that, like self-control, which affects adolescent choice, this factor also may be related to understanding moral choice. He suggests that willpower is affected by the cognitive skills (e.g., setting goals, future-time perspective) that youths carry into situations, which means that some of the same factors that hinder decision making in real-life situations may also forestall the emergence of a solidified, prosocial identity. For example, neurobiological factors that facilitate adaptive social behavior are also associated with moral thought and decision making (e.g., the medial and ventral prefrontal cortex in the brain) (Decety and Howard 2014). Still, opportunities available in the social environment will also drive such action, which means that adolescent activity patterns affect the application of a youth's attitudes and personality to the situation (Carlo 2014; Hart 2005). Some scenarios are generated by the youth herself because she helps shape the environment and its norms (Turiel 2006), but others are from external forces—even chance. The impact of these opportunities is evident in studies of Moffitt's (1993) hypothesized abstainers, or those who do not engage in delinquency during adolescence. Research suggests that these youths are not necessarily isolated but, rather, occupy a different social space in which they are engaged with prosocial peer groups that provide greater opportunity for action based on shared moral beliefs (Brezina and Piquero 2007; Chen and Adams 2010; Piquero et al. 2005).

Adolescents frequently try to "establish boundaries of personal jurisdiction" and therefore may apply moral considerations inconsistently (Smetana, Jambon, and Ball 2014, 36; see also Thoma and Rest 1999). Gertrude Nunner-Winkler (2007) studied consistency in moral motivation using a long-term follow-up of participants from Germany. Using a scenario-based measure of action and associated motivation, the author found a good deal of instability in moral motivation from childhood to late adolescence. She found a negative correlation between ages seven and eighteen (−0.21), reflecting a curvilinear pattern in moral motivation, and that there were rank-order shifts in the responses, reflecting instability over time. Adolescents may be implicitly challenging the moral lessons that they learned as children and engaging in relativistic application of those rules or norms. These findings suggest that early influences are not wholly determinative of later moral motivation, because that may shift until late adolescence before settling into a more consistent pattern in early adulthood.

While identity development might be perceived as an inward journey, or an isolated search for self, the literature suggests that it is actually a transactional, sociocognitive process between an adolescent and his or her environment (Bronfenbrenner 1979) that depends on factors that build to some coherence in identity (Lapsley and Hill 2009; McAdams 2009). This developmental process is ongoing as individuals move into legal adulthood age, and therefore the juvenile justice system should be cautious in inferring character at that stage. This process can be a double-edged sword as far as adolescent behavior is concerned. McAdams (2009) argues that openness to experience is a factor in the development of moral values but that experiential openness might also come with experimentation. Identity reflects influences in the youth's life—including experiences with the juvenile justice system. The theory and research suggest, however, that there must be some individuation and sense of responsibility if moral identity is to play a substantial and consistent role in individual decision making (Blasi 2005; Hardy 2006). At the same time, some of the developmental evidence presented here suggests that this might not occur until late in adolescence or early adulthood.

Moral Concerns, Aggression, and Delinquency

Although often considered separately (Arsenio and Lemerise 2004), moral identity development has been directly linked by a small body of research to delinquency and aggression. That investigation involves studying how variation in offender histories and offense types and seriousness is associated with variation in information processing in social situations and the moral considerations in the underlying behaviors (Dodge and Crick 1990; Huesmann 1988). Not unlike the studies of adolescent choice described previously, this research takes an especially close look at thought and behavior in social context and situations (Arsenio and Lemerise 2004; Tisak, Tisak, and Goldstein 2006), which is directly relevant in identity development, expression, and reinforcement. The potential linkage between dispositional aggression and identity is predicated on the idea of differences in interpreting social cues and the intentions of others. A lack of awareness of how actions will be received or hostile attribution of others' intentions may dampen the impact of moral concerns (Tisak and Jankowski 1996).

Studies have identified differences in social-information processing between delinquent and nondelinquent youths (e.g., Liau, Barriga, and Gibbs 1998; Slaby and Guerra 1988). Delinquent or aggressive youths view the intentions of others, for example, as more hostile, and their goals in responding to those scenarios are, for example, to exercise control over people or situations (Arsenio and Lemerise 2004). The expected outcomes of actions may also differ because of an inability to tap into prosocial solutions in ambiguous situations or those in which there is conflict (Tisak, Tisak, and Goldstein 2006). This is comparable to the limitations in the range of possible responses to social cues, or behavioral repertoire, exhibited by more serious delinquent offenders (Moffitt 1993).

Ronald G. Slaby and Nancy G. Guerra (1988) studied distortions in social-information processing related to relaxed moral constraints on aggressive and delinquent behavior in a sample of 144 incarcerated and community-located youths. Consistent with expectations, they found a gradient pattern and statistically significant differences across the low-aggression to high-aggression and incarcerated subgroups. Youths in the high-aggression and incarcerated groups more frequently saw hostility in ambiguous situations, had hostile goals in their possible responses, offered fewer prosocial solutions, and perceived fewer negative consequences from acting on their goals than those in the low-aggression groups. Their beliefs about aggression were more positive as well. Albert K. Liau, Alavaro Q. Barriga, and John C. Gibbs (1998) studied these relationships in a small sample ($n = 103$) split between incarcerated and community youths. They focused especially on cognitive distortions in social-information processing, dimensions of thought processes related to self-centeredness, externalizing blame, and assuming the worst in others' intentions. Not surprisingly, these distortions had greater traction in the delinquent sample and were related to problem behaviors. This research again links the situational and developmental context of adolescence to both delinquent choices and identity.

The Limits of the Pure Learner's Permit Perspective

Research on the teen brain, decision making in the adolescent environment, and developmental processes has become quite prominent and is an essential starting point for reevaluating the choices and character of delinquent youths for the purposes of juvenile justice intervention strategies. The presumed takeaway from that literature is a perception that "an understanding of the teen brain both supports the retention of a separate juvenile justice system and illuminates the proper perspective on the adjudication and treatment of young offenders" (Maroney 2010, 91). These works, which cross multiple fields, provide a good deal of support for the simple statement that youths and adult offenders are different from one another but also that their underlying determinants are complex. Despite these commonsense and empirical supported distinctions between adolescents and adults and evidence that serious adolescent offenders are treatable (e.g., Lipsey 1999), there is also much individual-level variation. Numerous cases of delinquency do not directly involve peers or they involve youths who have had repeated opportunities for rehabilitation that do not come to fruition. These cases are also distinct with respect to situational and individual circumstances that inevitably play a role in discretionary decision making.

The categorical distinction between youths and adults raises challenges when it comes to the discussion of specific cases—especially when balanced against potential public safety concerns and easily identified exceptions.

Research on the distinctions between adults and adolescents based on brain development has also acknowledged the within-group variation in adolescent decision-making processes and behavior (Dahl 2004; Galvan et al. 2007; Sisk and Zehr 2005; Steinberg et al. 2008). Dahl (2004), for instance, notes that while there is increased reward sensitivity at some points in adolescence, youths are likely to differ in that sensitivity. This may correlate with certain measurable personality traits, like impulsivity or emotionality (Byrnes 2002), or cognitive styles that emphasize rational choice (Reyna and Farley 2006). Similarly, Spear asserts that "biology is not destiny and is modifiable by social behavior and other experiences" (2000, 447).

The view of adolescence as a learner's permit coupled with the recognition of variation in the cases before the juvenile justice system (Zimring 2005a) creates challenges in operationalizing distinctions among cases and illustrates that prediction or explanation for a case, or collection of cases, can be precarious (e.g., Auerhahn 1999; Kazdin 2000; Silver and Miller 2002). Adolescents who appear to abuse the excuse of youth by repeatedly committing offenses—even after intervention by families, communities, and the juvenile justice system—therefore might not warrant the response from the juvenile justice system that others would get. This complexity is evident in the public opinion literature on how to respond to youth delinquency as well. In general, a child-saving instinct is deep rooted, but it is not without exception and is often tied to the types of cases under consideration (Applegate, Davis, and Cullen 2008; Bishop 2006).[2]

While the public, many policy makers, and those in the field certainly recognize those boundaries in most cases, some others question the strength of that distinction. Those critics argue that absolute categorical mitigation of delinquent offenses is not warranted by the evidence and that meaningful individual variation must be considered in court decisions (Maroney 2010). Often these arguments rest on assertions about parity in cognitive development between adults and late adolescents. If an individual knows that an action is wrong, then that person is accountable for it. Stephen J. Morse (1997, 1999) argues that treatability and responsibility are distinct, necessitating a mixed theory of punishment and intervention in determining what stance should be taken to delinquency and criminal cases. He identifies a lack of clarity in the research on adolescent immaturity and judgment that is due to the overlap in distributions among adolescents and adults on dimensions relevant to judging culpability like self-regulation and moral identity. Therefore, he argues, there is a distinction between the risk-taking endemic to adolescence and more serious "intentional criminal behavior" (Morse 1997, 55).

To underscore that point, Figure 3.2 shows the distribution of impulse control at one wave in the Pathways to Desistance study.[3] The graph illustrates three important points. First, there is a slight upward trend over time in impulse control among age groups, which is consistent with the research

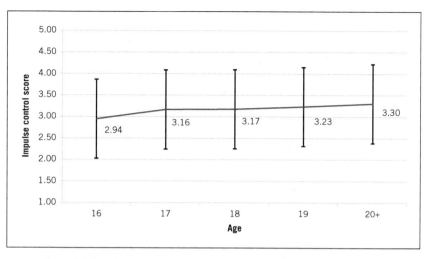

Figure 3.2 Impulse control by age in Pathways to Desistance study (*n* = 1,233)

described here. Second, there are statistically significant differences between age sixteen (mean = 2.94) and age nineteen (mean = 3.23) and twenty and older (mean = 3.30). Last, the bars surrounding the distribution of the mean, which represent the standard deviation values, suggest that age groups overlap in youths' level of impulse control. In other words, the distinctions are not so great that the younger and older age groups would not overlap at all in impulse control. This has implications for the usefulness of absolute categorical distinctions between adolescents and young adults because there is some comparability that necessitates caution in light of individual variation.

These perspectives find limits to the utility of the developmental research just described in responding to delinquent behavior—especially serious delinquency. Despite the confluence of factors that affect youths' decision making, youths retain a level of agency in engaging in acts that they understand to be wrong or potentially harmful to others. Thus, Morse argues that it is necessary to consider the individual youth's agency as a mediator of the different factors that affect judgment (e.g., real or perceived peer pressures, reward sensitivity) because there is still a core level of "normative competence" in most cases (1997, 23). This suggests that sanctions should be selected with this agency in mind, especially because the juvenile justice system may be a part of the social-interaction process that generates moral identity.

With these possible limitations to the unreserved use of research and philosophy on developmental distinctions, it is essential to consider whether and how these insights can be used in other practical ways in responding to delinquent youths. The criticisms just outlined reinforce the value of acknowledging and understanding differences in the broad group of adolescents who engage in delinquency, which some would characterize as a majority of the population (Moffitt 1993), and translating this to an appropriate response to delinquent behavior. Adolescents must successfully negotiate several tasks to set the stage for successful transitions to adulthood (Clausen 1991; Dahl 2004; Spear 2000), and justice-involved youths may face hurdles in reaching these milestones (Dmitrieva et al. 2012; Mulvey and Schubert 2011; Uggen and Wakefield 2005). Expanding the examination of delinquency in the context of the life course and folding it into responses within the system's day-to-day activities will establish the foundation for appropriate system response.

While the research informing reform proposals from the early twenty-first century is useful and now has the imprimatur of neurological and biological sciences, there are limitations to how that information can be practically applied in day-to-day operations. Unanswered questions in this research remain (e.g., Denno 2006; Males 2009; Maroney 2010; Sullivan and Newsome 2015), and therefore this emerging evidence is likely to be of greatest use as "one new input into the well-established interface between juvenile justice policy and developmental science" (Maroney 2010, 167) as opposed to the entire foundation for the juvenile justice system. A wide net is needed in assessing the evidence for how adolescents develop and make decisions (Reyna and Farley 2006)—especially those that may lead them to the juvenile justice system. This is especially true when it points to categorical distinctions that hold generally but that also reflect individual-level variation that overlaps with adult populations (Males 2009; Morse 1997, 1999). These within-population differences require specific attention because, while policy operates at a general level, individualization is inevitable when it comes to treatment and sanctions for delinquent youths.

Unquestionably, new biological and neuroscientific evidence has contributed significantly to understanding adolescence. The individual variability and interdependent nature of decisions and behavior—coupled with these processes not being determinative—require a multifaceted foundation for understanding and action (Dahl 2004; Spear 2000). Very clearly, capacity for judicious choice and execution of choice is not totally static, because the objectives of an individual's decision making will shift at least somewhat over time (Reyna and Farley 2006). This shifting is related to developmental factors but is also affected by the experience of having already made certain decisions (Byrnes 2002), such as those that lead to juvenile justice involvement. This expansion of context is a premise of developmental and life-course theories of offending, which are the subject of Chapter 4. The review and analysis in the next chapter, which draws on social and behavioral sciences, can be placed alongside the evidence described here to contextualize the place of juvenile justice response in the lives of delinquent youths with various offenses, pathways to and from the system, delinquency patterns, and risk and need profiles.

4

Expanding the Evidence Base for Developmental Juvenile Justice

T he evidence offered in support of a more developmental juvenile justice
system is valuable in reaffirming perceived differences between youths
and adults. Still, it does not fully delve into patterns of delinquency, its
etiology, and its long-term pathways in a way that matches the complexity of
the delinquency problem and the juvenile justice system's response to it.
Analysis of additional layers of developmental and life-course insights provides a more expansive and nuanced view of what drives aspects of delinquency and identifies the possibilities and challenges inherent in the juvenile
justice response to a heterogeneous population of adolescents.

Patterns and Deviations in Delinquency Trends

The variation in incidence and prevalence of delinquency suggests that, at a
minimum, it is necessary to disaggregate patterns of delinquent behavior as
they unfold over time if the system is to become more developmental. This
has been the focus of developmental and life-course studies of offending for
some time. Focused consideration of a single data set can help illustrate patterns and nuances in the broader findings on age and delinquent behavior.
In the Pathways to Desistance study, for several years researchers closely
followed 1,356 youths who were involved in the court systems in Philadelphia, Pennsylvania, and Phoenix, Arizona (Mulvey et al. 2004; Schubert
et al. 2004).

Figure 4.1 presents yearly delinquency curves for eight waves of measurement of twenty randomly selected cases.[1] The raw curves illustrate a few

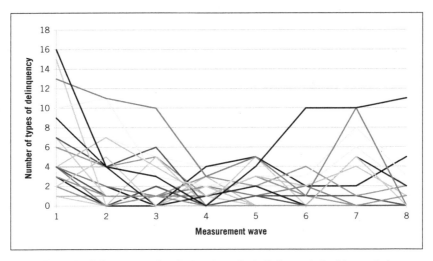

Figure 4.1 Delinquency variety for twenty youths in Pathways to Desistance study

key points about delinquency pathways. First, the initial time point, wave one, tends to be the highest level of self-reported offending for each youth, and the curves' starting points cluster at the lower end of the range, representing fairly low levels of offending. Although the average variety score, or number of types of offending, is roughly 5.5 at that point, the standard deviation of 4.2 is high, mostly owing to several cases that have scores at 1 or 2. This illustrates the distinct starting points for this sample. Mixing these youths with those who have not had contact with the juvenile court previously would produce even more variability.

Second, the trend lines very quickly begin to cluster toward the bottom of the types of delinquency scale, showing a drop-off across time—with a couple of clear exceptions. Third, individuals vary a good deal over the observation period, suggesting a lot of potential pathways following contact with the system—despite some commonalities. Fourth, most of these curves (sixteen) trend toward zero at the last observation point, and roughly half get there in the two waves before that (and remain there). Finally, the fluctuations or rebounds in some individual curves suggest that these types of pathways of delinquency are intermittent and nonlinear (Bushway, Thornberry, and Krohn 2003; Piquero 2004).

One common means of distilling and assessing these types of pathways is through semiparametric group-based trajectory modeling, or latent class growth analysis (see Muthén 2004; Nagin 2005). This approach usefully summarizes relatively common patterns of delinquency in this sample of justice-involved youths and provides a basis for further analysis of probabilistic groupings of cases. The latent class growth analysis conducted by Shaun M. Gann, Christopher J. Sullivan, and Omeed S. Ilchi (2015), shown in Figure 4.2, uses the Pathways sample. That analysis identified four estimated trajectory groups, which contain a few different average trends (see also Mulvey et al. 2010). This figure shows some commonalities with the raw curves in Figure 4.1, but it also conveys the estimated prevalence with which youths in the sample tend to follow these estimated pathways. First, despite the selection of justice-involved youths, 44 percent had little or no delinquency during the observation period. Although this analysis is based on self-reports, it reinforces other findings that a substantial proportion of youths tend to curtail their delinquency after initial contact with the juvenile justice system (e.g., Snyder 1998). Second, the most extreme latent subgroup identified in the statistical model, youths who begin with high variety scores and remain there for the duration of the observation window, makes up the smallest proportion of the sample (13 percent). This is characteristic of a high-rate, chronic offender group. Third, the other two groups decline in their offending relatively quickly, with roughly 25 percent fitting a profile of youths who start off with high levels of offending (a score of 8.2 on average) but drop toward zero over time. Interestingly, the levels for these two groups cross in the middle of the study follow-up, which exemplifies the within-individual variation in delinquency during adolescence.

While it is more challenging to identify pathways that these youths follow to the juvenile justice system, these groups serve as a loose starting point to consider such trends. The analysis of delinquency trajectories considered the degree of linkage between the age of onset of offending and these

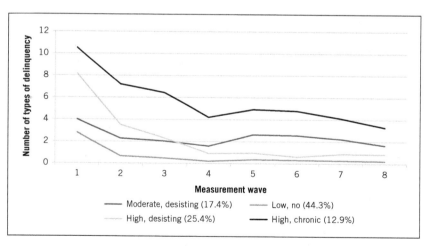

Figure 4.2 Trajectories of delinquency with latent classes in
Pathways to Desistance study (*n* = 825)
Source: Adapted from Gann, Sullivan, and Ilchi 2015. Used with permission
from Springer Nature. Copyright 2015.

empirically identified groups (Gann, Sullivan, and Ilchi 2015). The group characterized as having high initial-offending scores and chronic delinquency was used as a reference point, and the estimates show that those with later ages of onset were significantly more likely to be placed in the lowest offending group (38 percent greater odds) or the group that started high but desisted quickly (28 percent greater odds). Conversely, those who began offending earlier in life and had more prior contact with the system generally wound up with more extensive and sustained delinquency careers after adjudication. When using the low, no-offending group as a reference point, each increase in the number of juvenile petitions before the study began led to a statistically significant increase in the odds of placement in one of the more serious delinquency groups. The high, chronic group saw the largest effect. Each additional earlier petition led to 26 percent greater odds of winding up in that class as opposed to the lowest-offending group. The effects for the other two groups were less pronounced at roughly a 20 percent difference in the odds of placement in each of those versus the low, no-offending group. There is some continuity in the types of patterns leading to juvenile court involvement but also opportunities for turning points. This example shows variation in delinquency pathways across adolescence among justice-involved youths and that it may be linked to other key developmental influences for prediction or explanation.

Key Parameters in Delinquency Pathways

Contextualizing delinquency in a temporal sequence is part of the career paradigm for describing criminal behavior (Barnett, Blumstein, and Farrington 1987; Blumstein et al. 1986). The developmental perspective offers a framework for considering milestones in the process of engaging in delinquency, which may include mundane (e.g., hanging out with peers) or monumental experiences depending on the case (e.g., trouble at home that leads to divorce and subsequently loosens parental supervision). These influences or experiences are likely to be cumulative such that they materially affect what happens later in constraining or opening opportunities (see Evans, Li, and Whipple 2013; Loeber and Farrington 1998). A developmental framework identifies core aspects of delinquency that are worth investigating and explaining, like onset, duration, and desistance (Loeber and Le Blanc 1990).

Onset: Getting Started in Delinquency. Onset, which refers to the initial emergence of delinquency, is one of the strongest correlates of long-term offending (Loeber and Farrington 2000). This is axiomatic in that earlier onset often suggests a lengthier period of active offending simply by virtue of timing (DeLisi and Piquero 2011), but questions emerge from how age of onset might matter. Is this just another indication of latent behavioral problems (e.g., recalcitrance that started very early in life), or does it lead to other problems that prolong delinquency (e.g., education interruption, weakened prosocial ties)? Studies have found support for both explanations (Gann, Sullivan, and Ilchi 2015; Nagin and Farrington 1992; Tolan and Thomas 1995), generally reaffirming the complexity of the links between onset and later behavior (see e.g., Bacon, Paternoster, and Brame 2009; van Domburgh et al. 2009).

Two elements of this onset parameter are instructive in linking juvenile justice and adolescent development. First, its timing can be a demarcation point in establishing the underlying reasoning and long-term prospects for stability or change. Second, the circumstances and timing of onset can help in understanding delinquent youths, explicating their risks and problems, and projecting long-term behavioral patterns (Lahey, Waldman, and McBurnett 1999; Moffitt 1993). In that way, it is more than just a first offense at a point in time but, rather, a marker of a process in which individual and environmental factors play a role in determining the initial timing of problem behaviors and delinquency. For example, experiences very early in life may affect executive functioning and other sources of self-regulation that start youths on a long-term trajectory of delinquent behavior (Lahey, Waldman, and McBurnett 1999; Moffitt 1993). Conversely, later onset of delinquency may follow from peer relationships or routine time spent in a neighborhood environment where youths encounter delinquent opportunities in subtle ways.

The timing and nature of initiation could affect the later processes that lead to elongated or shorter delinquency careers as well. Onset may result from causal processes or an accumulation of problems that create obstacles to stopping the pattern, like academic problems or reduced connections to prosocial influences. In fact, some argue that delinquent behavior can begin after a conscious or involuntary weakening of ties to prosocial institutions like family or school (Sampson and Laub 1993),[2] which knifes off elements of a youth's life that prevent delinquent behavior (Maruna and Roy 2007). Youths adopt that role to a greater or lesser extent, which affects how their behavior is perceived—by self and others—and the informal and formal response to it. They may feel more freedom to commit delinquent acts than their peers who do not engage in delinquency (Hindelang 1970), but these youths may not be fully committed to a long-term pattern of behavior when first engaging in it either. A host of processes—both systematic and random—can generate delinquent pathways, and these different stories are pertinent to juvenile justice response.

Duration: Continuing in Delinquency. "Continuity" refers to how long a youth persists in his or her delinquency or criminal behavior (Blumstein and Cohen 1987). Rolf Loeber and Marc Le Blanc (1990) discuss this in terms of the maintenance of delinquency as opposed to the activation in onset. Research on stability in offending in adolescence and beyond characterizes its continuity and, where it is present, has sought explanations to distinguish those who continue their behavior from those who do not (see e.g., Greenwood and Abrahamse 1982). Most youths do not persist in legally prohibited behaviors into adulthood, but some segments of the delinquent population have a discernible degree of stability in delinquent behavior (Bushway 2013).

Given the nature of adolescence, some believe that adolescents who engage in any delinquency will continue to do so for much of their time as teenagers. This has implications for understanding delinquency and the juvenile justice system response. If the course of delinquency runs out only as youths age, then this calls into question what the juvenile justice system can do earlier to stop those delinquency careers. Just as there are multiple pathways to the juvenile court, multiple developmental contingencies might lead to its continuance or conclusion. These partly parallel the ways youths get into delinquency but are combinations of subsequent events and influences as well. First, the notion of cumulative continuity in risk is one way delinquent behavior might persist beyond a youth's early engagement (Moffitt 1993; Nagin and Paternoster 2000; Sampson and Laub 1993). This includes the possibility that the informal or formal juvenile justice response to the delinquent behavior affects whether the youth continues. Several studies have found, for instance, that early arrest has a significant impact on the risk of later school dropout and related educational outcomes (Hirschfield 2009; Kirk and Sampson 2013; Sweeten 2006), which will in turn generate increased risk of continuity in delinquency because of school withdrawal (see, e.g., Thornberry, Moore, and Christenson 1985).

Second, certain benefits—recall the allure of delinquent behavior in situational choices in adolescent social settings—accrue from continued involvement in delinquency, at least for a time. Elijah Anderson (1999) identifies and explains the use of street codes as a means of negotiating challenging urban environments where status can be essential to survival, and Mercer L. Sullivan (1989) considers how economic motivations might drive initiation and continuance of certain types of delinquency. More generally, Mark Warr (2002) discusses aspects of status with respect to peers and noted enhancing standing and avoiding losing face as motivators of delinquent behavior. As these motivations recede, juveniles are apt to respond differently to their social environment and curtail delinquent behavior (Moffitt 1993). The juvenile justice system must understand that individual and environmental factors—including its own intervention—may prolong delinquency.

Seriousness and Frequency of Delinquency. The mix of offenses in which youths engage is especially pertinent to system actors. For example, interviews about decision making with court officials routinely suggested that they prioritized types of offenses and more frequent offenders in processing (Sullivan, Latessa, et al. 2016). A statement from a focus group of police officers illustrates this point: "We have a core group of juveniles in each part of our city that are routine offenders. If a crime happens in a certain neighborhood, we know which juveniles to target." Similarly, in discussing detention decisions, a juvenile court official in an interview said, "Typically, youth are detained for armed robbery, domestic violence, and violations charges." This is in large part because these youths commit "most of the charges" and are "repeat offenders."[3]

Such dimensions of active criminal careers, which clearly resonate with system actors, inform understanding of youth delinquency in other ways as well. A basic premise of the developmental approach is that there is a relatively small group of high-frequency offenders (less than 10 percent) who contribute most of the overall offenses or juvenile court contacts (Blumstein et al. 1986; Piquero 2008b). This draws on the study of the Philadelphia birth cohort data by Marvin E. Wolfgang, Robert M. Figlio, and Thorsten Sellin (1972; see also Blokland, Nagin, and Nieuwbeerta 2005; D'Unger et al. 1998; Sullivan and Piquero 2011). These more serious, violent, and chronic offenders are a necessary focal point for the juvenile justice system (Snyder 1998). They do, however, make up a minority of cases despite the disproportionate attention they often receive in media, among politicians, and from the public. In this case, the research evidence perhaps alerts us to a place where the overall risk of delinquency is concentrated, which is a key aspect of assessing cases before fashioning effective intervention.

Desistance: Winding Down Delinquency. The reasons for conclusion of delinquency careers vary as well. Some may wind down because of informal influences or because sanctions or treatment in the juvenile justice system—or an interaction between formal and informal influences—trigger desistance. "Desistance" refers to the subsiding of a pattern of delinquency or criminal behavior. Contingent turning points in the desistance period generate that outcome (Bushway et al. 2001; Bushway, Thornberry, and Krohn 2003; Laub and Sampson 2001). Desistance is often nonlinear, involving some return to offending and intermittency before a full stop in delinquency (Piquero 2004). This is in part a drift away from delinquency as opposed to a concerted choice (Matza 1964; Laub and Sampson 2003). It is natural that juvenile justice decision makers will perceive a lesser probability of later change the more they have seen a youth in their court or program.

The descriptive reality of patterns of engagement in delinquency and subsequent desistance implies that the antisocial behavior usually does not endure. Most delinquent youths, even serious adolescent offenders, are likely to either drastically curtail or discontinue their offending during late adolescence and early adulthood (Loeber and Farrington 2012). For instance, Edward Mulvey and colleagues' (2010) study of trajectories of justice-involved youths found that roughly three of four youths were desisters. Such

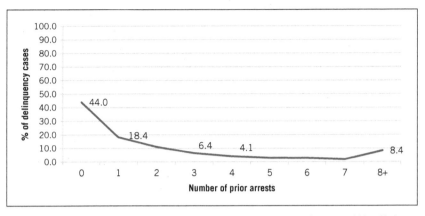

Figure 4.3 Number of prior arrests for delinquency cases in New Jersey and New York

findings offer a sensitizing point for the juvenile justice system, but it does not obviate the need to consider the possibility that delinquency could continue if the response is ineffective.

Juvenile justice involvement can tie into development in a few ways. Figure 4.3 contains a descriptive analysis of prior offenses by age using Aaron Kupchik's (2006) data on roughly 2,200 youths who encountered the justice system in New York and New Jersey.[4] Each of these youths was between age fifteen and seventeen, or in midadolescence. The figure shows that a sizable group was not arrested previously (44 percent). This pushes to more than 60 percent when including those with one prior arrest, meaning that most did not engage in repetitive contact with the juvenile justice system during adolescence. It also generally corresponds with the low, no-delinquency group identified in the Pathways data previously. Nevertheless, roughly 40 percent of youths had multiple prior arrests, with about 8 percent amassing eight or more arrests, and thirty youths with twenty or more prior arrests. The size of this group with longer official records tends to align with the size of the most serious group of delinquents in the Pathways study. Figure 4.3 shows the variation in prior offending among one sample of youths in the juvenile justice system but also indicates that the majority would not officially be chronic offenders (Snyder 1998).

Arnold Barnett, Alfred Blumstein, and David P. Farrington (1987) formally model the probability that an official delinquency career would continue or stop at a given point in the sequence of convictions. When studying only cases with multiple convictions, they found that a model characterized by between-youth variability in offending rates, as well as heterogeneous "termination probability," best fit the data (93). Two groups, frequent and occasional offenders, dominated in the data. The former group (43 percent of those with multiple convictions), averaged about 1.1 convictions per year. The latter group had an average of 0.41 convictions per year with a "termination probability per conviction" of 0.33 (98). The yearly conviction rate was fairly low among those with multiple recorded offenses, and the majority of that subgroup of eighty-two youths with at least two convictions had a low yearly offending rate and a fairly high probability of cessation at each subsequent offense.

A prospective look at juvenile justice system involvement also offers some insight on this question of chronic offending versus desistance (see Figure 4.4). Data on officially recorded convictions from age ten to twenty-four among cases in the Cambridge Study on Delinquent Development (Farrington and West 1990; Piquero, Farrington, and Blumstein 2007) show that among those convicted at any point in adolescence or early adulthood (136, or 33.9 percent) 36 percent had only one recorded conviction, suggesting that a reasonably sized group of those who encounter the justice system do not have another official contact. Some who have multiple offenses nevertheless stop while they are still at an age that falls under juvenile justice jurisdiction. Within the Cambridge study, this group makes up about 16 percent of those with at least one conviction.[5]

Of the many reasons for offender stoppage, turning points certainly can come from experiences with the juvenile justice system. The Office of Juvenile Justice and Delinquency Prevention (OJJDP 2000) report *Second Chances*, published to coincide with the juvenile court's centennial, contains narratives from several successful adults who credit juvenile court judges, probation officers, and treatment programs with helping them find alternative pathways. Understanding the prevalence of this group matters in responding to juvenile delinquency but so too does the potential for identifying markers for stopping delinquency before the transition to adulthood. Some adolescents curtail their offending because of delayed deterrence from jus-

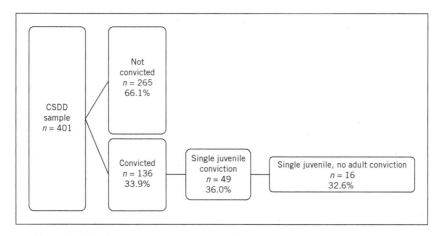

Figure 4.4 Conviction patterns in Cambridge Study on Delinquent Development (CSDD)

tice sanctions (Cusson and Pinsonneault 1986) or skill development in treatment (Lipsey 1999). Others may be like Stanley, the subject in Clifford Shaw's *The Jack-Roller*, who stated, "My reformation I attribute to the people I came into contact with after leaving the House of Corrections," rather than changes instigated by the justice system ([1930] 1966, 182). Others require greater age and maturation to separate from a pattern of delinquent behavior (Shover 1985).

Late adolescence and early adulthood often coincide with diminishment of delinquent behavior, which suggests that the transition between developmental stages plays a role in the shift from delinquency. Other youths will continue their offending into adulthood, however (Mulvey et al. 2010). Among youths in the Cambridge study convicted at least once, 43 percent continued to offend and then aged out of the juvenile justice system without desisting. These are the cases for whom the system either outright failed or was simply ineffectual against a youth's preexisting risks or other circumstances that emerged coincidental to (or following) juvenile justice involvement. Developmental research indicates that the system has little effect for some youths because of their accumulated risks and lost social capital. Still, it is also a reminder that the juvenile justice system does affect many of the youths that it encounters. For example, one juvenile court judge who identified a "lost cause" on his docket also expressed positive views of the "work" by several other youths and thought that only a minority of cases were beyond the help of the juvenile court.[6]

In the Pathways to Desistance data, delinquency clearly began to lessen toward the end of adolescence or early adulthood and, for a significant portion of that sample, began to taper off after initial involvement with the juvenile court. Still, the Cambridge study conviction patterns suggest that one-and-done delinquents are by no means the rule, and many delinquent youths pick up later convictions. These preceding analyses, using several sources of data, added to the types of delinquent youths, system responses, and youth choices and character, illustrate the many pathways *to* the juvenile justice system in terms of onset and continuity and *from* the system after it takes action (or not) with a given youth. Better understanding and explanation of the commonalities and divergence in those paths is a precursor to a more developmental juvenile justice. The general principles and specific explanations of development and the life course can be useful in understanding typical and atypical delinquency cases and informing the system's response.

Core Developmental and Life-Course Principles

Identification of patterns of delinquency and the extraction of common markers of careers offer useful information about the timing, duration, and conclusion of delinquency. Nevertheless, specification of the parameters of delinquency careers is not totally informative about influences, predispositions, and adolescent behavior. It is, therefore, necessary to specify connections between these patterns and processes underlying delinquency and its variation between and within youths. From a developmental or life-course standpoint, the linkage between these influences and patterns of stability and change places delinquency and its causes in a space that parallels other behaviors and experiences in the lives of children, adolescents, and young adults. This foundation is based on a general understanding of human development and common events in the life course and how certain predispositions, social relationships, events, or system exposure affect those patterns. In other words, it considers delinquency alongside key elements of youths' lives and offers a more holistic view of factors affecting youths' behavior and identifies potential modes of intervention.

If the objective of the juvenile court is to redirect lives, which was its initial aim and has experienced resurgence in the twenty-first century, insight on delinquency must be linked to these broader principles relevant to adolescent development. The National Research Council (NRC 2013) report on development and juvenile justice establishes the centrality of the interaction between a youth's individual risks and strengths and the social environment. Those interactions may create challenges and affect the opportunities that arise in youths' lives, paralleling integrated perspectives on prosocial and antisocial development in the life course of youths. This thinking on interactions that occur over time is often implicit in the court's fact-finding and dispositional decision making because of the desire to contextualize the youth's delinquency in other facets of his or her life (e.g., family, school, substance use) and consider past patterns of behavior and future possibilities. In hearings, for example, judges and magistrates frequently asked about the interaction between the youth and school with a subtext of its stark importance for his or her future. Three perspectives on development and the life-course establish key foundations with respect to delinquency. Each helps directly operationalize the National Research Council's (NRC 2013) view that a developmental juvenile justice system must focus on individuals in interaction with the social environment over time.

Developmental and Life-Course Frameworks

Ecological Model. The transactional ecological model of development by Urie Bronfenbrenner (1977, 1979) describes youths at the center of delinquent acts while also acknowledging and assessing their embeddedness in a family, peer group, school, and neighborhood, which both affects their behavior and is affected by it. Bronfenbrenner (1977, 1979) saw youth development as unfolding in nested ecological spaces in mutual interaction of the individual and his or her environment. He integrated developmental influences in "multiperson systems of interaction not limited to a single setting and . . . [that] take into account aspects of the environment beyond the immediate situations containing the subject" (1977, 514). The microsystem captures the child's or adolescent's interactions in the immediate social setting (e.g., parents, siblings, and peers). In the exosystem the youth interacts at different developmental stages, like schools or neighborhoods. The macrosystem comprises the broader societal structure and norms, laws, and rules. Those might be the policies that affect the response to juvenile delinquency and the legal statutes governing childhood, adolescence, and adulthood (Scott and Steinberg 2008). Bronfenbrenner considers not only objective states of social settings but also perception and reactions. For youths, these are reciprocal influences among the pairs and groups in which they are embedded and interactions in settings like juvenile courts and treatment agencies.

The juvenile justice system likely would fit into Bronfenbrenner's exosystem. Thinking developmentally requires awareness of how juvenile justice processes and outcomes absorb the effects of other interactive units, including the youth and the family, and of how it affects a youth's development in a direct sense and via his or her perception of it. Some of the specific interventions in the system illustrate this thinking about developmental ecology. Multisystemic therapy and functional family therapy draw on an ecological perspective by addressing youths and domains in which they interact, primarily the family (Henggeler 1997; Sexton and Alexander 2000). At the same time, the juvenile justice system is only one among several influences on youth development. These influences operate in cooperation or competition to affect youths' immediate and long-term behavior.

Dynamic Contextualism. Similarly, David L. Featherman and Richard M. Lerner (1985) consider whether the basis of development resided in the person, his or her environment, or the interaction between the two. Not surprisingly, they argued that behavior is contingent on both the person and the environment in an interaction, identifying a need for "complementarity" in explaining developmental patterns. Most importantly for this discussion, they explicitly proposed that individuals are "co-producers" of their development such that their environment affects them, but choices and actions also affect those external influences to generate constancy or change in developmental patterns (1985, 659–660). This is reminiscent of the transactional aspect of Bronfenbrenner's (1979) theory and relates to other perspectives that identify how individuals and environments coproduce stability or change in behavior (Caspi, Bem, and Elder 1989; Moffitt 1993; Sampson and Laub 1993). It also comports with the expectation that a youth will both affect the handling of his or her juvenile court case and be affected by it (Emerson 1969). Featherman and Lerner (1985) suggest that, while there is likely to be a degree of continuity in behavior on the basis of certain interdependent individual and environmental factors, observed behaviors are contingent on several factors and so—even in cases in which there appears to be a fair degree of certainty about future risk—outcomes can be unpredictable and change can emerge (Sampson and Laub 2005b; C. Sullivan 2013).

Life-Course Theory. Glen Elder's life-course theory bears some similarities in emphasis with these developmental approaches but also some distinctions. Elder (1998) recognizes the different ways that individual pathways might play out and that individuals help construct their own pathways and turning points in life, but he also argues that this does not occur in a vacuum (Featherman and Lerner 1985; Laub and Sampson 2003). Specifically, he argues that individuals exercise human agency (subjective choice) with some constraints from the social environment (structural forces). This necessarily means that there are contingencies in decision making such that both subjective and structural factors invariably play a role in delinquency pathways. Also, as contingencies change or external shifts occur, youth behavior may follow—both immediately and in long-term patterns.

More broadly, the life-course perspective emphasizes the need to think holistically about individual pathways and presents several relevant principles. General life-course theory considers the effects of (1) historical time and place, (2) timing in lives, (3) linked lives, and (4) human agency with an emphasis on transition experiences that affect trajectories. In delinquency, these principles are relevant to understanding its etiology in terms of onset, continuance, and desistance and also establish the potential impact of multiple levels of context around human choice and patterns of behavior. The opportunities available at certain times and places and linkages to families, communities, and peer groups structure the range of options that youths might see in the immediate situation and in long-term prospects for change or continued delinquent behavior.

The Nature of Continuity and Change

The contingencies highlighted in the life-course, dynamic-contextualism, and ecological-development frameworks are a gateway to analysis of continuity and change in behavior over time. The presence of continuity and change is an essential operating framework for considering the response to youth delinquency and juvenile justice in interactive fashion. While evidence suggests that continuity in offending is not the modal track followed by adolescents, understanding that subgroup requires concerted attention for identification, explanation, and intervention.

Homotypic and Heterotypic Continuity. Homotypic and heterotypic continuity are two ways of looking at behavioral stability (Rutter 1989). Homotypic continuity refers to sustained instances of the same behavior (e.g., repeated shoplifting throughout adolescence). Heterotypic continuity refers to distinct, but like, behaviors that recur over time and that are at least in part attributable to a similar underlying factor. This is especially relevant in identifying youths with behavioral issues that transcend delinquency because it focuses more on common underlying factors. Heterotypic continuity could, for example, indicate that dishonesty with teachers or parents might evolve into later shoplifting from a store.

Terrie E. Moffitt (1993) describes the related idea of contemporary continuity, in which the consistent behavior is an expression of an underlying factor that is relatively stable in its impact on that behavior. For example, cognitive ability or lack of self-control may hinder school performance or even reaction to the juvenile court process in a way that is not self-defeating, just as it also increases the likelihood of a youth engaging in delinquency to begin with. A youth displaying cross-situational consistency (Moffitt 1993) or varieties of antisocial behavior (see Bendixen, Endresen, and Olweus 2003; Sweeten 2012) indicates that the youth's actions transcend short-term situational circumstances and may reflect more entrenched attitudes, habits, and sources of risk. The extent of convergent behavior across school, home, and community at one point in time helps identify the processes that generate that behavior.

Interactional and Environmental Continuity. Avshalom Caspi, Daryl J. Bem, and Glen H. Elder (1989) consider cross-situational convergence in behavior in terms of interactional continuity, in which individual predisposition elicits from the environment negative or positive response that reinforces those behavioral patterns. These processes involve a reproduction, or stability, in social environments conducive to continuity of routine actions in conjunction with an inability or lack of willingness to change those circumstances. A persistent pattern of delinquency may be due in part to the repeated manifestation of an individual trait, but it could also be a product of continued embeddedness in a school or neighborhood with a high concentration of delinquent peers (Wikström and Sampson 2003; Zimmerman and Messner 2011).

The notion of organic or system-driven changes in behavior must account for the possibility of youths' exposure to disadvantaged situations from early childhood through adolescence that they have little power to change on their own. In interviews with juvenile court personnel, they frequently discussed the challenges of adolescents who go through programming designed to change antisocial thinking and attitudes and bolster prosocial alternatives but end up being undercut by their home, school, or community environment.[7] They reported that families in particular influenced stability in behavior despite attempts to foster change. One juvenile justice official said, "Our biggest obstacle is engaging parents. Behavior change is difficult, [especially] when kids share that they've tried to use problem-solving skills [gained through intervention of the court] and their parents are resistant." From this official's perspective, continuity in delinquency is related to the consistency and salience of the home environment in which the youth is embedded. This can place a drag on the individual aspiration for change and limit the impact of formal intervention.

This extends Moffitt's (1993) argument that the environmental circumstances of youths with early individual risk factors are not predisposed to remediating delinquent behavior. Those raised in disadvantaged community environments may simultaneously experience harsher disciplinary practices and lower responsivity or warmth at home (Leventhal and Brooks-Gunn 2000), meaning that there will be continuity in disadvantaged environments (see also Cairns and Hood 1983; Caspi and Roberts 2001; Sameroff 1995). A youth exposed to a family in which discipline is not constructive may also attend schools with similar problems.

Avshalom Caspi and Brent W. Roberts (2001) argue that this cumulative disadvantage may also result from interactions between individual and environment. "Cumulative continuity," an idea central to developmental and life-course theories of crime, refers to transactional processes that occur over time to generate an observed pattern of stability. In cumulative continuity, selection into environments that reinforce a given attitude or behavior help propel that disposition forward and foster recurrence (Caspi, Bem, and Elder 1989). Youths may select deviant peers who reinforce a propensity toward antisocial behavior, leading to its continuance. In that sense, continuity is affected partly by the underlying propensity and partly by the consequences that result from its earlier expression. The core trait could become less salient, but behavioral continuity results from factors like narrowed opportunities for prosocial behavior or solidification in habits or social interaction style. Juvenile justice intervention must be mindful of these processes because they generate a more holistic picture of patterns of delinquency and also may offer a sense of how best to intervene (or the challenges in doing so).

General Mechanisms of Continuity (and Change)

Population Heterogeneity and State Dependence. Drawing on earlier work by James J. Heckman (1981), Daniel S. Nagin and Raymond Paternoster (1991) relate observed stability in delinquency to two possible processes: state dependence and persistent population heterogeneity. Heckman argues that two processes generate observed behavioral continuity. First, individuals differ in their propensity to participate in a behavior, and that enduring feature will continue to manifest over time—suggesting apparent stability. Second, experiences and behavior may have a causal effect on later behavior by altering future preference for that activity or affecting a social dynamic related to it. Nagin and Paternoster (1991) found a diminished direct effect of prior offending to current offense after controlling for the effect of persistent heterogeneity. Reviewing research that appeared following their 1991 study, Nagin and Paternoster (2000) found evidence supporting persistent heterogeneity and some supporting state dependence as well. They propose a mixed model to account for stability and instability in offending over time (see also Sullivan and Piquero 2010; Sullivan, Ousey, and Wilcox 2016). Observed patterns of delinquency reflect variation both between youths at the start of adolescence and of factors consequent to that behavior that spur further delinquency. This implies that the pattern of delinquency over time is a contingent process and the juvenile justice system must identify both enduring and emerging factors that affect youths' behavior and address them in its responses.

Developmental Cascades. William Healy argues that understanding the interdependent contributing factors to current delinquency required an understanding of the "left-overs from the yesterdays of life" (1925, 41). These early observations about justice-involved youths reflect the notion of developmental cascades, which Ann S. Masten and Dante Cicchetti describe as the interactions and transactions between a youth, developmental settings, and interpersonal influences, which can "alter the course of development" (2010, 491). These effects may be direct and unidirectional (e.g., from parent to child), direct and bidirectional (e.g., between parent and child), or indirect through various pathways (e.g., from structural influences to school environment to the individual youth). Each cascade can affect the youth's development in proximal or distal fashion.

Kenneth A. Dodge and colleagues (2008) present a cascades model of early conduct problems. Their "cascades" are a series of steps in which one adversity, or risk, affects the next one until the process ends with adolescent violence, much like a domino effect. They suggest, for instance, that an adverse socioeconomic context can lead to harsh and inconsistent parenting, which triggers behavioral problems in childhood that lead to violent behavior in adolescence. Dodge and colleagues argue that each successive step might bring new risk but, most relevant to juvenile justice, also opportunity for intervention. On the other hand, these are complex patterns of interactions over time that, according to Moffitt (1993), limit options for behavioral change. In juvenile justice, this means that possible unanticipated harmful effects downstream can work against the system's desire to promote change or that there may be opportunities to intervene at some point in that chain of relationships to preclude later parts of the cascade process (Dodge et al. 2008). The sustained pattern of behavior operates in a past-as-prologue process in which prior behavior triggers a cascade that narrows the options for later change. As noted earlier, a youth might have his education interrupted by juvenile justice involvement and then become ensnared in continuous antisocial behavior when he might not have otherwise. There is some variation in cascade patterns.

Variability in Continuity: Multifinality and Equifinality

A developmental response to delinquency requires a sense of within-individual variation in delinquency trajectories. A developmental view explicitly assimilates the idea of a past narrative that leads to justice involvement as well as future possible pathways of prosocial or antisocial behavior. This is somewhat implicit in the evaluations made by juvenile justice actors anyway (Emerson 1969). This "diversity in process and outcome" is caused by youths being treated as "open systems" as opposed to fully formed (Cicchetti and Rogosch 1996, 597). This follows the notion of state dependence mentioned earlier and implies that social influences and life experiences affect youths developmentally. Also, the initial condition in which the juvenile court encounters them could have emerged from multiple distinct developmental processes. Finally, a youth's later outcomes will be only partly determined by her status at the point at which she encountered juvenile justice agencies. In equifinality, multiple pathways can generate the same outcome. In multifinality, the same initial condition leads to different outcomes, such as the classic notion of a "good boy in [a] high delinquency area" (Reckless, Dinitz, and Murray 1957, 18) or two brothers who grow up in the same household but behave quite differently (e.g., Plomin and Daniels 2011).

Just as numerous configurations of risk factors could lead to juvenile justice involvement, there are varying pathways from that event. While early juvenile justice involvement may produce a pattern that leads to adult offending, some pathways to prosocial adult outcomes do include juvenile justice involvement in adolescence. Lee Robins (1978) identifies this paradox in looking at the relationship between adult and childhood antisocial behavior, reinforcing the need to be careful in assuming too much weight for early experiences in explaining later patterns of behavior (see Sampson and Laub 2005b). Early experiences are certainly likely to have distal impacts and are important to understand the youth's case, but delinquency likely has proximal causes as well. These immediate factors may be more sensible as primary explanatory mechanisms or leverage points for intervention.

Table 4.1 exemplifies multifinality and equifinality as well as continuity and discontinuity in certain delinquency patterns in development using a random sample of twenty youths selected from the Rural Substance Abuse and Violence Project. The researchers administered surveys to a panel of 3,976 Kentucky adolescents. They were initially surveyed when in the seventh grade in 2001, and follow-ups took place in successive years through

TABLE 4.1 RISK AND BEHAVIOR PATTERNS WITH MULTIFINALITY AND EQUIFINALITY USING RURAL SUBSTANCE ABUSE AND VIOLENCE PROJECT DATA

Youth ID	Wave one			Wave two		Wave three		Wave four	
	Impulsivity	Peer risk	Delinquency	Peer risk	Delinquency	Peer risk	Delinquency	Peer risk	Delinquency
1	X	X	X	X	X	X	X	X	
2	X	X		X		X		X	
3	X	X	X	X	X	X	X	X	
4		X		X		X		X	
5		X		X					
6				X		X		X	
7	X			X	X	X		X	
8				X		X		X	
9		X		X		X		X	
10	X	X	X	X	X	X	X	X	
11						X	X	X	
12		X	X	X	X	X	X	X	X
13		X	X	X	X	X	X	X	X
14	X	X	X	X	X	X		X	
15		X		X		X		X	
16						X		X	
17	X	X	X		X	X	X	X	
18		X				X		X	
19		X	X	X	X	X	X	X	
20	X	X	X	X	X	X	X	X	X

2004. The indicators shown in the table reflect simple dichotomous characterizations of risk (high impulsivity, which was determined only in the first wave, or any association with delinquent peers) and delinquent behavior (yes/no). An X in the table indicates that the youth showed that risk or behavior at that wave of the study; no X indicates that that risk factor or behavior was not present at that time.[8]

Even in this relatively small sample, in the initial condition at wave one the presence of impulsivity is associated with several different subsequent patterns. Some of these involve sustained delinquency (e.g., youths 1, 3, 10, 20), and others correspond to little or no subsequent delinquency (e.g., youths 2, 7). This is an example of multifinality that is based on an initial condition. At the same time, high impulsivity is not a necessary condition for sustained delinquency (e.g., youths 12, 13, 19), and neither is concurrent or lagged peer delinquency. Likewise, it seems that delinquent behavior tapers off for several youths in the table, but different risk and behavioral patterns precede those occurrences. Both trends illustrate equifinality whereby any one of multiple different initial (or earlier) conditions may lead to the same later pattern of behavior. This provides just a small window into the range of influences that may affect the onset, continuance, and curtailing of delinquent behavior. As mentioned in Chapter 1, a rather substantial literature has developed around risk and protective factors for antisocial behavior and delinquency.

Delinquency Risk in a Developmental, Life-Course Context

Understanding delinquency from a developmental and life-course perspective aids in linking longitudinal patterns to information about risk and protective factors for delinquency (Catalano and Hawkins 1996; Farrington 2005b). It is a useful starting point for narratives about how delinquency begins, continues, and stops. It also places juvenile justice involvement in the broader context of youths' lives, which is valuable in considering how the system might redirect developmental pathways—either positively or negatively.

Accumulation and Interaction of Risks

The configuration of risk factors that contribute to a delinquent event or a pattern of chronic behavior is likely to vary significantly across cases just as the circumstances and nature of those events will. Shaw's ([1930] 1966) classic portrait of a serious delinquent, for example, paints the picture of a youth with enduring dispositional factors with different origins who is emboldened by certain situational contributors to his behavior. These risk factors seemed to act in an interdependent way, highlighting their accumulation and the internal relationships among them. Three passages from his delinquency history illustrate that collection of risk factors and their interplay. First, Shaw describes the criminogenic properties of one of the neighborhoods where his subject, Stanley, lived:

> In the light of the disorganized community situation back of the yards, the persistence of a high rate of delinquency is not at all surprising. With the marked changes in the composition of the population, diffusion of divergent cultural standards, and the rapid disorganization of the alien culture, the continuity of community traditions and cultural institutions is broken. Thus the effectiveness of the community in the control and education of the child is greatly diminished. (Shaw [1930] 1966, 37)

He then describes Stanley's home life in a way that reveals the risks and challenges present within that layer of his development:

> The family situation in which Stanley lived during his early childhood presents a rather complicated picture of human relationships. The situation was one in which family disorganization, emotional tensions, and marked confusion of moral standards were outstanding features. The significance of these conditions is probably reflected in the ineffectiveness of the family in the discipline and control of its members. (Shaw [1930] 1966, 40)

This identifies the family as a clear factor in his development and later behavior. Still, at some points in telling his own story, Stanley identifies other influences, such as peers and the side effects that sometimes come with formal justice intervention. These influences also contain an acknowledgment of the lures of delinquency and procrime attitudes, which indicate individual factors most highly correlated with repeat offending. Stanley says:

> Like all criminals, I wanted to get ahead in crime. I was always planning new crimes and longing for another chance to show my stuff. My mind ran in a gutter, and that gutter was crime. I always had been that way. . . . Crimes held lures and adventures for me that nothing else did. There was nothing else open for me. I couldn't think about anything else for thoughts about crime always crowded out everything else. (Shaw [1930] 1966, 108)

Building on these initial forays to understand delinquency by individuals like Shaw and Healy, juvenile justice agencies are now immersed in formal assessment of risks and needs with systematic tools. Regardless of the method used, a good deal of consistency is identifiable in risk markers for delinquency as well as the skills and attitudes that may promote change. The list of relevant influences also suggests that delinquency is multiply determined and crosses numerous domains. With the foundation of developmental and life-course principles as background, risk and protective factors can be conceived of as different aspects of individual lives that spark, continue, or stop patterns of delinquency.

As in equifinality, no single pathway to delinquency exists. Thomas Dishion, Deborah Capaldi, and Karen Yoerger (1999) note the difficulty of disentangling the effects of different risk factors and highlight that these influences often come in a collection, or package. Other research points toward an interaction among risk factors that creates a multiplicative effect, increasing the likelihood of negative outcomes (Elder 1998; Shader 2001). As the mass of problems in a youth's life increases and covers more domains, so too does the likelihood of delinquency, as in Healy's multiple factor approach (Laub 2000). This evidence suggests that a simplistic view of risk and delinquent pathways in juvenile justice is likely to miss important leverage points in intervention.

Risk Factors in Delinquent Development

Data from the Project on Human Development in Chicago Neighborhoods (PHDCN) depict some general findings about risk factors (Earls and Visher 1997).[9] Figure 4.5 shows the unconditional patterns of delinquency for 25 youths randomly selected from 752 members of one cohort of the PHDCN. Measurement occurred at approximately twelve, fourteen, and sixteen years of age. As shown in the plot, there is variation in youths' initial self-reported delinquency scores. Less apparent is that 13 of 25 have an initial delinquency score of zero, suggesting that—with a few exceptions—the PHDCN youths have relatively low levels of offending around age twelve. Beyond that, eight of those thirteen cases also have zero offending scores at the two subsequent waves. Several different offending patterns emerge for the other youths in this display. These include upward trends toward age sixteen that portend continued offending and others that show gradual declines across the three observation points. The formal latent growth curve modeling on which this figure is based showed significant variation in the components for the intercept, which represents the initial delinquency score, but had mixed findings for the variance of the longitudinal trend (C. Sullivan 2014).[10]

As did the analysis of the Pathways data earlier, this example indicates that there is variation inherent in the onset and continuance of delinquency, and it is affected by certain risk factors or protected by others. Although patterns are generally similar with system-involved youths such as those in the Pathways sample, it is possible to look at factors that affect delinquency patterns of youths selected not on the basis of their justice involvement but

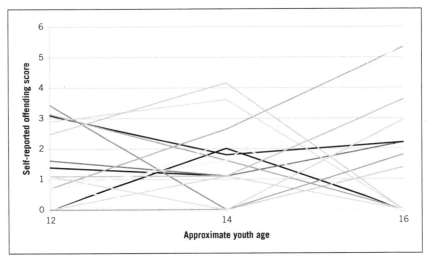

Figure 4.5 Self-reported offenses from Project on Human Development in Chicago Neighborhoods data ($n = 25$)

from a community-based sample (Huizinga et al. 2000). Figure 4.6 summarizes an analysis of the relationships between selected risk factor variables and the two components of delinquency patterns of PHDCN youths: initial levels (latent intercept) and trends (latent slope).[11]

Overall, self-control and exposure to delinquent peers had statistically significant and strong effects on the initial level of delinquency. A one-point increase in the delinquent peer measure was associated with a roughly three-point increase on the latent intercept for delinquency ($b = 3.34$) and self-control had a significant effect ($b = 0.23$), suggesting that a one-point increase in lack of self-control leads to a slight increase in the initial level of delinquency. Both parental warmth ($b = -0.08$) and social support ($b = -0.03$) had significant protective effects on the initial level of delinquency in the cohort analysis. There was also statistically significant variance in the initial level of delinquency among PHDCN neighborhoods, suggesting that initial risk of delinquent behavior is distributed unequally across communities. The positive effects for parenting and social support indicate that those with expected reductions in their initial levels of delinquency on the basis of the effects described previously tend to lose some of that protection over time. This is expected, because other behavioral influences take hold. However, the youths would still end up slightly better off on the strength of those initial influences.

This basic analysis of the relationship between risk or protective factors and delinquency follows several other points from the existing research in showing that risk factors for patterns of delinquency cut across multiple

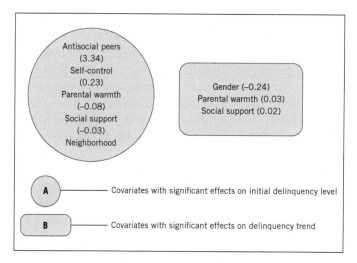

Figure 4.6 Risk and protective effects on delinquency patterns from Project on Human Development in Chicago Neighborhoods data (*n* = 752)

Note: Unstandardized estimates are in parentheses ($p < .05$). Predictors tested were gender, race, socioeconomic score, self-control score, parental lack hostility score, parental warmth score, parental monitoring score, total social support, antisocial peers, and neighborhood effect.

domains (individual, family, peers, and community). These relationships are complex, however, and early risk factors do not always steer expected patterns of delinquency and criminal behavior over time. This raises the question of how to explain variation in patterns in the relationship of risk and protective factors to longer-term trends in delinquency during adolescence and how to use that information to respond appropriately in the juvenile justice system.

Pairing this analysis with Table 4.1, showing risks and delinquency, offers a reminder that risk and protective factors and resultant behavioral patterns have several permutations that might lead to delinquency (Rutter 1989) or to resilience (Masten 2001). On their own, patterns of delinquency and risk factors do not offer a compelling narrative about how delinquency emerges, continues, and ceases. More than that, this narrative falls short in providing a sense of how those factors work in tandem to produce patterns and how to unwind those processes to forestall delinquency trajectories. A concerted effort to make juvenile justice more developmental requires understanding mechanisms to determine precisely how to intervene.

Delinquency and Developmental, Life-Course Criminology

Many of the core concepts of development and the life course discussed earlier are included in theory and research on crime and criminality. These perspectives emphasize the need for insight on the behavior of individuals and, from there, the need for awareness about within-individual change or stability and their respective causes (Loeber and Le Blanc 1990). Within this broad framework, multiple disciplines, emphasizing elements of behavior at a microlevel all the way to societal influences, can be informative (Phillips and Shonkoff 2000). Some have cautioned against becoming transfixed on systematic or orderly patterns of behavior and have instead highlighted the age-graded effects of life events and opportunity (Laub and Sampson 2003; Sampson and Laub 1993, 2005b).

The research and theory reviewed to this point suggest that risk and protective factors produce an infrastructure through which between-individual differences will play out over time, but later processes that might not be fully anticipated in evaluating youths at a single point in time (such as when they encounter the system) affect within-individual variation (Nagin and Paternoster 2000; Sampson and Laub 1995; Sullivan and Piquero 2011). This is a particularly good conceptual fit when trying to understand the variation observed in youths' pathways to and from the juvenile justice system. It is also a clue that reductive social or individual-centric explanations oversimplify the developmental process.

Several perspectives on delinquency and development draw on the principles described earlier to animate the factors that contribute to the onset and continuance of delinquent behavior (for extensive overviews, see Farrington 2005b; Thornberry 1997). The two most prominent perspectives are Moffitt's (1993) taxonomy of antisocial behavior and Robert J. Sampson and John H. Laub's (1993; Laub and Sampson 2003) age-graded social control perspective on criminal behavior. Other theories of delinquency can also contribute to a fuller understanding of adolescent delinquency onset, continuance, and desistance. Although differing somewhat in their main propositions, these theories have in common (1) integration across existing views of risk factors for delinquency like peer relationships, ties to prosocial others, and individual constitutional factors and (2) consideration of those risk factors in a dynamic developmental or life-course framework.

The Taxonomy of Antisocial Behavior. Moffitt's perspective on delinquency begins with the identification of possible groupings of offenders and then attempts to differentiate them on the basis of developmental patterns and the individual and social factors that generate such patterns. Moffitt's life-course-persistent (LCP) offenders are "few, persistent, and pathological" (Moffitt 2006, 277), which conforms with previous findings suggesting that a relatively small group of offenders was responsible for most offenses (e.g., Wolfgang, Figlio, and Sellin 1972). She attributes their behavior to a problematic convergence of neuropsychological deficits and disadvantageous environments, which are not fully deterministic but can set a youth on a challenging course early in life. It involves a series of transactions between youths disadvantaged by developmental risk factors and high-risk environments. In other words, a child may have traits that make her difficult to parent, and her parents will likewise tend to have limited resources and skills to appropriately manage that behavior. The by-product of that process is that the stream of opportunities to break free from this pattern of behavior is likely to have narrowed over time, and these issues may follow the youths across multiple developmental settings (Caspi, Bem, and Elder 1989). Adding to this trouble, LCP individuals often lack skills to take advantage of options even when they become available.

Moffitt's second taxonomic group has implications for juvenile justice policy and practice as well. Compared to the LCP group, adolescence-limited (AL) offenders are "common, relatively transient, and near normative" (Moffitt 2006, 277). The AL group will offend for a short period and for reasons that are not as threatening to their long-term prospects as LCP delinquents' reasons. AL youths' delinquent behavior is instrumental, situationally confined, and relatively short-lived. They may be mimicking their peers who are more entrenched in delinquency and who seem to them to be navigating this maturity gap well (Moffitt 1993). In the transitional period of adolescence some adultlike opportunities might present themselves (e.g., substance use, sex), but societal laws and norms preclude them from acting on them—for example, upper-level high school students getting together in the woods to drink and use recreational drugs. Offenses are unlikely to be as serious or diverse as those committed by LCP offenders, but they certainly can have serious repercussions if the situation leads AL adolescents to become involved with more harmful offenses (e.g., driving under the influence, illegal sexual contact).

Still, these youths are typically less likely to experience cumulative continuity, because they generally possess prosocial skills developed before adolescence. This gives them the flexibility to adjust their behavior to different contingencies of risk, reward, and the alternative sources of social control that often emerge toward the end of adolescence. They can more readily take advantage of opportunities to desist but may have continued difficulties if they encounter snares, including the development of substance dependencies and responses from the juvenile justice system and other formal agents like schools that may unwittingly foster continuance (e.g., Hussong et al. 2004; McGee et al. 2015).

Moffitt's theory was tested and modified using data from the Dunedin, New Zealand, Multidisciplinary Health and Development Study. The subjects were a birth cohort from a single hospital, studied in 1972–1973 when participants were about three years old. The 1,037 children, with roughly equal gender split, cover the socioeconomic-status spectrum of New Zealand. The researchers carried out eleven comprehensive assessments beginning at age three and up until age thirty-eight. The key measures included neuropsychological tests, personality inventories, employment and relationship status and problems, self-reported offending, use of court records, genetics, and biomedical data. The group also obtained reports from collaterals, like partners, friends, and family members.

The research on Moffitt's theory provided support in some ways and less in others. Terrie E. Moffitt, Donald R. Lynam, and Phil A. Silva (1994) found evidence consistent with the theory for neuropsychological scores at age thirteen and later offending (ages thirteen, fifteen, eighteen) (see also Piquero 2001). The same relationship did not hold with AL offenders. This is a core proposition about the mechanisms generating the groups and therefore requires consideration in identifying whether anticipated explanations have empirical support. Nagin and colleagues (1995) studied the properties of groups identified in previous trajectory modeling. They looked at three groups of offenders: low-level chronics, high-level chronics (roughly equivalent to Moffitt's LCP), and ALs. They found differences between AL and LCP groups but also a good deal of self-reported antisocial behavior in the AL group. A later study by Moffitt and colleagues (2002), using the same New Zealand cohort data, shows that the LCP group was clearly worse off across several outcome measures at age twenty-six (e.g., self-reported offending, mental health functioning). They were distinct from AL offenders, but the AL group still seemed to be poorly off relative to the expectations of the theory.

Moffitt (2006) acknowledges findings that challenge the theory or suggest that revisions are needed and mentions several areas that require further study. Torbjørn Skardhamar (2009) criticizes Moffitt's taxonomy on substantive and empirical grounds. He raises three main issues: (1) Should types be viewed literally? (2) Can the proposed mechanisms produce these types? (3) Is there empirical support for the taxonomy? These questions are worth considering because they influence whether the theory can be an effective vehicle to understanding and responding to delinquency. From a juvenile justice perspective, group-based theories can help simplify the understanding of recurring patterns, but the developmental variability described to this point suggests this must be done without overgeneralizing, stereotyping, or assuming that they represent real, immutable types (see Nagin and Tremblay 2005; Sampson and Laub 2005c).

One key distinction is that there is a different initial condition for the AL delinquent youths than for an LCP offender. A second is that the probability that a given youth will desist from offending differs between these groups. LCP offenders may transition to other antisocial behaviors as they grow up but will still be relatively more delinquent than others in their age cohort. Their prosocial opportunities have narrowed, and they also may lack the skills to take advantage of those opportunities. Additionally, the processes underlying their behavior are likely to differ from youths who have not been involved in antisocial behavior for very long. While the identification of groups by the system is at the center of Moffitt's perspective, the taxonomy is valuable because of the narratives it might produce about how different youths reach the system, the disposition of their cases, and how they proceed from that point.

Other Group-Based Perspectives. Moffitt's taxonomy of antisocial behavior is the most prominent group-based theory on delinquency and criminal behavior, but others can identify processes at work in patterns of continuity and change in delinquent behavior. Although their theory is not as explicitly group based, Benjamin Lahey, Irwin D. Waldman, and Keith McBurnett (1999) argue for distinctions between delinquents based on age of onset. In their integrative causal model, antisocial behavior results from transactions between the developing youth and his or her social environment, which generates an antisocial propensity. Their perspective is based heavily on between-youth differences, and they identified multiple individual traits (and skills) believed to play a causal role in antisocial propensity (e.g., oppositional temperament, cognitive skills). These individual factors are likely influenced by genetics and early experiences with the social environment. They distinguish aggressive from nonaggressive problem behavior and assert that each has different origins and patterns, which parallel the nature and etiology of the groups that Moffitt proposed. At the same time, they view delinquency's causes as similar for both groups but varying in salience with the age of onset. Group differences are identifiable by the seriousness of offenses and their linkage to age. These different typological perspectives predominately reflect between-individual differences that play out across time and developmental stages. While Lahey, Waldman, and McBurnett acknowledge interaction between the individual and social environment, they lean toward the notion of closed systems, in which within-individual change is limited once a behavioral pattern emerges, rather than open ones.

Age-Graded Social Control Theory. Life-course perspectives tend toward a continuous open system for large portions of individual lives. Sampson and Laub (1993; Laub and Sampson 2003) incorporate age into their propositions about crime and the life course but also argue very explicitly that their perspective on criminal behavior proceeds from a life-course vantage point in which change is prevalent. Further, they argue that general mechanisms underlie onset, continuance, and desistance from delinquent and criminal behavior (Sampson and Laub 2005b). This stands in contrast to group-based perspectives in which the mechanisms producing patterns of behavior vary in categorical ways. Their theory draws on several concepts discussed to this point, such as multifinality, state dependence, trajectories and turning points, and elements of the life-course perspective and dynamic contextualism. Their propositions also draw from existing criminological perspectives, especially Travis Hirschi's (1969) social control theory.

Making use of some of the core concepts described here, Sampson and Laub argue that, while it matters, early risk is not determinative and that stability in offending behavior is "far from perfect" (Laub and Sampson 1993, 309). This leads them to reject development as something that unfolds cleanly over time in favor of something that is socially reinvented over time based on individuals' experiences (see Sampson and Laub 2005b). This reflects the idea of state dependence. Laub and Sampson argue that early offending weakens social bonds that then affects later behavior. Similarly, restoration of those bonds can foster desistance (Laub and Sampson 2001, 2003). This explicitly incorporates life-course themes that "link social history and social structure to unfolding of human lives" (Laub and Sampson 2003, 33). The theory has moved through two iterations over time, and the later version elaborates the first's propositions and draws on concepts, like agency, omitted initially.[12] Stability and change owe to the ebb and flow and variation in informal social controls experienced over time. Specifically, weakened informal social controls get youths into delinquency, but social controls can also foster turning points and lead the way out of a criminal career.

Their later work explicitly articulates a place for situated choice in offending (cf. Modell 1994), acknowledging that perception of turning points may depend on subjective factors, and consequently, those must play a role in changing offending over time. Change in routine activities is a mechanism that might change offending (see Warr 1998). With that, some change results from "purposeful action," but unanticipated opportunities for going straight can emerge in subtle ways. These "side bets" accrue over time so that the individual ends up with a stake in conformity that builds a boundary around his or her future choices (Laub and Sampson 2003, 282).

This theory largely builds on Sampson and Laub's work in piecing together quantitative and qualitative data originally collected by Eleanor and Sheldon Glueck (1950, 1968) (see Laub and Sampson 1998). The data are from a longitudinal study of five hundred delinquent and five hundred nondelinquent boys matched on age, IQ, ethnicity, and neighborhood deprivation. The study blends data sources such as official records, observations, personal interviews (with follow-ups at ages twenty-five and thirty-two), and self-, parent-, and teacher reports. Laub and Sampson (2003) expanded the follow-up data using the Gluecks' original interviews and later conducted life-history interviews with fifty-two of the men in the sample (to age seventy in some cases).

They and others have found support for different propositions of their theory. John H. Laub, Robert J. Sampson, and Gary A. Sweeten (2006) argue that prior studies of social control theory provide support for Laub and Sampson's basic assertions about onset and persistence of offending. Sonja E. Siennick and D. Wayne Osgood (2008) found that social control variables at the heart of the age-graded theory's propositions about desistance generally have some support. Some critiques of this theory have argued that it is too heavily focused on change and does not fully account for between-individual differences that may lead individuals to take certain pathways and turning points. Laub and Sampson (1993) explicitly note that they found effects of marital attachment and job stability—after accounting for persistent heterogeneity between individuals. Similarly, Robert J. Sampson, John H. Laub, and Christopher Wimer (2006) found that within-individual change had a significant impact on offending and that a quality marriage had an even greater effect on offending after they controlled for baseline differences between individuals. The social bond of a quality marriage, rather than the mere existence of the relationship, is presumably what gives it effect.

Sampson and Laub's propositions about delinquency and development offer two points for consideration from the standpoint of juvenile justice response. First, they are adamant that change is a modal pattern in behavior over time, which is generally supported in studies of long-term trajectories of offending across developmental stages (see C. Sullivan 2013). Second, they assert that, while individual differences matter, certain elements of the social environment can promote continuity or change in patterns of delinquency. Though easier to operationalize in theory than in practice, this invites the justice system to promote positive social influences to override the behavioral pattern that caused the youth to reach the system in the first place. Later elements of Sampson and Laub's age-graded social control theory delve more into the situated choice of offending over the life course (see Laub and Sampson 2003), and this is at the heart of what the juvenile justice system is trying to understand and respond to, especially in promoting youths' agency to change pathways and replace problem habits—whatever their origins—with prosocial ones.

Interactional Theory of Delinquency. Terence P. Thornberry (1987) was one of the first criminologists to call for and propose a dynamic explanation for delinquency and crime. This perspective views delinquency as both an independent and dependent variable on the basis of its role at different parts of a causal chain. The relationships in the theory are reciprocal such that certain factors affect one another as a series of "causal loops" (874). Specifically, a belief in conventional values affects school commitment, but a youth's commitment and engagement with school may also weaken or strengthen her prosocial beliefs. The theory also has a role for structural influences like race and class in setting the initial conditions of this interactional model.

Like age-graded social control theory, the theory asserts that social bonds are malleable over time and are weakened or strengthened by the youth's interaction with his environment. Thornberry argues that weakened social controls indirectly lead to delinquency because there must also be an interactive setting for learning that behavior, carrying it out, and reinforcing it. Thornberry (1987) establishes support for interactional and reciprocal relationships in social influences in criminal behavior. Specifically, he identifies an over-time, reciprocal relationship between contact with delinquent peers, marijuana use, and religious commitment. The theory finds support in later work that more explicitly incorporated propositions from developmental and life-course theories, such as weakened bonds to prosocial others, strengthened ties to delinquent peers, and a persistent pattern of delinquency among early starters (Thornberry and Krohn 2005).

Social Development Model. Richard F. Catalano and J. David Hawkins (1996) describe a general theory of behavioral development that is holistic and covers a multidomain approach to explaining behavior—whether prosocial or antisocial. They draw on aspects of individual constitutional factors, the immediate environment (parents, peers), and the broader social structure. Using those different domains of influence, they integrate control, social learning, and differential association theories of crime. Like Bronfenbrenner's (1979), their perspective anchors individuals to a progression through social institutions, like junior high and high schools, across multiple developmental stages through transactional processes. This is double edged because these stage transitions offer opportunities for change, but the experiences and propensities from the previous phase can just as easily serve as a precursor for continued problems at the next.

The social development model's proposed theoretical mechanisms center on social processes that affect youth development and the social ties and opportunities that are in turn affected by the individual's behavior and choice. The perceived opportunity for participation in certain activities (be they pro- or antisocial) and interpersonal interactions lies at the center of the theory. Outcomes reflect the degree to which youths pursue these opportunities, their skills or abilities for taking advantage of them, and subsequent reinforcement. This process leads to the forging of a social bond—which can be pro- or antisocial—that helps sustain or change an existing behavioral pathway.

The Social Development Research Group, which has developed and evaluated the Seattle Social Development Model and Communities That Care delinquency prevention programs, has performed much of the evaluation of this theory. For example, Richard F. Catalano and colleagues (2005) found support for the distal effects of social structural and individual constitutional factors in the theory, but there were some unexpected findings as well.

Christopher J. Sullivan and Paul Hirschfield (2011) also found general support for the social development model in a sample of youths from Chicago Public Schools, but the youth skills domain seemed to behave slightly differently than suggested in the original model (there were direct effects on behavior). The model's core propositions generally hold in relevant studies, but the exact mechanisms have mixed support. The value of social relationships and skills articulated in the theory is evident in the applied aspect of the work of the Social Development Research Group (see, e.g., Hawkins et al. 1999, 2005). For juvenile justice, that suggests that shifting delinquent youth pathways will involve promoting skills necessary for prosocial interaction and ensuring opportunities and reinforcement for their expression.

Situated Action Theory. Per-Olof H. Wikström developed a theory that blends elements of the individual, his or her development, and the situations encountered in explaining delinquent and criminal behavior, which it views from the standpoint of morally suspect actions. Wikström argues that "individuals' knowledge and skills . . . are always applied to the particularities in the setting in which they take part. It is the interaction between an individual and his environment that determines his course of actions (inactions)" (2006, 87). This represents an intersection between who a youth is and where she is in terms of activity space, which may include community or social interactions. It clearly distinguishes propensity for behavior from actual acts (Wikström 2005). He argues that change or stability in behavior is due to an individual's change or stability in exposure to different social settings in which an individual develops and engages with the environment.

Using data from the Peterborough (United Kingdom) Youth Study, Per-Olof H. Wikström and David A. Butterworth (2006) found that individual variation in lifestyle factors—especially time spent with peers—was a strong predictor of offending levels. Other research from this group has offered support for the basic premises of the theory: there is variation in youths' exposure to criminogenic situations, and the degree to which they engage in delinquency is determined by that exposure, as well as their individual propensity. This follows other integrated perspectives and broader principles on how individuals develop and interact with their environments to produce delinquent behavior. Questions remain on how to inculcate and leverage moral action and self-control characteristics in at-risk and delinquent youths.

Expanding Insight for Developmental Juvenile Justice

The system of relationships identified by these developmental and life-course theories are, of course, stylized in certain ways. None can fully cover the multiple, complex causal processes driving delinquency. But in operational-izing key mechanisms that affect developmental pathways and turning points, they offer possible narratives of delinquency and ideas about inter-vention. In linking risk and protective factors in a formal way, these theories move beyond categorizing and counting risk factors (and strengths), which occurs regularly in juvenile justice assessments, to developing an under-standing of how the pieces fit together and what they mean for a youth's future development and delinquent behavior. Understanding the etiology of delinquency at that level is a necessary precursor to appropriate response by the juvenile justice system.

Several lessons emerge from these propositions about how risk turns into delinquent behavior. While researchers tend to focus more on the identifica-tion of patterns and possible explanations, unsurprisingly practitioners are typically more interested to know how this informs the justice system's day-to-day activities and broader mission (see e.g., Green 2006; Lueger 2002). There is now a greater focus on evidence-based practice in juvenile justice, so taking a step forward requires identifying where developmental insights can inform initiatives already underway in the system and where insights from practice suggest further research. Finally, the general question of im-pact in a developmental sense is crucial in thinking about the court's mission and assessing success. Part II considers how developmental and life-course insights can be thoughtfully practiced in the juvenile justice system.

PART II

Developmentally Informed
Juvenile Justice

5

Developmentally Suitable Treatment and Sanctions

Much of the discussion about the integration of developmental insight with the juvenile justice system focuses on the broad distinctions and necessary decisions in processing youths. But the day-to-day workings of the system are likely to be more determinative in successful reform. Given the full spectrum of delinquency cases, it is impossible to fully discuss changes without considering how youth and adolescent development informs juvenile justice treatment and sanctions for various types of cases given its existing capacity and operations.

This chapter begins by reiterating general lessons about juvenile justice intervention covered in previous chapters. The second section examines the system's assessment function and analyzes information from the previous chapters in terms of what it suggests about identifying youth risk and needs. The third section focuses on treatment within the juvenile justice system to synthesize what works (and does not) and for whom. Examples of effective and ineffective programs and references to systematic review studies (e.g., Curtis, Ronan, and Borduin 2004; Lipsey 1999; Lipsey et al. 2010) identify potential best practices in the system, linking them to developmental insights.

The second half of the chapter focuses on sanctions. Appropriate sanctions are in the mission of the juvenile justice system, but they receive less attention than treatment in research and discussion of best practices. The attention that they do receive is often negative. A renewed emphasis on developmental principles and research findings informs balanced juvenile justice policy and practice and provides support for discussing the role of well-thought-out sanctions for delinquent youths. I introduce key points along those lines to argue that the developmental research and principles discussed earlier have implications for assigning sanctions before I review common approaches like probation and correctional custody as well as newer approaches like systematic, graduated sanctions. The chapter concludes by bringing together the system's sanction and treatment objectives in an integrated way using developmental principles.

Effective Treatment and Developmental Juvenile Justice

Although seemingly obvious, the precise objectives of juvenile justice treatment can be somewhat difficult to pin down in a specific way. Often, they reduce to simply trying to get youths to change their behavior. The variation in the juvenile justice population and the diversity of possible responses make it challenging to identify unified objectives for addressing delinquency. Still, the parameters of delinquency careers and explanations for them can help guide a discussion of potential responses to delinquency. The juvenile justice system must respond to a range of individual case and youth characteristics from petty to extreme. Treatment must reflect the mechanisms underlying each youth's behavior.

Developmentally, the juvenile justice system attempts to address the outcome of three factors: (1) individual youth propensities, (2) environmental contingencies and social influences, and (3) the interaction between youths and the settings and institutions that they encounter. It is essential to understand the skills and deficits that youths face in development, the resources and deficits in the environments that surround them, and how youths navigate those influences. Taken together this means that the treatment process must address deficits and build skills, promote positive social support and influences when possible, and help equip youths to deal with the challenges in their environment when that is resistant to change. There may be multiple routes to successful treatment depending on the circumstances, but they all build on these core objectives, which have strong connections to the developmental processes discussed in Chapters 3 and 4.

While it is essential to take stock of what we know about delinquency, its etiology, and its consequences in thinking about treatment strategy for individual cases and different subsets of youths, it is equally necessary to consider what developmental research suggests about the limits of treatment. This injects an understanding of the challenges inherent in responses to delinquency and the anticipated outcomes from those efforts. The work of Terrie E. Moffitt (1993) and Robert J. Sampson and John H. Laub (1993) points to cumulative consequences that drive continued delinquent behavior and, later, crime. While this does not obviate efforts to treat even serious delinquency (Lipsey 1999), it does suggest that certain youths will require more intensive treatment and sanctions from the juvenile court and that some youths will continue to engage in delinquency despite those efforts. Assessment is an important starting point for effective treatment.

If a youth perceives benefits from delinquent behavior, this may limit the effect of juvenile justice treatment. Choosing delinquency is not necessarily an irrational choice from the standpoint of the social environment in which youths predominantly interact (Furby and Beyth-Marom 1992). The adaptive nature of delinquent behavior in adolescence is among the primary takeaways from the developmental literature. This is true both of youths who develop in challenging environments where assertions of strength or the by-products of delinquency help build reputation or status (see Anderson 1999; M. Sullivan 1989) and of youths who engage in risky behavior because of social imperatives or perceptions (Moffitt 1993; Singer 2014). The system and its personnel must start from that notion of youths' motivation to create a foundation for responding to delinquency in a developmentally informed way. Interventions in juvenile justice must provide plausible alternatives to gaps left by removing the benefits of delinquency and help youths build skills to take advantage of prosocial opportunities.

Developmental Insights and Juvenile Justice Assessment

Formal assessment of youth risk and needs has become far more common since the 1990s, and many agencies now use risk and needs assessments to identify factors for promoting change (Douglas and Skeem 2005; Schwalbe 2007). Although dynamic influences and potential change in behavior are part of a developmental perspective, such assessment processes do not necessarily give all the information needed to construct a developmentally informed treatment plan. The youth assessments frequently have a static perspective—although the field recognizes the dynamic nature of risk and needs—regarding the pathway to juvenile justice contact and the subsequent interactions with environment that produce later outcomes.

Developmental risk and needs assessment must include a desire to know more about the youth, his or her social environment (both current and earlier in development), and the interaction with the different contexts to which the youth is exposed. This overlaps but also exceeds current approaches to youth assessment. The practical implications of developmental insights start with risk and needs assessment, which should look backward at influences that shaped the youth's trajectory of interaction with environment and behavior to that point. The developmental approach requires a shift in thinking about risk factors, putting them together to understand mechanisms that drive behavior, understanding how criminogenic needs contribute to later developmental pathways, and identifying the barriers to desistance from delinquent behavior. The expanded developmental framework for considering risk also requires holistic assessment of the youth and his age-graded interactions with the social environment as a means of looking forward in time without fixating solely on risk (Ward, Melser, and Yates 2007).

Extraction of a set of risks and needs common to all youths supports a systematic response to the youths who come before the juvenile court, but Andre M. Van Der Laan, Martine Blom, and Edward R. Kleemans (2009) found that delinquent behavior is the product of both long-term, cumulative risk factors and short-term situational influences. This implies that risk crosses multiple dimensions and that a single domain, such as the family, could play a long-term role through socialization or parental attachment or a short-term role through exposure to opportunity that may come from an absence of guardianship. While these different family influences are certainly related, distinguishing among them can better direct the course of treatment for the youth. For example, is the familial risk an enduring matter of family management or parent-youth bonding or a by-product of the parent's need to secure the family financially? Understanding patterns of delinquent behavior from a career point of view draws on the timing, nature, and repetition of the delinquent act. After integrating a career point of view with assessment, developing a sense of the proximal and distal causes of delinquency is possible. If delinquency is chronic, search for the origin possibly should focus more on the youth; if a first-time offense—particularly later in adolescence—it may be more a product of a social or situational influence. In other words, the nature of the case and the youth's history can inform a narrative about what drove the behavior that landed him or her in the juvenile court. The treatment response should reflect that knowledge in a systematic and comprehensive way.

Current Risk Assessment in Developmental Context. A good assessment strategy is a necessary precursor to effective treatment in the justice system (Bonta 2002). Juvenile risk and needs assessment has a dichotomous, additive sense of risk, however. This is evident in reviewing two validated comprehensive risk and needs assessments frequently used for justice-involved youths.[1] The first, the Positive Achievement Change Tool (Baglivio 2009; Winokur-Early, Hand, and Blankenship 2012), is used by Florida's juvenile justice system.[2] The tool has both criminal and social history sections that contribute to the overall-risk score. Within those, the interview guide suggests that assessment administrators should be asking questions or using probes such as the following:

- In what kinds of circumstances are you most likely to use violence?
- What are some early signs that you are beginning to have a problem with some person, place, or thing?

- When you experience strong emotions like anger, fear, or depression, what kinds of things do you do to manage and work through those feelings?

These questions have some developmental elements because they ask about skills, situations, thoughts, and actions that may indicate patterns. They also ask about enduring risk factors like anger along with more proximal, situational influences. Such questions, and related later questions, do not seek the frequency of exposure to situational influences, whether the youth has experienced them continuously or only recently, or whether they might interact with their juvenile justice history in a way that increases the risk of behavior continuity. Each of these is an element of interest to developmental narratives for youth delinquency.

The Ohio Youth Assessment System interview guide contains some similar elements. A subpart focused on prosocial skills starts with a hypothetical scenario:

- If one of your friends asked you to go to a party, what would you do?
- What if you knew there would be alcohol and drugs there?
- What things lead you to get into trouble?
- Tell me of a time where you did not realize that you were headed for trouble but looking back on it should have seen it. (Latessa, Lovins, and Ostrowski 2009)

This information—especially when coupled with other self-report data and collateral reports from family or others—is useful in understanding risk and protective factors. It is situational in the sense that it is either asking about a given event or probing for those types of scenarios. This breaks down to three items on the assessment tool: "can identify triggers/high risk situations," "weighs pros/cons of a situation," and "demonstrates pro-social decision-making" (Latessa, Lovins, and Ostrowski 2009). As in the Positive Achievement Change Tool, formal assessment of repetitiveness or variation in response to situations is missing. Similarly, it is possible that information embedded in answers to those questions—or related to them—may be beneficial from a developmental standpoint. For instance, how often they miss signs of trouble is not evident here nor are the contingencies, like peer presence or efficacy in school, that may facilitate or mask that potential trouble.

From Assessment to Developmental Assessment. The developmental evidence suggests that the characteristics of the offender and situation vary between adults and youths, between youths, and even in one youth over time. This is a key foundational point in thinking about youth risk and needs assessment from a developmental perspective. Developmentally informed treatment requires enhancements to how those in the field gather and use information in intervention decisions. Greater use of developmental and life-course theory is necessary to both improve the usefulness of information and better align current system practice with developmental aims.

Apart from age of onset, these tools generally do not consider age or developmental status as factors in the assessment or as considerations of outcomes besides recidivism. These assessment details and relevant clinical notes create a narrative around the youth's behavioral pattern, its major influences, and its actual and potential consequences. This establishes an integrated, multifaceted picture of risk and needs from which to develop patterns and mechanisms underlying behavior as opposed to just a series of scores, which can be useful but are not all that well animated in developmental mechanisms.

Michael D. Maltz and Jacqueline M. Mullany (2000) developed a visual map of a portion of the life course that can be adapted to understanding risk, needs, and life-event information for justice-involved youths. In fact, their original graphs were based on life-course patterns for probationers as they moved through different ages, contact with key institutions and relationships, major life events, and proximal, situational risks for delinquency like drug use. Figure 5.1 presents a case history charted by age, but its time structure could be adapted and the overlaid information that is used to understand a given case could be changed. This type of plot can integrate different informational domains, drawing from formal assessment and case notes, to get an initial sense of risks, needs, and strengths and their pattern across time and the youth's juvenile justice contact. The chronological aspect also allows an integration of timing and patterns alongside common risk and needs information.

Risk and needs assessment tools must balance information yield against the time necessary to collect it and ability to process it. A set of more extensive measurement tools could tap into developmentally salient strengths, skills, and deficits for treatment plans to more effectively promote positive development goals. The distilled version of the process may leave out some desirable developmental data that could be useful in comprehensively understanding a youth's life. For instance, in the Positive Achievement Change Tool, when a youth loses his or her temper or what things lead a youth to get into trouble could be heavily situationally dependent or consistent across different settings. From the perspective of a developmental framework like Moffitt's, specifying that process is necessary in making attributions about the youth's behavior and its implications.

Information on long-term behavioral patterns and life-course events can and should be linked with the insight from the formal assessment process (Doyle and Dolan 2002; Shlonsky and Wagner 2005). Several dimensions of

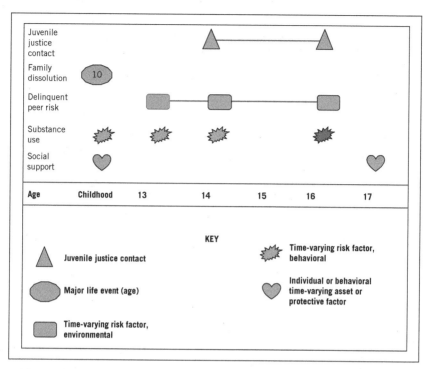

Figure 5.1 Example juvenile case visualization with key developmental events, influences
Source: Adapted from Maltz and Mullany 2000.

youth risks and needs are correlated with developmental risks or strengths that could be targets of treatment. A developmental assessment approach would also attempt to get an understanding of how youths respond to recurring situations to identify how individual factors interact with the environment to lead to delinquency. This is consistent with the contingent and situational nature of development, which aggregates to the long-term behavioral patterns that may be more apparent to researchers and practitioners (Horney 2001). Considering the immediate delinquency situation that brought the youth to the juvenile court as well as how the youth may have arrived at it is also possible.

Knowledge of the distinction between categorical attributions and individual assessments is required in analyzing the link between assessment information and case decisions; the age and developmentally graded nature of relationships among risk, protection, and behavior; the multicausal and complex nature of mechanisms that affect behavior in assessment and prediction; clearer integration of strengths and leverage points in assessment; and the role of clinical information and narrative in facilitating the best treatment response to youth risk and needs, as well as sanctions that fit the nature of their offense.

Age, Development, and Assessment. Acknowledgment of the relationship between age and delinquency should help in directing youth treatment plans. Responsivity factors are those that are not formal risk or protective factors but that moderate the effectiveness of treatment (Vieira, Skilling, and Peterson-Badali 2009). Contemporary understanding of development—and its conditioning effect on relevant qualities like cognitive ability in adolescence—certainly suggests that this be evaluated in thinking about effective treatment. Stage and age are necessary responsivity factors in understanding treatment in the juvenile justice system because the court is processing and overseeing youths who are aging and encountering developmental milestones that span from late childhood to early adulthood.

The juvenile justice system responds to youths at distinct places on the cognitive development scale across its typical age of jurisdiction. Thus, age and development, reflecting youths' skills at a point in time, should be important aspects of youth assessment for treatment. For instance, the timing of emergence of certain risk factors—like deviant peer associations—may indicate whether they are likely to be a developmental (Snyder et al. 2005) or situational influence on delinquent behavior (Osgood et al. 1996) and therefore how the system might treat that influence in responding to youths and their environments. Similarly, sanctions are likely to vary in effectiveness depending on how a youth is disposed to modify her behavior (or not) in response.

Going a step further, a developmental approach to the screening and assessment of justice-involved youths, not surprisingly, necessitates a strong focus on change and stability in risks and needs. Assessing immediate and potential distal risk factors driving those patterns requires (1) an understanding of the developmental progression of risk and needs and (2) routine reassessment to consider how the risk and needs profile has evolved over time. In responding to and treating youths, that information requires regular updating with respect to growth or worsening of circumstances and influences. Tracking changes in risks and needs is also a good first step in understanding the potential effect of the juvenile court on developmental outcomes. This has several implications, but the first is that assessments of a youth conducted at each stage of the juvenile justice process as well as from one contact with the court to the next should be pieced together. So, for instance, in one moderate-sized court in Ohio, a youth who was thirteen and a half years old when he reached the juvenile justice system had the pattern of contacts and scores shown in Figure 5.2.[3]

While repeated contact with the juvenile justice system may be a sign that some risks or needs have deteriorated or at least not changed, it is possible that a youth has made progress in some and backslid in others. This pattern of change or stability—beyond a static or stage-to-stage view of behavior—may be informative for understanding intervention processes and outcomes. If the assessment process is valid, domain scores may pinpoint what is driv-

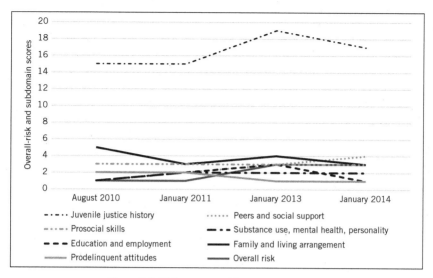

Figure 5.2 Risk score trend for an example youth

ing change over time or identify recalcitrant areas of need. One pertinent question raised by Figure 5.2 is what precipitated the increased overall-risk score in 2013, which included a move in designation from moderate to high, and then what drove it back down in the 2014 assessment. The subdomain score for family risk shows some fluctuation, as does that for peers and social network risk. Declines in risk from prodelinquent attitudes and education show some progress in the latter assessment. Still, the youth has continued to be involved in the juvenile court and therefore has some elevated risk as a result. A dynamic view of the process might identify factors that are obstacles to a youth changing course and those that might facilitate it.

The juvenile justice system must respond to youths during years that are known for their volatility and change. Assessment systems must consider this in understanding the degree of risk and need for a particular youth. This recognizes the fundamental premise that "timing in lives" matters (Elder 1998, 3) and that precocious contact with certain risks or events may have meaning different from contact occurring at more developmentally normative points. Characterizing different risk factors as ephemeral or situational versus enduring is a key element of developmental intervention. As alluded to earlier, a family problem could be due to enduring management problems that severely affect youth development or to a more situational influence related to a severe fight between siblings or parent and child. Likewise, a problem in school could be socially driven or could follow an interaction with a disliked peer as opposed to a recurring set of school disciplinary problems. The chronic-acute distinction should factor into the prioritization of that domain in treatment and the accompanying intervention strategy. The question of cross-situational consistency also comes into play here because the primary focus of treatment must reflect the relative balance of what youths import into situations and how they respond to them.

The notion of responsivity suggests that treatment modalities should be age graded so that the strategy employed corresponds to how that risk factor or need manifests at that developmental point. The juvenile justice system cannot wait to intervene if intervention is necessary, but transition points may present fruitful opportunities for intervention and should shape how the system responds. This requires elements of both short- and long-term thinking when delivering treatment. Clearly, the objective in these cases is to get the youth to change course as soon as possible to prevent further involvement with the system and reroute the developmental trajectory. It is also possible that change will come slowly with further delinquency in the interim. This is the zigzag pattern of offending identified by Laub and Sampson (2003, 196), which can play out also when considering treatment processes (for a discussion of substance use treatment relapse, see, e.g., Catalano et al. 1991).

Assessment of dynamic risks and needs focuses on factors that can change through treatment (Vincent, Guy, and Grisso 2012). Assessments must account for shifting life circumstances of youths over time and foster resilience to override intractable social risk factors. Struggles in treatment and related behavior problems can generate further involvement with or penetration into the juvenile justice system if left without a developmentally appropriate response. A developmental approach to monitoring and response to justice-involved youths is essential because the path to desistance is unlikely to be linear. As the path swerves, a developmental juvenile justice system must make repeated measurement and assessment of youths, whether those be skill or behavior based.

Additive versus Disaggregated and Integrated Assessment. The multicausal nature of delinquency and the presence of individual and social risk factors are well known and have long been part of understanding delinquent behavior. Developmental and life-course insights contribute to an understanding of key interactions and mediation relationships that require separation before effective treatment. Risk and needs across multiple domains inevitably require capturing how the risks—and potentially offsetting strengths—interact to affect youth behavior and involve youths in the juvenile justice system and how the system can best respond. As Helena Chmura Kraemer and colleagues point out, "Accumulating risk factors and either counting or scoring them does little to increase the understanding of etiologic processes or of how interventions might be optimally timed, constructed, or delivered to prevent or treat psychiatric conditions" (2001, 848).

Figure 5.3 shows three randomly selected cases from a youth residential facility that all have the same aggregate assessment score, which fell right around the average of 19 from that sample of youths in residential facilities.[4]

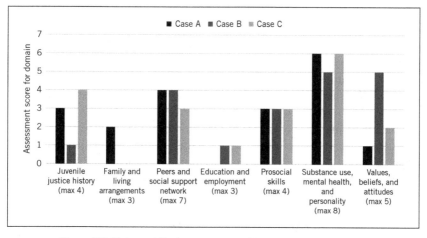

Figure 5.3 Risks contributing to a comparable overall risk assessment score of three case examples

The cases depicted show both similarities and differences in each score, which may suggest different etiology and courses of treatment. Case A appears to be in line with Cases B and C in terms of risk on three of the domains ("peers and social support," "prosocial skills deficits," and "substance use, mental health, and personality"), but it is distinctly lower in "values, beliefs, and attitudes" and much higher on "family and living arrangements." This package of risks implies that the youth's delinquency may come from multiple social mechanisms and the youth has fewer internalized values and beliefs that underlie recurring antisocial thinking. Case C has some commonalities with Cases A and B, but the "juvenile justice history" score is greater than that for the others and the "values, beliefs, and attitudes" domain is not as high a risk as it is for Case B. The youth in Case C seems to have an extensive juvenile justice history and several other risks but has not internalized those thinking patterns conducive to continued delinquency.

Risk factors are not additive in the sense that the scores of two different risk factors are summed. If those two risk factors both occur within the family and there are other social supports, those risks may be mitigated such that they are not so determinative in a youth's behavior. On the other hand, a family management risk indicator coupled with a youth's difficult temperament may have an interactive relationship that substantially affects the youth's behavior and its likelihood of continuance (Lahey, Waldman, and McBurnett 1999; Moffitt 1993). Thus, moving beyond a mere score or risk grouping may further illuminate the nature of risk and needs of justice-involved youths.

The salience, or weight, of risk factors is discrete in that a point system cannot capture which deficits may prove limiting in a youth's redirection to a more prosocial pathway or what single strength may be valuable in helping the youth move forward. The neuropsychological, executive functioning deficits central to Moffitt's (1993) assertions about life-course-persistent offenders, for instance, will affect skills like self-control and anger management and therefore a youth's situational and developmental interaction across multiple domains. Furthermore, early-appearing risk may create a sustained, solidified pattern of negative interaction and a string of accumulated consequences. At the same time, it is possible that a youth otherwise assessed as being high risk might benefit from one high-leverage social support or skill that can be an offset, as seems to occur in some cases studied by Laub and Sampson (2003). Such observations can fill in a developmental narrative around actuarial assessment systems and subsequently identify treatment priorities. The nature of the case before the court may necessitate different levels and types of information. A general screening tool is helpful at first, but more intensive data gathering is necessary to inform specific intervention.

Assessment, Categorization, and Individual Case Decisions. Some type of classification is endemic to decision making in any system, but it is important to consider how it affects individual case decisions. William S. Robinson (1950) initially cautioned against making inferences about individuals from aggregated data. That caution has relevance for relying too heavily on summarized patterns of behavior or risk scores to make decisions about individual youths as well. The multicausal and contingent view of behavior helps produce observed variation in origin points and outcomes of youths' lives. This variation in starting points and outcomes is a fundamental sensitizing principle in life-course research (Cicchetti and Rogosch 1996; Featherman and Lerner 1985; Laub and Sampson 2003). Though it is necessary to group cases to simplify how much certain risk factors take hold and drive behavior, delinquency trajectories are inherently contingent and probabilistic. Overreliance on aggregated groupings without attention to individual variation can raise problems in optimizing decision making. This also highlights the real limitations of assessment for predictive purposes. At best, most assessments have moderate predictive strength, suggesting some error. Developmentally, this is not surprising in light of the multifinality and equifinality described earlier.

The effectiveness of categorizations is related to how well they limit within-group variation and maximize between-group variation (Gottfredson 1987). This changes the focus of the juvenile justice system from the individual's characteristics to those of a statistically generated group (Osgood 2005; Raudenbush 2005; Silver and Miller 2002). While it is necessary to simplify information for the purposes of individual decision making, understanding the within-category variation is necessary when thinking about what happens next for a youth (Raudenbush 2005, 131).

Maintaining some individual decision-making discretion—within boundaries—is important in ensuring that discretion that takes account of developmental factors can enter the assessment process and subsequent decision making. Assessment processes allow these scenarios, which typically occur when juvenile justice personnel believe that scoring and classification is too low relative to their experience. Analysis of approximately 34,000 juvenile assessments in Ohio for 2015 found that roughly 3 percent, or 966, of cases were overrides.[5] Of those cases with a departure from the assessment, 96 percent, or 929, were from a lower to a higher risk level. Most departures pertained to youth cooperation with the process, ongoing presence in treatment, or the nature of their offense, which do not fully reflect the risk score and level (e.g., sex offenses, serious violent offenses), as opposed to developmental reasons.

The Role of Clinical Information. Developmental risk and needs assessment should proceed using narrative insight and awareness of contingencies that affect patterns of recent behavior and potentially predict later behavior, using structured decision making within that context. Those doing the assessments also require clear cues as to developmental risk and protective factors and an understanding of how those fit into judgments about the best course of action in responding to a case in a way that reaps the potential benefits of actuarial risk and needs assessment (e.g., greater structure, reduce disparities in decisions).

One important by-product of the move toward standardized assessment in juvenile justice and other areas of child services is that informed clinical judgment may be underused in responding to individual needs (Shlonsky and Wagner 2005). Interestingly, the idea of integrating these information sources traces back to Paul Meehl (1954), whose career largely focused on assessing clinical and actuarial judgment in diagnostics and outcomes and set the intellectual foundation for its current use in juvenile justice. Aron Shlonsky and Dennis Wagner developed a framework that brings all viable information into the assessment process. They focus on child service investigations, but many points of their framework carry over to juvenile justice:

The combined use of actuarial risk assessment and an objective, clearly articulated structure for documenting clinical assessment findings is intended to help agencies reduce subsequent maltreatment through improved targeting of limited resources for service intervention. For example, high risk families can be given priority for intensive case intervention services used to maintain families or reunify them, as well as worker case management activity and contact. However, a deep understanding of individual and family functioning may be required in order to select those services most likely to address key areas of need. (2005, 422)

Actuarial risk assessment tools for juvenile justice sometimes rely on items whose relevance depends on information that would be available only in a clinical interview. For example, the treatment implications of substance-use-related risk have different relevance depending on a youth's age, type of drug(s) used, and the context in which it is used. A developmental framework gives juvenile justice officials and researchers guidance on the basic necessary information and the understanding of a delinquent act and future delinquency.

Thomas M. Crea asserts, "While the predictive validity of actuarial assessments tends to be robust, these tools are limited by their narrow scope and their inherent subjectivity when completed by individual caseworkers" (2010, 198). A less restrictive, but still structured, decision-making model can help balance the generally derived insights on subgroups of juvenile justice cases with sources of variation that are apparent in the developmental and life-course research areas. This also dispenses with the half-truth that subjectivity does not come into play in assessment and instead harnesses it for greater developmental insight and sense of context. So in addition to potentially adding developmentally relevant items and questions, augmentation of the assessment information can explicitly call for related insights that may be useful to understanding a youth's pathway to the juvenile justice system and possible points on how he or she will fare under certain treatment approaches. While some such information may show up in other elements of case records and juvenile court predisposition reports (Rogers and Williams 1994), thereby contextualizing recommendations and decisions of the court, a developmental juvenile justice system requires systematic integration of information about the factors that require attention in treatment and those that may be obstacles to effective intervention if they are not simultaneously accounted for.

Both clinical judgment and actuarial assessment are useful in making decisions about youths and therefore are included in the information-gathering process and juvenile justice response (Mulvey and Iselin 2008). Mulvey and Iselin emphasize the need for consistency in the guidance provided to decision makers as well as linking structured decision making to ongoing management of risk and needs that recognizes the potential for change across adolescence. Integrating these elements of information gathering and decision making are necessary to move the juvenile justice system in a more developmental direction. Future research support for this may come from integration of data and text analysis techniques (see, e.g., Don et al. 2007).

Developmentally Informed Treatment in Juvenile Justice

Identifying and understanding individual and collective risk and needs offers a starting point for appropriately treating individual youths and allocating resources at the program or agency level. Next is delivery of effective, developmentally informed treatment strategies that address the risks and needs that contribute to delinquent behavior. While developmental literature often provides suggestions that fall outside the purview of the juvenile justice system (e.g., early intervention), developmental research and thinking is helpful for what should happen with treatment inside the system.

Richard F. Catalano and J. David Hawkins (1996) identify several relevant points that can be applied to developmentally informed treatment in the juvenile justice system. With general understanding of risk factors and processes that generate antisocial development and delinquency as a background, the system can proceed to "interrupt the causal processes that lead to antisocial outcomes and strengthen the processes that lead to prosocial outcomes" (182). Catalano and Hawkins provide guidelines for intervention that are based on that objective and that are adaptable for the juvenile justice system:

- Each aspect of the process that drives a youth's delinquency has potential for intervention.
- The multicausal nature of risk and protective factors suggests that multiple different treatment programs are often necessary.
- Treatment should attempt to change the mechanisms contributing to delinquency while also bolstering strengths that foster prosocial development and behavior.
- The cumulative and contingent nature of development necessitates the earliest intervention possible.
- Treatment must be appropriate to the youth—from the standpoint of both the risks and the environments that are salient at a given age.
- Points of transition, which may lead to changes in opportunities or social influences, are possible leverage points for intervention.

These organizing points build on relevant insight about development and youth behavior and provide a framework for intervention that is cognizant of the ways that individuals interact with their environments over time.

The current approach to treatment in the juvenile court is multifaceted and varies as much as the justice-involved youths described in Chapter 1. Treatment efforts in the juvenile justice system have their origins in dealing with the social context of juvenile delinquency. The youth's interaction with the social environment quickly came into focus, however. William Healy notes:

We have come to know that the deepest necessity in each and every case is for holding fast to the conception of "the situation" . . . [that is, the environment and the active person in it], the situation as a whole. This means the interplay, the interweaving of the individual and his environment, the universal and inevitable interrelation of these two. (1925, 40)

The question is what is the appropriate treatment and its packaging and delivery? Although access to quality programs is sometimes limited when considered at the youth level (see Greenwood 2014), an array of effective strategies can be used across the spectrum of youths who reach the juvenile justice system. This is certainly a useful basis for treating justice-involved youths and is a clear advance over treatments that do not recognize the situational interaction between youths and their environment in generating delinquency.

Treatment Aims and Developmental Needs. In the risk-needs-responsivity model that drives many of the current treatment modalities in juvenile justice and correctional settings, reducing criminogenic needs is essential to reduce later recidivism (Andrews and Bonta 2010). A developmental approach to juvenile justice treatment would certainly parallel that but requires some adjustments. First, risks and needs must be viewed in a developmental sense to understand what a youth currently faces. Other important principles from the developmental literature, such as understanding how those risks interact and accumulate and their progression over time, also require close attention in treatment. Second, and relatedly, there must be an expanded sense of the scope of outcomes of interest in a more developmental juvenile justice system. The goals of juvenile justice treatment should explicitly incorporate developmental outcomes like prosocial skill development.

The Contingency of Treatment. Effective treatment rests on high-quality interventions for youths, but a condition for their success is matching the right program to each youth (Sullivan and Latessa 2011), which is difficult when the youths who come into the juvenile justice system vary along with their risks and needs. Programming that corresponds to the results of the assessment for each youth at the appropriate developmental stage must also be available (Pawson and Tilley 1997). This is the Right Kid, Right Time, Right Program notion espoused by the National Council of Juvenile Family Court Judges (2016). The individual cannot be divorced from the program, so a move to a more developmental juvenile justice system must use that additional information to fine-tune youth placements. Treatment heterogeneity is a fact of life in the juvenile justice system as it is in other contexts (Kravitz, Duan, and Braslow 2004), so it is important to consider both general (categorical) and specific (individual) responsivity factors in understanding the potential effects of treatment.

Developmental insights—in interaction with case and youth characteristics—can help with this type of allocation. Two youths might have the same risk score on a negative peer association domain measure but nevertheless require different treatment strategies. One youth, for example, might have a more extensive juvenile justice history and the other might be before the court for the first time. The first youth will likely benefit from greater attention to his individual risk factors (e.g., prodelinquency attitudes) that are likely to generate a lengthier pattern of behavior. For the other youth, attention to peer refusal skills to help him identify risky situations and strategies for deflecting or extricating himself from situations may be a better option (Sullivan and Jolliffe 2012).

Recognizing Reward and Risk. The treatment process inevitably must consider mechanisms that more naturally promote desistance. Their implementation will account for decision-making contingencies, change in perceived choice and agency, increased opportunity for prosocial interactions, and aging itself. Treatment plans and protocols must recognize and deal with potential offsetting rewards that could come from delinquent behavior. Going a step further to bring the youth's age into the assessment process reinforces the need to focus more strongly on one risk or another. An older youth in the preceding peer-driven delinquency situation may not require the same treatment dosage as a younger one or in the first scenario. At the same time, the thought-action processes identified in the biopsychosocial research since the 1990s suggest that youths must be convinced of the rewards of engaging in treatment and developing skills. The long-term benefits of behaving differently because of the treatment process will likely be outweighed—at least for those youths who are embedded in delinquency—by more immediate rewards that accrue from continuing delinquent behavior. Some youths stand to gain a lot more from delinquent behavior than from ceasing it, so the treatment process and related incentives and sanctions must set and promote realistic expectations for short-term change.

Multiple, Cumulative, and Interactive Risks. Multifaceted interventions are frequently necessary to satisfactorily address the cumulative and interactive risk factors of serious juvenile offenders. The juvenile justice system's decision making is important in the effectiveness of those interventions. Right-sizing juvenile justice response—and its costs in time and resources—depends on the nature of the case. Frequently, risk factors are chained such that some have greater primacy than distal others. The individuals that a youth is hanging around with may affect delinquency, but developmentally, the youth's choice of those associations and length of unsupervised time with those peers can also be linked back to familial factors (Thornberry 1987). Youths with certain predispositions are also more apt to gravitate to those peers and situations, perhaps even shaping those circumstances with their decisions, which again points to unearthing the narrative and underlying processes of a youth's pattern of delinquency. It also suggests that treatment must address multiple risk domains in a way that considers the primary, or presenting, risk factors and those that may seem to be secondary but nevertheless reflect underlying causes.

Wraparound services that touch on multiple aspects of risk and needs are needed for many youths who encounter the juvenile justice system frequently and have multiple, interwoven risk factors. Wraparound services must be a system of parts as opposed to a single program (Rosenblatt 1996). The strategy is comprehensive in carefully identifying and responding to youths' needs (and risks) and mapping those developmentally before juvenile justice contact and continuing into adolescence and early adulthood. The related mechanism of systems of care points to a process that is multifaceted but also integrated in that meaningful connections among the different programs and agencies are relevant in treatment or sanctions for justice-involved youths. As Abram Rosenblatt (1996) notes, this can also involve other institutions, like the family (or school or community), that would be pertinent in responding to the factors that might affect developmental and situational risk for delinquency. This also requires someone, such as a case manager or probation officer, who can coordinate across the service providers and perhaps help the youth and his or her family put everything together so that the objectives are clear. This starts with a judge or magistrate but requires consistent enforcement by those overseeing the youth's case.

Informal Support and Developmental Scaffolding. Juvenile justice treatment must also be mindful of the interaction between a youth and his or her environment and how it affects the developmental process (Holmbeck et al. 2000). While it is useful to understand a youth's trajectory of delinquency, beginning with distal risk factors as the origin in his or her behavioral history, the juvenile justice system must concern itself with the proximal mechanisms driving behavior and aim to treat those. At the same time, knowing which risk factors contribute—even distal ones—to delinquent behavior is necessary to obtain a full understanding of the youth's behavior. For example, the presence of trauma or victimization should inform a youth's treatment plan regardless of whether it occurred recently or earlier in life (Espinosa, Sorensen, and Lopez 2013). Treatment and skill development inherently bring in the interaction of the youth with the situation and influences around him or her and require formal consideration of the obstacles and opportunities stemming from the different institutions and settings that play a role in the youth's development and behavior. Environmentally, this frequently points to family, peer, community, and school settings as areas for intervention, since there may be elements of these environments that increase the youth's risk of delinquency. For example, a lack of support in familial relationships may create space for other forms of antisocial peer association and bonding (Thornberry 1987).

Michael Doyle and Mairead Dolan (2002, 654) offer an integrated assessment and clinical judgment structure that generally follows this social scaffolding for youth behavior. It breaks down the individual narrative into historical presentation of risk and need, current presentation of risk and need with the specific manifestations, contextual factors that influence the etiology of the problem and further treatment, and protective factors that promote change. Doyle and Dolan highlight trauma and abuse as a historical factor, substance use as a presenting indicator at the assessment point, social support as a contextual factor in understanding the youth, and motivation for and responsiveness to treatment as a protective factor. Considering each case across related dimensions recognizes the interactive and cumulative nature of risk and strength in drawing information from assessment and clinical review in developmental terms.

Insertion of developmental principles into juvenile justice moves the process past a narrow scope of what might influence a youth to change offending behavior. Youths are entangled with many other influences and contexts besides the juvenile justice system and treatment agencies. These developmental and situational influences can be either barriers to effective outcomes or a potential scaffold on which juvenile justice intervention might build. This means that effective treatment for positive youth development must account for the individual but also be mindful of the other institutions that will inevitably affect their developmental outcomes. This is consistent with a systems of care perspective that draws in multiple agencies but goes further in understanding that youths must attain skills to appropriately engage with all environments, even as agencies make efforts to strengthen the family (Kumpfer, Molgaard, and Spoth 1996) or improve the capability of communities to prevent crime (Kim et al. 2015).

Bolstering Developmental Skills

A developmental context for treating delinquent youths applies to several skills that are relevant to reducing risk of later delinquency and promoting positive developmental pathways. Addressing deficits in social supports offered to justice-involved youths will inevitably be part of effective intervention, but developmentally informed intervention must also consider how antisocial attitudes and thinking patterns drive delinquent behavior—especially for categories of more serious offenders. Still, many of these treatments at varying dosages and points of emphasis are functional across the spectrum of justice-involved youths. Tailoring effective interventions requires multiple approaches. This knowledge can help identify important targets for intervention and inform intervention (Huey et al. 2000; Kazdin and Nock 2003; Ward et al. 2007).

Attitudes and Thinking Patterns. The change process will likely include cognitive elements (Giordano, Cernkovich, and Rudolph 2002; Maruna 2001; Mulvey et al. 2004; Paternoster and Bushway 2009), or how the youth thinks about his or her behavior, to address patterns before deconstructing and rebuilding toward more prosocial behaviors. Moving from delinquent thinking to script-based action requires that youths engage in alternative situational awareness and decision making. Interventions using cognitive-behavioral therapy (CBT) use cognitive restructuring to thwart criminal thinking patterns (e.g., Bush, Glick, and Taymans 1997). Youths often arrive in the juvenile justice system with deficits—as well as strengths—that require prioritization in treatment so they can better handle situations in the future. Philip Kendall, a leading researcher in this area, describes those challenges:

> Children and adolescents are in the process of developing ways to view their world, and cognitive-behavioral treatments provide educational experiences and therapist-coached reconceptualizations of problems to build a new "coping" template. That is, the treatment goal is for the child to develop a new cognitive structure, or a modified existing structure, through which he or she can look at formerly distressing situations. Therapy helps in reducing the support for dysfunctional schemata and in constructing a new schema through which the child can identify and solve problems. (1993, 236)

Need for a "coping template" is especially true given justice-involved youths' risks and needs and, for the most part, touches a large segment of the population that encounters the juvenile justice system.

The linkage between thought and behavior in the treatment of delinquency makes youths' cognitive framework for action a significant part of twenty-first-century research and thinking on development and sets a foundation for effective intervention. CBT programs in delinquency treatment help youths develop skills for interacting with and responding to their environment. Still, the pattern of behavior that they show will be contingent on both subjective and structural influences, as youth's environments may pose challenges. These negative, interactional thought-action scripts can be reinforced and persist across developmental stages if they go uninterrupted (Dodge 1993; Huesmann 1988). Aggressive actions in adolescence can be linked to patterns of social information processing, which can also be linked to cognitive-behavioral processes (Arsenio, Adams, and Gold 2009; Lemerise and Arsenio 2000).

Nana A. Landenberger and Mark W. Lipsey (2005) reviewed fifty-eight CBT studies of juvenile and adult offenders, of which seventeen, or 29 percent, were delinquent youths (see also Pearson et al. 2002). One category of programming included cognitive-skills training, such as Thinking for a Change and Moral Reconation Therapy, which elevates the perspective taking and moral reasoning that underlie youths' thoughts and behaviors (Bush, Glick, and Taymans 1997; Little and Robinson 1988). The authors also included some CBT programs for anger management training, like Aggression Replacement Training, which teaches exercising self-control in situations that provoke anger (Glick and Goldstein 1987). Landenberger and Lipsey (2005) found that those in CBT had a 25 percent, on average, lower rate of recidivism relative to a comparison group. There was significant variation around that average, but the researchers report no differences between juvenile and adult populations in program effectiveness. CBT, therefore, is likely to be one element of effective treatment—especially as it deals with the link between cognitive processes and behavior important to the developmental process. This programming also fosters skills in several pertinent developmental domains. For example, inability to control anger affects a youth's ability to form prosocial, romantic relationships and interact productively in employment settings.

Other studies have shown that CBT has effects on core elements of development as well—especially mental health outcomes. In 2006 Andrew C. Butler and colleagues reviewed sixteen studies that systematically examined the status of the research on CBT interventions (see also Hofmann et al. 2012). They found positive treatment effects on mental health outcomes like depression, post-traumatic stress disorder, and anxiety (which all saw large effects) and anger (moderate effects). Denis G. Sukhodolsky, Howard Kassinove, and Bernard S. Gorman (2004) reviewed forty studies on CBT and anger in children and adolescents and identified moderate treatment effects. The researchers note that a skill-development treatment style was among the most effective in reducing aggressive behavior and anger. Those approaches also strongly promoted social skills and self-control.

In the 1990s and 2000s, John E. Lochman and his colleagues conducted a series of important studies of a CBT anger-coping intervention with aggressive children (see Lochman 1992; Lochman et al. 2006). Some received a booster to the intervention in the year following their original involvement in the treatment. Lochman (1992) studied 145 boys in early to middle adolescence, following them up at two and three years after treatment. He found that the children who received the booster showed some improvement in functioning and substance use but did not show much difference in terms of general deviance. One important conclusion is that the length of time of the intervention and the use of a follow-up booster may be especially important with this population. Philip C. Kendall and Lauren Braswell's (1993) work on CBT focuses on impulsivity and externalizing behavior in children. They found much evidence for the viability of this approach with young people who are at risk for delinquent behavior.

The prominence of this treatment strategy and its connection to developmental principles make it a promising foundation on which to build developmental juvenile justice. Still, developmental research also suggests some variation in its effectiveness. Grayson N. Holmbeck and colleagues (2000) note three important elements in thinking about adolescent development and treatment. First, the objectives of treatment, or issues that require attention, may depend on the developmental stage of a youth, so that certain skill sets may be more relevant at particular points in the youth's life. Second, the success of a treatment strategy depends on the youth's stage of development. The need for skills training as opposed to skills training *and* cognitive restructuring depends on the youth's stage of development relative to the pattern of delinquent behavior. Third, the youth's individual risk level relative to developmental stage may have implications for treatment. If CBT and role-playing require certain baseline skills as a foundation for treatment and if those skills correlate with age, cognition and neurocognition levels should be assessed before treatment (Kendall and Choudhury 2003; Riggs et al. 2006; Weisz et al. 1995).

While the totality of the literature indicates that CBT can be efficacious across ages and developmental stages, cognitive development may be a responsivity factor in treatment methods (Holmbeck et al. 2000), and age affects elements of CBT programming (Durlak, Fuhrman, and Lampman 1991; Sukhodolsky, Kassinove, and Gorman 2004). This requires attention to moderators of effective treatment—particularly among adolescents—and identification of the skills necessary to help youths mitigate risks and bolster skills.

Self-Regulation. Self-regulation is relevant in understanding delinquency and development (Gottfredson and Hirschi 1990; Pratt and Cullen 2000; Vazsonyi, Mikuška, and Kelley 2017). Reverse engineering Moffitt's life-course-persistent pattern of antisocial behavior suggests that youths with early neuropsychological deficits develop a psychosocial interactional style that leads to problematic environmental responses that further entrench them in antisocial behavior (see also Caspi, Bem, and Elder 1989). James Heckman (2000) identifies noncognitive skills, like self-regulation, as instrumental in the development of human capital and later life outcomes. Further, he argues that these skills can be inculcated via appropriate early intervention programs. These characteristics are likely to be fairly set once a youth reaches adolescence (Gottfredson and Hirschi 1990), and adolescents may be more inclined toward risk seeking and avoiding the exercise of such control (Steinberg 2007). Nevertheless, it seems possible to instill a degree of self-regulation after childhood or compensate for deficits by fostering other skills to manage its expression.

The linkages between self-regulation and problem outcomes suggest that development of self-control skills is a necessary priority for many delinquent youths—even relatively nonserious cases in which ability to override impulses and risk seeking may be attenuated during adolescence. Nurturing self-regulation should be at the heart of any intervention plan that seeks to redirect justice-involved youths. Michael Gottfredson and Travis Hirschi (1990) suggest that parents must appropriately sanction problem behavior to foster self-control at early developmental stages. Prosocial influences, therefore, contribute to the development of self-control, but some evidence suggests it might be promoted synthetically.

A review of thirty-four intervention studies suggests that certain training activities can boost self-control at early developmental stages (Piquero et al. 2016). The intervention studies addressed self-control or behavioral outcomes like delinquency in youths. Many of the modalities identified overlap with or derive from elements of CBT strategies, such as skills development, coping strategies, training and role-playing, and strategies for delayed gratification. The average effect size was moderate (0.27) and statistically significant, but there was significant variability across studies—those focused on skill building tended to be more effective. The authors offer the caveat that the impact on delinquency is less pronounced. This review of intervention studies cannot really help in understanding whether these strategies might aid justice-involved youths, specifically, because the studies did not include these youths or age ranges in their study, but the review finds potential promise in such interventions.

Much of the research on developing youth self-control focuses on parental interventions meant to indirectly promote that skill development. For example, Matthew Sanders and Trevor Mazzucchelli (2013) found that the Positive Parenting Program affected youth self-regulation via changes in parental management strategies. Similarly, the Promoting Alternative Thinking Strategies curriculum addresses self-regulation training in school-based settings. In this curriculum, self-regulation is learned through training to facilitate inhibitory control and mindful planning via self-talk, or interior thinking about perceptions and actions, which mediates thinking and action (Greenberg et al. 1995; Humphrey et al. 2016).

Although research results are not totally clear about the effects of fostering self-control at the ages at which youths encounter juvenile justice, other findings from CBT studies and the literature on development of self-regulation in adolescence more generally can plausibly be used (Pokhrel et al. 2013). All in all, instilling self-control in justice-involved youths is a challenging proposition, but it is worth the effort; it shortens their delinquent and criminal careers and promotes other important developmental outcomes (Heckman, Stixrud, and Urzua 2006).

Peer Refusal. The individual mechanisms by which peers affect delinquency suggest that multiple approaches should be available in the juvenile justice system to counteract effects of deviant peer influence on youth behavior. The most appropriate approach likely depends on a youth's stage of development and how the peer social environment affects his or her behavior. In the public policy realm, the prominent use of media ads that tell youths to stay "above the influence" of deviant peers (Office of National Drug Control Policy 2011, 1) reflects blanket, educationally based initiatives that take a simplistic view of the different mechanisms at work in the peer-youth-delinquency relationship (Sullivan and Jolliffe 2012). Developmentally, the peer relationship operates in multiple ways (e.g., selection effect, socialization), which highlights the need for multiple distinct treatment strategies around peer influence. Some of the principles unearthed in this research likely resonate with the mechanisms driving youth delinquency—particularly for those involved in delinquency as a normative behavior. Some justice-involved youths, however, might be less amenable to interventions aimed at enhancing skills relevant to reduced involvement in social-group-driven delinquency because their behavior began before peer influence became important and thus results from enduring factors rather than proximate social environment.

A review turned up somewhat mixed evidence on peer refusal skills programs, most of which were school based and aimed at younger youths (Sullivan and Jolliffe 2012). Some research with a population of at-risk youths shows that these skills are teachable (Ngwe et al. 2004). An evaluation and longitudinal analysis of the Aban Aya Youth Project suggests moderate-to-strong effects on violence and school delinquency for at-risk boys. This was a broad, culturally informed social development curriculum delivered in school settings. The community-based component showed significantly stronger effects than the school-only curriculum (see Flay et al. 2004). The researchers also conducted a crude test of a mediation model that specified effects on violence operating through peer behaviors and peer group pressure. Their findings suggest that the program influenced longitudinal trends in violence at least partly because of the program's effect on peer risk. This suggests that programming might be effective in buffering the peer risk factor that frequently affects adolescent delinquency. It does, however, require thought about which youths to target and the type and intensity of the treatment.

Education and Vocational Skills. Educational attainment is critical for youths to achieve relevant developmental benchmarks and establish competencies for effective transition to adulthood (Clausen 1991). Given this, education must be a short-term focal end point for a youth, family, and juvenile justice system. In a developmental sense, treatment aimed at educational attainment goes beyond the pursuit of academic credentials or promotion of cognitive skills—although those are quite important. It instead requires a competence or human capital framework that is inevitably linked to some of the other important drivers of delinquency or prosocial pathways discussed here (e.g., self-regulation, social skills) (Heckman and Rubinstein 2001).

Educational intervention is especially challenging in the juvenile justice system owing to the prior academic challenges and classroom behavior issues that frequently co-occur with delinquency and the school interruptions that come with subsequent contact with the courts. Strategies also must support both youths who are involved with the justice system but remain in the community (and in school) and those who receive educational services in juvenile residential facilities (Ingersoll and LeBoeuf 1997). The system must intervene in other areas of need to ensure that youths have the skill set necessary to maintain their engagement with the educational process and progress in it as much as possible. Juvenile justice agencies and corrections facilities therefore must cultivate referral options or be able to effectively deliver academic content in alternative school environments. The evidence on these alternative educational programs successfully doing so is somewhat mixed (Cox 1999; Cox, Davidson, and Bynum 1995). Basic elements of promoting change and fostering positive development are relevant here. In their review of effective programs in the late 1990s, L. W. Sherman and colleagues (1998) highlight the importance of innovative environment, clear norms and rules for behavior and performance, and building social and thinking skills for crime prevention in school environments (see also Sherman et al. 2002).

Integrating Strengths and Mind-Set

The juvenile court still operates in a risk-centered framework (Barton and Butts 2008). That philosophy is likely to continue because its mission includes sanctioning delinquency on the community's behalf. Acknowledgment of potential strengths and protective factors signals a shift from an almost-exclusive focus on the problems and risks of delinquent youths to a multidimensional view of their needs and, subsequently, their potential resilience and strengths. This approach is premised on inverting the abnormal psychology or developmental psychopathology view of delinquency with one rooted in positive psychology (Lerner, Dowling, and Anderson 2003; Seligman and Csikszentmihalyi 2014). Laura Nissen describes this shift toward assets and resilience as "an organizing principle for a family of theories and practice strategies that focus on the generally untapped gifts, positive attributes, and under-developed capabilities of persons, families, and even communities" (2006, 41). For example, an individual's intelligence may be a protective factor, and good relationship with a parent may provide a social bond that acts as a buffer. These factors reduce the likelihood of delinquent behavior despite other problems or circumstances.

Rather than focus exclusively on the risk of negative outcomes, this paradigm seeks to understand and exploit strengths and assets. Richard F. Catalano and colleagues (2002) list several dimensions of positive developmental psychology, including promoting self-efficacy, broadly fostering youth competence, generating prosocial bonding opportunities, bolstering positive identity, supporting belief in the future, and introducing rewards for prosocial behavior. These objectives overlap with a developmental approach to juvenile justice that looks beyond recidivism alone. While much of the insight for framing response to delinquent youths considers how problem behavior develops in the life course, the science on positive development and related intervention can be a valuable component of a more developmental juvenile justice system.

The emphasis on promoting strengths and recognizing potential for prosocial outcomes is valuable in responding to the average case in the juvenile justice system, even though more serious cases often get the lion's share of attention (Butts, Mayer, and Ruth 2005). That emphasis coincides with the juvenile justice system's desire to route youths to positive behavioral pathways. Within this framework the key objective is not to dismiss the delinquent behavior but rather to also recognize a youth's assets; believe that he or she has a capacity for change; and promote attachment to conventional others and institutions, development of prosocial skills, and engagement in activities that help the youth grow those skills (Butts, Bazemore, and Meroe 2010). William H. Barton and Jeffrey A. Butts (2008) conducted an exploratory study of several intervention programs and agencies that use a positive youth development framework. They found some potential promise but acknowledge that it is still too early to tell how effective they will be (see also Schwartz 2001).

Educational psychology research on youth development has identified the benefits of instilling a growth mind-set in youth and adolescence (e.g., Claro, Paunesku, and Dweck 2016; Yeager et al. 2016). In this approach, based on the work of Carol Dweck (2008), outcomes only partly reflect initial conditions because there is room for learning and change over time. This is an inherent stance of the juvenile justice system, and its work would not be possible if it assumed that all youth behavior results from innate, unchangeable factors. A developmental approach uses that framework not just in addressing risks and needs but also in making an explicit effort to develop skills that will aid a youth's movement through adolescence into adulthood.

Summary

This insight that links development and current juvenile justice treatment identifies principles for treating youths to reduce future delinquency and promote positive outcomes effectively. Each of these ideas for intervention for justice-involved youths depends heavily on the infrastructure and support of the juvenile justice system and—in many cases—other societal institutions. The assessment of risks and needs and subsequent treatment often overlaps with developmental principles and can foster appropriate skills, but current practice does not fully embody developmental ideas. Treatment programs addressing developmental outcomes while also reducing risk for delinquency show some promise but have some limitations as well.

Effective Sanctions and Supervision for Delinquent Youths

The enduring legacy of the juvenile court is its treatment aims, and contemporary practice—and related discussion—still revolves around those. This is true among both its supporters, who tend to deemphasize sanctions, and its detractors, who fixate on its inadequacies in dealing with extreme cases. Balancing these perceptions in juvenile justice policy and practice can be difficult. The juvenile justice system must also be mindful of the messages it sends to delinquent youths and the broader community.

Development and Juvenile Punishment

The signal from the sanctions used by juvenile justice actors influences the effectiveness of juvenile justice response to youths. The premise of the juvenile court's response to delinquency is intervention, but response tends to focus on treatment or minimization of the problems that may follow from juvenile justice involvement, like missed developmental milestones. To the extent that there are coherent philosophies for sanctioning delinquent youths, they often appear to be analogues of the reasons for punishment in the adult system. But rehabilitation aims, which seek to bring about reform for the youths whom they treat, reign supreme in the juvenile justice system.

It is shortsighted, however, to ignore other possible aims of punishment, like deterrence, in assessing effective and developmental juvenile justice practice because some key stakeholders may view them as part of the reasons for sanctions. State codes authorizing juvenile justice systems (Feld 1988) underscore this point. For example, Texas's Family Code, which provides the infrastructure for juvenile justice, underwent revision in 1995 and now lists the following objectives:

- Strengthen public safety
- Promote the concept of punishment for criminal acts
- Remove, where appropriate, the taint of criminality from children committing certain unlawful acts
- Provide treatment, training, and rehabilitation that emphasize the accountability and responsibility of both the parent and the child for the child's conduct (Texas Attorney General 2016, 1)

The state's 1973 code did not include language about public safety or accountability. Similarly, the intent behind Wisconsin's current juvenile justice legislative code mixes objectives of community protection and accountability with a desire to help youths develop skills to produce later positive outcomes.[6]

As with treatment, juvenile justice sanctions that take account of youth development are more effective, because part of growing up is to gradually have freedom to make decisions and experience the effects of those decisions—but in a fashion that does not cripple long-term prospects (Zimring 2005a). This gradual extension of freedoms offers more latitude to choose and act and simultaneously gradually scales up responsibility. While this responsibility is a part of the juvenile justice process, it has played a less prominent role in considering how developmental research can inform the response to delinquency than has the general notion that youths and adults differ. This is unfortunate because fitting the objectives of the juvenile justice system to relevant elements of developmental research leads to important insights on how to respond to delinquency in a comprehensive way to promote positive development. Insights that inform treatment are also relevant to sanctions, and other research and principles might be particularly valuable to understanding and improving the sanctions process.

Knowledge of effective or promising treatment is only part of a more developmental system. The juvenile justice system inherently must consider both treatment and sanctions (O'Connor and Treat 1995). Although the juvenile court from its onset was disposed toward sanctions, it avoided severe sanctions—whether defined as transfer to adult court or more restrictive juvenile facilities—to whatever extent possible because of their potential costs. Still, developmentally informed sanction strategies must account for the full distribution of cases that come before the juvenile court. The system also requires some means of ensuring accountability.

While differential treatment of youths for transgressions against the law is desirable in most situations, it is also important that choice and character not be entirely dismissed with juveniles. Dismissal of responsibility may have detrimental side effects by removing youths' sense of agency for their actions and the ability to individuate from their family of origin and other socializing institutions. Also, a lack of sanctions may block youths' ability to understand that their character, while not set in stone in their teens, is shaped in some ways by their actions and that it will become part of how they are judged in formal and informal settings in adulthood.

In case studies from the juvenile justice system, youths seemingly have to go to a lot of trouble to elicit a serious sanction from the court. When assigning sanctions, harm avoidance can be a starting principle but requires some revision if the objective is to alter youths' long-term behavioral patterns. In the short term, for instance, juvenile court involvement—even when warranted—can disrupt ties to the community, prosocial peers, school, and families. In the long term, it can interrupt or prohibit achievement of milestones and weaken constraints on antisocial behavior. Research reviews have identified the potential criminogenic impact of juvenile court involvement, suggesting that it can have an iatrogenic effect (e.g., Gatti, Tremblay, and Vitaro 2009; Petrosino, Guckenburg, and Turpin-Petrosino 2010). An appropriate response to the behavior is necessary to preserve public safety or to express the will of the community, however, and the system must therefore find appropriately tailored sanctions that redirect youths toward better behavior later on and opportunities to build skills to help them attain important developmental milestones.

The Philosophy and Practice of Punishment in Juvenile Court

In his book comparing youths' processing in juvenile and adult courts, Aaron Kupchik lays out the typical progression of sanctions experienced by some youths in the juvenile court that he observed:

> The going rate of punishment follows a very predictable pattern of escalating sanctions. . . . For all offenses other than severe violence (violence leading to serious injury of the victim), on a first offense the juvenile is diverted from court before coming before a judge; on a second offense the judge diverts the case to a counseling program; on a third offense the judge sentences the defendant to a review period of six to twelve months (after which, if the offender has been compliant and not been arrested, the case is dismissed); and on a fourth offense the defendant receives probation. Probation might be given more than once, though with continued involvement offenders graduate to the two other available sanctions: suspended sentences (probation with an added threat of a prison term) or incarceration. (2006, 87)

Youths experience significant sanctions only after several steps in the process. Unfortunately, these cases reinforce the stereotypical view of the juvenile justice system as being lax in its sanctioning responsibility.

This is a symbolic problem for the juvenile court in garnering support for its mission, which requires a degree of latitude toward youths' behavior, from the public and politicians. It presents more substantive concerns as well. If the response to youth delinquency is intended to have a developmental impact, appropriate sanctions will align with that objective. Although the evidence is sparse, it is not hard to envision many youths being unfazed—even confused—by the process observed by Kupchik. Research by Barry Glassner and colleagues (1983) in New York shortly after the state adopted stringent laws for trying juveniles as adults elaborates on this point. They report that two-thirds of their interviewees referred to the impending possibility of adult court sanctions as a reason to curtail their offending (see also Levitt 1998). Although this does not fully address the impact of the juvenile justice sanctions process and being deterred does not align precisely with developmental progress, these findings suggest that the juvenile justice system should consider the implications of the signals sent to youths.

Robert M. Emerson (1969) suggests that court actors spend a good deal of time trying to make some determination of why youths have made the choice to engage in delinquency and what that offense and the rest of their profile suggests about their moral character. The manner in which adolescent choices unfold and their character not yet being set in stone suggest some need for mitigation of the sanction for delinquent actions (Scott and Steinberg 2008). Decisions with respect to handling individual delinquency cases come down to a consideration of the offense and the youth. Despite the desire of the system to redirect youths toward prosocial trajectories via treatment and least restrictive alternatives, it is also important that it takes its role in sanctioning delinquent behavior seriously.

Generally, justice sanctions reflect a few possible objectives and divide roughly into expressive goals, intended to send a message to the youth or public on behalf of society, and instrumental goals, emphasizing crime reduction objectives (Tonry 2006). Often, juvenile court dispositions seek to satisfy multiple objectives simultaneously. Some are more salient in criminal court, but they are worth discussing briefly to identify the logic underlying societal response to delinquency and assess juvenile justice sanctions in the context of youth development.

Rehabilitation. A utilitarian objective of punishment, rehabilitation seeks some attainable outcome in responding to a delinquent act. It takes only a glance at the many treatment programs directed at youths, which can stretch to double digits in even the smallest court, to understand that rehabilitation plays a primary role in the juvenile justice system. The delivery of sanctions often is calibrated to maximize the potential for rehabilitation. In some cases, this means eschewing sanctions altogether or suspending them if a youth engages in an alternative like community service or treatment. This emphasis on rehabilitation over other goals, such as protecting public safety, is a continual point of attention in juvenile justice policy and practice (Bernard and Kurlychek 2010; Fondacaro, Slobogin, and Cross 2006). Regardless of the precise balance, rehabilitation is an enduring objective in responding to delinquency cases. The other acknowledged goals of juvenile justice are deterrence, incapacitation, and retribution. These philosophies play a lesser role in the juvenile court than the criminal justice system perhaps, but they provide context for considering juvenile justice sanctions nevertheless.

Deterrence. Deterrence is a standard objective of any response to delinquent or criminal behavior. This is a utilitarian goal because the objective is to affect decision-making processes such that potential offenders reconsider their actions in light of possible punishment (Paternoster 2010; Tonry 2008). This suggests that youths contemplating delinquent acts will reconsider their options if consequences from the juvenile justice system seem likely. A general deterrence focus emphasizes sanctions on a class of youths in terms of its effects on others in that class who might commit delinquent acts in the future. Specific deterrence is more isolated in that it is intended to reorient the youth being sanctioned toward refraining from delinquent behavior in the future because of the punishment received for the current offense (Schneider and Ervin 1990).

A look at the evidence for the deterrability of young offenders provides a more complicated view of the potential impact of juvenile justice sanctions. A now-popular example of the limitations of deterrence-based sanctions for juveniles is that of the Scared Straight program, which aims to shock at-risk and delinquent youths to discourage further problem behavior. The program began in a New Jersey prison when inmates serving life sentences developed an awareness program to try to teach youths about the possible results of criminal behavior (Finckenauer and Gavin 1999). Unfortunately, the evidence on the program's effectiveness has not been favorable, and deterrence-based approaches to preventing delinquent behavior similar to this program have found limited support (e.g., Petrosino et al. 2013). This is consistent with broader developmental research that suggests that mitigation of substantial accumulated risk factors is unlikely after a short-term experience such as these awareness programs—if the youths sanctioned in this way even receive the message from the program in the way it is intended.

Juveniles' limited amenability to deterrence from sanction reflects the motives and situational constraints that produce delinquent behavior. The social nature of delinquency (Warr 2002) and adolescents' weighing of possible approbation from peers (real or sensed) relative to the disapproval of parents, school officials, and the justice system would seem to attenuate the possible usefulness of such an approach. More specifically, the argument for deterrence-based sanctioning of most juvenile offenders is tenuous owing to youths' heightened reward salience relative to adults (Fagan and Piquero 2007; Steinberg 2014).

The potential variation in justice-involved youths suggests that deterrent effects cannot be fully ruled out. This corresponds to certain juveniles possibly being "more deterrable than others; that is, they may react and adjust their sanction threat perceptions in heterogeneous ways" (Loughran et al. 2012, 7; see also Paternoster 2010). It is important to consider general variation in potential response to sanctions while also considering individual factors that may drive that response, such as cognitive deficits or prior experiences with sanctions or delinquency. But operationalizing deterrence objectives, using developmental insights, in the juvenile justice system is challenging for three important reasons—beyond the simplistic argument that the court is not tough enough. First, the nature of juvenile court processes and sanctions can make it difficult to introduce mechanisms aimed at deterrence in a broad sense. Juvenile courts often package sanctions and treatment, and disentangling and connecting them to the action that caused the youth to come before the court can be difficult. Second, the ongoing monitoring that occurs in a system that relies heavily on probationary dispositions means that repeated instances of behavior and consequence or reward will occur. Therefore, that interaction over time becomes part of the possible impact of sanctions—especially for specific deterrence. Third, the juvenile court has sufficient individualization that youths may not know exactly what happened in response to a transgression by others, severely limiting the potential for general deterrent effects.

Incapacitation in Juvenile Custody. Though not generally viewed as a primary objective of sanctions in juvenile justice, incapacitation may be a possible by-product of some responses to delinquent youths. It also is sometimes used in preadjudication detention when the court wishes to prevent further delinquency during case processing. This in turn limits the delinquency—and associated victimization and societal costs—that comes from that career (Greenwood and Zimring 1985). In some ways it is the converse of rehabilitation because it takes little formal stance on what happens to youths while they are in custody or being monitored. Christina Stahlkopf, Mike Males, and Daniel Macallair (2010) describe juvenile incarceration and youth crime trends in California and find little evidence of an incapacitation effect. Gary Sweeten and Robert Apel (2007) used a nationally representative sample of youths and found prevention of a substantial number of offenses—they estimate between six and fourteen—for each year of placement.

Any assessment of short-term reduction in delinquency must incorporate the long-term impacts on development and the likelihood of lengthening a career or extending it into adulthood, however (Scott and Steinberg 2008). This is particularly relevant from a developmental standpoint because the system must seek balance between crime control and the possible interruption of skill building and exposure to further detrimental risk factors. A study by Anna Aizer and Joseph J. Doyle (2015) illustrates this potential problem. They used a judicial random-case-assignment process in Chicago to control for shared individual and case factors, like prior record and offense seriousness, that could confound the relationship between incarceration as a juvenile and then as an adult. They identified a link between the two and then assessed whether this relationship occurred in part as a result of the interruption or termination of formal education concurrent to juvenile incarceration. They attribute this increased likelihood of adult incarceration based on juvenile incarceration to a loss of human capital, via higher risk of high school dropout, at an important developmental stage.

These results suggest that the system might observe some short-term lessening of delinquency from incapacitation, but youths' exposure to criminogenic settings and loss of key developmental opportunities, which lessens the likelihood that youths' careers will wind down later in adolescence or in the transition to adulthood, may counteract that effect. If too many youths receive those serious placements or their time in facilities lacks thoughtful planning, the system's response to delinquency could be a snare, which Moffitt (1993) describes as a factor that prolongs antisocial behavior in cases predicted to see it wind down.

Just Deserts in the Juvenile Court. Like deterrence and incapacitation, just deserts, especially when framed as a retributive process, is often anathema in the juvenile justice system. Just-deserts sentencing metes punishment for a transgression against another person, another's property, or society that fits well with the offense that was committed. Proportionality is central to this sanctioning philosophy (Von Hirsch 1992). This fits with the desire to express disapproval for the delinquent act as a rationale for punishment of juveniles.

Although not frequently named as an objective of juvenile courts' response to youth behavior, just-deserts sentencing is appropriate to think about from a developmental standpoint because it fits with an accountability-based approach to juvenile delinquency. Stephen J. Morse (1999) argues that deserving based on moral fault is necessary in fashioning appropriate sanctions for delinquency. His normative account of responsibility argues that, while the leverage points might differ as far as decision making, youths in their midteens have a reasonable sense for the wrongfulness of their delinquent acts. Therefore, restrained just-deserts objectives may be part of a set of responses designed to foster prosocial development—especially because evidence suggests that (1) youth identity forms in interaction with the social environment and (2) is still in progress into adulthood.

There is some evidence for the resonance of this approach when assessing how its target populations might consider juvenile justice sanctions. While college students are likely to be distinct from delinquent youths in important ways, they are relatively close in age and developmental stage and consequently share some qualities. Studies of college students by Kevin M. Carlsmith, John M. Darley, and Paul H. Robinson (2002) found that just-deserts motive for punishment resonated most strongly with those in the sample and across different offense types. Although the philosophy of just deserts evinces proportionality as a means in and of itself, there may be some instrumental benefits when developmental ideas are considered. Dennis Maloney, Dennis Romig, and Troy Armstrong (1988) assert that a sanction fitting the crime is more about accountability in the juvenile justice system than retribution. Therefore, sanctions aim to ensure that youths take responsibility, an instrumental goal in fostering moral development. The research provides an initial basis for considering how sanctions should be included in a multifaceted, developmental response to delinquent behavior.

Sanctions, Delinquent Youths, and Development

The juvenile justice system uses several common sanctions, which approximate ones available in the adult system to different degrees. In the juvenile justice system, a youth may receive a community-based custodial disposition that is treatment focused or be sent to a state-level facility that has a treatment orientation but is also focused on security and control. In the juvenile justice system, community-based sanctions might range from teen courts to a restitution-based program to intensive probation supervision. Although there are parallels, the relative distribution of those categories of sanctions differs between the juvenile and adult systems.

The juvenile court began to pay greater attention to the idea of effective sanctions in the first two decades of the twenty-first century. The question of which of those sanctions just discussed makes sense for juvenile offenders is, not surprisingly, conditional on the case and the individual youth. The system must prioritize three objectives: (1) expressing disapproval appropriately, (2) the utilitarian objective of trying to give the youth a sense of moral ownership of the behavior and its harm to foster prosocial identity development, and (3) avoiding overly harsh punishment that negatively affects later development through unnecessary restriction on treatment opportunities or other side effects (e.g., collateral consequences, missed developmental milestones). A developmentally informed system cannot simply rely on treatment to reduce recidivism and redirect youth trajectories. A comprehensive and thoughtful response will integrate these pieces to address risks and needs and foster skills while also not trivializing the youth's actions. Sanctions should not be detrimental to development, but some principled punishment is needed.

Avoiding an overly punitive juvenile justice system seems wise, but there are good reasons to maintain reasonable sanctions. Gordon Bazemore and Susan E. Day assert that "one does not have to believe in the value of deterrence, retribution, or even incapacitation to acknowledge that all societies and communities . . . define the norms of acceptable behavior; demonstrate disapproval of such unacceptable behavior; and acquire some means of imposing consequences on those who commit crimes" (1998, 2). The imperative is stronger when considering the need to help adolescents develop into citizens who respect norms and understand the necessity of some response to their violation. While there is sometimes perceived to be a duality in treatment and sanctions, that does not have to be the case, and, more importantly, appropriate juvenile justice sanctions should be used with treatment efforts to promote positive development. The degree to which that message resonates does, however, depend on how it is delivered.

The pendulum swings of juvenile justice policy and practice frequently carry buzzwords with them that capture some of the underlying reasoning for the arguments of their proponents. "Accountability" is one such term used by those who seek more balance between punishment and treatment in the juvenile justice system. Initiatives toward ensuring greater accountability for delinquent youths come in several forms, some seemingly minor sanctions as well as more serious responses. Accountability holds some just deserts because it seeks to hold a juvenile responsible through imposition of consequences proportionate to the delinquent act (Kurlychek, Torbet, and Bozynski 1999).

Accountability is something more than mere just deserts, or a punishment fitting the crime, when used in the juvenile justice system. Accountability and clear and explicit consequences for problem behavior can play a formative role in youths' lives. Even those who are concerned with the potential harm of deleterious adultlike sanctions for juveniles recognize that a degree of accountability is important in the juvenile court's response to offending:

> Affirming partial responsibility for youth constitutes a virtue. The idea of personal responsibility and accountability for behavior provides an important cultural counterweight to a popular culture that endorses the idea that everyone is a victim, that all behavior is determined, and that no one is responsible. The juvenile court elevated determinism over freewill, characterized delinquents as victims rather than perpetrators, and subjected them to an indeterminate quasi-civil commitment process. The juvenile court's treatment ideology denied youths' personal responsibility, reduced offenders' duty to exercise self-control, and eroded their obligations to change. If there is any silver lining in the current cloud of "get tough" policies, it is the affirmation of responsibility. (Feld 1999, 390)

These sanctions need not be overly harsh or noxious to achieve a developmental purpose. The principles underlying restorative justice and restitution, for example, fit into a developmental schema for punishment (NRC 2013). Restorative justice, which focuses on acknowledging the wrong done, includes stakeholders in the process of expressing the concern of the community to promote reparation. Rehabilitation is a potential by-product of that process (Stinchcomb, Bazemore, and Riestenberg 2006). Promoting accountability in the juvenile justice system involves increasing the likelihood of a consequence for the delinquent act, reducing delays between the offense and the sanction, and ensuring monitoring and enforcement of court orders (Griffin 1999a). With accountability, a youth should recognize the wrongfulness of the delinquency and must make appropriate amends for it. Patrick Griffin notes that these sanctions must be "swift, sure, coherent, and consistent" (1999a, 2). Adolescent development can be blended with each of those objectives because it is important to link the consequence to the offense in time, ensure that it is pretty certain to happen if it is to be a counterweight to potential rewards from delinquency, be clear in terms of its objectives so that the youth understands the reasoning, and apply it in a consistent way for the same offenses by any given youth.

Development of a moral identity is an interactive process, with each action and reaction between a youth and his parents, community, or the juvenile justice system having the potential to affect development. A decision to dismiss or divert a case—even for a first-time offender—is made on the assumption that a youth will think or behave differently in similar circumstances in the future. This decision might be made based on an expectation of either parental intervention or the belief that the youth will age out of the offense. A more proactive approach to sanctions for youths who have committed relatively nonserious delinquency builds on the notion that a moral identity develops in conjunction with one's environment (Markstrom-Adams 1992). Therefore this approach can not only make a statement about the wrongfulness of the action but also identify a tangible means of growing from that mistake.

Megan C. Kurlychek, Patricia M. Torbet, and Melanie Bozynski (1999) describe juvenile accountability and its emphasis on two key players in the juvenile justice system: judges and probation officers. These officials have the greatest capacity to ensure youth accountability. They also may play a frequently unacknowledged developmental role for youths. Sanctions should be applied swiftly and consistently and escalate with offense level or violation of court orders. High caseloads and increased juvenile court docket sizes present challenges to this approach, however. Thus, a greater focus on accountability requires system-wide transformation such that policies, practices, and personnel at multiple agencies internalize the philosophy.

A position statement on child discipline from the Canadian Paediatric Society begins with the premise that "discipline" is driven by the desire to "impart knowledge and skill—to teach"—but "is often equated with punishment and control" (Nieman, Shea, and Canadian Paediatric Society Community Paediatrics Committee 2004, 37). The sanctioning role in the juvenile justice system often serves a punishment and control function. However, it is clear that appropriate sanctions may also play a teaching and skill-building role that at least complements the treatment and intervention function. In this way, it redirects youths toward more prosocial outcomes. This is especially relevant since character development is part of an interactive process in which youths temporarily try on different roles and behaviors before character is solidified (McAdams 2009; Turiel 2006).

Juvenile Probation as a Developmental Sanction

Probation supervision is the most common response to juvenile delinquency and therefore must be part of any conversation on sanctions in juvenile justice (Griffin 1999a). This extends to the prospects of a more developmental juvenile justice system. The supervisory relationship presents a difficult line to walk for the probation officer in exercising control versus attempting to engage the youth in a way that fosters behavioral change (Schwalbe 2012). This can send mixed signals to youths in what probation means as a sanction or in facilitating alternative developmental trajectories. Given the extensive use of probation in the juvenile justice system, it is important to consider how it represents a consequence for youth delinquency—this is true both of the case disposition and the day-to-day process of being under probation supervision. The probation role is therefore central in any effort to make the juvenile justice system more developmental, and the signal that it presents to youths is important in fostering accountability and legal socialization.

The probation sanction places an added layer of supervision on a youth from prior transgressions. Thus, the main sanction a youth faces is in increased monitoring, and this is the control element of the juvenile probation process (Schwalbe 2012). Other elements—including skill building and risk reduction—are part of this process as well. The youth must also show progress in certain areas such as behaving better at home, improving school grades and attendance, reducing exposure to delinquent peers and risky situations, and curtailing drug and alcohol use. Consequently, this sanction aims to promote behavioral change through aspects of the supervision process (Walters et al. 2007).

Richmond, Virginia, for example, has a sanction system for its juvenile probationers that begins by defining the expectations, including attendance at all sessions, being honest in discussions with their probation officer, following rules and conditions, making progress on their probation plan, meeting expectations at home and school or work, and participating in programs to which they are referred. Supervisees then learn about three progressively more restrictive levels of possible sanction that accompany violations of those rules. They could receive an activity or curfew restriction at the first level of violation (minor), followed by increased supervision by the probation officer in frequency or its length of time (moderate), and finally, detention time or electronic monitoring (major) (Department of Criminal Justice Services 2000).[7]

This handling of technical violations offers a sense of how a developmental juvenile justice system might operate. First, clear communication of the violation to the youth is necessary such that she or he understands the previously defined rule that has been broken. This helps ensure an initial foundation of procedural justice. Next, the response should be proportionate to the offense and clearly an appropriate consequence of that misstep. If the youth progresses beyond that first violation, then the sanctions should gradually increase to reflect greater severity. Youths should, however, also be informed that the factors that grant leniency start to diminish as their behavior continues to violate the rules. This is especially true if they have been involved in programming designed to impart skills to mitigate risks that they may encounter. Some latitude is possible as they work on those skills, but transgressions cannot be continually ignored. Absent such programming it may be challenging to gain compliance from the youth—for perceptual reasons, because he or she has not amassed the skills to navigate risky situations, or because the other challenges in his or her environment overwhelm these still-developing skills. This process also should be mindful of the salience of rewards for adolescents—relative to risks—and attempt to foster buy-in through expansion of privileges or rewards for positive behavior.

A closer examination of the nature of probation supervision from a developmental standpoint identifies opportunities as well as potential pitfalls. First, probation supervision can serve as a developmental leverage point and potential source of support for redirecting the youth's trajectory. This does not require a sole focus on treatment or support but rather a firm but fair stance that recognizes a youth's need to grow in certain areas while also being cognizant of the strengths already possessed. Taking this further to identify implications for juvenile justice sanctions suggests two conclusions. First, probation supervision can be an effective sanction for delinquent youths in a developmental sense. Second, the youth–probation officer relationship requires greater consideration because of its implications for development. Full effectiveness likely requires reimagination to ensure that the probation officer serves as a developmental influence. The relationship must be appropriately calibrated to ensure that the response to negative *and* positive behavior on the part of the youth is appropriately recognized so that he or she can assimilate it into a developmental mind-set and also to consider how it can be leveraged to promote motivation for change (Schwalbe 2012). The size of the incentive-to-sanctions ratio is also relevant in the process of offender rehabilitation (e.g., Gendreau 1996; Long and Sullivan 2017; Senjo and Leip 2001), and monitoring plans for delinquent youths should reflect this factor because of the reward sensitivity of adolescents.

Urie Bronfenbrenner's (1977, 1979) ecological development model suggests that the relationship of a youth and his or her probation officer is dyadic and therefore shapes the youth's behavior and attitudes and affects how he or she interacts with other layers of the developmental context. At this point, there is relatively little direct information on how a probation officer might influence development, but research findings on effective supervision practices and the broader understanding of youth pathways can help generate some ideas. Principles from the literature on effective parental discipline should be a starting point in framing a developmental approach to juvenile probation.

Given its prevalence as a response to delinquency, the probation officer–youth relationship must reflect a developmental posture if the system is to move fully in that direction. While a youth can obtain appropriate treatment, it still occurs within the context of juvenile justice control, and therefore the central relationships between the youth and probation officer (and judges and other court personnel) must support treatment goals. At the same time, the process must proceed in a way that provides for developmentally effective legal socialization, identity formation, and skill building.

Graduated (and Encompassing) Sanctions

Graduated sanction schemes link responses to delinquency and violations of court or probation requirements to clear, progressive responses by the system. If applied correctly, these schemes can be an antidote to violations and may have broader implications for developmental juvenile justice. A graduated sanctions approach has the advantage of not involving a youth in the deeper end of the system if it is avoidable. It also links that process to behavior in a way that offers the youth some control over the outcomes and reflects a continuum of sanctions and care appropriate to youths' risks and needs. Barry Krisberg and colleagues (1995) consider graduated sanctions and treatment in the context of developmental principles but are open ended as to which ones. With less serious or first-time offenders, they suggest that predictable and immediate sanctions may be preferred to convey the consequences for such behavior and to provide early intervention. It is necessary to have some sanctions early in the process so there is some understanding of the consequences associated with that behavior (NRC 2013). Appropriate graduated sanctions offer alternatives that fit the individual and the offense, which in turn connect to initial treatment dispositions and monitoring of compliance and adjusting for change over time.

Graduated sanctions are developmental in at least three ways. First, at least as designed, sanctions can be reasonably age graded in the sense that youths who continue to be involved in the system will likely also penetrate it further over time. It may, therefore, run contrary to a growth or developmental model to resist a gradual enhancement in sanctions as youths encounter the juvenile justice system or violate conditions associated with the disposition of a previous case. The second developmental implication is that moral identity and character are still forming and are determined in part by the youth's assimilating the reaction of others to behavior. Third, clear conveyance of the graduated sanctions scheme, coupled with follow-through in supervision, may foster agency. Agency is an aspect of change in behavior and a general developmental scaffold. It suggests to the youth that she can control further system responses through her behavior and reaction to the court or supervision process.

Procedural Justice in Juvenile Court Contact and Sanctions

Youths face a great deal of show in the sanction process. Emerson (1969) describes youths receiving a suspended sentence to emphasize the possible outcome of their case or other scenarios in which judges made much of first suggesting the possibility of a harsh sanction like youth corrections before ultimately rolling that back to a community-based sanction. This has the potential to erode perceived legitimacy. At the lower end of seriousness, youths may get multiple strikes before the system responds with an official sanction. While some may be grateful for a break, such breaks can erode the authority with which youths view the court.

The perceived legitimacy of the system is especially important (see e.g., Fagan and Tyler 2005; Sampson and Bartusch 1998). Legal socialization is an important individual-social construction in youths' long-term stance toward social norms and the law (Piquero et al. 2005). Cynicism about the legal system and perceptions of its legitimacy affect behavior and response to justice institutions and, in turn, can affect behavioral pathways. Alex R. Piquero and colleagues (2005) found stability in a short snapshot in a juvenile offender sample but also significant variation in starting points. This suggests that orientation to the law and social norms develops over time but has begun at the time of juvenile justice contact. In that sense, the system is already disadvantaged in motivating youths and families to engage affirmatively in the process and therefore must be mindful of that possibility in processing youths and building skills.

For justice-involved youths, "following procedures that participants perceive to be fair helps to legitimize the entire process and increases the likelihood that participants will accept outcomes decided by those with decision-making authority" (Jackson and Fondacaro 1999, 102). Jeffrey Fagan and Tom R. Tyler (2005) also argue that youths' interactions with the law are important in their development and affect later moral identity and related attitudes and behaviors. They found that experiences with the law shaped youths' perceptions of legal actors and the rules underlying the legal system—even when controlling for individual personality and social context. In turn, legal socialization, measured by legal cynicism, perceived legitimacy of the system, and moral disengagement, was associated with self-reported delinquency.

Youths may perceive unfairness if the punishment that they receive for their transgression is too lenient or too harsh. The signal sent in requiring treatment may mean conflation of punishment and treatment in the youth's mind, which is problematic in attempting to build motivation for treatment. Specifically, Jesse Roest, Peer van der Helm, and Geert Stams (2016) argue that motivation is likely to be lower for youths who view treatment as compulsory, but the therapeutic alliance around the process can promote motivation for treatment and change. This linkage matters because it reflects how youths are processed in the court, supervised by probation officers, and treated by juvenile justice and affiliated agencies.

The central objective in procedural justice is to ensure that youths perceive that they are being treated fairly in the process—even if the result is undesirable. These ideas of accountability, identity development, and legal socialization parallel messages that emerge from research on youth internalization and development from parental discipline. Joan E. Grusec and Jacqueline J. Goodnow discuss the value of "pairing" the approach to parental discipline with the act committed by the child (1994, 8), which aligns with the process being coherent and reflecting the principles of authoritative parenting associated with positive developmental outcomes and reduced delinquency (Pettit, Bates, and Dodge 1997). Certainly, the accumulation of perceived unfairness across situations—especially when coupled with certain attitudinal factors—may have a significant developmental impact.

For the sanction system to be developmental, it will require coordination and must permeate juvenile courts and probation agencies because of the necessary suite of responses to the behavior of the youths before they encountered the juvenile justice system and to court orders and supervision once in the system. This goal of procedurally just interactions follows from the ecological-developmental stance laid out by Bronfenbrenner (see Jackson and Fondacaro 1999). The stage or timing of sanctions—and the clarity with which that happens—has implications for the signal sent to youths. Regardless of their label, there are scenarios in which treatment and sanctions of some type are introduced before or after adjudication. Some sanctions may also occur after disposition if a youth violates a condition of supervision. This has implications for procedural justice as well as whether sanctions affect development. The articulation of the purpose of sanctions can affect procedural justice and the accompanying legal socialization of youths. A youth detained before adjudication may not associate that with being found delinquent unless that previously served time is viewed as the result of that earlier action. Given their development status, youths may be particularly amenable to emphasis on approaches that build skills and values rather than harsher sanctions designed to deter (Tyler and Rankin 2012). Developmentally, the juvenile justice system must be mindful of the signals sent with sanctions to promote individuation and moral identity growth as well as skill building that will reduce the likelihood of recidivism and lead to other positive life outcomes.

Integrated Developmental Response to Delinquency

Given the variety and volume of delinquency cases that the juvenile justice system encounters, there may be an inclination to do relatively little if it is possible and seems prudent for a youth. This instinct is sound if one assumes that the system is mainly going to do harm—even unintended. This was the logic behind the idea of radical nonintervention (Schur 1973), but that idea is complicated when viewed from a developmental perspective. The cumulative nature of risk factors and developmental experiences of youths suggest that the system strategically intervene with most youths whom it encounters. This has implications for both treatment and sanctions because each can serve a developmental purpose. The expenditure of resources and time and the possibility of further contact cannot be ignored, but—at least from a developmental standpoint—some reaction is necessary in most cases encountered by the juvenile justice system. To have developmental effect, they must blend treatment and sanction.

The system loses a developmental opportunity if it artificially bifurcates the treatment aims of the juvenile court and the sanctioning function or if it is insufficiently thoughtful about the correspondence of the two. While it is more obvious with treatment goals, appropriate sanctions based on the offense and prior record of a youth can be developmentally beneficial. In such cases, youths learn that the behavior was inappropriate through sanction but also build constructive skills to prevent it from happening later. The benefits of being attentive to sanction are important in the context of the juvenile justice population described earlier—many of the more serious cases will have been subject to detrimental developmental influences that marked childhood and adolescence. Poor parental bonds and family management, which can manifest in inconsistent disciplinary practices, are frequent risk factors for juvenile justice involvement. Involvement with juvenile court offers an opportunity to engage in developmentally formative action if family is a risk factor for a youth. Of course, the youth benefits from the sanction only if it is fairly administered and appropriate to the case.

The widespread use of the word "accountability" when discussing sanction in juvenile justice is distinct in that it emphasizes future pathways more than deterrence or incapacitation. Accountability is desired in adults and is also responsive to the aims of the societal collective in that the individual can be counted on to consider the needs of others and acknowledge when he has made a mistake or fallen short. These relatively subtle shifts in the language around juvenile court objectives parallel developmental principles and research, opening up space to consider the role that sanctions play in that process.

Blending Treatment and Sanction

A more developmental juvenile justice system builds on effective or promising practices in the field. The need for clearer integration between treatment and sanctions is not novel, and that integration has been implemented in some circumstances previously. Developmental juvenile justice requires more thought about the factors driving delinquent behavior and the most appropriate reaction to that behavior. The developmental-situational interaction framework is instructive here because it leads to an understanding of current behavior and a projection of future behavior, which are central to deciding how to resolve a case. More agencies are moving toward treatment and sanction dispositional matrices to guide evidence-based decision making (Howell 2003), but they must be developmentally informed and linked to the delinquency career.

States and localities that use treatment and sanction grids frequently do so to develop appropriate dispositions for delinquent youths in a relatively systematic way. Washington State uses presumptive sentencing guidelines for juvenile offenders (Washington State Caseload Forecast Council 2017). These factor in the youth's age, seriousness of dispositional offense, and a criminal history score. The system largely provides a presumptive amount of time to be in custody for cases that reach higher levels on the grid and suggests local sanctions (community-based sanctions like probation) for cases with a combination of factors that fall lower on the grid. Adjustments for mitigating or aggravating factors are possible as well.

Florida's Department of Juvenile Justice developed a structured decision-making approach built on the offense type combined with risk and needs assessment information from their Positive Achievement Change Tool (Baglivio, Greenwald, and Russell 2015). This grid summarizes the youth's risk in a systematic way such that it can inform subsequent decisions. The department's grid suggests placement based on the seriousness of the offense and the risk level. Michael T. Baglivio, Mark A. Greenwald, and Mark Russell (2015) demonstrate that it performed well in predicting recidivism in a sample of roughly 38,000 juvenile offenders in the Florida Department of Juvenile Justice database.

The matrix illustrates that, with few exceptions, a sanction is necessary. Even Level 1 cases that are nonserious are eligible for civil citation, which is diversion with a community-service-based sanction (Sullivan et al. 2010). From there, the matrix is at least nominally integrative in that community supervision sanctions (Levels 3b and 3c) have some services attached, such as aggression replacement treatment or multisystemic therapy. Gina Vincent and Brian Lovins (2015) note that more integration of treatment services is necessary to promote change in delinquent youths and reduce long-term offending; determining where youth needs fit into the matrix and integrating service needs more prominently would also be valuable. Those factors drive some of the choices made with respect to which skills or CBT programs are required in any given case. The most appropriate developmental intervention also affects choices.

The assessment of criminogenic needs is beneficial, but a developmental juvenile justice system must break away from an exclusive or predominant focus on risk management. Gina M. Vincent, Laura S. Guy, and Thomas Grisso (2012) present a service referral matrix of youth risk and needs along multiple, developmentally relevant dimensions. It identifies a series of presenting conditions or risk factors (e.g., disruptive behaviors, family issues) as they cross low, moderate, and high levels of risk or need. So, for example, a moderate-risk youth who exhibits disruptive behavior would warrant a "community-based cognitive-behavioral skills intervention" (70), while a high-risk youth with disruptive behavior might require similar services but in an intensive community-based or residential setting. Functional family therapy and multidimensional-treatment foster care, respectively, fit youths at those risk and need levels who also have treatment needs in the family area. This matrix, then, focuses on treatment needs while being mindful of risks, but the Florida grid focuses more on sanction and placement decisions that take into account appropriate treatment.

Combining risk level and possible service types recognizes that treatment settings and intensity require adjustment depending on other aspects of a youth's case. Delinquency history may preclude community-based treatment in some cases, and therefore selection of developmentally appropriate treatments must consider presenting risks and needs in multiple settings. Individualization will always be necessary in this process, but having available an array of well-performing services across environments, given risk and needs levels and developmental stages, is a prerequisite for an effective system.

Figure 5.4 offers a more explicit integration of these ideas. It elaborates on key considerations for sanctioning, providing treatment, and supervising youths to optimize developmental leverage points. This approach helps in visualizing risk and needs information across multiple domains and can simultaneously provide a sense of case offense severity and criminal history. Each plotted score can guide treatment decisions when mapped to services and sanctions. In Figure 5.4 the juvenile justice history and current offense score is high at 8, so the youth would likely be placed in a community or state residential facility. His or her treatment would focus on delinquent thinking and attitudes (using training such as Thinking for a Change) with some concurrent emphasis on building developmental skills. Strengths or assets could also be overlaid on this plot to develop a more comprehensive assessment of

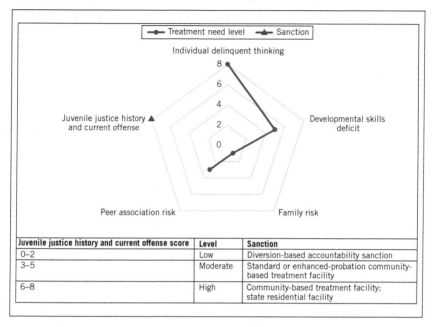

Juvenile justice history and current offense score	Level	Sanction
0–2	Low	Diversion-based accountability sanction
3–5	Moderate	Standard or enhanced-probation community-based treatment facility
6–8	High	Community-based treatment facility; state residential facility

Figure 5.4 Radar plot of integrated treatment needs and sanction assessment

the youth and identify ways of capitalizing on those in treatment and under supervision.

The objective of a developmental system is to work with particular youths and those around them to reduce their overall package of dynamic risks, promote skill development, and reduce the likelihood of later delinquent and criminal behavior. Treatment programs may overlap with the objectives of sanctions. Michael Baglivio and Katherine Jackowski (2013a) conducted an experimental study of a victim awareness program with 320 incarcerated juveniles in Florida. The idea was to promote empathy, which aids development of a moral identity, through a series of guided interactions about how victims are affected by different crimes. After roughly twenty-four hours of group sessions, the treatment group had greater awareness of their own feelings and better understood others' feelings relative to the control group. This suggests that the right type of restorative-justice programs may help develop moral identity and be a useful complement to other programming.

Figure 5.5 shows what a system with a greater developmental pathway focus would aspire to see. The dotted vertical lines are ages at which a youth encountered the juvenile justice system. This youth had three juvenile justice contacts, at around ages fourteen, fifteen, and sixteen. While his self-reported delinquency did increase initially, the highest risk area began to diminish after the most serious contact at sixteen, and skills began to improve gradually.

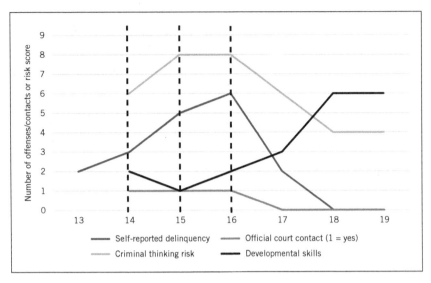

Figure 5.5 Visualizing risk and delinquency reduction and skill promotion goals in juvenile justice

The Central Role of the Probation Officer in Developmental Juvenile Justice

Probation supervision is a sanction in the juvenile court, but it is a significant part of a developmental approach as well. The probation officer integrates the sanction and treatment process, balances the two, and ensures that the youth understands the objectives of the package of responses from the court. The probation officer may be able to offer a clear sense of how elements of the disposition, including routine supervision and treatment, fit with developmental aims. In this dyad, every interaction between a youth and probation officer has the potential to affect the youth's performance while under supervision and later in development.

Many youth probationers distrust the system and perhaps have had low levels of adult support and monitoring in the past. Youths are likely to be sensitive to how the system identifies and responds to transgressions. Belief that responses are arbitrary may harm the interlocked supervision and treatment process at the core of the juvenile justice process. Probation and sanctions (treatment) should be appropriate to a youth's developmental status and environmental influences. For example, it is not enough for a probation officer to insist that a youth disassociate with certain friends. A developmental approach builds up skills for interacting with those friends while also alerting youths to opportunities to seek prosocial peers and settings (see Catalano and Hawkins 1996).

Maloney, Romig, and Armstrong (1988) identify two important objectives of the probation officer as developmental driver when they discussed the balance between accountability and competency development. Although the latter is more obviously aligned with a developmental approach to juvenile justice, both objectives have implications for fostering skills and developing a prosocial identity that will help in restructuring youths' pathways. Balanced probation starts by laying out the continuum of sanctions and the expectations for a youth under supervision. For the youth and probation officer, this is an opportunity to set realistic expectations about the skills necessary to take steps toward a more prosocial pathway and the conditions to satisfy to remain accountable to the contract. In setting expectations, graduated rewards and sanctions become linked to particular conditions and identify milestones for successful completion of the supervision term.

From a developmental standpoint, sanctions must accord with positive discipline to ensure success. Returning to the parallel between the juvenile justice system and the parental approach to discipline, the probation officer–youth relationship will affect the internalization and response to discipline in a given instance and across the supervision period (American Academy of Pediatrics 1998). Building rapport to foster social capital is an important aspect of the probation officer's role, and the probation officer is essential to the success of the probationer (Skeem and Manchak 2008).

Restructuring the relationship between probation officers and youths to take a more developmental approach requires a system in which a youth on probation receives appropriate treatment resources to mitigate risks, build skills, and develop a supportive, but fair, relationship with the probation officer. If insufficient attention is given to the agreement between the probation officer and the youth, however, much of the potential benefit from the relationship is lost. If the youth perceives an arbitrariness in sanctions or cannot get access to needed skill-building treatments, the youth will likely be tethered to the system for a longer time, and another transgression might lead to more substantial sanctions. If the probation officer can balance fostering accountability and supporting competency development, then the youth will have a stronger chance of assimilating those. Probation is just one aspect of juvenile justice, but given its high usage, it has an outsized impact on the system. Making probation supervision more developmental will bring together treatment and sanction aims, providing a foundation for other elements to work more effectively.

Juvenile Incarceration, Treatment, and Development

Secure placement in a state facility is the most severe sanction available to the juvenile justice system. It may take a lot of exposure to the system before a youth reaches a residential placement. Although a small part of the delinquency population, juveniles in residential placement are particularly relevant to questions of integrating sanction and treatment for development. The setting in those facilities may not promote positive development (Sedlak and McPherson 2010) and may interrupt key developmental milestones, which can have detrimental effects on later life outcomes (Mulvey and Schubert 2012; Uggen and Wakefield 2005). Juvenile justice policy and practice toward residential placement has implications for individual youths and their development as well as the efficiency and effectiveness of the system as a whole.

Given the underlying philosophy of youths as works in progress (see NRC 2013), great effort is typically taken to limit the use of secure residential placement, which is the most restrictive of the sanctions available to juvenile justice decision makers. Institutional placement and the length of stay show negligible effects on recidivism (Lin 2006; Loughran et al. 2009), which suggests at best marginal returns to public safety from the use of secure juvenile placement. Factoring in the potential for detrimental effects on development (see Mulvey and Schubert 2012; Scott and Steinberg 2008) and the certainty that these juveniles will eventually return to the community, the number of youths sent to residential facilities must be limited to only necessary cases.

Placement is an undesirable, but sometimes required, worst case, so what occurs in those facilities must be maximally productive in attenuating youths' risks for recidivism and promoting their ability to achieve prosocial developmental milestones upon release. From a developmental standpoint, placement should occur rarely and thoughtfully. Developmental outcomes should be considered while youths are in the facility, which can be challenging because of security concerns. There is some evidence that juvenile correctional officials recognize the need to make treatment and redirection strong priorities in the facilities. Tory Caeti and colleagues (2003) surveyed juvenile correctional administrators and found consensus on pertinent questions about priorities and attitudes toward the types of goals that inevitably are part of a developmental juvenile justice system. The results suggest that they see the juvenile correctional system as setting the stage for redirecting youths once they leave custody.

Treatment can be effective in juvenile residential placement settings as well. Mark W. Lipsey (1999) found that factors such as intervention type, service provider, and implementation quality had impacts on recidivism among institution-based treatments. He used this evidence to argue that even relatively serious young offenders are treatable under the right circumstances. A review by Doris MacKenzie and Rachel Freeland (2012) of facility climate and the nature of treatment as potential moderators of the generally negative effects of institutional placement has similar findings to Lipsey's (1999) but also suggests that the broader treatment context matters.

These studies show that it is possible to both treat and sanction youths effectively across the entire spectrum of cases processed by the juvenile justice system. Still, facilities and the system should mitigate potential negatives, like stigma and developmental obstacles associated with secure confinement. These youths must transition back into the community and at the same time transition into later stages of adolescence or early adulthood. Positive reentry into the community is promoted through appropriate supervision and services and attention to the developmental transition that coincides with that process. Some findings suggest that fairly administered sanctions can satisfy that aspect of the juvenile court's mission while also promoting accountability and prosocial identity development.

Principles of Integrated Developmental Dispositions

An integrated, developmentally informed system of treatment and sanctions follows a few key principles. First, intervention must be comprehensive and based on a youth's risks, needs, and strengths. It should also account for the most salient risks and needs that generate delinquency (and risks and needs interaction). For instance, a youth with disruptive behavior across situations may require a strong focus on individual needs. On the other hand, if delinquency is predominately a product of the peer environment or substance use, a different course of action may be required.

Second, sanctions should impose a penalty for the behavior but should not be so onerous that they are a detriment to a youth's opportunities to develop in a prosocial fashion. A developmental juvenile justice system recognizes opportunities to help a youth change course but also is aware that juvenile justice contact can be a causal variable in later behavioral problems and life-course outcomes. Thus, there should be some well-communicated and appropriate sanction for delinquent behavior that also allows space for fostering skills in treatment and provides programming to help a youth develop tools to avoid future such behavior. Additionally, the demarcation between sanction and treatment must be clear to the youth and signal the purpose of each (see Ward 2010) so that motivation for treatment is not compromised (Parhar et al. 2008). In other words, treatment should not be the only vehicle for imparting a sense of responsibility to the youth (Maloney, Romig, and Armstrong 1988). That may send a mixed message and hinder youth development.

Third, a clear promotive approach focused on the youth's growth must ensure that developmental objectives are considered. Like the assessment tools described previously, which can open up a discussion of how to view youth processing, placement, and treatment more developmentally, sanction and treatment grids are potentially valuable not only for how they diminish the likelihood of recidivism but also on their contributions to developmental outcomes. If a youth has a skill deficit that impedes ability to achieve developmental milestones (e.g., anger management), then that must be part of the treatment plan. How the desired skill aids the youth's later development should be clearly conveyed to the youth and his or her developmental supports. The skill must be continually measured to identify points of progress and potential reversion.

Fourth, case processing and supervision require a developmental view. Details about the timing of aspects of the juvenile justice process, disposition, and sanctions matter developmentally. Communication must be reasonably consistent across different aspects of the process so that youths understand the opportunity for growth and development—in addition to the need for taking responsibility. In part accountability is about legal socialization and procedural justice but potentially goes deeper into the youth's individual development. Barry C. Feld (1990) calls attention to bureaucratic routines in case processing and decision making and argues that a more developmental juvenile justice system inevitably requires changes to those routines. This developmental stance must permeate court hearings, treatment contacts, and interactions among juvenile justice personnel and youths and families.

Fifth, positive youth development and agency building must be part of the developmental treatment of justice-involved youths. Many youths face risks in their day-to-day lives and can consequently adopt a fatalistic stance on the future that can promote moral disinhibition. The supervision and treatment process should foster a sense that although some or even most risk factors are out of their control, these factors can be mitigated. Treatment will target risks and diminish them, but ideally youths should also develop general skills and self-efficacy as they emerge from juvenile-justice-related programming. The skills and self-efficacy will help them identify and pursue appropriate prosocial opportunities. If part of the developmental process involves taking responsibility, it is essential that the system help youths develop the necessary tools to make positive decisions. Agency and self-efficacy are abstract ideas, but it is clear that some elements of cognition, outlook, and ownership come into play when individuals change their behavior. This is true whether looking at the research on developmental pathways (Giordano, Cernkovich, and Rudolph 2002; Maruna 2001) or treatment research (e.g., Landenberger and Lipsey 2005).

Embedding Youth Development in Juvenile Justice Practice

Early twenty-first-century juvenile justice has seen momentum in a push toward a developmentally informed response to juvenile delinquency that relies heavily on distinctions between youths and adults, which has manifested in important case law regarding punishment of juveniles for serious violent offenses and legislative shifts in juvenile and adult court jurisdiction. The by-product of these efforts is a renewed emphasis on redirecting youth pathways, which was a core objective of the early juvenile court. A great deal of work has been done to identify effective intervention practices in juvenile justice, but less emphasis has been placed on applying that research to important developmental principles and outcomes. For this philosophy to fully affect the practices of the juvenile justice system, it must inform the system's dual mission of treatment and sanctions for delinquent youths. Developmental research offers insight for both.

Developmental considerations factor into aspects of the system's current operations, but revisiting those operations and considerations will identify further services and sanctions. For example, developmental considerations might suggest more intensive services for a younger youth who is "low risk" (e.g., limited prior record) but has other needs requiring more attention. Such a youth could fall between the prevention and juvenile justice pieces of the comprehensive strategy outlined by James C. Howell (2003). A developmental approach may require more intervention with low-risk-high-need cases—in terms of both sanctions and services. However, placing young, low-risk-high-need youths in a skills-based treatment program with other youths who are more serious offenders is contrary to the objective of reducing risk of later recidivism (Dodge, Dishion, and Lansford 2007). Instead, those youths should receive treatment in community-based settings (e.g., school, home), and structured activities should be preferred (Greenwood 2007).

Developmental juvenile justice interventions overlap with general principles of intervention with youths but also sensitize the system to delinquency cases that veer from the typical and require commensurate responses. Sanctions can be a useful developmental influence. The identity established in adolescence and early adulthood builds from the interaction between the individual and the responses of the social environment. The formal effect of the juvenile justice system and informal social controls, on the other hand, play a part in how youths build this identity. This reflects the legal socialization and skill-development objectives of the juvenile court.

The developmental approach to juvenile justice certainly does not consider adolescents to be too similar to adults, but it also does not infantilize youths in a way that sends the wrong signal about responses to delinquency. Part of the challenge of implementing new programming and broader reform in the juvenile justice system is working in a way that brings along various stakeholders who tend to have different orientations toward a specific program or broader intent for the changes sought. It is important to remember that, while research clearly shows that the public values appropriate treatment for juveniles, those studies also show the public's belief in accountability.

Youths may appreciate the harm resulting from the delinquent acts that they commit, but they respond better to behavioral rewards than to negative reinforcement incurred for problem behavior (Steinbcrg 2014). The response to delinquent behavior must balance the identification of the wrongful act and imposition of a reasonable sanction that reinforces disapproval with the creation of contingencies based on positive outcomes that correct future behavior. Thus, the juvenile justice system is not only treating delinquency but also altering the choice structure for future behavior. Counteracting the immediate rewards associated with delinquent behavior is important because those rewards are likely to be more tempting to youths. Youths' developmental origins and interaction with the adolescent social environment make immediate rewards attractive. The system and related programs should therefore identify meaningful tangible and intangible rewards as replacements.

Integrating developmental research into the juvenile justice system requires acknowledgment and understanding of the potential direct and indirect impacts of system contact and its response on youth behavior and development. In certain situations, like those in which serious, violent, or chronic delinquent youths have interdependent risk factors, a significant sanction is necessary but also must be mindful that it and other responses should help the youth move to a different pathway. Discipline and sanction are an express part of the broader research on development. Decisions regarding sanctions require consideration in a general developmental sense of the signal that youths receive from sanctions in light of their individual profile and the nature of their delinquency. There are certainly tensions between punishment and treatment in a developmental framework, but that is compatible with the system established in 1899.

The juvenile justice system's dual mission and existing day-to-day tasks point to a challenging agenda underlying the call to become more developmentally focused. While some evidence already supports and informs this process, the accumulation of more research findings is a necessary, but not sufficient, condition for effecting changes. As research on youth development and effective practice in juvenile justice has accumulated, another set of researchers and practitioners has simultaneously identified important obstacles to real-world implementation and developed useful strategies for overcoming them. Chapter 6 considers how to use those strategies to move to a more developmental juvenile justice system. It looks at the challenges that have come up in the discussion of treatment and sanctions in this chapter, attempting to identify guideposts for implementation of a developmental approach to juvenile justice.

6

Implementation Science and
Juvenile Justice Reform

Chapter 5 lays out an evidence base and ideas for treatment and sanction schemes in developmental juvenile justice, offering an idealized view of what has been effective in some juvenile justice systems and what could be effective on the basis of developmental and life-course research and principles. Programs must be introduced in a way that fits the current landscape of juvenile justice and also address the sheer amount of variability confronted by juvenile justice agencies; heed the procedures that they use in processing, sanctioning, and treating youths; and be aware of the context in which they perform those operations. Numerous ideas for developmental juvenile justice work in principle but may be difficult to implement fully in practice, and so it is essential to explicitly enumerate and analyze the factors that will affect implementation.

Any recommendations for more developmental juvenile justice could profoundly affect decision making from intake to reentry, dispositional decisions about treatment referral and sanctions, treatment strategy, and youths' interaction with system personnel. In short, the proposed changes would affect the organizations implementing them, personnel inside those organizations, youths who encounter the system, and other community stakeholders. The recommended changes are also multilayered in the sense that they require changes to policy as well as case-level decision making and individual treatment and sanctions. For instance, a more developmental system would have to enhance its assessment process to more fully capture the complexities and pathways underlying youth delinquency. A research base on program effectiveness is only one part of implementing effective programs and, surprisingly, given the challenges in reaching that point, adding to it may be the easier part (Fixsen et al. 2009; Fixsen et al. 2013; Laub 2016). Greg Berman and Aubrey Fox (2010) compare the failure of evidence-based reforms in justice settings to the likelihood of success for new start-up businesses, in which relatively few initiatives are unqualified successes. To avoid programs that plateau following initiation, program implementation must be considered carefully in assessing possible future pathways for the juvenile justice system.

Given how much the juvenile justice system depends on networked partners and treatment providers (Howell et al. 2003), the system arguably has even more layers and constituencies that vary in their views, objectives, and constraints than other implementation settings. This leads to a diffuse implementation environment because most states have numerous courts, which serve multiple constituencies, and frequently rely on private agencies as collaborators and referral destinations for youths. The implementation process therefore is difficult to traverse, with a "litany of impediments" (Klein 1979, 186). Researchers and practitioners can analyze the reform process to understand its key characteristics (Miller, Ohlin, and Coates 1977), and there is a growing body of research on implementation from which to draw to determine the feasibility of change and enhance the chances of success.

This chapter takes stock of the juvenile justice system from the standpoint of readiness for change and offers ideas about how to implement the suggestions discussed to this point. The first section reflects on the context of contemporary juvenile justice and what it means for implementing developmental policy and practice. This facilitates a transition to a discussion in the second section of implementation science before focusing specifically on the juvenile justice system. The third section then evaluates aspects of the juvenile justice system's readiness for the introduction and use of evidence-based policy and programs. The fourth section offers a conclusion, making the point that development of an evidence base is a necessary step but so too is paying careful attention to implementation—especially in the unique context of the juvenile justice system.

The Juvenile Justice Implementation Landscape

The two-pronged mission of the juvenile court—of justice and community safety objectives and of treatment—has produced some volatility in policy and practice as preferences change, significant cases spur new policy and law, and adjustments are made toward more or less restrictive policy and practice (Bernard and Kurlychek 2010). The shifting preferences that underlie these trends mean that agreement with existing and proposed policies and practices among the different constituencies that have a stake in the court's mission will vary. Elizabeth S. Scott and Laurence D. Steinberg (2008) and the National Research Council (NRC 2013) argue that the political and social landscape early in the twenty-first century is open to juvenile justice reform, with some clear examples coming in legislative action, court decisions, and introduction of developmentally responsive programming and sanctions. Still, the current climate and enduring characteristics of the juvenile justice system also make a more developmental approach somewhat difficult. Unanticipated consequences are also possible, which some have argued was the case with the due process decisions made by the U.S. Supreme Court in the 1960s that may have indirectly led to use of more adult like sanctions for juvenile delinquency decades later (Feld 2003).

Mechanisms of Change in Juvenile Justice

Enumerating the mechanisms by which change happens is useful for understanding the prospects for implementation. These paths to system and agency change inherently set the broader context for the introduction, support, and development of new juvenile justice initiatives. They also speak to the historical and legal or policy context for implementing innovative programs and practices (Green 2001) and whether organizations can identify opportunities in potentially challenging situations (Greenwood 2014). Legislative and judicial mandate lies at one end of the spectrum, but the many softer directives for change have different meanings for implementation.

The history of the juvenile court has seen catalysts for change that range from rapid and radical to methodical and mundane. Figure 6.1 lists categories of catalysts, each followed by general and specific examples of being put into practice. The processes that lead to change are distinct but not mutually exclusive. Friend of the court briefs and arguments from litigants often draw on expert testimony or research that would fall in the advocate-and-implement category in instances outside the courtroom. Expert testimony or research can also enter the legislative process, in which lobbying, or advocacy, is quite common. In some cases lobbying and expert testimony may, in fact, be better ways to move research evidence into practice because they shape the content and process of change as opposed to merely identifying the need for it. An example is the inclusion of language pertaining to elements of the Comprehensive Strategy on Serious, Violent, and Chronic Juvenile Offenders (e.g., risk and needs assessment) in legislation that facilitated that strategy's implementation in North Carolina (Howell 2003; see also Greenwood 2014).

The paths to change have distinct origins and motivations for reform, which influence implementing the changes under consideration. Moving from top to bottom of the figure, catalysts for change vary in the degree to

---

Legislatively mandate

- A new law mandates a change to juvenile justice practice
- Efforts in New York and North Carolina to raise the age of adult court jurisdiction to eighteen years old

Judicially mandate

- A legal decision alters the range of procedures and decisions available to the system
- Warren Court decisions beginning in the 1960s extended procedural rights to juvenile offenders
- U.S. Supreme Court decisions forbid the use of the death penalty and limited mandatory life sentences for crimes committed as juveniles

Litigate and monitor

- An individual or class-action lawsuit leads to a settlement or consent decree mandating specific reform
- *S.H. v. Stickrath* settlement in Ohio led to reforms in juvenile incarceration; U.S. Department of Justice settlement agreement with Memphis and Shelby County, TN, reduced racial disparities in decision making

Administratively direct

- Those in oversight roles pursue a change to agency policy or practice
- Implementation of uniform risk and needs assessment practices across a state, like the Ohio Youth Assessment System

Financially motivate

- Agencies or individuals in the position to distribute grant or contract funding encourage recipients to adopt new policies or practices
- Assessment and response to disproportionate minority contact in federal Juvenile Justice and Delinquency Prevention Act; justice reinvestment initiatives, which encourage local agencies to develop and use alternatives to referral to state residential facilities

Advocate and implement

- Local officials and stakeholders within the system decide to adopt an alternative approach based on their objectives and evidence of efficacy or effectiveness
- Kansans United for Youth Justice pushes for state legislation to make changes such as limiting youth incarceration, reinvesting in community-based alternatives, and limiting case processing and probation supervision times; other states, like Pennsylvania, have moved toward evidence-based practices via the input of policy advisory boards

---

Figure 6.1 A typology of processes for shift in juvenile justice policy and practice

which the source for change is imposed from outside or comes from grassroots initiatives involving local agency stakeholders and implementation settings. Legislative and judicial mandates leave little room for maneuver by the juvenile justice system. Legislative shifts in the boundaries of juvenile status and adulthood require that courts change how they make decisions, which leave courts with little control. Similarly, U.S. Supreme Court decisions have restricted dispositional options for youths in criminal courts, which in effect imposed changes on local systems and personnel. But agencies have some choice in how to respond to those decisions. For instance, raise-the-age laws in New York and North Carolina limit the number of offenses eligible for adult court transfer (Blythe 2017; McKinley 2017), but prosecutors have discretion in how they apply the laws.

Other mechanisms for change in policy and practice proceed differently in the balance of mandate versus local discretion in adopting and implementing new approaches. The consent decree model, for example, lies somewhere between the two poles. In such cases, litigation or an investigation generates a monitored settlement with a clear expectation for change, but the relevant parties can negotiate the exact route by which it occurs before monitoring. The now-concluded settlement agreement in *S.H. v. Stickrath* in Ohio is a good example (Owen and Larson 2017). The agreement stipulated how to handle juvenile cases, but involved agencies had a voice in how the goals would be met. In this instance the stick was perhaps more prominent than the carrot in instigating and implementing changes, but local agencies could contribute to the agreement's provisions.

In other cases, a tangible incentive to change practice is what drives the process. States and federal funders may provide financial incentives and technical assistance that encourage adopters to alter their policies and practices. Several U.S. states have implemented such approaches in an attempt to shift youths from custodial dispositions to less costly, evidence-based community alternatives (Butts and Evans 2011). This is quite distinct from a fully mandated approach to change but is still directed or motivated from outside the local agency.

These approaches contrast with catalysts for change generated by attempts to align policy and practice with evidence about effectiveness and, sometimes, cost-effectiveness. This requires activism and promotion of system change without the leverage that comes from a mandate or immediate incentive. Without that leverage, moving research into practice is more challenging because the cost to benefit of altering policy and practice versus maintaining the status quo is weighed differently than in the other scenarios (Green 2001). This approach is likely to work best in combination with some of the other catalysts because they can provide some cover and incentives for adopting alternatives. Peter W. Greenwood (2014) describes some U.S. states, such as Pennsylvania, that have gradually moved toward more evidence-based practices without any precipitating event or agreed-on problem (e.g., significant overuse of state residential facilities for youth placement). The means by which change emerges in a broader sense has implications for its implementation in juvenile justice settings that affect youth.

Current Sociopolitical Climate

The juvenile justice system today seems receptive to change. Scott and Steinberg (2008) and the National Research Council (NRC 2013) identify a receptive sociopolitical landscape in their suggestions for reforming the juvenile justice system. At the same time, discussion about the system is often relatively polarized, pitting rehabilitation against punishment (Bishop 2006; Mears 2002). The system is subject to critique for failure on both fronts. Nancy E. Dowd states:

> Our goal for all youth should be support, opportunity, and success. . . . Yet we have a juvenile justice system that in large part is a

failure. It disserves youth, increases criminal conduct and threats to public safety, functions in a racially and ethnically biased way, and harms the youth that come within its doors. . . . The existing system does not serve society, and it does not serve the youth who come into contact with the system. (2015, 2–3)

Contrast this perspective with that of police officers in a focus group conducted in conjunction with the Ohio Disproportionate Minority Contact Assessment study described in previous chapters. Officers from a small agency serving about fifty thousand residents mentioned the need for juvenile justice reform but believed that reinforcing consequences for the criminal actions of youths was the primary objective. In their view, leniency within the juvenile justice system led to escalation in the prevalence and seriousness of youth offending, and its reform would come from enhanced penalties. In particular, they saw as important updating and expanding their local juvenile detention center, suggesting that if there was a place to send the more serious youth offenders, sentencing would not be so lenient within their jurisdiction. A real threat of punishment, rather than just a slap on the wrist, would reduce their frequent contacts with juveniles. The dissatisfaction expressed by Dowd differs in intent and emphasis from the concerns of these officers, but both ultimately suggest that the juvenile justice system is failing and reform is necessary.

This contrast reflects the complex political landscape around juvenile delinquency despite receptivity to change. For example, raising the age of juvenile court jurisdiction receives wide but not unconditional support. Twenty-first-century legislative changes at the state level roll back policies from the 1970s to 1990s (Eckholm 2016) but do not fully turn back the clock. New York State's effort to raise the age for adult jurisdiction to eighteen for most cases met with questions about whether the new law did enough to reverse the provisions of earlier laws that were among the strictest in the nation (McKinley 2017). Similarly, after many years of research and debate, North Carolina passed a raise-the-age bill that had provisions for violent offenses and felonies to remain in adult court jurisdiction (Blythe 2017). These successful efforts suggest that there is a new openness to change with respect to handling juvenile offenders, but the efforts do not necessarily completely align with developmental views. In both New York and North Carolina, for instance, some legislators changed their mind only when convinced of cost savings or when provisions were added to ensure that some cases would continue to be processed in adult court. Total immersion in a developmental approach is unlikely unless it fits in a framework that considers the best interests of youths from a developmental standpoint and is mindful of sanctioning and public safety. It also must be considerate of the day-to-day practices of juvenile justice because this is where many of those broad policies will play out and affect youths.

Initial Conditions and Readiness for Change

Even with strong support, agencies will not find it easy to implement programs and sanction practices that simultaneously promote community safety and positive youth development. While implementation of evidence-based practices in juvenile justice is growing, such programming is still not the norm for many youths (Greenwood 2014). In addition, a period with less receptivity to change may be just around the corner and enthusiasm for these reforms is not universal—inside or outside the system. Articulation of a strategy and evidence of positive effects is necessary to maintain enthusiastic champions and garner resources for evidence-based policies and programs (Howell and Higgins 1990; Savaya, Spiro, and Elran-Barak 2008).

The catalyst for change often sets the tone for implementation because it establishes the costs and benefits and the supports and resources of the process. Thomas E. Backer summarizes the chief obstacles in implementing change in policy and practice, even in cases in which incentives or mandates are involved:

> Many of the challenges of innovation and change reflect complicated human dynamics. People need to feel rewarded for changing and to be involved in planning for changes that will affect them. They need to work through their fears, resistances, and anxieties about change. When ignored, this human dimension often causes technology transfer efforts to fail or to have a reduced impact because successful technology transfer requires individuals and organizations to change. . . . *Readiness for change* is one of these challenges—one often neglected in planning and implementing technology transfer. (1995, 21; emphasis in original)

Given this, fostering "readiness for change" is essential to the prospects and potential problems in altering course in any system, much less one with the dual missions and complex, interdependent parts of the juvenile justice system (Butts and Evans 2011).

Joseph A. Durlak and Emily P. DuPre's (2008) comprehensive review of implementation research, which includes individual studies and meta-analyses, found that well-thought-out and evidence-based implementation strategies had more chance of success. They reviewed 542 interventions and often found flawed implementation on the basis of their indicators (e.g., program reach, adaptation). Most studies showed that about 60 percent followed the implementation plan. Few were above 80 percent in fidelity to implementation planning, but the effect sizes for well-implemented programs were two to three times greater than for those that were not.

They identified a few especially important contributors to this success. First, capacity for implementation, which includes funding and policy infrastructure, makes a difference at a broad level. Second, at the front line, the skills and beliefs of those implementing the intervention are essential for success. Duncan C. Meyers, Joseph A. Durlak, and Abraham Wandersman (2012) designate these as support (capacity) and delivery (skills and beliefs) systems, which involve organizations and individuals working together cooperatively. These mediators of implementation success and sustainability result from other factors, such as whether the implementation shared decision making and collaborative processes that fostered local ownership for the new practice (Durlak and DuPre 2008). Together, these various orientation points set a foundation for looking at implementation of the types of policies and practices advocated in calls for a more developmental juvenile justice system.

The prospects for implementing change are, of course, localized, but this does not preclude a review of some general aspects of juvenile justice to better understand potential implementation. Implementation is transactional and cumulative in the sense that the context and climate of the organization undergoing the shift will influence individuals' perceptions of change, and their overall readiness follows from their level of buy-in (Backer 1995). Individual capacity for implementation is a by-product of skills, experience, and motivation (Wandersman et al. 2008), but it is embedded in an interactive, organizational context. An interdependent, ecological framework, therefore, is useful for disaggregating the implementation process (Aarons, Hurlburt, and Horwitz 2011; Chinman et al. 2005; Durlak and DuPre 2008; Greenhalgh et al. 2004; Wandersman 2003) and corresponds well with the complex, interactive aspects of the juvenile justice system and its responses to delinquent youths.

Implementation Context

Implementation context refers to the environmental influences or infrastructure features that directly or indirectly affect adherence to practices prescribed by the new policy or procedure. Environment can affect other dimensions of implementation like choices about target populations and fidelity to evidence-based practice. Organizational and community or political support can help or hinder implementing evidence-based programs if, for instance, key decision-making personnel do not believe it appropriate or safe to divert certain youths from secure detention or placement to the community. A lack of readiness in the agencies involved and infrastructure may affect implementation of new programs, so this assessment must occur before implementation begins (Edwards et al. 2000; Fagan et al. 2008; Feinberg, Greenberg, and Osgood 2004).

Gregory A. Aarons, Michael Hurlburt, and Sarah M. Horwitz (2011) argue that public program implementation involves exploration, adoption decision and preparation, active implementation, and sustainment, but these processes result from a multilayered implementation context that covers both inner and outer influences. The inner dimension of implementation consists of organizational characteristics close to the intervention itself, while the outer context consists of sociopolitical and financial supports. Examples of outer context are state-level funding, oversight on policy directives, or technical assistance relationships with program developers.

In justice reinvestment, for example, states shift resources to local settings as an alternative to more costly state-level placements. When federal resources and technical assistance are necessary, formally leading implementation from the federal level is made difficult by the tremendous variation within and across states, even with support and strong planning from states. Implementation can be difficult at the state level as well. For example, Ohio has eighty-eight counties and a home-rule system that allows the counties to consider and respond to their specific needs as they see fit (Cianca 1993). Greenwood (2014) argues that implementation diffused across local agencies has hindered the adoption of evidence-based practices in California. In contrast, Maine has state-level directives supporting implementation.

Charles Frazier and Donna Bishop (1990) discuss these challenges in the context of the mandates from the Juvenile Justice and Delinquency Prevention Act of 1974, which required changes in youth detention practices. They concluded that even agency reform imposed by legal mandates faces implementation challenges. These aspects of the implementation context can also affect the infrastructure and resources for change (Aarons, Hurlburt, and Horwitz 2011; Fixsen et al. 2013). In justice settings, implementation invariably requires support from public officials and government agencies (Berman and Fox 2010). Aarons, Hurlburt, and Horwitz (2011) identify multiple aspects of the context for implementation pertinent to the juvenile justice implementation landscape. Figure 6.2 summarizes these elements and their linkages to the juvenile justice system. The outer context encompasses three interrelated aspects of implementation. First, in the juvenile justice system, the case processing and service environment is a key piece of the process. It reflects the sociopolitical will for the prospective changes and the resources for them. Deficits in financial support for developmentally informed programming for youths will inevitably affect implementation. Interorganizational networks and advocacy and support for proposed changes are the other two aspects of implementation.

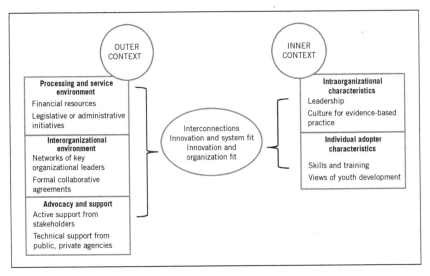

Figure 6.2 Conceptual implementation model in juvenile justice
Source: Adapted from Aarons, Hurlburt, and Horwitz 2011.

Network Context for Juvenile Justice Innovation Implementation. Perhaps no aspect of implementation in juvenile justice is as essential as interorganizational networks. As Aarons, Hurlburt, and Horwitz (2011) assert, agencies affiliated with the focal organization (the juvenile court) can facilitate or impede adoption of evidence-based practices. Subparts of agencies and larger organizations typically must work together to implement new programs in juvenile justice systems. Contract agencies can often deliver appropriate specialized services to youths more efficiently and effectively, but this common practice adds another layer of variability in implementation and makes the direct experiences of youths with the system from the standpoint of developmental effects contingent on other agencies and stakeholders.

The juvenile justice system's reliance on outside providers to deliver services on a per-case basis is evident in data from the Census of Juveniles in Residential Facilities, which shows that of the 48,043 youths held in custody in the United States in 2015, about 15,000 (32.3 percent) were held in private facilities. This is a slight increase from 1997 when 28 percent of the 105,055 youths were in private facilities (Sickmund, Sladky, and Kang 2017). This service rate is even greater in community-based services, which make up a great deal of juvenile justice agency spending. Sarah Armstrong (2002) reported that six private nonprofits received $23 million in contracts from the Massachusetts Department of Youth Services during one year in the late 1990s.

Comprehensive reform is therefore difficult because both lead agencies and their affiliates must buy into new ways of doing things, despite distinct organizational cultures, resource differentials, and the pull of current practice. Given this, the collaborative capacity of the juvenile court and its network is essential to implementation (Chinman et al. 2005; Foster-Fishman et al. 2001) because the process may require reshaping relationships and expectations of partner agencies and building new connections with others. These changes are somewhat unavoidable in light of the specialized practice and skills necessary for some interventions, but this identifies a consequential barrier to seamless implementation. This barrier may emerge despite contractual oversight and the ability to refer youths (or not) to those programs because whether those options are exercised may be affected by other available referral options. Networks may also be influenced by the market for service providers (Auger 1999) in a jurisdiction, which can be thin in the specialized context of youth treatment (Hubel et al. 2013). Consequently, the ability to identify appropriate agencies and ensure adherence to best practices may be curtailed and hard to subject to ongoing quality control. Furthermore, the process of moving to contract systems for services sometimes hollows out such oversight capacity (Greenwood 2014; Van Slyke 2003).

Entrenched networks around the juvenile justice system are a double-edged sword because the infrastructure that supports implementation may require enhancements (Hubel et al. 2013)—especially in moving to more developmental juvenile justice. While these legacy networks and existing relationships may promote collaboration, changes in course will be harder to implement given agencies' existing strengths and weaknesses. Current practices may have powerful supporters that bend toward the status quo (Greenwood 2014). New providers may have trouble getting a foothold in the process (Van Slyke 2003), but sufficient market competition is often necessary to realize the gains from privatization of services and can also constrain or open up the potential adaptability of those agencies (Hubel et al. 2013).

Inner Context for Juvenile Justice Innovation Implementation. The climate and support for change in a juvenile justice agency affects how successful it will be in introducing change. If it struggles in balancing treatment and sanction objectives, it will be difficult for those working in the agency and its stakeholders to identify where and how a more developmental approach fits with existing practices and even more challenging to operationalize relevant practices. On the other hand, juvenile justice agencies may be strong in their routine practices but struggle with new initiatives that require institutional support for monitoring and feedback. Those within the organization may believe that existing practices work well and therefore see no need to change them. This is especially troublesome in scenarios in which there is no strong tangible mandate or incentive to change at a local level. Even when such mandates or incentives are part of the implementation context, it will be challenging to introduce new policy and practice without the existence of other preconditions for a sustainable implementation environment (Bowen and Zwi 2005).

The culture and climate of an agency implicitly or explicitly proscribes certain responses to individual cases and to general initiatives that are undertaken because of internal or external pressures (Cooke and Rousseau 1988). In turn, individuals and agencies are more or less suited to absorbing the new policy or practice and sustaining it (Cohen and Levinthal 1990; Klein and Knight 2005). The success of the innovation depends on belief that the new direction being taken fits with the objectives and tasks of an agency (Aarons, Hurlburt, and Horwitz et al. 2011; Bowen and Zwi 2005). Demonstrating a need for the change also facilitates adoption (Greenhalgh et al. 2004).

This connection between organizational culture and norms and the desired change is an important bridge for implementing evidence-based practices (Caccia-Bava, Guimaraes, and Harrington 2006). An orientation toward organizational and individual growth and learning is necessary to build flexibility and tolerance for error during transitional periods (Klein and Knight 2005; Meyers, Durlak, and Wandersman 2012). Such an orientation ensures that the new practice is an ongoing part of organizational culture as opposed to a single implementation step (Green 2001).

People in the Implementation Process

A supportive organizational culture for implementation is likely to increase quality assurance and adherence to the protocol of an innovative program or practice (Greenhalgh et al. 2004). Still, implementation is likely to fail without appropriate buy-in and know-how from the personnel in the inner context. The juvenile justice system has components that set this inner context for implementation, but the importance of people as the delivery system for change cannot be overemphasized. Implementation across multiple levels and agencies in juvenile justice allows inputs into the process that generate opportunities to extend the reach of the desired change, but the diffusion also adds opportunities for deviation in introduction, execution, and sustenance of new approaches. Differences between line personnel and managers seeking to implement changes may cause deviations as might line staff who have their own orientation to the new approach. The variety of constituencies, particularly among those who will actually deliver the new policy and practice and the variety within and between those groups pose implementation challenges. For example, some juvenile justice agencies likely have greater capacity for discussion about issues of race based in part on their personnel composition, organizational history, and current initiatives. In turn, initiatives related to disproportionate minority contact depend on organizational context, such as receptivity to dialogue (Sullivan, Latessa, et al. 2016).

Aarons, Hurlburt, and Horwitz discuss the importance of what they call "individual adopter characteristics" (2011, 9). In juvenile justice, the personnel involved in an implementation process may have different backgrounds, goals, and perceptions of not only their role in the agency but also the need for change. They also likely vary in their views on youth development and how it should inform policy and practice (Kupchik 2006). Unlike with a program that is just starting, change to contemporary juvenile justice policy and practice in an existing agency will be implemented by individuals who play distinct roles in the system and have different attitudes toward innovation and aptitude for delivering its key components. Understanding people as central inputs in implementation is essential in navigating the information environment that accompanies innovation and implementation—particularly in convincing people of the usefulness of the shift in approach (Bowen and Zwi 2005).

Individual and organizational predispositions set the stage for implementation success. Some of these may be obstacles in managing change (Klein and Knight 2005, 244). The innovative practice that is being introduced:

- Often has limitations
- May require new technical knowledge or skills to implement
- May have been decided on at a higher level of an organization, but line staff are the ones implementing it
- May require changes to day-to-day activities and norms
- Will take a good deal of effort and time, and gains may not pay off immediately
- May be resisted by organizational inertia

These factors are notable because they originate from individual beliefs and actions—that can accumulate to the organizational level—and therefore require attempts to accommodate the views and routines of system personnel.

Adopter characteristics also interact with the nature of the juvenile justice system, in which routine change seems to be the norm. David J. Rothman highlights the certainty of the original juvenile court: "[The reformers] were confident that they knew how to analyze the causes of criminality, what should constitute the proper kind of treatment, and how it should be implemented" (1980, 50). Sanford J. Fox describes a similar attitude in Judge Ben Lindsey in Denver, who saw the juvenile court as a "vigorous machine for social engineering" (1996, 34) that could bring about profound change in youths' lives. This disposition certainly is not universal among personnel, agencies, and sites, but it does contribute to the context for implementation in creating a potential tension between frequent change and the predisposition of agency actors toward helping justice-involved youths.

If leaders move from one trend to the next without thought, implementation fatigue in line staff sets in, so there is a definite need to balance new and existing practices (Klein and Knight 2005). Likewise, those arguing for a change should offer a clear sense of what it might add to the agency's practice, using metrics to show that current practice is not working sufficiently well (Greenwood 2014). Change can be perceived as risky or threatening, which means that obtaining buy-in is essential in implementing innovative practices and programs (Greenhalgh et al. 2004).

The level at which the decision is made to adopt an evidence-based practice frequently differs from that at which it will be implemented (Greenhalgh et al. 2004). Who conveys the alternative approach to those who will implement it and how it is conveyed may affect its adoption. Anne L. Schneider (2009) reports that leadership styles based on inclusiveness and free information flow led to more success in implementation. An "implementation by edict" practice (also see Fixsen and Blase 2008), which is destined to breed discontent even with some support for the practice at the center of it, is described by Paul C. Nutt:

> Implementation by edict involved sponsors' using control and personal power while avoiding any form of participation. . . . Sponsors merely announced changes and prescribed expected behavior using memoranda, formal presentations, or on-the-job instructions that dictated the expected behavior of users. (1986, 249–250)

A line staff that sees implementation of evidence-based practices as an edict from administrators will delay the intended changes. If sponsors cannot answer questions about important aspects of the program or the rationale for it, buy-in from those whose day-to-day activities implement the change will be hindered. If personnel have opportunities to engage in the planning process and understand its objectives, implementation will proceed more smoothly (Bryson 2004; Greene 1988; Meyers, Durlak, and Wandersman 2012).

In one implementation study surveys of staff who were required to integrate actuarial assessment of youths into their job tasks illustrate the barriers that can emerge even with some degree of cooperative implementation.[1] Support for risk and needs assessment was associated with items reflecting whether staff perceived the process as ineffective or inconsistent (gamma = −0.33 on a scale from 0 to 1.00), whether the assessment was easy to use and interpret (gamma = 0.55), and whether there was staff support for implementation (gamma = 0.59). Obtaining buy-in is essential because, in many aspects of these reforms, agency personnel and their interactions with youths are at the center of the intervention. This has led Dean Fixsen and his colleagues to go as far as to say that "the practitioner is the intervention," meaning that leaving them out of the adoption and implementation process increases the chances of failure (2009, 532).

Implementation and the Juvenile Justice Population

Challenges in the implementation context are magnified when they interact with important features of justice-involved youth populations and the system's response to those populations. Which populations are targeted and the broader intentions behind new policies and practices relate to choices, values, and assumptions about expected outcomes (Ingram and Schneider 1991). In monitoring target populations, it is necessary to account for particular subgroups that may be more or less receptive to the new approach. In the case of developmental juvenile justice it is important, for instance, to consider the many samples of youths that generate research evidence and to precisely understand their insights and limitations for policy and practice.

The ability to assess risks and needs, maintain a range of programs for addressing them while also appropriately sanctioning for an offense, and implement with fidelity the program for youths drives the feasibility of effective intervention (Elliott and Mihalic 2004; Welsh, Sullivan, and Olds 2010). Introduction of a program to cases outside its proper scope may lead to poor outcomes; this potential heterogeneity in program effects requires attention in the implementation of broader reforms and individual programs (Flay et al. 2005; Lipsey 2009). This includes attention to barriers like ancillary substance use needs and missing pieces like cultural refinements to youth treatment to ensure individual success.

When the target of the intervention is unclear, delivering the program or policy in a way that will maintain adherence to its intended objectives is difficult. Even when the target is initially clear, complications may arise from differences among the juvenile justice population. Mark W. Lipsey's (2009) meta-analysis of delinquency treatment studies found that intervention programs tended to have stronger recidivism-reduction effects on youths with higher levels of delinquency risk but increased likelihood of recidivism for those with more prior aggression. If replicated, such studies are important in generating ideas of how to match a program or practice to a youth in the target population. Evidence-based intervention efficacy frequently applies to relatively circumscribed target groups (Welsh, Sullivan, and Olds 2010). The diversity in juvenile justice populations therefore is especially pertinent because intervention effectiveness hinges on the fit between a youth *and* the strategies for processing, sanctioning, and treating him or her. Multiproblem youths may require interventions that cut across modalities—some with different philosophies and strategies. This requires care in applying categorical distinctions and groupings because effective intervention outcomes are a product of interdependence between youths and juvenile justice responses to their behavior.

Scott W. Henggeler and colleagues designed the multisystemic therapy program for youths who have already had encounters with the juvenile justice system and are "experiencing serious antisocial behavior" and for their families (2009, 1). Similarly, intensive drug treatment and accompanying monitoring is intended for youths and adults with severe drug problems. These programs may be ineffective, however, for adolescent populations engaged in developmentally normative substance use or experimentation (Sullivan, Blair, et al. 2016). Given the reality that treatment setting and intensity matters in light of youth-level differences, the range of different types of risk and need profiles might interact with the programs that are selected, developed, and implemented in juvenile justice contexts. For instance, the applicability of the multisystemic therapy program depends on a youth's age, family influence, the seriousness of his or her delinquency, and whether family contributes to the youth's behavior. Likewise, restorative justice varies in appropriateness (and effectiveness) depending on an individual youth and focal offense (Bergseth and Bouffard 2013; Rodriguez 2007).

The individualized nature of the juvenile justice system, which often requires a package of sanctions and treatment combined with a choice of interventions and responses, means that standardization, or approaches straight from a manual, may be difficult to implement. This complicates delivering a routine package of services and sanctions. At the other end of the spectrum, to redirect youth trajectories means intervention for low-risk-high-need youths, which can lead to misalignment with the risk principle suggesting that intensive treatment be reserved for those at the highest risk levels (Andrews et al. 1986). This is a variant of the net-widening problem that comes with the introduction of broad processing and disposition-matching initiatives (Decker 1985; Ezell 1989). The program or practice is not implemented as intended when this and related responses, such as relabeling of case types to ensure treatment as usual, materialize as by-products of the change process.

The target population for an intervention includes other points of potential influence, such as youth age, race, and gender. The very notion of a more developmental juvenile justice raises concerns about fitting interventions to subgroups of youths across age. As children and adolescents move through developmental stages, interventions vary in appropriateness, potentially affecting their impact on the intended target. A program or sanction that has efficacy in one targeted age range may lose value when applied to those at a different age or developmental stage. Friedrich Lösel and Andreas Beelmann (2006) found that the effects of social skills training programs on antisocial behavior were different across age subgroups. The effects were larger for adolescents (ages thirteen and older) than for younger children, which suggests that youths in the juvenile justice age range can still learn and apply those important skills (see also McCart et al. 2006).

Similarly, James C. Howell (2003) highlights the different delinquency career types as objects of intervention. These, in turn, reflect some broader developmental processes relevant to intervention. Equifinality and multifinality suggest that youths are open systems (Cicchetti and Rogosch 1996), for instance. Youths who are seemingly on the same trajectory can be affected by juvenile justice intervention in different ways and therefore have different outcomes (multifinality). A lot of developmental and life-course perspectives have interactive principles at their heart (Bronfenbrenner 1977, 1979; Featherman and Lerner 1985; Laub and Sampson 2003), which inherently suggests that the result of any juvenile justice system intervention will depend on its nature and the youth.

Because of cultural differences in family management, different family-based interventions could lead youths to the same outcomes in terms of prosocial behavior (equifinality). Programs developed with one target population in mind are sometimes then introduced to slightly different ones (Dodge 2001; Spoth, Kavanagh, and Dishion 2002). Cultural differences may emerge. Juvenile justice programs that target parenting practices offer one example. Different cultures tend to observe different norms in socializing children, such as disciplinary practices (e.g., Forehand and Kotchick 1996), and cultural factors may attenuate the effectiveness of programs that demonstrated efficacy on other populations (Durlak and DuPre 2008). Cultural factors can affect the willingness of participants to engage in a process like parent training as well as the uptake of the essential elements of programs (e.g., appropriate boundary setting). Interviewees in a study of disproportionate minority contact,[2] for example, raised the question of how the system interacts with minority families and whether this generates two-way distrust that is a hindrance in effectively dealing with delinquency. One said, "Families [especially minority families] have difficulty relating to staff. It's important they feel comfortable and that staff are empathetic to needs. That's part of the job." Another said, "Although resources are limited, the court's biggest barrier is families' lack of trust and reluctance to engage in the court." This raises essential questions about fit of intervention modality to different subgroups in the system, especially those that may be overrepresented because of limited resources or options for alternative placements (Devine, Coolbaugh, and Jenkins 1998). These concerns affect central aspects of the intervention but also more practical issues linked to service delivery (e.g., location, hours).

Gender is another important factor in thinking about target populations ahead of implementation (Kempf-Leonard 2012). Although the juvenile justice population is predominantly male, practice based on developmentally informed policy requires attention to influences that may differentially affect boys and girls. Gender-responsive programs may improve outcomes on factors relevant to development and, possibly, recidivism (e.g., education, employment, and self-efficacy) (Zahn et al. 2009). Knowledge about the nature of the target population helps, but the uncertainty of whether specific programs are necessary can also raise some challenges in terms of identifying the most fruitful implementation strategy.

Fidelity to the Model

Determining whether the program or practice is delivered as intended starts with an appropriate target population. Policy and programming generally are effective because of certain active ingredients, however, and when those elements are absent, the prospects for success are far less clear (Carroll et al. 2007; Dusenbury et al. 2005). As in other dimensions discussed to this point, the juvenile justice system's individualized nature of responses and need for integrating a variety of different elements makes it difficult to coalesce around a developmental approach (treatment, sanction, case processing, and policy). At the treatment level, multimodal interventions that address multiple developmental risk factors can become complex in that it must account for interdependent influences on behavior while also fostering alternative prosocial skills (Bruns et al. 2004).

Program fidelity is how well a program adheres to its original conceptualization and program theory (Carroll et al. 2007), which includes an evidence-based practice, delivery of components, and their duration or sequencing. In juvenile justice reform, this requires that the broad principles and practices—as well as individual programs—align with a developmental understanding of adolescence and delinquency. Christopher Carroll and his colleagues (2007) note that the frequency, duration, and coverage of the practice determine adherence to its original intent. They also identify some moderators of adherence, which can complicate attainment and maintenance of fidelity. These include the complexity of the program or practice, whether adequate resources or strategies are in place to facilitate implementation, quality of its delivery, and how participants respond to the intervention. Developmental juvenile justice can build on existing evidence-based approaches, but fidelity likely requires expansion in some areas of assessment, treatment, and graduated sanction and supervision and in staff training and monitoring.

Implementation context affects fidelity. Linda Dusenbury and colleagues (1997) found that slippage from protocols in drug prevention trials, a marker of poor fidelity, often came from staff turnover and introducing the new procedures too quickly. The complexity of the protocol also had some bearing on adherence. Very clearly, this is relevant to adopter characteristics like prior training and education, the core elements necessary for fidelity, and determination of how to tailor training and other technical assistance to the local context. Training, technical assistance, and monitoring are closely related to fidelity, and the way those elements enter the process matters (Durlak and DuPre 2008; Meyers, Durlak, and Wandersman 2012). Durlak and DuPre argue that, to promote successful implementation and effectiveness in practice, training must

> prepare providers effectively for their new tasks, but this means training should not only help providers develop mastery in specific intervention skills, but also address their expectations, motivation, and sense of self-efficacy, because the latter can affect their future performance in and support of the new innovation. (2008, 338)

This type of training corresponds to an interactive implementation environment as opposed to one that is unidirectional from the top down. In general, prioritizing this type of buy-in and cultivating human resources is essential in driving fidelity. Prioritization like this seems to have been a factor in the adoption and implementation of innovative practices in juvenile justice (Howell 2003).

A more developmental juvenile justice system requires multiple levels of implementation fidelity. At the court or system level, developmentally appropriate placements are made for youths at certain ages and risk levels. In an aggregate sense, appropriate options are available and used effectively. At the individual-case level, developmentally informed sanctions breed greater responsibility and developmentally informed treatment strategies promote positive skill development. In the cognitive-behavioral therapy interventions described in Chapter 5, specific components such as self-monitoring, situational thinking, and role-playing for subsequent actions facilitate change between thought and action (Lipsey, Landenberger, and Wilson 2007). In multisystemic therapy programs, involving the entire family is a core part of the model treatment and therefore a key ingredient of fidelity (Henggeler et al. 2009). The nature of fidelity depends on whether the focus is on policy, practice, or specific programming, but achievement of the main objectives is predicated on adherence to well-supported resource allocation, decision-making strategies, monitoring methods, and intervention protocols. The scope and elements of the developmental approach must be clear to all involved in its implementation for this to occur.

Core Implementation Drivers and Juvenile Justice

As described earlier, several factors affect scale-up of promising programs and practices, which is an inherent objective of reforms to juvenile justice

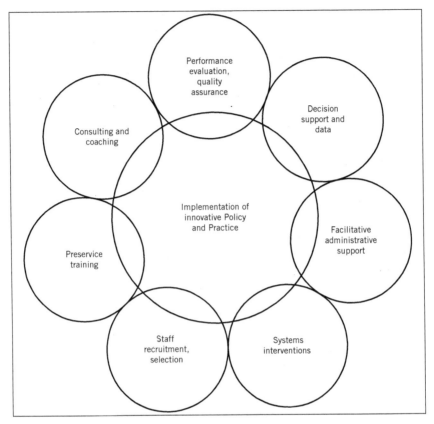

Figure 6.3 Core implementation factors
Source: Adapted from Fixsen et al. 2009.

policy and practice. Given the different elements of implementation just described, it is useful to consider core factors necessary to any change process. Dean Fixsen and his colleagues at the National Implementation Research Network have identified several key implementation components (Fixsen et al. 2009). Figure 6.3 summarizes those elements. The diagram shows components, their integration, and their organization around the central objective of implementation of evidence-based policy and practice.

Staff Recruitment and Selection

New policies and procedures may be codified externally by experts or those at upper levels of the system, but ultimately, frontline personnel make decisions about delivery because they have meaningful contacts with the target population. This was a key lesson from implementation of multisystemic therapy programs: resource allocation and staffing decisions affect "service parameters," like personnel who deliver the intervention (Henggeler and Schoenwald 2011, 10). Programs frequently differ in their core requirements, which affect implementation feasibility. In some instances, requirements interact with the innovation's fit into the existing practices of the agency and its human resources (e.g., skill sets, education, and orientation). From a management perspective, staff in the adopting agency help or hinder implementation depending on the degree of change in their routines and their self-efficacy for the new approach (Henderson, MacKay, and Peterson-Badali 2006; Turner, Nicholson, and Sanders 2011). Some have found that, although more experienced staff can be critical of newer approaches, they also implement them with greater fidelity (Dusenbury et al. 2005). This suggests that it is worth leveraging experience to improve implementation of evidence-based practices where possible.

Practitioners' skill sets must match the program or policy. A risk and needs assessment, which can set the course for later decisions in the system, ideally requires strong interview skills and rapport building to elicit the best information (Bonta et al. 2001). An intake official may conduct a detention screening while a probation officer prepares predisposition assessments. The skills and job responsibilities of the personnel who deliver the process must match it. Even with training, some will believe they cannot adapt to the practice and may be reluctant to change (Backer 1995). This is relevant to multiple parts of the implementation process, such as selection and recruitment and consulting and coaching.

Preservice and In-Service Training

Training is the most efficient and effective way of introducing the background and philosophy underlying a new approach, identifying its key components and objectives, and offering key personnel the chance to work with the new skills and protocols and receive advice on further developing them (Fixsen et al. 2009). Ideally, training should identify a rationale for the programs and policies while also teaching and providing feedback on the practitioner performance of its specific elements. Still, though training is necessary, it is not sufficient in supporting effective implementation. It must be tied to ongoing technical assistance, monitoring, and necessary modification for full effect. These components should be interactive and offer an ongoing opportunity to gain buy-in from those implementing the procedures on the ground (Wandersman et al. 2008). Greenwood (2014) discussed Florida's initial introduction of two evidence-based practices, multisystemic therapy and functional family therapy, as an example in which implementation support did not match the evidence base for the program. Contact with the developer and technical assistance team was curtailed after training, which diluted the quality of service delivery and results.

Consultation and Coaching

Optimal implementation practices require ongoing monitoring, feedback, and coaching for those who are delivering key components of the innovative policy or practice. The application of training knowledge must be considered in day-to-day activities to fully diagnosis places for improvement (Fixsen et al. 2009). A staged implementation with pilot testing of the new initiatives can help in developing buy-in, setting an infrastructure, and identifying possible glitches in the new practices (Greenwood 2014). Despite training on new tactics, staff may revert to existing knowledge or make modifications after the implementation process begins (especially over time). Because implementation occurs in the context of existing caseloads and processes, a new, somewhat assimilated approach may be less efficient than an old, fully operationalized one. Staff may also master skills in an abstract sense without fully implementing them in their work. For example, probation officers can be trained to assess youth risk and needs with a standardized tool, but the gains on youth development and behavioral outcomes are mainly realized in linking that information to case planning. In an implementation survey on risk and needs assessment, about one-third of respondents (34.2 percent of 544 respondents) said that they were not certain that or disagreed that the results of the assessment process helped in making treatment planning decisions for youth. While the assessments helped in establishing risk levels, agencies lost some of the value of implementing the alternative practice because the practice was not fully linked to the system's broader treatment objectives. In a case like this, a second wave of coaching and consultation might focus on how to use assessments and identify some examples of cases that demonstrate effective and efficient applications that reduce recidivism and improve other developmental outcomes. The skill development and cognitive-behavioral interventions, which are part of developmentally focused interventions for delinquent youths, likewise require adequate training, feedback, and ongoing coaching to maximize their effectiveness (Landenberger and Lipsey 2005).

Performance Evaluation and Quality Assurance

Evaluation and quality assurance identify how well staff implemented the evidence-based policy or practice and adhered to the protocol on which they originally trained (Fixsen et al. 2009). A diversion strategy to limit the penetration of offenders into the system may initially target low- and moderate-risk youths, but it is possible that external pressures can cause those who make screening and disposition decisions to focus solely or predominantly on low-risk youths, which ultimately defeats the purpose of such initiatives. James Austin and Barry Krisberg (1981) discuss the problem that arose when the Office of Juvenile Justice and Delinquency Prevention (OJJDP) encouraged alternative placements for status offenders in the mid-1970s. This led system personnel to alter delinquency charges, subtly resulting in relabeled youths who were processed formally in the juvenile justice system anyway. Ongoing evaluation and quality assurance can curtail—or at least limit—such modifications by evaluating adherence to the core practices and documenting outcomes. If adoption is inconsistent or partial, those leading and operationalizing the implementation need to know. Similarly, tracking outcomes can find slippage in implementing the new policy or practice.

Decision Support Systems

For evaluation and feedback, agencies must have an infrastructure that delivers information on the implementation process, assesses its status, and corrects procedures and policies as needed. This component is sometimes perceived as ancillary to the primary focus of implementation but supports and facilitates that process. In the risk and needs implementation study described earlier, there was a reasonably strong relationship between user satisfaction with the computer interface for the tool and general satisfaction with the assessment and its implementation (gamma = 0.65 on a scale from 0 to 1.00).[3] Integration of supportive infrastructure in day-to-day practice can also feed information back into the implementation process to generate appropriate modifications. For developmental juvenile justice, this requires assessing some nonroutinely measured outputs, such as prosocial interaction skills and whether youths attain key developmental milestones like work or fostering prosocial romantic relationships.

Facilitative Administration

Frontline personnel must be fully involved in the implementation process throughout its lifespan, but moving innovative policy and practice to the field requires upper-level backing and oversight too. Supervisors must ensure that the frontline staff moving the principles and evidence into practice stay focused on adherence to fidelity and the objectives at the center of the implementation. All aspects of policy, procedure, and culture should support that mission (Fixsen et al. 2009). Relatedly, systems intervention relies on administrators to foresee resource needs—whether financial, service availability, or personnel-based—and find ways to construct an infrastructure that facilitates success. Such an infrastructure in developmental juvenile justice entails having sufficient sanctions and treatment options that reflect those principles and being able to coach contract agencies on how to introduce those policies and principles into their routine practices (Howell 2003; OJJDP 1995).

The review of these implementation drivers in the context of developmental juvenile justice collectively suggests potential implementation challenges but also identifies ways to cultivate readiness for successful implementation. Organizational and individual preparedness for implementation is promoted through attention to implementation drivers that foster readiness for change (Backer 1995). Although change is always challenging for individuals and organizations, it is important that it is "intentional and positive" (Simpson 2002, 171). Keeping the core implementation drivers in mind sensitizes juvenile justice agencies and personnel to necessary inputs, but there are several pertinent strategies to consider in overcoming implementation challenges in juvenile justice.

Implementation Tactics in Developmental Juvenile Justice

The history, culture, and resources of a policy implementation environment are an important aspect of their introduction and success (Bowen and Zwi 2005). Useful advice on implementation of evidence-based practice and policy comes from fields such as medicine or education, but juvenile justice differs from these fields in practices, key stakeholders, and intended outcomes. Its current landscape and its longevity also allow consideration of what has (or has not) worked in responding to delinquency in the recent and more distant past. The research on implementation just reviewed here supports the value of fully understanding the characteristics and operations of organizations and individuals who are involved with implementation. In the juvenile justice system this generally requires a sense of day-to-day factors, like caseloads and treatment resources, that affect the operations of courts, probation, and corrections agencies as well as community partners. The formalization of juvenile courts has brought large dockets and caseloads—even with lower juvenile crime rates. The need to process this large group of diverse cases is a potential countervailing cost of engaging in new implementation efforts.

Beyond routine changes, juvenile justice agencies frequently undertake large-scale initiatives like detention reform or reducing disproportionate minority contact that require time and resources. Given the potential complexities that come with executing multiple large planning or implementation processes at one time, it is important that those in the organization and key stakeholders understand how those pieces fit together and address a broader set of aims. The mix of public and private agencies involved in the juvenile justice process also may produce tension because oversight and accountability in these arrangements can be difficult (Armstrong 2002; Curran 1988). Larger juvenile courts might have dozens of partner agencies and many parties involved in implementing change. The juvenile justice system operates with multiple overarching objectives, and implementation must address them all while developing strategic, well-thought-out approaches. Implementation strategy starts with understanding elements that may be especially relevant to developmental juvenile justice.

Effectively Convey the Evidence Base

To gain buy-in, those seeking change must precisely and effectively convey the underlying knowledge base to those who will implement it. The translation of evidence through some distillation is necessary for effective communication (Wandersman et al. 2008), but so too is avoidance of oversimplification and extrapolation beyond the evidence. The manner in which policy makers and practitioners consider the evidence (objective inputs) underlying implementation of new policy and practice in light of their existing beliefs (subjective inputs), whether from ideology or other sources, sets the baseline for its use in the field (see Bowen and Zwi 2005; Weiss and Bucuvalas 1980). The evidence often is probabilistic, contested, or still in a developmental stage (Greenhalgh et al. 2004; Wandersman 2003). Even when there is agreement that certain programs are effective, summaries may give slightly different answers (Greenwood and Welsh 2012). The evidence base for a new policy or practice requires thorough vetting before it is conveyed to those in the field. This is especially true when working with audiences who are generally skeptical of these efforts or have seen other approaches come and go during their time in the field.

The body of research on knowledge use suggests that—even when those in the field buy into research evidence—it may reach policy and practice in an indirect manner (Bowen and Zwi 2005; Weiss and Bucuvalas 1980). In their classic study on knowledge use among federal, local, and state officials, Carol H. Weiss and Michael J. Bucuvalas report that decision makers use research on the basis of multiple frames of reference and that "direct and immediate applications of research to decisions are rare—given the nature of organizational decision-making processes" (1980, 306).

The prospects for a more developmental juvenile justice system in relation to the evidence marshalled thus far are affected by a few key factors. Much of the extant research establishes differences between juveniles and adults and therefore (1) it is broader than needed to inform understanding of specific developmental interventions and sanctions, (2) it carries some concerns about extrapolation of findings to other groups of youths in the juvenile justice system, and (3) insight on implementation is lacking. As evidence on development grows, it is important to use it to refine developmentally informed juvenile justice policy and practice. Typically, research evidence comes from studies that seek to ensure internal validity—often imperfectly— but dissemination and implementation rest on concerns about whether a strategy or program will hold up in other places or populations or have external validity (Green 2001). The evidence is often more idiosyncratic than acknowledged and there is a real chance that the program or practice will work differently in a different setting. This creates obvious problems in trying to implement a broad reform strategy that is partly philosophical across scores of settings. In the case of developmental strategies, then, this problem might be mitigated by presenting not only the evidence on the differences between adult and juvenile decision-making practices but also the mediating and moderating factors that affect behavior in justice-involved youths and how that might affect intervention outcomes.

Focus on Feasibility

Models for implementation of evidence-based practices typically consist of phases for intentional planning, development of buy-in, appropriate identification and training of staff, monitoring and technical support, and continuous improvement (Aarons, Hurlburt, and Horwitz 2011; Simpson 2002). Organizational and individual change in service settings usually require careful consideration and monitoring—especially in diffuse implementation contexts like juvenile justice. Change is a deliberate process as opposed to something that organizations and individuals pull off effortlessly. In a review of state-level best practice implementation, Greenwood (2014) found that successful agencies used a deliberate and strategic approach (see also Durlak and DuPre 2008). Contingency planning and what-if questions are essential in thinking about strategic implementation (Begun and Heatwole 1999; Sullivan, Welsh, and Ilchi 2017). Given the way that many juvenile justice agencies operate, it is likely that an agency has seen previous efforts to innovate. In looking at the outer and inner context for implementation, strategic planning must consider where previous efforts have been successful or not and why that was the case. They must also identify the most suitable evidence-based approach for that implementation environment (Greenwood and Welsh 2012).

Meyers, Durlak, and Wandersman (2012) reviewed and synthesized the literature on implementation to develop a more streamlined conceptualization of the implementation process. Their process comprised four interdependent steps: initial consideration of the setting, developing a structure for implementation, structure after implementation, and improving future applications. Assessing needs and feasibility are essential first steps in fully establishing the potential of broad reform or specific programmatic changes and assessing probability of implementation and sustainability (Majchrzak

1984). This is an effort to identify whether the potential implementation setting has the elements of effective implementation or can develop them. Consequently, it must focus on characteristics like organizational resources and needs, fit between the desired program or practice and the organization, and organizational readiness (Meyers, Durlak, and Wandersman 2012). This focus can be challenging in juvenile justice because implementation often affects multiple agencies with different profiles on these implementation drivers. Analyzing and establishing feasibility is necessarily a localized process (see Wandersman 2003). The National Research Council report's (NRC 2013) emphasis on establishing state-level stakeholder groups to guide juvenile justice reform reflects that understanding. Potential obstacles must be identified as part of the planning process, and implementing agencies must then find ways to overcome them (Meyers, Durlak, and Wandersman 2012). This early assessment of the feasibility of implementation of evidence-based practice informs the strategy for the implementation process. Early and sustained attention to these aspects of implementation in juvenile justice will bring more successful change in juvenile justice (see Table 6.1).

Prioritizing Buy-In across Levels and Networks

Success in implementation is very much contingent on getting adopters to accept the changes. Acceptance depends on factors in the implementation environment, and some tactics are liable to be more successful than others. Promotion of buy-in must occur at multiple levels in the system because reservations will invariably come with the adoption of novel approaches (Backer 2000). Ongoing information sharing that fosters feedback and response is essential to this process (Greene 1988). If the objective is to implement developmentally informed policy and practice, the way in which those in the field conceive of the problem—and proposed solutions—must be considered. In turn, dissemination and implementation of evidence-based processes must be considered with the understanding of practitioners in mind. For example, if practitioners who are more inclined toward juvenile accountability can see that a developmental approach recognizes the importance of a constructive sanction, they may be more apt to buy into changes than if they perceive this as merely softening the system's approach.

Listening to staff, youths, and families before implementation is fully cemented is essential, especially given the array of different initiatives pushed into juvenile justice settings. Listening involves consultation with line personnel to identify evidence-based approaches that resonate with them. While evidence must support any suggestions, blending the preferences of those in the field into the new practices will more likely achieve sustainable change. This consultation is explicit and ongoing and recognizes the costs of change to those working in the system in terms of learning

TABLE 6.1 FEASIBILITY OF IMPLEMENTATION AND SUSTAINABILITY: ASSESSMENT QUESTIONS

Policy or practice	**Efficacy of approach** • Has the impact been demonstrated in rigorous research? • Is it developmental in nature? **Actionable program theory** • Can key components of the policy or practice be identified to inform further implementation? **Demonstrated replication and external validity** • Has the approach proved effective in multiple settings and with subgroups in the target population?
Implementation context, outer	**Political climate** • Is there support and a champion for the change in practice and to observe a deliberate and interactive implementation process? **Resources** • Are there sufficient funds and other infrastructure support (monetary, time, personnel)? • Are appropriate services or sanctions available in the juvenile justice system or networked agencies? **Interorganizational ties** • Do the juvenile justice agency and implementation group have sufficient relationships to facilitate an interactive change process and sustain it? If not, can they be built in time to support the implementation process?
Implementation context, inner	**Organizational readiness** • Is agency leadership, at multiple levels, prepared to introduce the new practice or policy and implement it in an interactive way? Is the culture of the organization suitable or primed for the anticipated change? If not, can it be made so while fostering staff buy-in? • Does the organization have informational resources and feedback processes in place to support implementation and continuous improvement? **Individual readiness** • Do agency staff have the dispositions and skill sets for the desired change, and are they prepared for it? • Do staff see potential usefulness in the innovation that will be implemented? • Do they perceive that there is sufficient support from the organization and its leadership?

new practice and procedure and identifying the benefits that accrue to the population with whom they work. Adoption is even more likely when benefits are demonstrated for the agency and, perhaps, the individual staff person as well. Too often those who are pushing for change see only the potential benefits of a new approach and do not take stock of the associated costs or convey the time frame for observing anticipated benefits (Ford, Ford, and D'Amelio 2008). This is especially important in juvenile justice settings where comprehensive efforts can take years to mature (see Howell 2003).

The implementation research carried out to the 2010s is consistent on a few things. The need for attention to the views and responsibilities of those who are implementing change comes up repeatedly in work focused on planning for and carrying out change. For instance, some of the resistance to actuarial assessments comes, not from an irresolvable philosophical disagreement about the relative value of practitioner versus research-based knowledge, but from the perception that some points of emphasis in formal assessments cover irrelevant dimensions or fail to tap themes that are more relevant to practitioners.[4] Interviewees in the Multi-method Study on Risk Assessment Implementation and Youth Outcomes in the Juvenile Justice System frequently called out items that they saw as irrelevant to their population (e.g., a question on self-esteem) and therefore a waste of time to ask youth about. Empty responses that do not firmly acknowledge those concerns, provide a rationale for those items, or investigate whether they are useful and modify accordingly are likely to erode buy-in for a change.

Although there are sure to be holdouts who are unconvinced that the new way of doing things is worth it, a lot of the resistance will dissipate with an inclusive approach that respects the professional judgment of the individual adopter enough to clearly convey the reasons for the change while staying true to the relevant evidence. It is even more effective if the process is collaborative and participatory, making it as useful as possible to those implementing it (Greenhalgh et al. 2004; Wandersman 2003; Wandersman et al. 2008). Those promoting the change must ensure that there is more than token participation from the staff involved and that those staff perceive that the person advocating for the change shares their interests and values (Greenhalgh et al. 2004). Sponsors of change efforts sometimes overlook the need to obtain sincere buy-in, but understanding and accounting for the values and interests of the personnel implementing the innovation may promote it (Nutt 1986). Two-way communication is also necessary when elements of the new initiative require adjustment during implementation (Bowen and Zwi 2005; Durlak and Dupre 2008; Greenhalgh et al. 2004).

Implementation in juvenile justice settings must take account of the entire network involved with youths and take stock of its complexity in structure and process (Greenhalgh et al. 2004). This has implications for both the implementation process and the potential sustainability of that work. The networked nature of juvenile justice requires that each court or juvenile justice agency that wishes to change direction—or even enhance its practices—must bring along its affiliated partner agencies. The promotion of new approaches involves persuasive communication, but contractual relationships predicated on certain practices may facilitate adoption (Aarons, Hurlburt, and Horwitz 2011) and ensure clarity in the roles and responsibilities in implementation (Hubel et al. 2013). At a minimum, implementation in networked systems requires thorough analysis of the linkages already in place (or not) to understand their implications for the proposed strategy (Begun and Heatwole 1999).

The Potential Role of Working Groups

Collaboration is essential to implementation of a more developmental juvenile justice system (Wilson and Howell 1995). James C. Howell and colleagues note that "the youth service field is littered with failed collaboration initiatives" (2003, 149). Collaboration requires dialogue and, potentially, transactional decision making among key representatives of agencies and other stakeholders in the juvenile justice process. In line with implementation science, this requires deliberate planning, attention to organizational and collective resources, and shared vision and culture as facilitators of adoption and sustainability of evidence-based practices.

Working groups or task forces are now relatively common vehicles to address shared concerns in juvenile justice and collaborate through information gathering, strategic planning, and implementation. This was a key recommendation of the National Research Council report on developmental juvenile justice. Two approaches have been useful in generating support for change: "(1) the use of bipartisan, multi-stakeholder task forces or commissions to promote consensus and long-term follow-through and (2) collaboration with foundations, OJJDP, and other youth-serving organizations to leverage resources" (NRC 2013, 326). While multifaceted working groups can be productive, simply bringing various stakeholders to the table can have pitfalls. Thus, organizers should encourage stakeholder participation but also structure it to give them the opportunity to contribute to but not impede the implementation process (Greenwood 2014). In general, the planning and implementation process must accommodate multiple perspectives and roles (Wandersman et al. 2008), but success requires strategic consideration of when and how to bring different voices to the table (Berman and Fox 2010). Participant selection should be based on each one's potential contribution to the process and need to be at the table. Once the relevant stakeholders and agencies are involved, it is important that they agree on a reasonable set of objectives for the innovation, as well as on key elements of the implementation process (Meyers, Durlak, and Wandersman 2012).

In the Comprehensive Strategy on Serious, Violent, and Chronic Juvenile Offenders, for example, community-based teams develop a strategic plan and then identify infrastructure supports to promote effective implementation (Howell 2003). Similarly, the Communities That Care program combines data gathering and planning processes with community members (Hawkins et al. 2009). A strategic plan around the identified goals and implementation needs can provide fixed objectives and success markers when changes seem to provoke instability (Begun and Heatwole 1999). These short- and long-term success markers emerge from a shared vision and identification of "superordinate goals" (Foster-Fishman et al. 2001, 244). Ideally, these markers have short- and long-term measurable objectives. Goals must reflect the dual mission of the juvenile justice system and accommodate the somewhat varied objectives of its constituencies and agencies as much as possible. Organizations working within such groups must be open to constructive suggestions on how their practices fit into the broader mission of the reform and be willing to make needed changes. Making changes should be cooperative, and each agency and its representatives must recognize where the implemented changes have consequences for others (Begun and Heatwole 1999). The problem solving and learning orientation that coincides with such openness is not foreign to the DNA of juvenile justice; it has frequently taken on such initiatives.

Balancing Adherence and Adaptation

The research on evidence-based practice supports the need to closely adhere to the initial protocols used in establishing the efficacy of that practice. In some cases, this can leave organizations and system personnel at a loss in thinking about potential change because they have a general sense that what works in one place will not necessarily work in another. This concern is supported by research on treatment heterogeneity. In juvenile justice, stakeholders also work within an environment that historically has looked at individual cases to identify appropriate sanctions and treatment strategies. Practitioners can frequently point to clear instances of how their implementation context or target population differs from other settings in which that program or practice has been effective (e.g., fewer resources, different composition of the target population).

The question of flexible adaptation versus strong fidelity is crucial to program dissemination and effective implementation (Castro, Barrera, and Martinez 2004; Durlak and DuPre 2008; Dusenbury et al. 2005). Delbert S. Elliott and Sharon Mihalic (2004), for example, reviewed the evidence for adaptation versus fidelity in programs for Blueprints for Violence Prevention and assert that local adaptation was not necessary, negotiated, or ultimately successful. This led them to recommend against any divergence from the initial program model. Others suggest, however, that some adaptation may be beneficial or, at least, not matter that much to the program's effectiveness. Craig H. Blakely and colleagues (1987) include four case studies of criminal justice programs in their research on the fidelity-adaptation question. They characterize the adaptations with respect to the original model, distinguishing especially between additions to the program and removal of active elements. Additions to the original program model generally resulted in greater effectiveness, and subtractions did not have a statistically significant effect on outcomes.

All adaptations must be well thought out and not constitute a watering down of the model program:

> An intervention cannot always be implemented fully in the real world. Local conditions may require it to be flexible and adaptable. Some specifications of interventions allow for local adaptation. Even if they do not explicitly do this, local adaptations may be made to improve the fit of the intervention within the local context. Indeed, the proadaptation perspective implies that successful interventions are those that adapt to local needs. (Carroll et al. 2007, 44)

These recommendations are not carte blanche to reconfigure important aspects of interventions. Without initial fidelity to the model or a clear sense of the rationale for modifications, it is difficult to attribute success or failure to the original idea under implementation or develop a sense of what elements are central to a program's success and therefore required (Carroll et al. 2007; Wandersman et al. 2008). The stated objectives of the initiative, the underlying theory for why it is promising, and the standards for judging its efficacy must be clear (Pawson 2003; Weiss 1995). Those who are implementing and monitoring the change should identify objectives to serve as fixed benchmarks and to ensure deliberate adaptation to promote better performance rather than merely for the sake of expediency.

A broad shift toward a more developmental juvenile justice system requires local adjustments to existing models. Each agency involved may have a different preexisting orientation to the underlying objectives. They will also have distinct implementation contexts and organizational cultures, and consequently implementation leaders must be cognizant that a one-size-fits-all approach that ignores initial conditions will end in failure or dilution of the program. In short, implementation procedures should follow prescribed elements but also be flexible enough to accommodate local circumstances and feedback (Chinman et al. 2005).

Adherence to Originally Stated Goals across Time and Place

Juvenile justice officials must avoid goal displacement if the push toward developmental juvenile justice is to be successful and sustainable. Without this avoidance, the objectives for system reform or individual evidence-based programs may shift over time to suit immediate practicalities as opposed to enduring benchmarks (Leone, Quinn, and Osher 2002). This is especially important as political changes take hold or the general climate for juvenile justice shifts over time (Bernard and Kurlychek 2010). Early twenty-first-century calls for a more developmental juvenile justice system in the United States came amid a sustained drop in official juvenile crime rates and presidential administrations that appeared to be more inclined than past administrations to integrate developmental principles with the prevention of and response to offending (White House Office of Press Secretary 2016). This undoubtedly helped fuel some of the recent changes that have occurred in processing juvenile offenders—particularly legislatively. Even with adherence to broad insights on the implementation process and successful case studies, challenges in moving research to practice will emerge.

Implementation of broad system reforms requires attention to variation in processes and outcomes in juvenile courts so that benefits accrue as widely as possible to youths, families, and communities. Types of offenses and their victims require attention in assessing the current landscape of the juvenile justice system because that affects local perceptions of delinquent offenses and offenders and thus decision making and resource allocation and usage (Bray, Sample, and Kempf-Leonard 2005; Feld 1991). Delinquency is, at least in part, a matter of what communities will tolerate or wish to respond to (Singer 2014), which influences the decisions made by justice system actors (e.g., police, intake and prosecutors, court staff), affecting the implementation of new reforms or programs.

The complex reasons for these differences include court organization and practices, local and state cultural predispositions toward delinquent youths, and placement resources (Bray, Sample, and Kempf-Leonard 2005). Reports that stratify delinquency cases by type of jurisdiction show a relation between those factors and juvenile justice decisions. Using the broad discretion of juvenile court actors as context, Barry Krisberg, Paul Litsky, and Ira Schwartz (1984) examined youth placement in juvenile correctional facilities. They began with how youths reach state residential facilities (e.g., court disposition decisions, parole revocation) or detention centers (e.g., intake decisions, hold for probation and parole). Admission rates varied, and some states contributed proportionally more (e.g., California, Delaware) or less (e.g., Massachusetts, Vermont) than their share of the eligible population of children in custody nationwide. Length of stay and resource expenditures per youth also had large differences among states.

Despite a legal framework that is applicable across the United States via court decisions that settle law pertaining to juvenile court procedure and funding mechanisms that can emphasize certain priorities, it is difficult to create uniformity in processing and decision making within and across states because of competing influences and interdependencies. Barry C. Feld refers to this as "varieties of juvenile courts" (1991, 209). The distribution of power to states for legislation and policy related to juvenile justice means that local priorities and predispositions are likely to drive juvenile justice policy and practice. For example, available alternatives to detention can affect multiple aspects of court procedure and practice (Austin, Dedel, and Weitzer 2005). Likewise, resource disparities and different concerns at the local level contribute to differences within states. Given this variety, changes to policy and practice will occur with some unevenness in their application across states and local courts. As Krisberg, Litsky, and Schwartz note, "The highly pluralistic and increasingly decentralized nature of our society"—which seems to have become even more so in the time since—makes it difficult to envision fully standardized decision making across courts (1984, 179). The planning and development of juvenile justice reform strategies must account for this difficulty.

Implementation Science and Developmental Juvenile Justice

Despite the shortcomings of the juvenile justice system and its sometimes-aborted attempts at improvement, much evidence suggests that juvenile justice policy and practice can have meaningful effects. Despite proclamations of the death of the original objectives of the court and that it has not aged well, it retains many of the same philosophies that it had when it began (Crippen 1999; Mears 2002; Sullivan, Piquero, and Cullen 2012). The juvenile justice system is unlikely to be substantially altered soon. Consequently, the system's limitations and missed opportunities offer some cautionary advice on implementation, but the juvenile justice system does have some elements necessary for more developmental juvenile justice.

The juvenile justice system, and general policy toward juvenile offenders, has moved in a direction that considers developmental insights. Juvenile crime rates seem to have mostly declined since the late 1990s as well. Counterintuitively, these successes, while perhaps not all that advocates wanted, may create less impetus for further change. While the culture of the juvenile court is to continually find improvements to policy and practice that will benefit youths, institutional inertia based on initial success may come into play (Audia, Locke, and Smith 2000), affecting whether agencies see the need or opening to engage in more change. This agency tendency accords with Rogers's notion of establishing "relative advantage" in adopting an innovation (1995, 212; see also Greenhalgh et al. 2004) and can come from either previous failure or success. Howell (2003) notes that much of the advantage in aspects of juvenile justice reform may bear fruit only years later. This, unfortunately, can raise obstacles for individual and organizational readiness to change that must be overcome to move toward a more developmental juvenile justice system.

Local agencies control aspects of juvenile justice, both sanctioning and treatment, but other entities are also involved. Court staff are unlikely to have much say in state-level legislation of youthful offenses. It is, however, possible to consult them in working through new assessment and case planning procedures or use their knowledge in identifying programs and service providers that are more developmentally informed. They can also contribute to identifying intermediate implementation benchmarks and expected outputs. Agency personnel must perceive the legitimacy of evidence for the implementation process (Bowen and Zwi 2005). Unfortunately, research on implementation is replete with examples of the need for organizational change, and the strategy used did not consider viewpoints of line staff, or worse, did not clearly articulate the reasons for it to those who would implement the policies and practice on the ground. Successful implementation requires a different approach.

Change for organizations and individuals is relative to what was in place beforehand (Armstrong 2002). This has important implications for the move toward more developmental juvenile justice. Without an outside catalyst for change, such as a strong push to raise the age from legislative champions or a U.S. Supreme Court decision regarding the most serious cases, change is less likely. Since the late 1990s, several initiatives have used developmental findings to make basic changes to policy and law, so it is unclear whether more wide-ranging policies to make the juvenile justice system more developmental will be adopted without further impetus from within the system.[5] The potential positive in this situation is that many actions that would make the system more developmental might be accomplished with changes that perhaps do not require extensive new implementation (e.g., use of different referral options). They still require significant motivation on the part of local agencies and their personnel, however.

While challenges to effective implementation in the juvenile justice system seem daunting, there are several reasons for optimism. System change is about both organizations and individuals (Backer 1995). One of the greatest assets for facilitating implementation of effective practices is those who work in the juvenile justice system. Much of this orientation corresponds to the mission of the juvenile court—including recognizing developmental distinctions between youths and adults and the desire to reroute problem trajectories. Roughly five hundred juvenile justice personnel completed surveys as part of the study of implementation and use of risk and needs assessment described earlier. Those who agreed with the statement that the tool "made their job easier" were very likely to express a high degree of satisfaction with it (gamma = 0.70). Still, that relationship was not quite as strong as that for the statement "the assessment benefits youths" (gamma = 0.78). This suggests that these practitioners judged the new practice on the basis of its potential contribution to their mission of appropriately processing, treating, and sanctioning youths. Therefore, how the practice helps youths is likely to be a driving force in receptivity to change in juvenile justice practice and policy. Understanding how practice helps youth is also essential in the system more generally—and would continue to be in a developmental system. Appeal for participation to those working in the system—as well as showing the evidence—can be a strong incentive toward implementing desired changes. This is parallel to the retail politics and ground game of political settings, in which grassroots contact with constituents is prioritized, and is a cause for optimism when considering potential adopter characteristics described in implementation science.

The policy context for implementing evidence-based practices can either facilitate or hinder their adoption (Henggeler and Schoenwald 2011). Implementation must account for both big-picture shifts in policy and the core functions of the juvenile justice system because that is the only way to ensure that the developmental principles identified here and elsewhere become embedded in the system's operations. Numerous decision points, agencies, and individuals are involved with each juvenile court case. A response optimized to the needs and risks of justice-involved youths in a developmentally informed fashion across agencies and stakeholders requires effective priorities and structure. This requirement stems from programming and dispositional options, but it also involves moving to a new normal in juvenile justice processes. Even if they appreciate Urie Bronfenbrenner's (1977, 1979) developmental dyads intellectually, for example, probation officers are unlikely to easily change their interaction style with youths. Consequently, at a system level, the implementation process must be cooperative and encourage sought-after changes as opposed to decreeing them.

Much evidence on implementation now exists to support a more developmental juvenile justice system, but there is still some uncertainty in those findings. Avoiding failures in translation of research to practice (Green 2001), requires attention to implementation science. There are numerous examples of failed reforms, as well as implementation efforts subjected to frontline adjustment and goal shifting, that rendered the new way of doing things a lot like the status quo. To avoid such failure, the evidence for youth development and effective intervention and sanction must meet the fertile but challenging twenty-first-century juvenile justice implementation context. Basic evidence on youth development is needed, as well as research on effective processing and disposition of juvenile justice system cases. Simultaneously, reform advocates and leaders can more closely apply implementation science to the unique context of juvenile justice and its existing evidence-based practices to ensure initial and sustained success in implementing these developmental principles and findings.

Conclusion

Deliberately toward More Developmental Juvenile Justice

The developmental framework for assessing and responding to delinquency helps sensitize juvenile justice operations and informs its response to the individual cases and youths that it encounters. The research and policy making over the last twenty years has largely focused on the broad role of juvenile and adult courts in responding to youths, using the evidence to inform response to moderate-to-serious young offenders through developmentally informed boundary ages for juvenile and adult court jurisdiction (Scott and Steinberg 2008). Even the National Research Council (NRC 2013) report on making the juvenile justice system more developmental addresses more of the big picture than the day-to-day processing, treatment, and sanction decisions that are likely to affect the full range of juvenile justice cases.

Whatever its scope, discussion of the need for developmental juvenile justice follows in part from recent research evidence from multiple fields, including psychology and neurological and biological sciences. But many of the key points from that discussion have not yet been fully integrated with valuable insights and research on youth development and the life course. Both areas are sources for identifying next steps in effective juvenile justice—especially concerning treatment and sanction of youths who are processed and adjudicated in the juvenile justice system. Similarly, linkage of developmental evidence to the key day-to-day operations of juvenile justice, which involve both treatment toward rehabilitative ends and sanction meant to promote youths' appreciation of wrongfulness and accountability, has not occurred. Knowledge bases on youth development and juvenile justice intervention have seen parallel progress in terms of identifying effective practices in recent decades, but reconciling those practices is a necessary step in determining how to blend knowledge of juvenile development with contemporary juvenile justice. Related fields, like public health and education, have turned from focusing primarily on efficacious and effective practices and toward promoting movement of evidence to the field. Juvenile justice should pay close attention to that area of research and practice as well.

The first section of this chapter recaps key discussion points and findings presented in this book. The second picks up from that by considering how to pursue the best policy and practice possible—given the risks, needs, and potential developmental outcomes of youths who encounter the juvenile justice system. It covers several suggestions for a more developmental juvenile justice system on the basis of the synthesis of research and data analysis in the preceding chapters. The third section is relatively brief and closes the book with a note on the challenges facing a more developmental juvenile justice system but also identifies available solutions. Given the stakes, it is worth trying to overcome obstacles to promote promising strategies for developmental juvenile justice.

A Platform for Developmental Juvenile Justice: Review of Key Points

Routine juvenile justice practice comes in many forms. The system is inherently rehabilitative in that it is meant to facilitate solving the problems that brought the youth to the court in the first place and that might also hinder later positive development. At the same time, the juvenile court has a responsibility in expressing the disapproval of the community by levying appropriate sanctions for juvenile delinquency. This aim has become more prominent since the late 1990s, as is evident in the promotion of accountability-based juvenile justice and the recalibration of the state legislation codes for juvenile courts. Pursuit of these goals requires multiple approaches to case processing, disposition, treatment, and sanction from a number of personnel groups, who range from the intake stage at the front end of the process to institutional corrections and aftercare for youths who reach its deepest end.

Foundations for a More Developmental Juvenile Justice System

Early chapters of the book describe the footprint of the juvenile justice system and the considerable variability of the youths and behaviors to which it responds. Juvenile delinquency has been in near continual decline since the 1990s, but the number of youths who reach the court is still high because of increased formality in responding to delinquency. Youths who reach the system range from those who are situationally involved in delinquency and unlikely to return after the initial petition to those who have compiled extensive records or engaged in serious offenses that significantly harmed victims, some in early adolescence. The factors that spur their delinquency and associated challenges may also lead to their involvement in other social service systems and heighten their intervention needs.

The juvenile justice system is a complex system and pursuit of a more developmental paradigm ultimately requires an understanding of the pathways to and from the system for youths. Infusion of developmental evidence on the etiology and patterns of delinquent behavior has proved useful in informing court decisions and affecting the legislative process in several instances. The understanding of the neurobiological underpinnings and behaviors as youths interact with the social environment provides specific answers to how delinquency should (and should not) be addressed. Still, this science cannot resolve all questions with respect to the system's response to delinquency. Understanding adolescent development as an interactive, cumulative process with multiple influences adds perspective on youth choices and character. The way that the juvenile justice system and other social influences respond to delinquency has consequences. Understanding the variation in cases before the court, their extensive possible origins, and the later pathways of the youths is a basis for more developmental juvenile justice.

Practice in a More Developmental Juvenile Justice System

Chapter 5, on effective treatment and sanctions, suggests that the juvenile justice system can affect short- and long-term outcomes of youths who have contact with it. The juvenile justice system's dual tasks of treating and sanctioning juvenile offenders offer context for moving this evidence to practice. Juvenile justice actors gather and synthesize a great deal of information on the youths and cases for which they will make decisions. Effective, developmentally informed assessment of the cases before the court is a necessary first step in preventing delinquency and in redirecting youth pathways. Assessment currently includes some potentially useful developmental information, but that might be enhanced through greater understanding of over-time patterns and the mechanisms that drive youth behavior, including the linkages (chains) of different risk factors and the contingencies under which they are more or less potent. Though they often have close alignment, current evidence-based programs and practices do not always fall in line with a more developmental juvenile justice system either. For example, the system's underlying risk-needs principles strongly tilt toward recidivism, whereas a developmental approach is as concerned with skill development and has a pluralistic, integrated view of youth outcomes like education and prosocial relationships. The developmental approach also considers age and developmental status as strong responsivity factors in identifying and implementing appropriate treatment and sanctions. Going a step beyond that, a full developmental profile of a youth—particularly one that seeks to promote positive pathways—requires comprehensive and integrative information on strengths, skills, and supports.

This assessment information provides a starting point for identifying important risks and needs for youth treatment. The system emphasizes redirecting trajectories of justice-involved youths, and treatment strategies must often address multiple, interlinked developmental factors. Some best practices, like cognitive-behavioral therapy and multisystemic therapy, are examples of evidence-based practices that have developmental underpinnings, but practices should, ideally, address the factors driving a youth's delinquent behavior (Lochman et al. 2006). Treatment programming in the juvenile justice system has begun to integrate developmental principles, and this can form a useful structure for delivering effective services to delinquent youths.

As noted in the National Research Council report (NRC 2013), developmental principles should also apply to the sanctioning aspect of the juvenile justice system's mission. As with treatment, this affects the full spectrum of youths who encounter the juvenile court. Categorical or individual excuses related to developmental factors should not lead the court or other influences like parents or schools to downplay delinquent behavior. This risks missing an opportunity to correct in a fair but firm way the behavior of individual youths who have transgressed. This learner's permit view, with gradual enhancement in responsibility and associated consequences as adolescents move toward adulthood, is as appropriate to the developmental process as is latitude granted for youthful mistakes (Zimring 2005a). Sanctions should therefore reflect that the juvenile justice system is one element of youths' developmental ecosystems. Fostering moral identity and legal socialization must account for an array of social interactions, including those with the juvenile justice system and police. This requires the juvenile court to be thoughtful about sanctions such that youths are accountable for their actions but in a way that does not unduly put up roadblocks to the treatment and skill development necessary for redirecting their pathway away from the juvenile justice system. The system must have a range of possible sanctions at its disposal as well as a willingness to communicate the developmental reasons for using them to youths, parents, and significant community stakeholders.

Implementing Developmental Juvenile Justice

Clarity and sobriety about the nature and strength of the evidence for a more developmental juvenile justice system is essential, because the findings that inform effective juvenile justice practice may be differentially applicable to particular subpopulations of justice-involved youths. Those effects can also be contingent on the settings in which they were first identified. Even then, developing the evidence base is really just one step in a multistage process. As the cycle of juvenile justice lurches back and forth it both progresses and regresses in the sense that any changes that are made as a result of trying to be more developmental could have a positive, null, negative, or—quite likely—varying effect on the system and justice-involved youths. Changes can also be co-opted in such a way that they become a part of the routine operations of the court but have little appreciable effect when considered against their main objectives. Although it is flexible, the juvenile court is a legacy institution, not a start-up, so the existing operations of juvenile justice agencies will inevitably offer context for the use of new evidence-based practices. Implementation must proceed carefully for effective, sustainable change.

Fortunately, the system can transcend many obstacles by using evidence-based best practices for organizational change and implementation of innovative approaches. Among the most important practices is to establish why proposed changes matter for youths and how they can help practitioners on the ground, like probation officers and intake staff, to better meet their objectives. The system is in the unenviable position of having to handle the particular problems of specific youths and cases in great depth while also having to devote attention to a portfolio of bigger-picture initiatives that can drain resources and divert attention from casework. This tension affects implementation when it causes system actors to reflexively recoil from changes sought by policy makers and administrators on the basis of research findings or advocacy. While there are certainly obstacles to more developmental juvenile justice practice, some straightforward steps can be taken to shepherd innovative initiatives as they are adopted and implemented. This starts with taking stock of the implementation context in making changes to policy and practice and being mindful of the knowledge and efforts of those who are responsible for pursuing the objectives of the juvenile justice system.

Principles for a More Developmental Juvenile Justice System

The lines of thinking and research evidence described in this book inform several key guiding principles for a more developmental system that does as much good as possible for youths while minimizing potential harms to them and society in the process. The need to think simultaneously at the system, agency, case, and youth levels can make implementation difficult because several contingencies and moving parts are inherent in each. When the levels are put together the challenges grow exponentially. The starting points for these processes involve laying out the objectives of the proposed response and identifying who or what are its primary targets. These principles are not exhaustive, providing a manual, but rather elements to consider when integrating developmental ideas into the juvenile justice process. They are based on reflections about who encounters the juvenile justice system and the processes and decisions that happen within it, an expansive view of developmental and life-course principles and research, a review of effective treatment and sanction practices, and the growing area of implementation science. Inevitably, the juvenile justice system can be made more developmental only one case, court, agency, facility, and staff member at a time. These ideas guide thinking about how the juvenile justice system, and its personnel and key stakeholders, can accomplish that goal.

Variability as a Rule

Above all else, there is a great deal of variability in the youths who become involved in the juvenile court and the circumstances of their cases. This variability grows when looking backward and forward in their lives. Thus, fully systematized approaches to decision making—whether for treatment or sanction—are bound to fall short. It is nevertheless possible to develop guidelines for handling these cases—especially with respect to the sanctions for given offenses and the array of treatment options that may reduce risk and promote skill development. Identifying and explaining the variability of delinquency cases and careers is an essential first step in any developmental policy or practice. This is true both in research and practice, and the system must reconsider its central questions in assessing delinquent youths for decisions that are relevant to developmental juvenile justice. This is true of those making intake decisions; probation officers who conduct investigations, make recommendations, and monitor youths; judges and magistrates who make disposition decisions; and corrections and treatment officials who deliver interventions and monitor progress.

Development Is Cumulative, Contingent, and Constant

The developmental approach is interventionist in nature. All contacts with the system—whether day to day or more extensive—are opportunities to foster positive development and diminish risk of later problem trajectories. The process of development is continuous; the juvenile justice system and the personnel within it are part of a youth's developmental influences, and every hearing and meeting can have an immediate or enduring impact on the youth. Youths' risks and needs can range from basics like food, clothing, and shelter to more complex mental health diagnoses, trauma, and skill deficits. They also will frequently have multiple, interlinked layers of criminogenic risk that foster delinquent behavior that must be addressed to prevent recidivism and promote positive development. Nevertheless, many youths exhibit tremendous resilience and possess strengths and protective factors to seize on in enacting positive change in their life-course pathways. Identification, understanding, and response to these constellations of risk, needs, and strengths offer an orienting point for assessment and intervention with delinquent youths.

A focus on dynamic development and growth recognizes that all youths must meet important developmental milestones to successfully transition to adulthood. These include obvious pursuits like education and work but also building a positive individual identity and improving self-efficacy around social interactions and adult responsibilities. The system must (1) take stock of where youths are with respect to skills at the point of juvenile justice involvement (e.g., problem solving and social engagement repertoire) and (2) make an effort to bolster skills where needed to enhance youths' ability to navigate those processes.

Parens Patriae Meets Supportive but Strong

The role of developmental caretaker fits the philosophy of the juvenile justice system. While the juvenile justice system can do well for youths, it can also do unintended harm. Youths entering the juvenile justice system have committed an infraction, which means that the court's response must promote accountability. This can lead to an overemphasis on punishment, but developmental findings point toward rightsized sanctions that promote accountability without undercutting youths' long-term life chances.

Constructive sanctions are an important aspect of developmental juvenile justice. The notion that individual youths are totally separable from the incident that brought them to the attention of the system is contrary to the juvenile court's role of appropriately expressing community disapproval and the youth's and community's interest in later positive developmental outcomes. This ties developmental juvenile justice with discipline for positive development. Just as effective parenting requires consistency, clarity, and adjacency in responding to problem behavior, juvenile justice must respond to delinquent youths with effective treatment and appropriate sanction, as well as effective communication of the process and intent underlying the response. Youths receive signals that inform their view of the law and shape the moral identity that is still under construction in adolescence. Part of the developmental process is learning from mistakes. Recognizing this is less about appearing to be tough on delinquent youths than it is about using accountability for developmental purposes.

Take a "What Happens Next" Focus

Juvenile justice decision making about sanctions and treatment must balance past and future. This is true whether considering the offense that led to the court petition or the set of risks and strengths that youths carry into the juvenile justice system. While evidence suggests that delinquency has much stability and that between-youth differences matter in understanding long-term patterns of offending, it is also true that the typical youth will not return to the juvenile justice system after a first offense. Given that, there is both opportunity and peril in how youths are treated and sanctioned in the system. The knowledge that the court and correctional and treatment agencies will be among the interactional environments that are simultaneously both a result of and a potential influence on youths' antisocial and prosocial behavioral pathways must be a central premise of developmental juvenile justice. For some youths juvenile justice contact may be a blessing in disguise if they receive needed services that they have yet to encounter in other community-based agencies or institutions, but they may also be labeled as delinquent, experience iatrogenic intervention, or miss important developmental milestones if they are held in custody over a long period of time.

Developmentally informed juvenile justice suggests a need to consider not only the immediate offense but also the pathway to it and from it. Some discussion of this "before and after" is necessary in framing how juvenile justice balances a focus on the case and the individual youth. Use of detention is a good example. Juvenile justice officials sometimes talk about a youth being in crisis in interviews and in court hearing observations, as they did in the Ohio Disproportionate Minority Contact Assessment study, an acute situation in which they see an immediate safety issue for the youth, family, or community. At the same time, if there is no reconsideration of that stance after the immediate crisis has passed, the developmental consequences could be troublesome. This requires thought about the positive or negative outcomes that might follow from the reaction of the system and placing well-thought-out boundaries around potentially problematic, albeit well-intended, responses. This is an essential tension of a developmental juvenile justice system, which is inherently interventionist but must also be judicious when intervening.

Youths and Juvenile Justice as Coproducers

The evidence from developmental and life-course research in behavioral and social sciences clearly points toward individuals as coproducers of their developmental outcomes. Though some who encounter the system have drifted into delinquency—rather than being fully committed to an antisocial lifestyle—there is still an element of agency involved (Matza 1964). Appreciation of agency should affect decisions about both treatment and sanction. In treatment, this notion of youth as coproducer leads to consideration of the fit of youth to the program for producing positive outcomes. If one argument underlying a more developmental juvenile justice system is that youth character is still unformed (Scott and Steinberg 2008), then all elements of the system's response can be thought of as a potential input in that process, and therefore the sanction must be one that positively changes the youth's pathway.

Probation officers will play an especially important role in this move to a more developmental system by virtue of the sheer number and array of justice-involved youths with whom they have contact. In addition to supervision and service brokering, juvenile probation sets up youth–probation officer relationships that form an essential dyad in a developmental juvenile justice system. The probation process must be an active one that urges the youth toward behavioral change as opposed to being a minimal supervisory or extreme control function. Juvenile probation personnel must consistently take this active stance to both major and minor interactions with youths if a developmental approach is to take hold.

The challenge for the juvenile justice system lies in determining how to embed core developmental principles and findings into intake, diversion, disposition, and corrections procedures. This cannot be relegated merely to treatment or sanctions but rather must become part of the infrastructure and process of the system to explicitly inform how judges, probation officers, and other juvenile justice staff monitor and sanction youths.

Maintain Experimental Approach While Mindful of Evidentiary Limitations

Research on the juvenile justice system—whether historical, legal, policy, or practice focused—supports the idea that it is a restless institution that incrementally tries to improve on its mission. Those in the system—despite any flaws it may have—work to improve its response to delinquency and children in need of services. This is illustrated nicely by the many diversion programs aimed at specific subgroups of youths like those with mental health problems. These efforts are not always successful, and there are certainly grounds for criticism about whether the juvenile justice system meets its goals. Still, a move toward a more developmental juvenile justice system will require further trial and error in introducing new ideas and implementing programs and practices based on those ideas. The ideas and research considered in this book identify strategies that are worth continuing and attempting in new settings. The system should show the same malleability that it hopes to see in the youths whom it encounters.

While there is a great deal of evidence to support elements of the developmental agenda for juvenile justice, there are also places where the developmental response may not be a perfect fit to the case at hand or align with the resources of the agency or skills of its personnel. Similarly, no evidence base is perfect or informative for all aspects of practice. Knowing where the evidence supporting particular efforts starts and ends can be useful in creating a bridge for implementation and in fostering openness to change initially and later on when new initiatives are not successful or require adjustment.

Demonstrate Why This Is Different, What It Means,
and How It Works

Regardless of the strength of the evidence, it is almost certainly a fallacy to think that system decisions and day-to-day practice will proceed solely on findings from research. There is much to gain by better understanding the implementation context and leverage points in the agencies where change is sought. Executing juvenile justice policy and practice involves numerous stakeholders with a variety of missions, which complicates the process of moving evidence to day-to-day practice. The reality is that true change requires significant buy-in and winning both minds and hearts in the implementation process.

As in the broader cycle of juvenile justice (Bernard and Kurlychek 2010), a steady stream of new initiatives can build up a well of resentment in line staff. Also some skepticism is inevitable in moving toward a more developmental juvenile justice system. Adding new practices to the existing day-to-day operations of the juvenile court in a way that minimizes disruption for already pressed staff must occur in a deliberate and thoughtful way. There will inevitably be some cost—at least in the short term—accompanying any benefits to changing practices and policies. Recognizing and addressing that cost is important in securing buy-in for new ways of doing things. Stakeholders—particularly those who will be doing the frontline work—must have a genuine voice in implementation processes. Those seeking change must demonstrate the usefulness of the innovation from multiple vantage points—including the benefits that will accrue both to the youths and to those being asked to change what they are doing in their day-to-day work. Displaying the outcomes of cases identified by peer staff members may be especially effective in conveying how a developmental approach or intervention was beneficial in handling a particular youth or in organizational decision making.

Development, Juvenile Justice, and Cautious Optimism

The juvenile court's founders were forward looking and confident about their ability to help youths in redirecting their lives, which would create a fairer, safer, and more benevolent society. Research has reaffirmed many of the fundamental ideas about youths that sparked the establishment of the juvenile justice system in the first place. Other research identifies areas where its effectiveness might be improved. Although individual differences are important in driving trajectories, it is abundantly clear that adolescence is a dynamic time of mistakes and learning is social interactions and not merely a playing out of a series of predestined events and behaviors. The dynamics of adolescence and patterns of delinquency careers identify opportunities to intervene effectively—even with more serious cases. Well-thought-out treatment programs can make good on that opportunity when matched to youths appropriately and implemented effectively. Appropriate sanctions need not be objectionable and can complement the developmental mission of the juvenile justice system.

The recommendations here are a mix of tested ideas and promising, plausible, but not-yet-tested ideas from relevant research and scholars' and laypersons' thinking on youth development and juvenile justice. The laudable goal of a more developmental system will likely take much work. Just having this knowledge is not enough. The history of the juvenile justice system and the research on juvenile delinquency requires a cautious but open-minded stance to the possibilities for reform. Looking back now, the early notion that the juvenile court could be an effective social engineer seems naïve and has likely contributed to some of the criticism that it has, perhaps appropriately, received in the latter part of the twentieth century (Scott and Steinberg 2008). But it is equally wrong to assume that the system cannot do anything to prevent further delinquencies or to improve the lives of the youths and families. In promoting developmental goals, the juvenile justice system can be a moral agency and a problem solver, balancing its mission to take an authoritative but helpful stance toward delinquent youths.

Advocates must overcome implementation challenges in moving toward more developmental juvenile justice. As David Tanenhaus notes, "The idealized juvenile court . . . never actually existed, nor could have. For any court system that mixed children of widely ranging ages, circumstances, and offenses was bound to handle its share of hard cases" (2004, 164). This, of course, remains the reality in modern juvenile justice and must be held firmly in mind when assessing the prospects for change. Still, the orientation of the personnel who work in the juvenile justice system, previous efforts at system improvement, the basic and applied research evidence base that has emerged over time, and the developmental institutions that stand ready to become involved in the lives of delinquent youths provide a fine foundation for redirecting pathways. Careful consideration of calls for reform, coupled with systematic efforts to implement a more developmental approach, has the potential to effectively blend the service and sanction missions of the juvenile justice system.

The juvenile justice process can affect whether and how certain youths will grow into adults. Developmental juvenile justice needs to be responsive to multiple concerns that have been recurring obstacles in previous policy discussions. Those across the political spectrum can assimilate this balanced approach based on developmental knowledge and innate beliefs about childhood, adolescence, and adulthood. The size and nature of the population that reaches the juvenile justice system suggest that the stakes in responding to delinquency are extraordinarily high. Looked at developmentally, getting juvenile justice right has potential immediate and long-term impacts on delinquency and crime as well as other major social indicators like work and citizenship. The field has made a great deal of progress in research and implementation of effective practices in areas relevant to developmental juvenile justice. This work extends the scope and depth of what the founders of the juvenile court intended. A careful look at the evidence behind these practices suggests that it is possible not only to make juvenile justice more developmental but also more effective. When that occurs, youths at the center of the juvenile justice process have better prospects, and those benefits move outward toward other aspects of the developmental ecosystem, like families, communities, and society as a whole.

Appendix

Methods

Ohio Disproportionate Minority Contact Assessment
Court Hearing Observation Data

From 2012 to 2016 the Ohio Department of Youth Services funded the Ohio Disproportionate Minority Contact Assessment study. The study collected police and court records and direct qualitative data from police agencies and courts in counties across the state. Systematic observations of hearings gathered information on processes and decisions in each of the thirteen juvenile courts.

The sample of cases selected for observation was dictated by the court's docket on any given day. The research team attempted to observe cases at the stages of the court process (initial hearing, detention, progress reviews, adjudication, and dispositions) and observe hearings led by judges and magistrates. This yielded a total sample of 133 distinct observations. A structured observation form was used for each hearing. The form denoted the type of hearing (e.g., detention, dispositional). Other key items included legal factors and outcomes (e.g., level and type of offense, supervision or treatment compliance, legal representation, sanction), administrative information provided by court staff (e.g., risk and need assessment recommendations, supervision recommendations), and factors related to the youths involved in the hearing (e.g., family or living environment, parent or guardian attendance at court). Field notes recorded the nature of the proceeding or exchanges between court actors and youths (e.g., content and tone of exchanges between court staff and youths).

The initial step of the analysis identified recurring patterns in the close-ended items to describe the hearings by reviewing code sheets and performing quantitative analysis on the compiled data. All comments and notes on observation forms were transcribed and systematically reviewed to find recurring themes in the hearings—both within and across courts. Last, representative examples of patterns observed in the hearings elucidated important themes that had emerged in the previous steps.

Juvenile Justice Interview Data

In total, 129 key-informant interviews were conducted in thirteen juvenile courts in Ohio between late 2012 and 2014. Interviewees were selected on the basis of their knowledge of the decision making that normally occurred at a relevant stage of the juvenile justice process. The final sample comprised court administrative staff (twenty-two); detention center staff (fourteen); intake and assessment staff (ten); supervision and programming staff (sixty); and magistrates and judges (twenty-five). Personnel with specific knowledge of disproportionate minority contact (DMC) initiatives were prioritized for interviews.

Interviews lasted thirty to ninety minutes depending on subjects' amount of knowledge about the topics of interest and the depth of their responses. The semistructured interview protocol consisted of anchor items and open-ended follow-up questions in several areas (e.g., minority youth contact with juvenile justice and the court; key factors in the decision-making process and policies regarding juvenile delinquency; the role of family in the decision-making process; and legal and social services available in the court). Discussion questions asked about community assets and strategies to address DMC—both past initiatives and ideas for the future. The focal question was followed by probes and general discussion (Patton 1990). Interviewers were thoroughly trained on the protocol before going into the field.

Data analysis used a grounded theory approach to identify and assess emergent themes (see Corbin and Straus 1990). The research team reviewed transcripts for themes and recurring patterns, summarized and grouped those themes (Braun and Clarke 2006), conducted an independent review by research staff to ensure accuracy and reliability, and identified representative quotes and examples to further contextualize key findings.

Police Focus Group Data

Seventeen focus groups and two interviews were conducted in law enforcement agencies across nine of the Ohio counties in the Ohio Disproportionate Minority Contact Assessment study. A purposive selection approach identified officers who had higher rates of contact with youths in their jurisdiction (in collaboration with a key liaison at each agency). These focus group sessions included 130 police officers.

To increase participation and engagement, the focus groups and interviews were facilitated by trained police consultants and conducted on-site at each agency. Each facilitator used a semistructured discussion outline with lead questions designed to generate discussion in a topic area. Participants discussed several general themes and especially those related to minority youths. For example, the focus groups touched on juvenile crime trends, the strengths and weaknesses of the juvenile justice system, and DMC and its factors. The protocol also covered the role of police in the community and identifying departmental policies, procedures, or initiatives relevant to juvenile crime in their community (especially areas that were predominately minority). As with the interview data for key informants in juvenile justice described earlier, the data were analyzed using a grounded theory approach to identify and assess emergent themes.

Assessment, Court, and Corrections Record Data

Case records from courts and state juvenile corrections facilities were collected and analyzed. These were usually either random samples from court case lists or full extractions from their administrative record systems. The final court sample contained 75,946 cases referred to thirteen juvenile courts in 2010 and 2011. The courts were mostly large and moderate size. Measures tapped six case outcomes: diversion, detention, dismissal, adjudication, secure placement, and waiver to adult court (bindover). Relevant characteristics of each case (e.g., seriousness, number of charges) and the involved youths (prior offenses, age) were analyzed as well. The analysis was descriptive but also used comprehensive statistical models that considered the impact of race alongside generally recognized legally relevant factors in obtaining estimates of possible DMC. Supplemental tests looked for possible sensitivity in the initial results.

The Ohio Department of Youth Services provided a stratified sample of state residential facility data for 2010 to 2014, which included 1,514 youths and was weighted toward the counties with court data. Measures in the data file included number of disciplinary infractions, time in seclusion, length of stay, school participation, and treatment received. Importantly, like some courts, the state corrections agencies provided extensive data on treatment referrals, the basis for important descriptive analyses presented in this book.

Multi-method Study on Risk Assessment Implementation and Youth Outcomes in the Juvenile Justice System

Personnel Surveys and Interviews

The University of Cincinnati studied implementation and monitoring of risk and needs assessment (RNA) tools used in system decisions and interventions and RNA's impact on youth recidivism and other developmental outcomes. The study, funded by the Office of Juvenile Justice and Delinquency Prevention (2014-MU-FX-0006), began in 2015 and concluded in 2019. It focused on three states at different stages of implementing versions of the same assessment instrument, the Ohio Youth Assessment System (see Latessa, Lovins, and Ostrowski 2009). The study used a multifaceted approach to develop recommendations for best practices for training in, monitoring of, and use of RNA instruments. Given the importance of RNA in current juvenile justice practice, the responses in surveys and interviews have implications for many of the themes in this book and the potential of further change in juvenile justice policy and practice.

A web-based survey was distributed to a wide range of assessment administrators and juvenile justice system personnel to understand their perceptions of the tool, its implementation, and its impact on their agency and the youths with whom they work. Participants were selected from training session rosters and lists from state partners, contacted directly by email, and given the URL to the informed consent documentation and the survey itself. Systematic follow-up protocols were used to maximize response rates. Roughly a thousand individuals across the three states responded to the survey, a response rate of 32 percent. The survey asked about respondents' role in RNAs, their perceptions of the implementation process, and whether they found the information from the tools useful in their job and to their agency. Key survey items and scales were modified from the Survey for Probation and Parole Officers (Hubbard, Travis, and Latessa 2001), Community Organizational Assessment Tool (Pratt and Hernandez 2003), and the National Criminal Justice Treatment Practices Survey (Taxman et al. 2007). An important aspect of the study sought to determine the relationship between general attitudes and perceptions performance of the RNA tools. Bivariate analyses were carried out to consider such questions.

Complementary data collection also occurred through intensive interviews with 217 staff at twenty-two juvenile justice agencies. Relevant personnel (e.g., judges; intake, diversion, and detention staff; probation and parole officers; treatment providers; and state-level administrators) were selected through a systematic process using existing contacts with state research partners. Trained interviewers administered the protocol, which combined themes and questions that tapped into attitudes and processes pertinent to risk assessment tools and their implementation. In total, the interview guide consisted of fifty-eight items (fifteen of which overlapped with the web-based agency personnel survey described earlier) and offered an opportunity for discussion and elaboration. The interviews included questions about agency and population characteristics, general approach to risk and needs assessment, implementation, use of the assessment information, and sustainability and quality assurance practices. The interviews lasted thirty to sixty minutes, depending on respondents' roles in their agency and in the RNA implementation. The responses were analyzed to elaborate on findings from the web-based survey and thematically to further identify RNA implementation drivers, similar to the process described earlier for the key-informant interviews.

Assessment and Case Record Data

The Multi-method Study on Risk Assessment Implementation and Youth Outcomes in the Juvenile Justice System also links implementation and case processing to the outcomes of justice-involved youths. Research staff sampled and extracted official record data from assessments conducted between 2013 and 2016 in the three states to create a random sample of 6,222 cases for further study. Youth sociodemographic information and all relevant assessment data (i.e., domain scores and overall risk score, or risk level) were extracted. Disposition, treatment exposure, and recidivism data were collected for select cases to find relationships between decision making that was based on the assessment tools and youth outcomes.

The record data used in the analyses from this study in this book come from assessment procedures administered early in the juvenile justice process (e.g., detention), at case disposition, or during youth intake at a residential facility. The exact composition of items and subdomains differs across those stages but generally consists of risks and needs that reflect youth juvenile justice history, familial problems, prodelinquency attitudes, association with delinquent peers, and substance use and mental health problems. These data also contain information on youth sociodemographic characteristics, offense, and treatment. The size of the subsamples differed according to whether the full database or a subset of cases was used (e.g., the descriptions in Figure 5.3 are from a sample of six hundred youths from one state).

Ohio Juvenile Justice Reform: Assessment and Case Record Data

Assessment data covering 2009 to 2015 were collected in association with a study of reform efforts in Ohio (OJJDP-2015-JF-FX-0064). The study identified and assessed an initiative to reduce rates of institutional placement on individual youths across multiple levels of risk, focusing specifically on recidivism and receipt of appropriate treatment services. It evaluated the relative effectiveness and costs and benefits of alternative placements. A state-level assessment database was used as a sampling frame. County size and assessment usage stratified cases before their random selection for the study. Descriptive analyses presented here are based on 4,750 disposition assessment cases from 2010 to

2015 of the Ohio Youth Assessment System. Measures included sociodemographic characteristics (sex, age, race), risk and needs score and level overall and for individual subdomains, and program referrals and dispositions.

Secondary Analysis of Pathways to Desistance Data

A study by Shaun M. Gann, Christopher J. Sullivan, and Omeed S. Ilchi (2015) used data from the Pathways to Desistance study (Mulvey et al. 2004; Schubert et al. 2004) to investigate mechanisms underlying the relationship between age of onset and long-term, continuous offending. The Pathways study used long-term, multifaceted data collection with a sample of adjudicated young offenders from Phoenix, Arizona, and Philadelphia, Pennsylvania. That sample is used here to consider the long-term offending groups identified in those analyses and their relationships with some relevant influences. Additional analyses also draw on the rich set of Pathways measures and unique sample of justice-involved youths to illustrate key points regarding different characteristics of delinquent youths (e.g., impulse control).

Participants were 1,354 adolescents who were adjudicated delinquent for a serious offense. Ages fourteen to seventeen at the start of the study, they were predominately minority (41.3 percent African American, 33.5 percent Hispanic) and male (86.4 percent). The analytic sample for this study comprises 792 males who had data on at least 70 percent of the possible assessments. Some sample restrictions were imposed to have these analyses correspond as closely as possible to previous studies using Pathways data (see Piquero et al. 2012).

The data consist of extensive individual and social history interviews spread over ten waves. The interviews occurred every six months at first, but later data collection occurred yearly. At each wave, the respondents answered a series of questions about offenses they committed, if any, during the recall period. At the first wave, they reported their offending over the previous year. The key repeated measure for the analysis presented here was a delinquency variety score (see Bendixen, Endresen, and Olweus 2003, Sweeten 2012). Respondents reported twenty-two types of potential offenses and were coded as 1 if they did engage in it and 0 if not. As with previous research with these data (see Mulvey, Schubert, and Chassin 2010; Piquero et al. 2012), responses combined to create a variety score of self-reported offending for each youth at each wave.

Latent class growth analysis (LCGA) curve models were estimated using the Mplus software package. LCGA models describe underlying latent subgroups made up of longitudinal trends in self-reported offending (Muthén 2004; Nagin 2005). All models use a full-information maximum likelihood estimator for data missing at random. Models were selected on the basis of several measures of fit and classification quality (see Nylund, Asparouhov, and Muthén 2007). The two key estimates produced with LCGA are latent growth factors and latent class probabilities. Individual cases are assigned to latent classes through modal class probabilities and their observed repeated measures data. Latent class probabilities estimate the relative prevalence of the groups in the sample. The four-group model shows the best fit (see Gann, Sullivan, and Ilchi 2015), and covariates were added to consider factors associated with different longitudinal offending patterns (Muthén 2004).

Secondary Analysis of Kupchik's Case Record Data

Aaron Kupchik (2006) conducted a mixed-methods, comparative study of adolescents processed in traditional juvenile courts and those remanded to adult court. He used pertinent cases from two adjacent states (New York and New Jersey) with different laws and policies. He conducted extensive observations and interviews in courts. He also developed a sample ($n = 2,223$) of case records from three courts in each state, based on age criteria (fifteen and sixteen). He collected measures for each case (e.g., sociodemographic factors, age, current offense, prior official juvenile or criminal history, and case disposition or sentence). The key measures were age and the number of prior arrests, which allowed description of whether youths—from the standpoint of official records—had limited or more extensive prior contacts with the justice system.

Secondary Analysis of Rural Substance Abuse and Violence Project

The Rural Substance Abuse and Violence Project (RSVP) is a panel study of adolescents and their school contexts in Kentucky. Data collection started in spring 2001, when the youths were in the seventh grade, and there were four total yearly survey waves. Researchers implemented a multistage sampling design in which seventy-four schools in thirty counties were initially selected, and sixty-five of those agreed to participate. The two metropolitan counties in the state were included to attain a representative sample from a predominantly rural state that would still reflect a continuum of rural to urban counties. A 43 percent youth response rate resulted in 4,102 seventh graders as potential respondents for the wave one study; completed surveys came from 3,692 students. This declined to 3,040 students for the final follow-up survey administration (wave four), but the demographic profile of the sample remained stable. These data have been used extensively in the study of adolescent development and delinquency.

The study captures a great deal of self-reported data on risky and delinquent behavior and associated risk and protective factors. Delinquency measures, for instance, asked youths about the frequency with which they had committed acts such as assault and larceny during the school year. Youths also reported impulsivity and association with delinquent peers, which represent two sources of possible risk for delinquency. The measure of impulsivity was based on responses to eleven survey items assessing frustration, temper control, attention span, and restlessness. The top 25 percent of impulsivity scores were considered at risk. The measure of delinquent peer associations tapped whether the respondents' closest friends participated in sixteen specific delinquent behaviors during the current school year (1 = yes, 0 = no). The study defined any association with delinquent peers as risk. These measures are analyzed descriptively to exemplify possible patterns of equifinality and multifinality. Further details on the data and related usage appear in the work of Christopher J. Sullivan, Graham C. Ousey, and Pamela Wilcox (2016) and Pamela Wilcox and colleagues (2014).

Secondary Analysis of Project on Human Development in Chicago Neighborhoods Data

In a study funded by the National Institute of Justice, Christopher J. Sullivan (2014) analyzed longitudinal cohort data from the Project on Human Development in Chicago Neighborhoods (PHDCN). The PHDCN is a large study of youths, families, and communities to collect systematic information about development and connect that to broader social institutions and settings (Earls and Visher 1997).

The data analyzed are from three waves for three age cohorts ($n = 752$ for cohort nine, 752 for cohort twelve, and 626 for cohort fifteen). Each cohort was interviewed approximately two years apart. Units of observation have a multistage design in a random sample of 343 neighborhood clusters. Eighty of these clusters were then selected on the basis of a stratified sampling strategy that focused on socioeconomic and racial composition. The selection of participants for the longitudinal cohort study followed from that process (Earls and Visher 1997). Roughly 75 percent of invited participants in each cohort participated (Molnar et al. 2004). Residents (twenty-five to fifty per neighborhood) in seventy-eight neighborhoods were queried about their perceptions of their neighborhood (Earls and Visher 1997; Liberman 2007).

Substance use items asked about the frequency of use of alcohol, marijuana, cocaine, inhalants, and other illicit drugs (National Institute on Drug Abuse 1991). The scores of the delinquency scale were based on item response theory and Rasch analysis (Huizinga, Esbensen, and Weihar 1991; Kirk 2006). Covariates were measured at wave one. A self-control measure was based on the Emotionality, Activity, Sociability, and Impulsivity (EASI) temperament instrument (Buss and Plomin 1975). Parental warmth, parental lack of hostility, and parental monitoring and supervision were measured in the Home Observation for Measurement of the Environment inventory (Caldwell and Bradley 1984). The social support measure came from the Provision of Social Relationships instrument, which asks whether youths feel respected and have people (family, friends) whom they can count on (Turner, Frankel, and Levin 1983). Peer influence measures were a set of fifteen items that asked youth participants about their friends' delinquent activities and substance use (Huizinga et al. 1991). The final stage of the analysis included community-level variables.

The analysis (1) assessed sample-average initial levels (intercept) and trends (slope) and their variance estimates, (2) plotted observed and expected trends across ages nine to nineteen, (3) tested group (cohort) differences in the latent growth factors, and (4) incorporated covariates and neighborhood variation to consider influence on the delinquency pathways. Several LGCA models were estimated using Mplus 6.0 with full information maximum likelihood. The estimation of the initial models provided a general description of trajectories of adolescent antisocial behavior in the PHDCN sample. Two sets of estimates were then assessed at the next stage of the process. Key indicators representing the domains described above, measured at wave one, were incorporated to determine whether these influences affect the growth factors (intercept, slope).

Secondary Analysis of McCord and Conway's Philadelphia Co-offending Data

A study by Jean Marie McGloin and colleagues (2008) used data previously collected by Kevin Conway and Joan McCord (2002) of a random sample of four hundred delinquent youths in Philadelphia who had official arrest records. The researchers then collected full juvenile histories for them by a records search from the late 1970s to early 1990s. They were particularly interested in charting a history of co-offending for the youths in their sample. Like Howard N. Snyder's (1998) study in Maricopa County, Arizona, this process gave complete juvenile system contact histories for the youths. Descriptive analysis used the number, continuity, and type of official-record contacts to construct a profile of that random sample of cases from Philadelphia. On average these youths had 4.5 arrests (SD = 3.78), with a range up to 24.

Notes

Introduction

1. See the Appendix for an overview of this study (Ohio Disproportionate Minority Contact Assessment), data collection, and analytic procedures.

2. This increase is estimated using data on youth population ages twelve to seventeen compiled by the Forum on Child and Family Statistics (2016) based on U.S. Census Bureau's *Current Population Reports* for 1950 to 2014.

3. For a critique of the application of this body of evidence to reach the *Roper v. Simmons* decision, see Denno 2006.

4. See the Appendix for overview of this study and data collection process.

Chapter 1

1. This does not account for reduced boundary ages that many states have (see Griffin et al. 2011) or for extended definitions of adolescence based on developmental science that may warrant additional consideration of how delinquency and criminal behavior are handled into early adulthood (see Loeber and Farrington 2012). After grouping arrests for those up to age twenty-four, their share of total court cases increases to about 43 percent.

2. See the Appendix and Chapter 4 for additional discussion of the secondary analysis of Pathways to Desistance data.

3. Responses for the diversion measure are missing for 22.1 percent of the cases. Some counties in the sample provided information only on nondiverted cases or on cases that included sealed records and were therefore unavailable.

4. Exclusion of conduct disorder diagnoses is a necessary sensitivity check in these types of prevalence studies, since symptoms of conduct order inherently overlap with delinquency.

5. Ohio Youth Assessment System data were extracted as part of a larger study on disproportionate minority contact with the juvenile justice system in thirteen counties in Ohio. See the Appendix for more details on that study, the Ohio Disproportionate Minority Contact Assessment. This is a validated assessment tool that attempts to summarize a youth's criminogenic risks and needs for the purposes of juvenile system decision making.

6. See the Appendix for more detail on the Multi-method Study on Risk Assessment Implementation and Youth Outcomes in the Juvenile Justice System.

7. With the Ohio Youth Assessment System, which is geared to the stage of the juvenile justice process, only two items contribute to the juvenile justice history domain: age of first contact with juvenile justice before age fourteen and prior adjudications.

8. See the Appendix for more details on the secondary analysis of Conway and McCord's Philadelphia co-offending data.

Chapter 2

1. A small minority of youths are transferred to the adult court through the juvenile court system. Patrick Griffin and colleagues (2011) report that legislative changes since the 1970s, but more frequently in the 1990s, mean that many more cases have been transferred and filed directly in criminal courts. Those are not captured by this figure or discussed in great detail here. They represent the extreme end of the range of cases over which the juvenile justice system has decision-making control.

2. Proportionally fewer prosecutors (4.8 percent of all respondents, or twenty-two prosecutors) took part in the Ward and Kupchik (2009) survey compared to other occupational groups like judges, defense attorneys, and probation officers.

3. See the Appendix for more detail on the Ohio Disproportionate Minority Contact Assessment study from which these data are drawn.

4. See the Appendix for more information on the methods and measures in the Ohio Disproportionate Minority Contact Assessment study.

5. David Steinhart (2006) acknowledges that this may be more challenging in practice. Thus far, findings on the parity in performance of these tools across race subgroups are mixed (see, e.g., Baglivio and Jackowski 2013b; Schwalbe et al. 2006).

Chapter 3

1. Points of convergence in adults and adolescents are discussed in this chapter to illustrate the boundaries of those insights (Byrnes and McClenny 1994).

2. An illustration of this complexity as it enters law and public policy is Deborah W. Denno's (2006) conclusion that the U.S. Supreme Court reached some correct decisions with respect to adolescent development and the law in cases like *Roper v. Simmons* (2005) but that its application of the underlying research base in arriving at those decisions was questionable. The court's decision-making process may suggest that it fell back on the notion that kids are different, which is more descriptive than prescriptive in its implications for the application of this evidence to juvenile justice policy and practice.

3. See the Appendix for an overview of the study, measures, and analytic approach to the secondary analysis of Pathways to Desistance data.

Chapter 4

1. For discussions of the relative advantages and disadvantages of scoring based on the number of types of offending, or variety scores, see Bendixen, Endresen, and Olweus 2003 and Sweeten 2012. The Appendix contains further description of the sample, measures, and analytic process of Pathways to Desistance data.

2. Weakened or strengthened bonds affect the continuation or desistance of delinquency and criminal behavior as well (Sampson and Laub 2005a).

3. See the Appendix for more detail on study methods of the Ohio Disproportionate Minority Contact Assessment.

4. See the Appendix for an overview of this study.

5. This subgroup (those with multiple offenses who stop delinquency while juveniles) may be hard to identify, because a youth may continue offending but is not formally detected and recorded (see Farrington et al. 2003). Terence P. Thornberry and Marvin D. Krohn's (2000) review of the research suggests between 70 and 95 percent concordance in self-reports and official records of delinquency and criminal behavior. The authors, using data from the Rochester Youth Development Study, later confirmed that self-reports and official records had much overlap (Thornberry and Krohn 2003). Some studies found greater divergence between the two, however—even in cases in which a record exists (see, e.g., Huizinga and Elliott 1986; Kirk 2006).

6. See the Appendix for an overview of the Ohio Disproportionate Minority Contact Assessment.

7. See the Appendix for discussion of the interview process and study methods of the Ohio Disproportionate Minority Contact Assessment.

8. See the Appendix for more detail on the study sample and measures.

9. For more on this sample and its measures and analytic approach, see C. Sullivan 2014 and the Appendix.

10. The latent slope variance estimate was statistically significant in a multilevel model with covariates, however, which is discussed next.

11. A description of predictors considered is provided in the Appendix.

12. Sampson and Laub (2016) elaborate on the possible role of agency in a way that suggests further refinement in their views.

Chapter 5

1. The depth of coverage of risk and needs assessments depends on whether they are merely an early screen for potential needs (Vincent, Guy, and Grisso 2012). More extensive assessments are needed as a youth moves deeper into the system. The examples used here occur around the time of disposition, meaning their intent is comprehensive assessment.

2. This tool is similar to the Youth Assessment and Screening Instrument discussed in Chapter 1.

3. These data are drawn from the Ohio Disproportionate Minority Contact Assessment. See the Appendix for more detail.

4. The sample comes from the Multi-method Study on Risk Assessment Implementation and Youth Outcomes in the Juvenile Justice System. See the Appendix for more details.

5. See the Appendix for more details on the Ohio Juvenile Justice Reform study.

6. See the Wisconsin Juvenile Justice Code, chap. 938, available at https://docs
.legis.wisconsin.gov/statutes/statutes/938.

7. For more details, see the home page of the Richmond Department of Justice
Services Division of Juvenile Community Programs, at http://www.richmondgov.com/
JusticeServices/DivisionJuvenileCommunityPrograms.aspx.

Chapter 6

1. See the Appendix for an overview of the Multi-method Study on Risk Assessment Implementation and Youth Outcomes in the Juvenile Justice System study
methods.

2. See the Appendix for discussion of the Ohio Disproportionate Minority Contact
Assessment study, the data collection, and its analytic process.

3. See the Appendix for further details on the Risk and Needs Assessment Implementation and Outcome study.

4. Seemingly, the scientific process could be beneficial when practitioners make
assertions about the usefulness of given processes, which are testable.

5. For an assessment on the prospects of moving boundary ages further into adulthood, see Cauffman 2012.

References

Aarons, G. A., M. Hurlburt, and S. M. Horwitz. 2011. "Advancing a Conceptual Model of Evidence-Based Practice Implementation in Public Service Sectors." *Administration and Policy in Mental Health and Mental Health Services Research* 38 (1): 4–23.

Abrams, L. S. 2006. "From Corrections to Community: Youth Offenders' Perceptions of the Challenges of Transition." *Journal of Offender Rehabilitation* 44 (2–3): 31–53.

Adams, G. R., and S. K. Marshall. 1996. "A Developmental Social Psychology of Identity: Understanding the Person-in-Context." *Journal of Adolescence* 19 (5): 429–442.

Agnew, R., and D. M. Petersen. 1989. "Leisure and Delinquency." *Social Problems* 36 (4): 332–350.

Ainsworth, J. E. 1990. "Re-imagining Childhood and Reconstructing the Legal Order: The Case for Abolishing the Juvenile Court." *North Carolina Law Review* 69:1083–1133.

Aizer, A., and J. J. Doyle Jr. 2015. "Juvenile Incarceration, Human Capital, and Future Crime: Evidence from Randomly Assigned Judges." *Quarterly Journal of Economics* 130 (2): 759–803.

American Academy of Pediatrics Committee on Psychosocial Aspects of Child and Family Health. 1998. "Guidance for Effective Discipline." *Pediatrics* 101 (4): 723–728.

Anderson, E. 1999. *Code of the Street.* New York: W. W. Norton.

Andrews, D. A., and J. Bonta. 2010. *The Psychology of Criminal Conduct.* 5th ed. New York: Routledge.

Andrews, D. A., J. J. Kiessling, D. Robinson, and S. Mickus. 1986. "Risk Principle of Case Classification: An Outcome Evaluation with Young Adult Probationers." *Canadian Journal of Criminology* 28 (4): 377–384.

Applegate, B. K., R. K. Davis, and F. T. Cullen. 2009. "Reconsidering Child Saving: The Extent and Correlates of Public Support for Excluding Youths from the Juvenile Court." *Crime and Delinquency* 55 (1): 51–77.

Armstrong, M. L. 1998. *Adolescent Pathways: Exploring the Intersections between Child Welfare and Juvenile Justice, PINS, and Mental Health.* New York: Vera Institute of Justice.

Armstrong, S. 2002. "Punishing Not-for-Profit: Implications of Nonprofit Privatization in Juvenile Punishment." *Punishment and Society* 4 (3): 345–368.

Arsenio, W. F., E. Adams, and J. Gold. 2009. "Social Information Processing, Moral Reasoning, and Emotion Attributions: Relations with Adolescents' Reactive and Proactive Aggression." *Child Development* 80 (6): 1739–1755.

Arsenio, W. F., and E. A. Lemerise. 2004. "Aggression and Moral Development: Integrating Social Information Processing and Moral Domain Models." *Child Development* 75 (4): 987–1002.

Audia, P. G., E. A. Locke, and K. G. Smith. 2000. "The Paradox of Success: An Archival and a Laboratory Study of Strategic Persistence following Radical Environmental Change." *Academy of Management Journal* 43 (5): 837–853.

Auerhahn, K. 1999. "Selective Incapacitation and the Problem of Prediction." *Criminology* 37 (4): 703–734.

Auger, D. A. 1999. "Privatization, Contracting, and the States: Lessons from State Government Experience." *Public Productivity and Management Review* 22 (4): 435–454.

Austin, J., K. Dedel, and R. J. Weitzer. 2005. *Alternatives to the Secure Detention and Confinement of Juvenile Offenders.* Washington, DC: U.S. Department of Justice.

Austin, J., and B. Krisberg. 1981. "NCCD Research Review: Wider, Stronger, and Different Nets: The Dialectics of Criminal Justice Reform." *Journal of Research in Crime and Delinquency* 18 (1): 165–196.

Ayers, C. D., J. H. Williams, J. D. Hawkins, P. L. Peterson, R. F. Catalano, and R. D. Abbott. 1999. "Assessing Correlates of Onset, Escalation, De-escalation, and Desistance of Delinquent Behavior." *Journal of Quantitative Criminology* 15:277–306.

Backer, T. E. 1995. "Assessing and Enhancing Readiness for Change: Implications for Technology Transfer." *NIDA Research Monograph* 155:21–41.

———. 2000. "The Failure of Success: Challenges of Disseminating Effective Substance Abuse Prevention Programs." *Journal of Community Psychology* 28:363–373.

Bacon, S., R. Paternoster, and R. Brame. 2009. "Understanding the Relationship between Onset Age and Subsequent Offending during Adolescence." *Journal of Youth and Adolescence* 38:301–311.

Baglivio, M. T. 2009. "The Assessment of Risk to Recidivate among a Juvenile Offending Population." *Journal of Criminal Justice* 37:596–607.

Baglivio, M. T., M. A. Greenwald, and M. Russell. 2015. "Assessing the Implications of a Structured Decision-Making Tool for Recidivism in a Statewide Analysis." *Criminology and Public Policy* 14 (1): 5–49.

Baglivio, M., and K. Jackowski. 2013a. "Evaluating the Effectiveness of a Victim Impact Intervention through the Examination of Changes in Dynamic Risk Scores." *Criminal Justice Policy Review* 26 (1): 7–28.

———. 2013b. "Examining the Validity of a Juvenile Offending Risk Assessment Instrument across Gender and Race/Ethnicity." *Youth Violence and Juvenile Justice* 11 (1): 26–43.

Barnett, A., A. Blumstein, and D. P. Farrington. 1987. "Probabilistic Models of Youthful Criminal Careers." *Criminology* 25:83–108.

Barrows, S. J. 1904. *Children's Courts in the United States: Their Origin, Development, and Results.* Washington, DC: U.S. Government Printing Office.

Barton, W. H. 2012. "Detention." In *The Oxford Handbook of Juvenile Crime and Juvenile Justice,* edited by B. C. Feld and D. Bishop, 636–663. New York: Oxford University Press.

Barton, W. H., and J. A. Butts. 2008. *Building on Strength: Positive Youth Development in Juvenile Justice Programs.* Chicago: Chapin Hall Center for Children.

Bazemore, G., and S. E. Day. 1998. "Beyond the Punitive Lenient Duality: Restorative Justice and Authoritative Sanctioning for Juvenile Corrections." *Corrections Management Quarterly* 2:1–15.

Bazemore, G., and M. Umbreit. 1995. "Rethinking the Sanctioning Function in Juvenile Court: Retributive or Restorative Responses to Youth Crime." *Crime and Delinquency* 41 (3): 296–316.

Begun, J., and K. B. Heatwole. 1999. "Strategic Cycling: Shaking Complacency in Healthcare Strategic Planning." *Journal of Healthcare Management* 44 (5): 339–351.

Bendixen, M., I. M. Endresen, and D. Olweus. 2003. "Variety and Frequency Scales of Antisocial Involvement: Which One Is Better?" *Legal and Criminological Psychology* 8:135–150.

Benekos, P. J., and A. V. Merlo. 2008. "Juvenile Justice: The Legacy of Punitive Policy." *Youth Violence and Juvenile Justice* 6 (1): 28–46.

Bennett, T., K. Holloway, and D. Farrington. 2008. "The Statistical Association between Drug Misuse and Crime: A Meta-analysis." *Aggression and Violent Behavior* 13 (2): 107–118.

Bergseth, K. J., and J. A. Bouffard. 2013. "Examining the Effectiveness of a Restorative Justice Program for Various Types of Juvenile Offenders." *International Journal of Offender Therapy and Comparative Criminology* 57 (9): 1054–1075.

Berman, A. M., S. J. Schwartz, W. M. Kurtines, and S. L. Berman. 2001. "The Process of Exploration in Identity Formation: The Role of Style and Competence." *Journal of Adolescence* 24 (4): 513–528.

Berman, G., and A. Fox. 2010. *Trial and Error in Criminal Justice Reform: Learning from Failure.* Washington, DC: Urban Institute.

Bernard, T. J., and M. C. Kurlychek. 2010. *The Cycle of Juvenile Justice.* New York: Oxford University Press.

Beyth-Marom, R., L. Austin, B. Fischhoff, C. Palmgren, and M. Jacobs-Quadrel. 1993. "Perceived Consequences of Risky Behaviors: Adults and Adolescents." *Developmental Psychology* 29 (3): 549–563.

Binder, A., and G. Geis. 1984. "Ad Populum Argumentation in Criminology: Juvenile Diversion as Rhetoric." *Crime and Delinquency* 30 (4): 624–647.

Bishop, D., and C. Frazier. 2000. "Consequences of Transfer." In *The Changing Borders of Juvenile Justice: Transfer of Adolescents to the Criminal Courts,* edited by J. Fagan and F. Zimring, 227–276. Chicago: University of Chicago Press.

Bishop, D. M. 2006. "Public Opinion and Juvenile Justice Policy: Myths and Misconceptions." *Criminology and Public Policy* 5 (4): 653–664.

Bishop, D. M., and M. Leiber. 2012. "Race, Ethnicity, and Juvenile Justice: Racial and Ethnic Differences in Delinquency and Justice System Responses." In *The Oxford*

Handbook of Juvenile Crime and Juvenile Justice, edited by D. Bishop and B. Feld, 445–484. New York: Oxford University Press.

Blair, J., A. Marsh, E. Finger, K. Blair, and J. Luo. 2006. "Neuro-cognitive Systems Involved in Morality." *Philosophical Explorations* 9 (1): 13–27.

Blakely, C. H., J. P. Mayer, R. G. Gottschalk, N. Schmitt, W. S. Davidson, D. B. Roitman, and J. G. Emshoff. 1987. "The Fidelity-Adaptation Debate: Implications for the Implementation of Public Sector Social Programs." *American Journal of Community Psychology* 15 (3): 253–268.

Blasi, A. 2005. "Moral Character: A Psychological Approach." In *Character Psychology and Character Education*, edited by D. K. Lapsley and F. C. Power, 67–100. South Bend, IN: Notre Dame University Press.

Block, J., J. H. Block, and S. Keyes. 1988. "Longitudinally Foretelling Drug Usage in Adolescence: Early Childhood Personality and Environmental Precursors." *Child Development* 59:336–355.

Blokland, A. A., D. Nagin, and P. Nieuwbeerta. 2005. "Life Span Offending Trajectories of a Dutch Conviction Cohort." *Criminology* 43:919–954.

Blumstein, A., and J. Cohen. 1979. "Estimation of Individual Crime Rates from Arrest Records." *Journal of Criminal Law and Criminology* 70:561–585.

———. 1987. "Characterizing Criminal Careers." *Science* 237:985–991.

Blumstein, A., J. Cohen, J. Roth, and C. Visher, eds. 1986. *Criminal Careers and "Career Criminals."* Washington, DC: National Academies Press.

Blythe, A. 2017. "NC Becomes Last State to 'Raise the Age' of Teens in Court." *Raleigh News and Observer*, June 20. Available at http://www.newsobserver.com/news/politics-government/article157219234.html.

Bonta, J. 2002. "Offender Risk Assessment: Guidelines for Selection and Use." *Criminal Justice and Behavior* 29 (4): 355–379.

Bonta, J., B. Bogue, M. Crowley, and L. Motiuk. 2001. "Implementing Offender Classification Systems: Lessons Learned." In *Offender Rehabilitation in Practice: Implementing and Evaluating Effective Programs*, edited by G. A. Bernfield, D. W. Farrington, and A. W. Leschied, 227–245. New York: Wiley and Sons.

Bowen, S., and A. B. Zwi. 2005. "Pathways to 'Evidence-Informed' Policy and Practice: A Framework for Action." *PLoS Medicine* 2 (7): e166. Available at https://doi.org/10.1371/journal.pmed.0020166.

Braun, V., and V. Clarke. 2006. "Using Thematic Analysis in Psychology." *Qualitative Research in Psychology* 3 (2): 77–101.

Bray, T., L. Sample, and K. Kempf-Leonard. 2005. "'Justice by Geography': Racial Disparity and Juvenile Courts." In *Our Children, Their Children: Confronting Racial and Ethnic Differences in American Juvenile Justice*, edited by D. F. Hawkins and K. Kempf-Leonard, 270–299. Chicago: University of Chicago Press.

Brennan, P. A., and A. Raine. 1997. "Biosocial Bases of Antisocial Behavior: Psychophysiological, Neurological, and Cognitive Factors." *Clinical Psychology Review* 17:589–604.

Brezina, T., and A. R. Piquero. 2007. "Moral Beliefs, Isolation from Peers, and Abstention from Delinquency." *Deviant Behavior* 28 (5): 433–465.

Bridges, G. S., and S. Steen. 1998. "Racial Disparities in Official Assessments of Juvenile Offenders: Attributional Stereotypes as Mediating Mechanisms." *American Sociological Review* 63 (4): 554–570.

Bronfenbrenner, U. 1977. "Toward an Experimental Ecology of Human Development." *American Psychologist* 32:513–531.

———. 1979. *The Ecology of Human Development: Experiments by Nature and Design.* Cambridge, MA: Harvard University Press.

Bronner, A. 1925. "The Contribution of Science to a Program for Treatment of Juvenile Delinquency." In *The Child, the Clinic, and the Court: A Group of Papers*, edited by J. Addams, 75–92. New York: New Republic.

Bruns, E. J., J. D. Burchard, J. C. Suter, K. Leverentz-Brady, and M. M. Force. 2004. "Assessing Fidelity to a Community-Based Treatment for Youth: The Wraparound Fidelity Index." *Journal of Emotional and Behavioral Disorders* 12 (2): 79–89.

Bryson, J. M. 2004. "What to Do When Stakeholders Matter: Stakeholder Identification and Analysis Techniques." *Public Management Review* 6 (1): 21–53.

Bursik, R. J., and H. G. Grasmick. 1993. *Neighborhoods and Crime: The Dimensions of Effective Community Control.* Lanham, MD: Lexington Books.

Bush, J., B. Glick, and J. Taymans. 1997. *Thinking for a Change.* Longmont, CO: National Institute of Corrections.

Bushway, S. 2013. "Life-Course-Persistent Offenders." In *Oxford Handbook of Criminological Theory*, edited by F. Cullen and P. Wilcox, 189–204. New York: Oxford University Press.

Bushway, S. D., and A. M. Piehl. 2007. "The Inextricable Link between Age and Criminal History in Sentencing." *Crime and Delinquency* 53 (1): 156–183.

Bushway, S. D., A. R. Piquero, L. M. Broidy, E. Cauffman, and P. Mazerolle. 2001. "An Empirical Framework for Studying Desistance as a Process." *Criminology* 39:491–516.

Bushway, S., T. P. Thornberry, and M. Krohn. 2003. "Desistance as a Developmental Process: A Comparison of Static and dynamic Approaches." *Journal of Quantitative Criminology* 19:129–153.

Buss, A. H., and R. Plomin. 1975. *A Temperament Theory of Personality Development.* New York: Wiley.

Butler, A. C., J. E. Chapman, E. M. Forman, and A. T. Beck. 2006. "The Empirical Status of Cognitive-Behavioral Therapy: A Review of Meta-analyses." *Clinical Psychology Review* 26 (1): 17–31.

Butts, J., S. Mayer, and G. Ruth. 2005. *Focusing Juvenile Justice on Positive Youth Development.* Chicago: Chapin Hall Center for Children.

Butts, J. A., G. Bazemore, and A. S. Meroe. 2010. *Positive Youth Justice: Framing Justice Interventions Using the Concepts of Positive Youth Development.* Washington, DC: Coalition for Juvenile Justice.

Butts, J. A., and D. N. Evans. 2011. *Resolution, Reinvestment, and Realignment: Three Strategies for Changing Juvenile Justice.* New York: John Jay College of Criminal Justice.

Byrnes, J. P. 2002. "The Development of Decision-Making." *Journal of Adolescent Health* 31:208–215.

Byrnes, J. P., and B. McClenny. 1994. "Decision-Making in Young Adolescents and Adults." *Journal of Experimental Child Psychology* 58 (3): 359–388.

Caccia-Bava, M., T. Guimaraes, and S. J. Harrington. 2006. "Hospital Organization Culture, Capacity to Innovate and Success in Technology Adoption." *Journal of Health Organization and Management* 20 (3): 194–217.

Caeti, T. J., C. Hemmens, F. T. Cullen, and V. S. Burton Jr. 2003. "Management of Juvenile Correctional Facilities." *Prison Journal* 83 (4): 383–405.

Cairns, R. B., and K. E. Hood. 1983. "Continuity in Social Development a Comparative Perspective on Individual Difference Prediction." In *Life-Span Development and Behavior*, edited by P. G. Baltes and O. G. Brim, 301–358. New York: Academic Press.

Caldwell, B. M., and R. H. Bradley. 1984. *Home Observation for Measurement of the Environment*. Little Rock: University of Arkansas at Little Rock.

Caldwell, R. G. 1961. "The Juvenile Court: Its Development and Some Major Problems." *Journal of Criminal Law and Criminology* 51:493–511.

Cantelon, S. L. 1994. *Family Strengthening for High-Risk Youth*. Washington, DC: Office of Juvenile Justice and Delinquency Prevention.

Carlo, G. 2014. "The Development and Correlates of Prosocial Moral Behaviors." In *Handbook of Moral Development*, vol. 2, edited by M. Killen and J. G. Smetana, 208–234. New York: Psychology Press.

Carlsmith, K. M., J. M. Darley, and P. H. Robinson. 2002. "Why Do We Punish? Deterrence and Just Deserts as Motives for Punishment." *Journal of Personality and Social Psychology* 83 (2): 284–299.

Carroll, C., M. Patterson, S. Wood, A. Booth, J. Rick, and S. Balain. 2007. "A Conceptual Framework for Implementation Fidelity." *Implementation Science* 2 (1): 40–49.

Casey, B. J., R. M. Jones, and T. A. Hare. 2008. "The Adolescent Brain." *Annals of the New York Academy of Sciences* 1124 (1): 111–126.

Casey, B., N. Tottenham, C. Liston, and S. Durston. 2005. "Imaging the Developing Brain: What Have We Learned about Cognitive Development?" *Trends in Cognitive Sciences* 9 (3): 104–110.

Caspi, A., D. J. Bem, and G. H. Elder. 1989. "Continuities and Consequences of Interactional Styles across the Life Course." *Journal of Personality* 57:375–406.

Caspi, A., and B. W. Roberts. 2001. "Personality Development across the Life Course: The Argument for Change and Continuity." *Psychological Inquiry* 12:49–66.

Castro, F. G., M. Barrera Jr., and C. R. Martinez Jr. 2004. "The Cultural Adaptation of Prevention Interventions: Resolving Tensions between Fidelity and Fit." *Prevention Science* 5 (1): 41–45.

Catalano, R. F., M. L. Berglund, J. A. Ryan, H. S. Lonczak, and J. D. Hawkins. 2002. *Positive Youth Development in the United States: Research Findings on Evaluations of Positive Youth Development Programs*. Washington, DC: American Psychological Association.

Catalano, R. F., and J. D. Hawkins. 1996. "The Social Development Model: A Theory of Antisocial Behavior." In *Delinquency and Crime: Current Theories*, edited by J. D. Hawkins, 149–197. Cambridge: Cambridge University Press.

Catalano, R. F., J. D. Hawkins, E. A. Wells, J. Miller, and D. Brewer. 1991. "Evaluation of the Effectiveness of Adolescent Drug Abuse Treatment, Assessment of Risks for Relapse, and Promising Approaches for Relapse Prevention." *International Journal of the Addictions* 25 (suppl. 9): 1085–1140.

Catalano, R. F., S. Oesterle, C. B. Fleming, and J. D. Hawkins. 2004. "The Importance of Bonding to School for Healthy Development: Findings from the Social Development Research Group." *Journal of School Health* 74 (7): 252–261.

Catalano, R. F., J. Park, T. W. Harachi, K. P. Haggerty, R. D. Abbott, and J. D. Hawkins. 2005. "Mediating the Effects of Poverty, Gender, Individual Characteristics, and External Constraints on Antisocial Behavior: A Test of the Social Development

Model and Implications for Developmental Life Course Theory." In *Integrated Developmental and Life-Course Theories of Offending*, edited by D. P. Farrington, 93–124. New Brunswick, NJ: Transaction.

Cauffman, E. 2012. "Aligning Justice System Processing with Developmental Science." *Criminology and Public Policy* 11:751–758.

Cauffman, E., and L. Steinberg. 2012. "Emerging Findings from Research on Adolescent Development and Juvenile Justice." *Victims and Offenders* 7:428–449.

CDC (Centers for Disease Control and Prevention). 2018. "YRBSS Data and Documentation." Available at https://www.cdc.gov/healthyyouth/data/yrbs/data.htm#anchor _1528921231.

Chaiken, J. M., and M. R. Chaiken. 1990. "Drugs and Predatory Crime." In *Crime and Justice: A Review of Research*, vol. 13, edited by M. Tonry and N. Morris, 203–239. Chicago: University of Chicago Press.

Chambers, R. A., J. R. Taylor, and M. N. Potenza. 2003. "Developmental Neurocircuitry of Motivation in Adolescence: A Critical Period of Addiction Vulnerability." *American Journal of Psychiatry* 160 (6): 1041–1052.

Chandler, J. J., and E. Pronin. 2012. "Fast Thought Speed Induces Risk Taking." *Psychological Science* 23 (4): 370–374.

Chein, J., D. Albert, L. O'Brien, K. Uckert, and L. Steinberg. 2011. "Peers Increase Adolescent Risk Taking by Enhancing Activity in the Brain's Reward Circuitry." *Developmental Science* 14 (2): F1–F10.

Chen, X., and M. Adams. 2010. "Are Teen Delinquency Abstainers Social Introverts? A Test of Moffitt's Theory." *Journal of Research in Crime and Delinquency* 47 (4): 439–468.

Chief Justice Earl Warren Institute on Law and Social Policy. 2012. "JDAI Sites and States: An Evaluation of the Juvenile Detention Alternatives Initiative; JDAI Sites Compared to Home State Totals." Available at https://www.law.berkeley.edu/wp -content/uploads/2015/04/JDAI-Rep-1-FINAL.pdf.

Childs, K. K., and C. J. Sullivan. 2013. "Investigating the Underlying Structure and Stability of Problem Behaviors across Adolescence." *Criminal Justice and Behavior* 40 (1): 57–79.

Childs, K. K., C. J. Sullivan, and L. M. Gulledge. 2010. "Delinquent Behavior across Adolescence: Investigating the Shifting Salience of Key Criminological Predictors." *Deviant Behavior* 32:64–100.

Chinman, M., G. Hannah, A. Wandersman, P. Ebener, S. B. Hunter, P. Imm, and J. Sheldon. 2005. "Developing a Community Science Research Agenda for Building Community Capacity for Effective Preventive Interventions." *American Journal of Community Psychology* 35 (3–4): 143–157.

Chitsabesan, P., L. Kroll, S. Bailey, C. Kenning, S. Sneider, W. MacDonald, and L. Theodosiou. 2006. "Mental Health Needs of Young Offenders in Custody and in the Community." *British Journal of Psychiatry* 188 (6): 534–540.

Cianca, S. 1993. "Home Rule in Ohio Counties: Legal and Constitutional Perspectives." *University of Dayton Law Review* 19:533–562.

Cicchetti, D., and F. A. Rogosch. 1996. "Equifinality and Multifinality in Developmental Psychopathology." *Development and Psychopathology* 8:597–600.

Claro, S., D. Paunesku, and C. S. Dweck. 2016. "Growth Mindset Tempers the Effects of Poverty on Academic Achievement." *Proceedings of the National Academy of Sciences* 113 (31): 8664–8668.

Clausen, J. S. 1991. "Adolescent Competence and the Shaping of the Life Course." *American Journal of Sociology* 96 (4): 805–842.

Cocozza, J. J. 1992. "Introduction." In *Responding to the Mental Health Needs of Youth in the Juvenile Justice System*, edited by J. J. Cocozza, 1–6. Seattle, WA: National Coalition for the Mentally Ill in the Criminal Justice System.

Cohen, W. M., and D. A. Levinthal. 1990. "Absorptive Capacity: A New Perspective on Learning and Innovation." *Administrative Science Quarterly* 35:128–152.

Cohn, L. D., S. Macfarlane, C. Yanez, and W. K. Imai. 1995. "Risk-Perception: Differences between Adolescents and Adults." *Health Psychology* 14 (3): 217–222.

Coleman, J. S. 1961. *The Adolescent Society: The Social Life of Teenagers and Its Impact on Education*. Westport, CT: Greenwood Press.

———. 1994. *Foundations of Social Theory*. Cambridge, MA: Harvard University Press.

Collins, W. A., and B. Laursen. 2004. "Changing Relationships, Changing Youth: Interpersonal Contexts of Adolescent Development." *Journal of Early Adolescence* 24:55–62.

Conway, K. P., and J. McCord. 2002. "A Longitudinal Examination of the Relation between Co-offending with Violent Accomplices and Violent Crime." *Aggressive Behavior* 28 (2): 97–108.

Cook, P. J., and J. H. Laub. 1998. "The Unprecedented Epidemic in Youth Violence." In *Crime and Justice: A Review of Research*, vol. 24, edited by M. Tonry, 27–64. Chicago: University of Chicago Press.

———. 2002. "After the Epidemic: Recent Trends in Youth Violence in the United States." In *Crime and Justice: A Review of Research*, vol. 28, edited by M. Tonry, 1–37. Chicago: University of Chicago Press.

Cooke, R. A., and D. M. Rousseau. 1988. "Behavioral Norms and Expectations: A Quantitative Approach to the Assessment of Organizational Culture." *Group and Organization Studies* 13 (3): 245–273.

Corbin, J. M., and A. Strauss. 1990. "Grounded Theory Research: Procedures, Canons, and Evaluative Criteria." *Qualitative Sociology* 13 (1): 3–21.

Côté, J. E. 1996. "Sociological Perspectives on Identity Formation: The Culture-Identity Link and Identity Capital." *Journal of Adolescence* 19 (5): 417–428.

Council of State Governments. 2015. "Closer to Home: An Analysis of the State and Local Impact of the Texas Juvenile Justice Reforms." Available at https://csgjustice center.org/youth/publications/closer-to-home.

Cox, S. M. 1999. "An Assessment of an Alternative Education Program for At-Risk Delinquent Youth." *Journal of Research in Crime and Delinquency* 36 (3): 323–336.

Cox, S. M., W. S. Davidson, and T. S. Bynum. 1995. "A Meta-analytic Assessment of Delinquency-Related Outcomes of Alternative Education Programs." *Crime and Delinquency* 41 (2): 219–234.

Crea, T. M. 2010. "Balanced Decision Making in Child Welfare: Structured Processes Informed by Multiple Perspectives." *Administration in Social Work* 34 (2): 196–212.

Crippen, G. 1999. "The Juvenile Court's Next Century—Getting Past the Ill-Founded Talk of Abolition." *University of Pennsylvania Journal of Constitutional Law* 2:195–222.

Csikszentmihalyi, M., R. Larson, and S. Prescott. 1977. "The Ecology of Adolescent Activity and Experience." *Journal of Youth and Adolescence* 6:281–294.

Curran, D. J. 1988. "Destructuring, Privatization, and the Promise of Juvenile Diversion: Compromising Community-Based Corrections." *Crime and Delinquency* 34 (4): 363–378.

Curtis, N. M., K. R. Ronan, and C. M. Borduin. 2004. "Multisystemic Treatment: A Meta-analysis of Outcome Studies." *Journal of Family Psychology* 18 (3): 411–419.

Cusson, M., and P. Pinsonneault. 1986. "The Decision to Give Up Crime." In *The Reasoning Criminal*, edited by D. B. Cornish and R. V. Clarke, 72–82. New York: Springer-Verlag.

Dahl, R. E. 2004. "Adolescent Brain Development: A Period of Vulnerabilities and Opportunities." *Annals of the New York Academy of Sciences* 1021 (1): 1–22.

Dalton, J. M. 1997. "At the Crossroads of Richmond and Gault: Addressing Media Access to Juvenile Delinquency Proceedings through a Functional Analysis." *Seton Hall Law Review* 28:1155–1229.

D'Amico, E. J., M. O. Edelen, J. N. Miles, and A. R. Morral. 2008. "The Longitudinal Association between Substance Use and Delinquency among High-Risk Youth." *Drug and Alcohol Dependence* 93 (1): 85–92.

Dawson, R. O. 1990. "The Future of Juvenile Justice: Is It Time to Abolish the System?" *Journal of Criminal Law and Criminology* 81:136–155.

Deal, T., C. Ely, M. Hall, S. Marsh, W. Schiller, and L. Yelderman. 2014. *School Pathways to the Juvenile Justice System Project: A Practice Guide.* Reno, NV: National Council of Juvenile and Family Court Judges.

De Avila, J. 2015. "Gov. Malloy Wants Minimum Age to Be Tried as Adult Set at 21." *Wall Street Journal*, December 28. Available at https://www.wsj.com/articles/gov-malloy-wants-minimum-age-to-be-tried-as-adult-set-at-21-1451354757.

Decety, J., and L. H. Howard. 2014. "A Neurodevelopmental Perspective on Morality." In *Handbook of Moral Development*, vol. 2, edited by M. Killen and J. G. Smetana, 454–474. New York: Psychology Press.

Decker, S. H. 1985. "A Systematic Analysis of Diversion: Net Widening and Beyond." *Journal of Criminal Justice* 13 (3): 207–216.

DeLisi, M., and A. R. Piquero. 2011. "New Frontiers in Criminal Careers Research, 2000–2011: A State-of-the-Art Review." *Journal of Criminal Justice* 39:289–301.

Dembo, R., and R. Brown. 1994. "The Hillsborough County Juvenile Assessment Center." *Journal of Child and Adolescent Substance Abuse* 3 (2): 25–44.

Denno, D. W. 2006. "The Scientific Shortcomings of Roper v. Simmons." *Ohio State Journal of Criminal Law* 3:379–396.

Department of Criminal Justice Services. 2000. "Evaluation of the Richmond City Continuum of Juvenile Justice Services Pilot Program." Available at http://www.jrsa.org/awards/winners/00_Evaluation_of_the_Richmond_Cityam_Final_Report.pdf.

Devine, P., K. Coolbaugh, and S. Jenkins. 1998. *Disproportionate Minority Confinement: Lessons Learned from Five States.* Washington, DC: U.S. Department of Justice, Office of Justice Programs, Office of Juvenile Justice and Delinquency Prevention.

Dilulio, J. 1995. "The Coming of the Super-Predators." *Weekly Standard* 1 (11): 23.

Dishion, T. J., D. M. Capaldi, and K. Yoerger. 1999. "Middle Childhood Antecedents to Progressions in Male Adolescent Substance Use: An Ecological Analysis of Risk and Protection." *Journal of Adolescent Research* 14:175–205.

Dmitrieva, J., K. C. Monahan, E. Cauffman, and L. Steinberg. 2012. "Arrested Development: The Effects of Incarceration on the Development of Psychosocial Maturity." *Development and Psychopathology* 24 (3): 1073–1090.

Dodge, K. A. 1993. "Social-Cognitive Mechanisms in the Development of Conduct Disorder and Depression." *Annual Review of Psychology* 44 (1): 559–584.

———. 2001. "The Science of Youth Violence Prevention: Progressing from Developmental Epidemiology to Efficacy to Effectiveness to Public Policy." *American Journal of Preventive Medicine* 20 (1S): 63–70.

Dodge, K. A., and N. R. Crick. 1990. "Social Information-Processing Bases of Aggressive Behavior in Children." *Personality and Social Psychology Bulletin* 16 (1): 8–22.

Dodge, K. A., T. J. Dishion, and J. E. Lansford, eds. 2007. *Deviant Peer Influences in Programs for Youth: Problems and Solutions.* New York: Guilford Press.

Dodge, K. A., M. T. Greenberg, P. S. Malone, and Conduct Problems Prevention Research Group. 2008. "Testing an Idealized Dynamic Cascade Model of the Development of Serious Violence in Adolescence." *Child Development* 79:1907–1927.

Don, A., E. Zheleva, M. Gregory, S. Tarkan, L. Auvil, T. Clement, B. Schneiderman, and C. Plaisant. 2007. "Discovering Interesting Usage Patterns in Text Collections: Integrating Text Mining with Visualization." Paper presented at the Proceedings of the Sixteenth ACM conference on Conference on Information and Knowledge Management, November 6–8, Lisbon, Portugal.

Douglas, K. S., and J. L. Skeem. 2005. "Violence Risk Assessment: Getting Specific about Being Dynamic." *Psychology, Public Policy, and Law* 11 (3): 347–383.

Dowd, N. E., ed. 2015. *A New Juvenile Justice System: Total Reform for a Broken System.* New York: New York University Press.

Doyle, M., and M. Dolan. 2002. "Violence Risk Assessment: Combining Actuarial and Clinical Information to Structure Clinical Judgements for the Formulation and Management of Risk." *Journal of Psychiatric and Mental Health Nursing* 9 (6): 649–657.

D'unger, A. V., K. C. Land, P. L. McCall, and D. S. Nagin. 1998. "How Many Latent Classes of Delinquent/Criminal Careers? Results from Mixed Poisson Regression Analyses." *American Journal of Sociology* 103:1593–1630.

Durlak, J. A., and DuPre, E. P. 2008. "Implementation Matters: A Review of Research on the Influence of Implementation on Program Outcomes and the Factors Affecting Implementation." *American Journal of Community Psychology* 41 (3–4): 327–350.

Durlak, J. A., T. Fuhrman, and C. Lampman. 1991. "Effectiveness of Cognitive-Behavior Therapy for Maladapting Children." *Psychological Bulletin* 110 (2): 204–214.

Dusenbury, L., R. Brannigan, W. B. Hansen, J. Walsh, and M. Falco. 2005. "Quality of Implementation: Developing Measures Crucial to Understanding the Diffusion of Preventive Interventions." *Health Education Research* 20 (3): 308–313.

Dusenbury, L., M. Falco, A. Lakem, R. Brannigan, and K. Bosworth. 1997. "Nine Critical Elements of Promising Violence Prevention Programs." *Journal of School Health* 67 (10): 409–414.

Dweck, C. S. 2008. *Mindset: The New Psychology of Success.* New York: Random House.

Earls, F. J., and C. A. Visher. 1997. *Project on Human Development in Chicago Neighborhoods: A Research Update.* Washington, DC: National Institute of Justice.

Eccles, J. S., C. Midgley, A. Wigfield, C. M. Buchanan, D. Reuman, C. Flanagan, and D. M. Iver. 1993. "Development during Adolescence: The Impact of Stage-Environment Fit on Young Adolescents' Experiences in Schools and in Families." *American Psychologist* 48 (2): 90–101.

Eckholm, E. 2016. "States Move toward Treating 17-Year-Old Offenders as Juveniles, Not Adults." *New York Times*, May 13. Available at https://www.nytimes.com/2016/05/14/us/states-move-to-treat-17-year-old-offenders-as-juveniles.html.

Edwards, L. P. 1996. "The Future of the Juvenile Court: Promising New Directions." *Future of Children* 6:131–139.

Edwards, R. W., P. Jumper-Thurman, B. A. Plested, E. R. Oetting, and L. Swanson. 2000. "Community Readiness: Research to Practice." *Journal of Community Psychology* 28 (3): 291–307.

Eisenberg, N. 2000. "Emotion, Regulation, and Moral Development." *Annual Review of Psychology* 51 (1): 665–697.

Elder, G. H. 1998. "The Life Course as Developmental Theory." *Child Development* 69:1–12.

Ellickson, P., H. Saner, and K. A. McGuigan. 1997. "Profiles of Violent Youth: Substance Use and Other Concurrent Problems." *American Journal of Public Health* 87 (6): 985–991.

Elliott, D. S., and S. Mihalic. 2004. "Issues in Disseminating and Replicating Effective Prevention Programs." *Prevention Science* 5 (1): 47–53.

Elliott, D. S., W. J. Wilson, D. Huizinga, R. J. Sampson, A. Elliott, and B. Rankin. 1996. "The Effects of Neighborhood Disadvantage on Adolescent Development." *Journal of Research in Crime and Delinquency* 33:389–426.

Emerson, R. M. 1969. *Judging Delinquents*. New Brunswick, NJ: Transaction.

Erikson, E. 1968. *Youth: Identity and Crisis*. New York: W. W. Norton.

Ernst, M., D. S. Pine, and M. Hardin. 2006. "Triadic Model of the Neurobiology of Motivated Behavior in Adolescence." *Psychological Medicine* 36 (3): 299–312.

Esbensen, F. A., and D. Huizinga. 1993. "Gangs, Drugs, and Delinquency in a Survey of Urban Youth." *Criminology* 31 (4): 565–589.

Espinosa, E. M., J. R. Sorensen, and M. A. Lopez. 2013. "Youth Pathways to Placement: The Influence of Gender, Mental Health Need and Trauma on Confinement in the Juvenile Justice System." *Journal of Youth and Adolescence* 42 (12): 1824–1836.

Evans, G. W., D. Li, and S. S. Whipple. 2013. "Cumulative Risk and Child Development." *Psychological Bulletin* 139:1342–1396.

Ezell, M. 1989. "Juvenile Arbitration: Net Widening and Other Unintended Consequences." *Journal of Research in Crime and Delinquency* 26 (4): 358–377.

Fader, J. J., P. W. Harris, P. R. Jones, and M. E. Poulin. 2001. "Factors Involved in Decisions on Commitment to Delinquency Programs for First-Time Juvenile Offenders." *Justice Quarterly* 18 (2): 323–341.

Fagan, A. A., K. Hanson, J. D. Hawkins, and M. W. Arthur. 2008. "Bridging Science to Practice: Achieving Prevention Program Implementation Fidelity in the Community Youth Development Study." *American Journal of Community Psychology* 41 (3–4): 235–249.

Fagan, J. 2008. "Juvenile Crime and Criminal Justice: Resolving Border Disputes." *Future of Children* 18 (2): 81–118.

Fagan, J., and A. R. Piquero. 2007. "Rational Choice and Developmental Influences on Recidivism among Adolescent Felony Offenders." *Journal of Empirical Legal Studies* 4 (4): 715–748.

Fagan, J., and T. R. Tyler. 2005. "Legal Socialization of Children and Adolescents." *Social Justice Research* 18 (3): 217–241.

Farrington, D. P. 1986. "Age and Crime." In *Crime and Justice: A Review of Research*, vol. 8, edited by M. Tonry, 189–250. Chicago: University of Chicago Press.

———. 1991. "Childhood Aggression and Adult Violence: Early Precursors and Later-Life Outcomes." In *The Development and Treatment of Childhood Aggression*, edited by D. J. Pepler and K. H. Rubin, 5–29. Hillsdale, NJ: Lawrence Erlbaum.

———. 2005a. "The Integrated Cognitive Antisocial Potential (ICAP) Theory." In *Integrated Developmental and Life-Course Theories of Offending*, edited by D. P. Farrington, 73–92. New Brunswick, NJ: Transaction.

———. 2005b. "Introduction to Integrated Developmental and Life-Course Theories of Offending." In *Integrated Developmental and Life-Course Theories of Offending*, edited by D. P. Farrington, 1–14. New Brunswick, NJ: Transaction.

Farrington, D. P., D. Jolliffe, J. D. Hawkins, R. F. Catalano, K. G. Hill, and R. Kosterman. 2003. "Comparing Delinquency Careers in Court Records and Self-Reports." *Criminology* 41:933–958.

Farrington, D. P., D. Jolliffe, R. Loeber, and D. L. Homish. 2007. "How Many Offenses Are Really Committed per Juvenile Court Offender?" *Victims and Offenders* 2 (3): 227–249.

Farrington, D. P., R. Loeber, and J. C. Howell. 2012. "Young Adult Offenders." *Criminology and Public Policy* 11:729–750.

Farrington, D. P., and B. C. Welsh. 2007. *Saving Children from a Life of Crime*. Boulder, CO: Westview.

Farrington, D. P., and D. J. West. 1990. *The Cambridge Study in Delinquent Development: A Long-Term Follow-Up of 411 London Males*. London: Springer.

Featherman, D. L., and R. M. Lerner. 1985. "Ontogenesis and Sociogenesis: Problematics for Theory and Research about Development and Socialization across the Lifespan." *American Sociological Review* 50:659–676.

Feinberg, M. E., M. T. Greenberg, and D. W. Osgood. 2004. "Readiness, Functioning, and Perceived Effectiveness in Community Prevention Coalitions: A Study of Communities That Care." *American Journal of Community Psychology* 33 (3–4): 163–176.

Feld, B. C. 1984. "Criminalizing Juvenile Justice: Rules of Procedure for the Juvenile Court." *Minnesota Law Review* 69:141–276.

———. 1988. "Juvenile Court Meets the Principle of Offense: Punishment, Treatment, and the Difference It Makes." *Boston University Law Review* 68:821–916.

———. 1990. "Transformation of the Juvenile Court." *Minnesota Law Review* 75 (3): 691–726.

———. 1991. "Justice by Geography: Urban, Suburban, and Rural Variations in Juvenile Justice Administration." *Journal of Criminal Law and Criminology* 82 (1): 156–210.

———. 1997. "Abolish the Juvenile Court: Youthfulness, Criminal Responsibility, and Sentencing Policy." *Journal of Criminal Law and Criminology* 88 (1): 68–136.

———. 1998. "Juvenile and Criminal Justice Systems' Responses to Youth Violence." *Crime and Justice* 24:189–261.

———. 1999. "Transformation of the Juvenile Court, Part II: Race and the 'Crack Down' on Youth Crime." *Minnesota Law Review* 84 (2): 327–395.

———. 2003. "The Politics of Race and Juvenile Justice: The 'Due Process Revolution' and the Conservative Reaction." *Justice Quarterly* 20 (4): 765–800.

———. 2009. "Violent Girls or Relabeled Status Offenders? An Alternative Interpretation of the Data." *Crime and Delinquency* 55 (2): 241–265.

Fergusson, D. M., and L. J. Horwood. 1995. "Early Disruptive Behavior, IQ, and Later School Achievement and Delinquent Behavior." *Journal of Abnormal Child Psychology* 23 (2): 183–199.

Finckenauer, J. O., and P. W. Gavin. 1999. *Scared Straight! The Panacea Phenomenon Revisited.* Prospect Heights, IL: Waveland Press.

Fischhoff, B. 2008. "Assessing Adolescent Decision-Making Competence." *Developmental Review* 28 (1): 12–28.

Fixsen, D., and K. Blase. 2008. "Implementation Drivers." Available at http://nirn.fpg.unc.edu/learn-implementation/implementation-drivers.

Fixsen, D. L., K. A. Blase, A. Metz, and van Dyke, M. 2013. "Statewide Implementation of Evidence-Based Programs." *Exceptional Children* 79:213–230.

Fixsen, D. L., K. A. Blase, S. F. Naoom, and F. Wallace. 2009. "Core Implementation Components." *Research on Social Work Practice* 19:531–540.

Flaherty, C., C. Collins-Camargo, and E. Lee. 2008. "Privatization of Child Welfare Services: Lessons Learned from Experienced States regarding Site Readiness Assessment and Planning." *Children and Youth Services Review* 30 (7): 809–820.

Flay, B. R., A. Biglan, R. F. Boruch, F. G. Castro, D. Gottfredson, S. Kellam, E. K. Mościcki, S. Schinke, J. C. Valentine, and P. Ji. 2005. "Standards of Evidence: Criteria for Efficacy, Effectiveness and Dissemination." *Prevention Science* 6 (3): 151–175.

Flay, B. R., S. Graumlich, E. Segawa, J. L. Burns, M. Y. Holiday, and Aban Aya Investigators. 2004. "Effects of Two Prevention Programs on High-Risk Behaviors among African-American Youth." *Archives of Pediatric and Adolescent Medicine* 158:377–384.

Fondacaro, M. R., C. Slobogin, and T. Cross. 2006. "Reconceptualizing Due Process in Juvenile Justice: Contributions from Law and Social Science." *Hastings Law Journal* 57:955–1367.

Forbes, E. E., and R. E. Dahl. 2010. "Pubertal Development and Behavior: Hormonal Activation of Social and Motivational Tendencies." *Brain and Cognition* 72 (1): 66–72.

Ford, J. D., L. W. Ford, and A. D'Amelio. 2008. "Resistance to Change: The Rest of the Story." *Academy of Management Review* 33 (2): 362–377.

Ford, J. D., D. J. Grasso, J. Hawke, and J. F. Chapman. 2013. "Poly-victimization among Juvenile Justice-Involved Youths." *Child Abuse and Neglect* 37:788–800.

Forehand, R., and B. A. Kotchick. 1996. "Cultural Diversity: A Wake-Up Call for Parent Training." *Behavior Therapy* 27 (2): 187–206.

Forum on Child and Family Statistics. 2016. "America's Children: Key National Indicators of Well-Being, 2016." Available at https://www.childstats.gov/pdf/ac2016/ac_16.pdf.

Fox, B. H., N. Perez, E. Cass, M. T. Baglivio, and N. Epps. 2015. "Trauma Changes Everything: Examining the Relationship between Adverse Childhood Experiences and Serious, Violent and Chronic Juvenile Offenders." *Child Abuse and Neglect* 46:163–173.

Fox, S. 1996. "The Early History of the Court." *Future of Children* 6:29–39.

Frazier, C. E., and D. M. Bishop. 1990. "Obstacles to Reform in Juvenile Corrections: A Case Study." *Journal of Contemporary Criminal Justice* 6 (3): 157–166.

Frazier, C. E., and J. K. Cochran. 1986. "Official Intervention, Diversion from the Juvenile Justice System, and Dynamics of Human Services Work: Effects of a Reform Goal Based on Labeling Theory." *Crime and Delinquency* 32 (2): 157–176.

Furby, L., and Beyth-Marom, R. 1992. "Risk Taking in Adolescence: A Decision-Making Perspective." *Developmental Review* 12 (1): 1–44.

Furdella, J., and C. Puzzanchera. 2015. *Delinquency Cases in Juvenile Court, 2013.* Washington, DC: Office of Juvenile Justice and Delinquency Prevention.

Galvan, A. 2010. "Adolescent Development of the Reward System." *Frontiers in Human Neuroscience* 4:116–124.

Galvan, A., T. A. Hare, C. E. Parra, J. Penn, H. Voss, G. Glover, and B. Casey. 2006. "Earlier Development of the Accumbens Relative to Orbitofrontal Cortex Might Underlie Risk-Taking Behavior in Adolescents." *Journal of Neuroscience* 26 (25): 6885–6892.

Galvan, A., T. Hare, H. Voss, G. Glover, and B. Casey. 2007. "Risk-Taking and the Adolescent Brain: Who Is at Risk?" *Developmental Science* 10 (2): F8–F14.

Gann, S. M., C. J. Sullivan, and O. S. Ilchi. 2015. "Elaborating on the Effects of Early Offending: A Study of Factors That Mediate the Impact of Onset Age on Long-Term Trajectories of Criminal Behavior." *Journal of Developmental and Life-Course Criminology* 1:63–86.

Gardner, M., and L. Steinberg. 2005. "Peer Influence on Risk Taking, Risk Preference, and Risky Decision Making in Adolescence and Adulthood: An Experimental Study." *Developmental Psychology* 41 (4): 625–635.

Gatti, U., R. E. Tremblay, and F. Vitaro. 2009. "Iatrogenic Effect of Juvenile Justice." *Journal of Child Psychology and Psychiatry* 50 (8): 991–998.

Ge, X., R. D. Conger, and G. H. Elder Jr. 2001. "The Relation between Puberty and Psychological Distress in Adolescent Boys." *Journal of Research on Adolescence* 11 (1): 49–70.

Gebo, E., and C. J. Sullivan. 2014. "A Statewide Comparison of Gang and Non-gang Youth in Public High Schools." *Youth Violence and Juvenile Justice* 12 (3): 191–208.

Gendreau, P. 1996. "The Principles of Effective Intervention with Offenders." In *Choosing Correctional Options That Work*, edited by A. Harland, 117–130. Thousand Oaks, CA: Sage.

Giordano, P. C., S. A. Cernkovich, and J. L. Rudolph. 2002. "Gender, Crime, and Desistance: Toward a Theory of Cognitive Transformation." *American Journal of Sociology* 107 (4): 990–1064.

Glassner, B., M. Ksander, B. Berg, and B. D. Johnson. 1983. "A Note on the Deterrent Effect of Juvenile vs. Adult Jurisdiction." *Social Problems* 31 (2): 219–221.

Glick, B., and A. P. Goldstein. 1987. "Aggression Replacement Training." *Journal of Counseling and Development* 65 (7): 356–362.

Glueck, S., and E. T. Glueck. 1950. *Unraveling Juvenile Delinquency.* Cambridge, MA: Harvard University Press.

———. 1968. *Delinquents and Nondelinquents in Perspective.* Cambridge, MA: Harvard University Press.

Gordon, R. A., B. B. Lahey, E. Kawai, R. Loeber, M. Stouthamer-Loeber, and D. P. Farrington. 2004. "Antisocial Behavior and Youth Gang Membership: Selection and Socialization." *Criminology* 42 (1): 55–88.

Gottfredson, D. M. 1987. "Prediction and Classification in Criminal Justice Decision Making." *Crime and Justice* 9:1–20.

Gottfredson, M. R., and T. Hirschi. 1990. *A General Theory of Crime*. Stanford, CA: Stanford University Press.

Graham v. Florida. 2010. 560 U.S. 48.

Green, L. W. 2001. "From Research to 'Best Practices' in Other Settings and Populations." *American Journal of Health Behavior* 25 (3): 165–178.

———. 2006. "Public Health Asks of Systems Science: To Advance Our Evidence-Based Practice, Can You Help Us Get More Practice-Based Evidence?" *American Journal of Public Health* 96 (3): 406–409.

Greenberg, D. F. 1977. "Delinquency and the Age Structure of Society." *Crime, Law and Social Change* 1 (2): 189–223.

———. 1985. "Age, Crime, and Social Explanation." *American Journal of Sociology* 91:1–121.

Greenberg, M. T., C. A. Kusche, E. T. Cook, and J. P. Quamma. 1995. "Promoting Emotional Competence in School-Aged Children: The Effects of the PATHS Curriculum." *Development and Psychopathology* 7 (1): 117–136.

Greene, J. G. 1988. "Stakeholder Participation and Utilization in Program Evaluation." *Evaluation Review* 12 (2): 91–116.

Greenhalgh, T., G. Robert, F. Macfarlane, P. Bate, and O. Kyriakidou. 2004. "Diffusion of Innovations in Service Organizations: Systematic Review and Recommendations." *Milbank Quarterly* 82 (4): 581–629.

Greenwood, P. W. 2006. *Changing Lives: Delinquency Prevention as Crime-Control Policy*. Chicago: University of Chicago Press.

———. 2007. "Promising Solutions in Juvenile Justice." In *Deviant Peer Influences in Programs for Youth: Problems and Solutions*, edited by K. A. Dodge, T. J. Dishion, and J. E. Lansford, 278–295. New York: Guilford Press.

———. 2014. *Evidence-Based Practice in Juvenile Justice: Progress, Challenges, and Opportunities*. New York: Springer.

Greenwood, P. W., and A. F. Abrahamse. 1982. *Selective Incapacitation*. Santa Monica, CA: Rand.

Greenwood, P. W., and B. C. Welsh. 2012. "Promoting Evidence-Based Practice in Delinquency Prevention at the State Level." *Criminology and Public Policy* 11 (3): 493–513.

Greenwood, P. W., and F. E. Zimring. 1985. *One More Chance: The Pursuit of Promising Intervention Strategies for Chronic Juvenile Offenders*. Santa Monica, CA: Rand.

Griffin, P. 1999a. "Developing and Administering Accountability-Based Sanctions for Juveniles." *Juvenile Accountability Incentive Block Grants Program Bulletin*, September. Available at https://pdfs.semanticscholar.org/5a3a/f7e942bb5cf6a13e88c7f770 dcdc18ab5e76.pdf.

———. 1999b. *Juvenile Probation in the Schools*. Pittsburgh, PA: National Center for Juvenile Justice.

Griffin, P., S. Addie, B. Adams, and K. Firestine. 2011. "Trying Juveniles as Adults: An Analysis of State Transfer Laws and Reporting." *Juvenile Offenders and Victims National Report Series Bulletin*, September. Available at http://www.ncjj.org/pdf/ Transfer_232434.pdf.

Grisso, T., and A. Kavanaugh. 2016. "Prospects for Developmental Evidence in Juvenile Sentencing Based on Miller v. Alabama." *Psychology, Public Policy, and Law* 22 (3): 235–249.

Grusec, J. E., and J. J. Goodnow. 1994. "Impact of Parental Discipline Methods on the Child's Internalization of Values: A Reconceptualization of Current Points of View." *Developmental Psychology* 30 (1): 4–19.

Haberman, C. 2014. "When Youth Violence Spurred 'Superpredator' Fear." *New York Times*, April 6. Available at https://www.nytimes.com/2014/04/07/us/politics/killing-on-bus-recalls-superpredator-threat-of-90s.html.

Habermas, T., and S. Bluck. 2000. "Getting a Life: The Emergence of the Life Story in Adolescence." *Psychological Bulletin* 126 (5): 748–769.

Hall, G. S. 1904. *Adolescence: Its Psychology and Its Relations to Physiology, Anthropology, Sociology, Sex, Crime, Religion and Education.* New York: Sidney Appleton.

Hardy, S. A. 2006. "Identity, Reasoning, and Emotion: An Empirical Comparison of Three Sources of Moral Motivation." *Motivation and Emotion* 30 (3): 205–213.

Hart, D. 2005. "The Development of Moral Identity." *Nebraska Symposium on Motivation: Moral Motivation through the Lifespan*, vol. 51, edited by G. Carlo and C. P. Edwards, 165–196. Lincoln: University of Nebraska Press.

Hawkins, J. D., R. F. Catalano, R. Kosterman, R. Abbott, and K. G. Hill. 1999. "Preventing Adolescent Health-Risk Behaviors by Strengthening Protection during Childhood." *Archives of Pediatrics and Adolescent Medicine* 153:226–234.

Hawkins, J. D., R. F. Catalano, and J. Y. Miller. 1992. "Risk and Protective Factors for Alcohol and Other Drug Problems in Adolescence and Early Adulthood: Implications for Substance Abuse Prevention." *Psychological Bulletin* 112:64–105.

Hawkins, J. D., T. Herrenkohl, D. P. Farrington, D. Brewer, R. F. Catalano, and T. W. Harachi. 1998. "A Review of Predictors of Youth Violence." In *Serious and Violent Juvenile Offenders: Risk Factors and Successful Interventions*, edited by R. Loeber and D. Farrington, 106–146. Thousand Oaks, CA: Sage.

Hawkins, J. D., R. Kosterman, R. F. Catalano, K. G. Hill, and R. D. Abbott. 2005. "Promoting Positive Adult Functioning through Social Development Intervention in Childhood: Long-Term Effects from the Seattle Social Development Project." *Archives of Pediatrics and Adolescent Medicine* 159:25–31.

Hawkins, J. D., S. Oesterle, E. C. Brown, M. W. Arthur, R. D. Abbott, A. A. Fagan, and R. F. Catalano. 2009. "Results of a Type 2 Translational Research Trial to Prevent Adolescent Drug Use and Delinquency: A Test of Communities That Care." *Archives of Pediatrics and Adolescent Medicine* 163 (9): 789–798.

Haynie, D. L., and D. W. Osgood. 2005. "Reconsidering Peers and Delinquency: How Do Peers Matter?" *Social Forces* 84:1109–1130.

Healy, W. 1912. "The Problem of Causation of Criminality." *Journal of the American Institute of Criminal Law and Criminology* 2:849–857.

———. 1913. "Present Day Aims and Methods in Studying the Offender." *Journal of the American Institute of Criminal Law and Criminology* 4 (2): 204–211.

———. 1925. "The Psychology of the Situation: A Fundamental for Understanding and Treatment of Delinquency and Crime." In *The Child, the Clinic, and the Court: A Group of Papers*, edited by J. Addams, 37–52. New York: New Republic.

———. 1933. "The Prevention of Delinquency and Criminality." *Journal of Criminal Law and Criminology* 24 (1): 74–87.

Heckman, J. J. 1981. "Heterogeneity and State Dependence." In *Studies in Labor Markets*, edited by S. Rosen, 91–140. Chicago: University of Chicago Press.

———. 2000. "Policies to Foster Human Capital." *Research in Economics* 54 (1): 3–56.

Heckman, J. J., and Y. Rubinstein. 2001. "The Importance of Noncognitive Skills: Lessons from the GED Testing Program." *American Economic Review* 91 (2): 145–149.

Heckman, J. J., J. Stixrud, and S. Urzua. 2006. "The Effects of Cognitive and Noncognitive Abilities on Labor Market Outcomes and Social Behavior." *Journal of Labor Economics* 24 (3): 411–482.

Henderson, C. E., D. W. Young, N. Jainchill, J. Hawke, S. Farkas, and R. M. Davis. 2007. "Program Use of Effective Drug Abuse Treatment Practices for Juvenile Offenders." *Journal of Substance Abuse Treatment* 32 (3): 279–290.

Henderson, J. L., S. MacKay, and M. Peterson-Badali. 2006. "Closing the Research-Practice Gap: Factors Affecting Adoption and Implementation of a Children's Mental Health Program." *Journal of Clinical Child and Adolescent Psychology* 35 (1): 2–12.

Henggeler, S. W. 1997. "Treating Serious Anti-social Behavior in Youth: The MST Approach." *Juvenile Justice Bulletin*, May. Available at https://files.eric.ed.gov/fulltext/ED412438.pdf.

Henggeler, S. W., and S. K. Schoenwald. 2011. "Evidence-Based Interventions for Juvenile Offenders and Juvenile Justice Policies That Support Them." *Social Policy Report* 25 (1): 1, 3–20.

Henggeler, S. W., S. K. Schoenwald, C. M. Borduin, M. D. Rowland, and P. B. Cunningham. 2009. *Multisystemic Therapy for Antisocial Behavior in Children and Adolescents*. New York: Guilford Press.

Henning, K. 2004. "Eroding Confidentiality in Delinquency Proceedings: Should Schools and Public Housing Authorities Be Notified." *New York University Law Review* 79:520–611.

Henry, D. B., P. H. Tolan, and D. Gorman-Smith. 2001. "Longitudinal Family and Peer Group Effects on Violence and Nonviolent Delinquency." *Journal of Clinical Child Psychology* 30:172–186.

Hindelang, M. J. 1970. "The Commitment of Delinquents to Their Misdeeds: Do Delinquents Drift?" *Social Problems* 17:502–509.

Hinshaw, S. 1992. "Externalizing Behavior Problems and Academic Underachievement in Childhood and Adolescence: Causal Relationships and Underlying Mechanisms." *Psychological Bulletin* 111 (1): 127–155.

Hirschfield, P. J. 2008. "Preparing for Prison? The Criminalization of School Discipline in the USA." *Theoretical Criminology* 12 (1): 79–101.

———. 2009. "Another Way Out: The Impact of Juvenile Arrests on High School Dropout." *Sociology of Education* 82:368–393.

Hirschi, T. 1969. *Causes of Delinquency*. Berkeley: University of California Press.

Hirschi, T., and M. Gottfredson. 1983. "Age and the Explanation of Crime." *American Journal of Sociology* 89:553–585.

———. 1994. "The Generality of Deviance." In *Advances in Criminological Theory*. Vol. 12 of *Control Theories of Crime*, edited by C. Britt and M. Gottfredson, 1–22. New Brunswick, NJ: Transaction.

Hoagwood, K., P. S. Jensen, T. Petti, and B. J. Burns. 1996. "Outcomes of Mental Health Care for Children and Adolescents: I. A Comprehensive Conceptual Model." *Journal of the American Academy of Child and Adolescent Psychiatry* 35 (8): 1055–1063.

Hockenberry, S. 2016. "Juveniles in Residential Placement, 2013." *Juvenile Justice Statistics National Report Series*, May. Available at https://www.ojjdp.gov/pubs/249507 .pdf.

Hockenberry, S., and C. Puzzanchera. 2014. "Delinquency Cases in Juvenile Court, 2011." *Juvenile Offenders and Victims National Report Series*, December. Available at http://www.ncjj.org/pdf/248409.pdf.

———. 2015. *Juvenile Court Statistics, 2013*. Washington, DC: Office of Juvenile Justice and Delinquency Prevention.

Hofmann, S. G., A. Asnaani, I. J. Vonk, A. T. Sawyer, and A. Fang. 2012. "The Efficacy of Cognitive Behavioral Therapy: A Review of Meta-analyses." *Cognitive Therapy and Research* 36 (5): 427–440.

Holman, B., and J. Ziedenberg. 2006. *The Dangers of Detention: The Impact of Incarcerating Youth in Detention and Other Secure Facilities*. Washington, DC: Justice Policy Institute.

Holmbeck, G. N., C. Colder, W. Shapera, V. Westhoven, L. Kenealy, and A. Updegrove. 2000. "Working with Adolescents: Guides from Developmental Psychology." In *Child and Adolescent Therapy: Cognitive-Behavioral Procedures*, edited by P. C. Kendall, 334–385. New York: Guilford Press.

Horney, J. 2001. "Criminal Events and Criminal Careers: An Integrative Approach to the Study of Violence." In *The Process and Structure of Crime: Criminal Events and Crime Analysis*, vol. 9, edited by R. F. Meier, L. W. Kennedy, and V. F. Sacco, 141–168. New Brunswick, NJ: Transaction.

Howell, J. C. 2003. "Diffusing Research into Practice Using the Comprehensive Strategy for Serious, Violent, and Chronic Juvenile Offenders." *Youth Violence and Juvenile Justice* 1:219–245.

Howell, J. C., M. Kelly, J. Palmer, and R. Mangum. 2003. "Integrating Child Welfare, Juvenile Justice, and Other Agencies in a Continuum of Services." *Child Welfare* 83 (2): 143–156.

Howell, J. M., and C. A. Higgins. 1990. "Champions of Change: Identifying, Understanding, and Supporting Champions of Technological Innovations." *Organizational Dynamics* 19 (1): 40–55.

Hubbard, D. J., L. F. Travis, and E. J. Latessa. 2001. *Case Classification in Community Corrections: A National Survey of the State of the Art*. Cincinnati, OH: Center for Criminal Justice Research. Available at https://www.uc.edu/content/dam/uc/ccjr/docs/reports/project_reports/NIJCommunityCorrections2001.pdf.

Hubel, G. S., A. Schreier, D. J. Hansen, and B. L. Wilcox. 2013. "A Case Study of the Effects of Privatization of Child Welfare on Services for Children and Families: The Nebraska Experience." *Children and Youth Services Review* 35 (12): 2049–2058.

Huesmann, L. R. 1988. "An Information Processing Model for the Development of Aggression." *Aggressive Behavior* 14:13–24.

Huey, S. J., Jr., S. W. Henggeler, M. J. Brondino, and S. G. Pickrel. 2000. "Improved Family and Peer Functioning." *Journal of Consulting and Clinical Psychology* 68 (3): 451–467.

Huff, C. R. 1998. *Comparing the Criminal Behavior of Youth Gangs and At-Risk Youths: Research in Brief*. Washington, DC: National Institute of Justice.

Huizinga, D., and D. S. Elliott. 1986. "Reassessing the Reliability and Validity of Self-Report Delinquency Measures." *Journal of Quantitative Criminology* 2:293–327.

Huizinga, D., F. A. Esbensen, and A. W. Weiher. 1991. "Are There Multiple Paths to Delinquency?" *Journal of Criminal Law and Criminology* 82:83–118.

Huizinga, D., and C. Jakob-Chien. 1998. "The Contemporaneous Co-occurrence of Serious and Violent Juvenile Offending and Other Problem Behaviors." In *Serious and Violent Juvenile Offenders: Risk Factors and Successful Interventions*, edited by R. Loeber and D. Farrington, 47–67. Thousand Oaks, CA: Sage.

Huizinga, D., R. Loeber, T. P. Thornberry, and L. Cothern. 2000. *Co-occurrence of Delinquency and Other Problem Behaviors.* Washington, DC: Office of Juvenile Justice and Delinquency Prevention.

Humphrey, N., A. Barlow, M. Wigelsworth, A. Lendrum, K. Pert, C. Joyce, E. Stephens, L. Wo, G. Squires, and K. Woods. 2016. "A Cluster Randomized Controlled Trial of the Promoting Alternative Thinking Strategies (PATHS) Curriculum." *Journal of School Psychology* 58:73–89.

Hussong, A. M., P. J. Curran, T. E. Moffitt, A. Caspi, and M. M. Carrig. 2004. "Substance Abuse Hinders Desistance in Young Adults' Antisocial Behavior." *Development and Psychopathology* 16:1029–1046.

Hyland, N. 2018. *Delinquency Cases in Juvenile Court, 2014.* Washington, DC: U.S. Department of Justice.

Inderbitzin, M. 2009. "Reentry of Emerging Adults: Adolescent Inmates' Transition Back into the Community." *Journal of Adolescent Research* 24 (4): 453–476.

Ingersoll, S., and D. LeBoeuf. 1997. *Reaching Out to Youth Out of the Education Mainstream.* Washington, DC: U.S. Department of Justice.

Ingram, H., and A. Schneider. 1991. "The Choice of Target Populations." *Administration and Society* 23 (3): 333–356.

In Re Gault. 1967. 387 U.S. 1.

International Association of Chiefs of Police. 2014. *Law Enforcement's Leadership Role in Juvenile Justice Reform.* Washington, DC: International Association of Chiefs of Police.

Ireland, T. O., C. A. Smith, and T. P. Thornberry. 2002. "Developmental Issues in the Impact of Child Maltreatment on Later Delinquency and Drug Use." *Criminology* 40 (2): 359–400.

Jackson, S., and M. Fondacaro. 1999. "Procedural Justice in Resolving Family Conflict: Implications for Youth Violence Prevention." *Law and Policy* 21 (2): 101–127.

James, C., G.J.J. Stams, J. J. Asscher, A. K. De Roo, and P. H. van der Laan. 2013. "Aftercare Programs for Reducing Recidivism among Juvenile and Young Adult Offenders: A Meta-analytic Review." *Clinical Psychology Review* 33 (2): 263–274.

Jessor, R., and S. Jessor. 1997. *Problem Behavior and Psychosocial Development: A Longitudinal Study of Youth.* New York: Academic Press.

Jessor, R., J. Van Den Bos, J. Venderryn, F. M. Costa, and M. S. Turbin. 1995. "Protective Factors in Adolescent Problem Behavior: Moderator Effects and Developmental Change." *Developmental Psychology* 31:923–933.

Jones, N. J., S. L. Brown, D. Robinson, and D. Frey. 2015. "Incorporating Strengths into Quantitative Assessments of Criminal Risk for Adult Offenders: The Service Planning Instrument." *Criminal Justice and Behavior* 42 (3): 321–338.

———. 2016. "Validity of the Youth Assessment and Screening Instrument: A Juvenile Justice Tool Incorporating Risks, Needs, and Strengths." *Law and Human Behavior* 40 (2): 182–194.

Justice Policy Institute. 2013. *Juvenile Justice Reform in Connecticut: How Collaboration and Commitment Have Improved Public Safety and Outcomes for Youth*. Washington, DC: Justice Policy Institute.

Kaeble, D., and L. Glaze. 2016. *Correctional Populations in the United States, 2016*. Washington, DC: Bureau of Justice Statistics.

Kahneman, D. 2003. "A Perspective on Judgment and Choice: Mapping Bounded Rationality." *American Psychologist* 58 (9): 697–720.

Kaufman, I. R. 1980. *Juvenile Justice Standards Relating to Adjudication*. Cambridge, MA: Ballinger.

Kazdin, A. E. 2000. "Understanding Change: From Description to Explanation in Child and Adolescent Psychotherapy Research." *Journal of School Psychology* 38 (4): 337–347.

Kazdin, A. E., and M. K. Nock. 2003. "Delineating Mechanisms of Change in Child and Adolescent Therapy: Methodological Issues and Research Recommendations." *Journal of Child Psychology and Psychiatry* 44 (8): 1116–1129.

Kempf-Leonard, K. 2012. "The Conundrum of Girls and Juvenile Justice Processing." In *Oxford Handbook of Juvenile Crime and Juvenile Justice*, edited by B. C. Feld and D. Bishop, 485–525. New York: Oxford University Press.

Kendall, P. C. 1993. "Cognitive-Behavioral Therapies with Youth: Guiding Theory, Current Status, and Emerging Developments." *Journal of Consulting and Clinical Psychology* 61 (2): 235–247.

Kendall, P. C., and L. Braswell. 1993. *Cognitive-Behavioral Therapy for Impulsive Children*. New York: Guilford Press.

Kendall, P. C., and M. S. Choudhury. 2003. "Children and Adolescents in Cognitive-Behavioral Therapy: Some Past Efforts and Current Advances, and the Challenges in our Future." *Cognitive Therapy and Research* 27 (1): 89–104.

Kent v. United States. 1966. 383 U.S. 541.

Kilpatrick, D. G., B. E. Saunders, and D. W. Smith. 2003. "Youth Victimization: Prevalence and Implications." *NIJ Research in Brief*, April. Available at https://www.ncjrs.gov/pdffiles1/nij/194972.pdf.

Kim, B.K.E., K. M. Gloppen, I. C. Rhew, S. Oesterle, and J. D. Hawkins. 2015. "Effects of the Communities That Care Prevention System on Youth Reports of Protective Factors." *Prevention Science* 16 (5): 652–662.

Kirk, D. S. 2006. "Examining the Divergence across Self-Report and Official Data Sources on Inferences about the Adolescent Life-Course of Crime." *Journal of Quantitative Criminology* 22:107–129.

Kirk, D. S., and R. J. Sampson. 2013. "Juvenile Arrest and Collateral Educational Damage in the Transition to Adulthood." *Sociology of Education* 86:36–62.

Klein, K. J., and A. P. Knight. 2005. "Innovation Implementation: Overcoming the Challenge." *Current Directions in Psychological Science* 14 (5): 243–246.

Klein, M. W. 1979. "Deinstitutionalization and Diversion of Juvenile Offenders: A Litany of Impediments." *Crime and Justice* 1:145–201.

Koepke, S., and J.J.A. Denissen. 2012. "Dynamics of Identity Development and Separation-Individuation in Parent-Child Relationships during Adolescence and Emerging Adulthood: A Conceptual Integration." *Developmental Review* 32 (1): 67–88.

Kohlberg, L. 1969. *Stages in the Development of Moral Thought and Action*. New York: Holt, Rinehart, and Winston.

Kraemer, H. C., E. Stice, A. Kazdin, D. Offord, and D. Kupfer. 2001. "How Do Risk Factors Work Together? Mediators, Moderators, and Independent, Overlapping, and Proxy Risk Factors." *American Journal of Psychiatry* 158 (6): 848–856.

Kravitz, R. L., N. Duan, and J. Braslow. 2004. "Evidence-Based Medicine, Heterogeneity of Treatment Effects, and the Trouble with Averages." *Milbank Quarterly* 82 (4): 661–687.

Kreager, D. A., K. Rulison, and J. Moody. 2011. "Delinquency and the Structure of Adolescent Peer Groups." *Criminology* 49 (1): 95–127.

Krisberg, B., and J. Austin. 1993. *Reinventing Juvenile Justice.* Newbury Park, CA: Sage.

Krisberg, B., E. Currie, D. Onek, and R. G. Wiebush. 1995. "Graduated Sanctions for Serious, Violent, and Chronic Juvenile Offenders." In *A Sourcebook: Serious, Violent, and Chronic Juvenile Offenders,* edited by J. C. Howell, B. Krisberg, J. D. Hawkins, and J. J. Wilson, 142–170. Thousand Oaks, CA: Sage.

Krisberg, B., P. Litsky, and I. Schwartz. 1984. "Youth in Confinement: Justice by Geography." *Journal of Research in Crime and Delinquency* 21 (2): 153–181.

Kumpfer, K., V. Molgaard, and R. Spoth. 1996. *Preventing Childhood Disorders, Substance Abuse, and Delinquency.* Thousand Oaks, CA: Sage.

Kupchik, A. 2006. *Judging Juveniles: Prosecuting Adolescents in Adult and Juvenile Courts.* New York: New York University Press.

———. 2010. *Homeroom Security: School Discipline in an Age of Fear.* New York: New York University Press.

Kurlychek, M. C., P. M. Torbet, and M. Bozynski. 1999. "Focus on Accountability: Best Practices for Juvenile Court and Probation." *Juvenile Accountability Incentive Block Grants Program Bulletin,* August. Available at https://www.ncjrs.gov/pdffiles1/177611.pdf.

Lahey, B., and I. Waldman. 2005. "A Developmental Model of the Propensity to Offend during Childhood and Adolescence." In *Integrated Developmental and Life-Course Theories of Offending,* edited by D. P. Farrington, 15–50. New Brunswick, NJ: Transaction.

Lahey, B., I. D. Waldman, and K. McBurnett. 1999. "The Development of Antisocial Behavior: An Integrative Causal Model." *Journal of Child Psychology and Psychiatry* 40:669–682.

Landenberger, N. A., and M. W. Lipsey. 2005. "The Positive Effects of Cognitive-Behavioral Programs for Offenders: A Meta-analysis of Factors Associated with Effective Treatment." *Journal of Experimental Criminology* 1 (4): 451–476.

Lapsley, D. K., and P. L. Hill. 2009. "The Development of the Moral Personality." In *Personality, Identity, and Character,* edited by D. Narvaez and D. K. Lapsley, 185–213. Cambridge: Cambridge University Press.

Latessa, E., B. Lovins, and K. Ostrowski. 2009. *The Ohio Youth Assessment System: Final Report.* Cincinnati, OH: University of Cincinnati Center for Criminal Justice Research.

Laub, J. H. 2000. "A Century of Delinquency Research and Delinquency Theory." In *A Century of Juvenile Justice,* edited by M. Rosenheim, F. Zimring, D. S. Tanenhaus, and B. Dohrn, 179–205. Chicago: University of Chicago Press.

———. 2016. "Life Course Research and the Shaping of Public Policy." In *Handbook of the Life Course,* vol. 2, edited by M. Shanahan, J. T. Mortimer, and M. K. Johnson, 623–637. New York: Springer.

Laub, J. H., and R. J. Sampson. 1993. "Turning Points in the Life-Course: Why Change Matters to the Study of Crime." *Criminology* 31:301–325.

———. 1998. "Integrating Qualitative and Quantitative Data." In *Methods of Life Course Research*, edited by J. Z. Giele and G. H. Elder, 213–230. Thousand Oaks, CA: Sage.

———. 2001. "Understanding Desistance from Crime." In *Crime and Justice: A Review of Research*, vol. 28, edited by M. Tonry, 1–69. Chicago: University of Chicago Press.

———. 2003. *Shared Beginnings, Divergent Lives: Delinquent Boys to Age 70.* Cambridge, MA: Harvard University Press.

Laub, J. H., R. J. Sampson, and G. A. Sweeten. 2006. "Assessing Sampson and Laub's Life-Course Theory of Crime." In *Taking Stock: The Status of Criminological Theory*, edited by F. T. Cullen, J. P. Wright, and K. R. Blevins, 313–333. New Brunswick, NJ: Transaction.

Lemerise, E. A., and W. F. Arsenio. 2000. "An Integrated Model of Emotion Processes and Cognition in Social Information Processing." *Child Development* 71 (1): 107–118.

Lemert, E. 1951. *Social Pathology: A Systematic Approach to the Study of Sociopathic Behavior.* New York: McGraw-Hill.

Leone, P., M. M. Quinn, and D. M. Osher. 2002. *Collaboration in the Juvenile Justice System and Youth Serving Agencies: Improving Prevention, Providing More Efficient Services, and Reducing Recidivism for Youth with Disabilities.* Washington, DC: American Institutes for Research.

Lerner, R. M., E. M. Dowling, and P. M. Anderson. 2003. "Positive Youth Development: Thriving as the Basis of Personhood and Civil Society." *Applied Developmental Science* 7 (3): 172–180.

Leventhal, T., and Brooks-Gunn, J. 2000. "The Neighborhoods They Live In: The Effects of Neighborhood Residence on Child and Adolescent Outcomes." *Psychological Bulletin* 126:309–337.

Leventhal, T., V. Dupéré, and J. Brooks-Gunn. 2009. "Neighborhood Influences on Adolescent Development." In *Handbook of Adolescent Psychology*, vol. 2, edited by L. Steinberg and R. Lerner, 411–443. New York: Wiley.

Levitt, S. D. 1998. "Juvenile Crime and Punishment." *Journal of Political Economy* 106 (6): 1156–1185.

Liau, A. K., A. Q. Barriga, and J. C. Gibbs. 1998. "Relations between Self-Serving Cognitive Distortions and Overt vs. Covert Antisocial Behavior in Adolescents." *Aggressive Behavior* 24 (5): 335–346.

Liberman, A. 2007. *Adolescents, Neighborhoods, and Violence: Recent Findings from the Project on Human Development in Chicago Neighborhoods.* Washington, DC: National Institute of Justice.

Lin, J. 2006. "Exploring the Impact of Institutional Placement on the Recidivism of Delinquent Youth." Ph.D. diss., New York University.

Lipsey, M. W. 1999. "Can Intervention Rehabilitate Serious Delinquents?" *Annals of the American Academy of Political and Social Science* 564 (1): 142–166.

———. 2009. "The Primary Factors That Characterize Effective Interventions with Juvenile Offenders: A Meta-analytic Overview." *Victims and Offenders* 4 (2): 124–147.

Lipsey, M. W., J. C. Howell, M. R. Kelly, G. Chapman, and D. Carver. 2010. "Improving the Effectiveness of Juvenile Justice Programs." Washington, DC: Center for Juvenile Justice Reform.

Lipsey, M. W., N. A. Landenberger, and S. J. Wilson. 2007. "Effects of Cognitive-Behavioral Programs for Criminal Offenders." Available at https://campbell collaboration.org/media/k2/attachments/1028_R.pdf.

Little, G. L., and K. D. Robinson. 1988. "Moral Reconation Therapy: A Systematic Step-by-Step Treatment System for Treatment Resistant Clients." *Psychological Reports* 62 (1): 135–151.

Lochman, J. E. 1992. "Cognitive-Behavioral Intervention with Aggressive Boys: Three-Year Follow-Up and Preventive Effects." *Journal of Consulting and Clinical Psychology* 60 (3): 426–432.

Lochman, J. E., N. R. Powell, J. M. Whidby, and D. P. Fitzgerald. 2006. "Aggressive Children: Cognitive-Behavioral Assessment and Treatment." In *Child and Adolescent Therapy: Cognitive Behavioral Procedures*, edited by P. C. Kendall, 33–81. New York: Guilford Press.

Loeber, R. 1982. "The Stability of Antisocial and Delinquent Child Behavior: A Review." *Child Development* 53:1431–1446.

———. 2012. "Does the Study of the Age-Crime Curve Have a Future?" In *Future of Criminology*, edited by R. Loeber and B. C. Welsh, 11–19. Oxford: Oxford University Press.

Loeber, R., and D. P. Farrington, eds. 1998. *Serious and Violent Juvenile Offenders: Risk Factors and Successful Interventions*. Thousand Oaks, CA: Sage.

———. 2000. "Young Children Who Commit Crime: Epidemiology, Developmental Origins, Risk Factors, Early Interventions, and Policy Implications." *Development and Psychopathology* 12:737–762.

———, eds. 2012. *From Juvenile Delinquency to Adult Crime: Criminal Careers, Justice Policy and Prevention*. New York: Oxford University Press.

Loeber, R., D. P. Farrington, M. Stouthamer-Loeber, and W. B. Van Kammen. 1998. *Antisocial Behavior and Mental Health Problems: Explanatory Factors in Childhood and Adolescence*. Mahwah, NJ: Lawrence Erlbaum.

Loeber, R., and D. Hay. 1997. "Key Issues in the Development of Aggression and Violence from Childhood to Early Adulthood." *Annual Review of Psychology* 48:371–410.

Loeber, R., and M. Le Blanc. 1990. "Toward a Developmental Criminology." In *Crime and Justice: A Review of Research*, vol. 12, edited by M. Tonry and N. Morris, 375–473. Chicago: University of Chicago Press.

Loeber, R., and M. Stouthamer-Loeber. 1986. "Family Factors as Correlates and Predictors of Juvenile Conduct Problems and Delinquency." *Crime and Justice* 7:29–149.

Loeber, R., and P.-O. H. Wikström. 1993. "Individual Pathways to Crime in Different Types of Neighborhoods." In *Integrating Individual and Ecological Aspects of Crime*, edited by D. P. Farrington, R. J. Sampson, and P.-O. H. Wikström, 169–204. Stockholm, Sweden: National Council for Crime Prevention.

Long, J., and C. J. Sullivan. 2017. "Learning More from Evaluation of Justice Interventions: Further Consideration of Theoretical Mechanisms in Juvenile Drug Courts." *Crime and Delinquency* 63 (9): 1091–1115.

Lösel, F., and A. Beelmann. 2006. "Child Social Skills Training." In *Preventing Crime: What Works for Children, Offenders, Victims, and Places*, edited by B. C. Welsh and D. P. Farrington, 33–54. New York: Springer.

Loughran, T. A., E. P. Mulvey, C. A. Schubert, J. Fagan, A. R. Piquero, and S. H. Losoya. 2009. "Estimating a Dose-Response Relationship between Length of Stay and Future Recidivism in Serious Juvenile Offenders." *Criminology* 47 (3): 699–740.

Loughran, T. A., A. R. Piquero, J. Fagan, and E. P. Mulvey. 2012. "Differential Deterrence: Studying Heterogeneity and Changes in Perceptual Deterrence among Serious Youthful Offenders." *Crime and Delinquency* 58 (1): 3–27.

Lueger, R. J. 2002. "Practice-Informed Research and Research-Informed Psychotherapy." *Journal of Clinical Psychology* 58 (10): 1265–1276.

Mack, J. 1909. "The Juvenile Court." *Harvard Law Review* 23:104–122.

MacKenzie, D. L., and R. Freeland. 2012. "Examining the Effectiveness of Juvenile Residential Programs." In *The Oxford Handbook of Juvenile Crime and Juvenile Justice*, edited by B. Feld and D. Bishop, 771–798. New York: Oxford University Press.

Maggard, S. R. 2015. "Assessing the Impact of the Juvenile Detention Alternatives Initiative (JDAI): Predictors of Secure Detention and Length of Stay before and after JDAI." *Justice Quarterly* 32 (4): 571–597.

Maguin, E., and R. Loeber. 1996. "Academic Performance and Delinquency." *Crime and Justice* 20:145–264.

Majchrzak, A. 1984. *Methods for Policy Research*. Newbury Park, CA: Sage.

Males, M. 2009. "Does the Adolescent Brain Make Risk Taking Inevitable? A Skeptical Appraisal." *Journal of Adolescent Research* 24 (1): 3–20.

Maloney, D., D. Romig, and T. Armstrong. 1988. *Juvenile Probation: The Balanced Approach*. Reno, NV: National Council of Juvenile and Family Court Judges.

Malti, T., and S. F. Ongley. 2014. "The Development of Moral Emotions and Moral Reasoning." In *Handbook of Moral Development*, vol. 2, edited by M. Killen and J. G. Smetana, 163–183. New York: Psychology Press.

Maltz, M. D., and J. M. Mullany. 2000. "Visualizing Lives: New Pathways for Analyzing Life Course Trajectories." *Journal of Quantitative Criminology* 16 (2): 255–281.

Manktelow, K. I. 2012. *Thinking and Reasoning: An Introduction to the Psychology of Reason, Judgment and Decision Making*. London: Psychology Press.

Markstrom-Adams, C. 1992. "A Consideration of Intervening Factors in Adolescent Identity Formation." In *Adolescent Identity Formation*, edited by G. R. Adams and R. Montemayor, 173–192. Newbury Park, CA: Sage.

Maroney, T. A. 2010. "The False Promise of Adolescent Brain Science in Juvenile Justice." *Notre Dame Law Review* 85:89–176.

Maruna, S. 2001. *Making Good: How Ex-convicts Reform and Rebuild Their Lives*. Washington, DC: American Psychological Association.

Maruna, S., and K. Roy. 2007. "Amputation or Reconstruction? Notes on the Concept of 'Knifing Off' and Desistance from Crime." *Journal of Contemporary Criminal Justice* 23:104–124.

Masten, A. S. 2001. "Ordinary Magic: Resilience Processes in Development." *American Psychologist* 56:227–238.

Masten, A. S., and D. Cicchetti. 2010. "Developmental Cascades." *Development and Psychopathology* 22 (3): 491–495.

Matthews, B., and D. Hubbard. 2007. "The Helping Alliance in Juvenile Probation: The Missing Element in the 'What Works' Literature." *Journal of Offender Rehabilitation* 45 (1–2): 105–122.

Matza, D. 1964. *Delinquency and Drift*. New Brunswick, NJ: Transaction.

Mayer, G. R. 2001. "Antisocial Behavior: Its Causes and Prevention within Our Schools." *Education and Treatment of Children* 24:414–429.

Mazor, A., and R. D. Enright. 1988. "The Development of the Individuation Process from a Social-Cognitive Perspective." *Journal of Adolescence* 11 (1): 29–47.

McAdams, D. P. 2009. "The Moral Personality." In *Personality, Identity, and Character: Explorations in Moral Psychology*, edited by D. Narvaez and D. K. Lapsley, 11–29. Cambridge: Cambridge University Press.

McCafferty, J. T. 2016. "The Importance of Counties: Examining the Predictive Validity of a State Juvenile Risk Assessment Instrument." *Journal of Offender Rehabilitation* 55 (6): 377–395.

McCart, M. R., P. E. Priester, W. H. Davies, and R. Azen. 2006. "Differential Effectiveness of Behavioral Parent-Training and Cognitive-Behavioral Therapy for Antisocial Youth: A Meta-analysis." *Journal of Abnormal Child Psychology* 34 (4): 525–541.

McCord, J., C. S. Widom, and N. A. Crowell, eds. 2003. *Juvenile Crime, Juvenile Justice*. Washington, DC: National Academies Press.

McGee, T. R., M. R. Hayatbakhsh, W. Bor, R. L. Aird, A. J. Dean, and J. M. Najman. 2015. "The Impact of Snares on the Continuity of Adolescent-Onset Antisocial Behaviour: A Test of Moffitt's Developmental Taxonomy." *Australian and New Zealand Journal of Criminology* 48:345–366.

McGloin, J., C. J. Sullivan, A. R. Piquero, and S. Bacon. 2008. "Investigating the Stability of Co-offending and Co-offenders among a Sample of Youthful Offenders." *Criminology* 46 (1): 155–188.

McGowan, A., R. Hahn, A. Liberman, A. Crosby, M. Fullilove, R. Johnson, E. Moscicki, L. Price, S. Snyder, F. Tuma, J. Lowy, P. Briss, S. Cory, G. Stone, and Task Force on Community Preventive Services. 2007. "Effects on Violence of Laws and Policies Facilitating the Transfer of Juveniles from the Juvenile Justice System to the Adult Justice System: A Systematic Review." *American Journal of Preventive Medicine* 32 (4): 7–28.

McGrath, A. 2008. "The Effect of Diversion from Court: A Review of the Evidence." *Psychiatry, Psychology and Law* 15 (2): 317–339.

McKinley, J. 2017. "'Raise the Age,' Now Law in New York, Is Still a Subject of Debate." *New York Times*, April 10. Available at https://www.nytimes.com/2017/04/10/nyregion/raise-the-age-new-york.html.

McLoyd, V. C., and B. Lozoff. 2001. "Racial and Ethnic Trends in Children's and Adolescents' Behavior and Development." In *America Becoming: Racial Trends and Their Consequences*, vol. 2, edited by N. J. Smelser, W. J. Wilson, and F. Mitchell, 311–350. Washington, DC: National Academies Press.

McReynolds, L. S., G. A. Wasserman, R. E. DeComo, R. John, J. M. Keating, and S. Nolen. 2008. "Psychiatric Disorder in a Juvenile Assessment Center." *Crime and Delinquency* 54 (2): 313–334.

Mears, D. P. 2002. "Sentencing Guidelines and the Transformation of Juvenile Justice in the 21st Century." *Journal of Contemporary Criminal Justice* 18 (1): 6–19.

———. 2012. "The Front End of the Juvenile Court: Intake and Informal vs. Formal Processing." In *Handbook of Juvenile Crime and Juvenile Justice*, edited by B. Feld and D. Bishop, 573–605. New York: Oxford University Press.

Mears, D. P., and W. R. Kelly. 1999. "Assessments and Intake Processes in Juvenile Justice Processing: Emerging Policy Considerations." *Crime and Delinquency* 45 (4): 508–529.

Mears, D. P., and J. Travis. 2004. "Youth Development and Reentry." *Youth Violence and Juvenile Justice* 2 (1): 3–20.

Meehl, P. E. 1954. *Clinical versus Statistical Prediction: A Theoretical Analysis and a Review of the Evidence*. Minneapolis: University of Minnesota.

Mendel, R. A. 2014. *Juvenile Detention Alternatives Initiative Progress Report, 2014.* Baltimore, MD: Annie E. Casey Foundation.

Meyers, D. C., J. A. Durlak, and A. Wandersman. 2012. "The Quality Implementation Framework: A Synthesis of Critical Steps in the Implementation Process." *American Journal of Community Psychology* 50 (3–4): 462–480.

Miller v. Alabama. 2012. 132 S. Ct. 2455.

Miller, A. D., L. E. Ohlin, and R. B. Coates. 1977. *A Theory of Social Reform: Correctional Change Processes in Two States.* Cambridge, MA: Ballinger.

Modell, J. 1994. "Review of *Crime in the Making: Pathways and Turning Points through Life* by Robert J. Sampson and John H. Laub." *American Journal of Sociology* 99 (5): 1389–1391.

Moffitt, T. E. 1990. "The Neuropsychology of Juvenile Delinquency: A Critical Review." *Crime and Justice* 12:99–169.

———. 1993. "Adolescent-Limited and Life-Course Persistent Antisocial Behavior: A Developmental Taxonomy." *Psychology Review* 100:674–701.

———. 2005. "The New Look of Behavioral Genetics in Developmental Psychopathology: Gene-Environment Interplay in Antisocial Behaviors." *Psychological Bulletin* 131:533–554.

———. 2006. "A Review of Research on the Taxonomy of Life-Course-Persistent versus Adolescence-Limited Antisocial Behavior." In *Taking Stock: The Status of Criminological Theory Advances in Criminological Theory*, vol. 15, edited by F. T. Cullen, J. P. Wright, and K. R. Blevins, 277–311. New Brunswick, NJ: Transaction.

Moffitt, T. E., A. Caspi, H. Harrington, and B. J. Milne. 2002. "Males on the Life-Course-Persistent and Adolescence-Limited Antisocial Pathways: Follow-Up at Age 26 Years." *Development and Psychopathology* 14:179–207.

Moffitt, T. E., D. R. Lynam, and P. A. Silva. 1994. "Neuropsychological Tests Predict Persistent Male Delinquency." *Criminology* 32:101–124.

Molnar, B. E., M. J. Miller, D. Azrael, and S. L. Buka. 2004. "Neighborhood Predictors of Concealed Firearm Carrying among Children and Adolescents: Results from the Project on Human Development in Chicago Neighborhoods." *Archives of Pediatrics and Adolescent Medicine* 158 (7): 657–664.

Moore, M. H., and M. Tonry. 1998. "Youth Violence in America." In *Crime and Justice: A Review of Research*, vol. 24, edited by M. Tonry, 1–26. Chicago: University of Chicago Press.

Morse, S. J. 1997. "Immaturity and Irresponsibility." *Journal of Criminal Law and Criminology* 88 (1): 15–67.

———. 1999. "Delinquency and Desert." *Annals of the American Academy of Political and Social Sciences* 564:56–80.

Mulvey, E. P., and A.-M. R. Iselin. 2008. "Improving Professional Judgments of Risk and Amenability in Juvenile Justice." *Future of Children* 18 (2): 35–57.

Mulvey, E. P., and N. D. Reppucci. 1988. "The Context of Clinical Judgment: The Effect of Resource Availability on Judgments of Amenability to Treatment in Juvenile Offenders." *American Journal of Community Psychology* 16 (4): 525–545.

Mulvey, E., and C. Schubert. 2012. "Youth in Prison and Beyond." In *The Oxford Handbook of Juvenile Crime and Juvenile Justice*, edited by B. C. Feld and D. Bishop, 843–870. New York: Oxford University Press.

Mulvey, E. P., C. A. Schubert, and L. Chassin. 2010. "Substance Use and Delinquent Behavior among Serious Adolescent Offenders." *Juvenile Justice Bulletin*, December. Available at https://www.ncjrs.gov/pdffiles1/ojjdp/232790.pdf.

Mulvey, E. P., L. Steinberg, J. Fagan, E. Cauffman, A. R. Piquero, L. Chassin, G. P. Knight, R. Brame, C. A. Schubert, T. Hecker, and S. Losoya. 2004. "Theory and Research on Desistance from Antisocial Activity among Serious Adolescent Offenders." *Youth Violence and Juvenile Justice* 2:213–236.

Mulvey, E. P., L. Steinberg, A. R. Piquero, M. Besana, J. Fagan, C. Schubert, and E. Cauffman. 2010. "Trajectories of Desistance and Continuity in Antisocial Behavior following Court Adjudication among Serious Adolescent Offenders." *Development and Psychopathology* 22:453–475.

Muthén, B. O. 2004. "Latent Variable Analysis: Growth Mixture Modeling and Related Techniques for Longitudinal Data." In *The Sage Handbook of Quantitative Methodology for the Social Sciences*, edited by D. Kaplan, 345–368. Thousand Oaks, CA: Sage.

Nagin, D. 2005. *Group-Based Modeling of Development.* Cambridge, MA: Harvard University Press.

Nagin, D. S., and D. P. Farrington. 1992. "The Stability of Criminal Potential from Childhood to Adulthood." *Criminology* 30:235–260.

Nagin, D. S., D. P. Farrington, and T. E. Moffitt. 1995. "Life-Course Trajectories of Different Types of Offenders." *Criminology* 33 (1): 111–139.

Nagin, D. S., and R. Paternoster. 1991. "On the Relationships of Past to Future Delinquency." *Criminology* 29:163–189.

———. 2000. "Population Heterogeneity and State Dependence: State of the Evidence and Directions for Future Research." *Journal of Quantitative Criminology* 16:117–144.

Nagin, D. S., A. R. Piquero, E. S. Scott, and L. Steinberg. 2006. "Public Preferences for Rehabilitation versus Incarceration of Juvenile Offenders: Evidence from a Contingent Valuation Survey." *Criminology and Public Policy* 5 (4): 627–651.

Nagin, D. S., and R. E. Tremblay. 2005. "Developmental Trajectory Groups: Fact or a Useful Statistical Fiction?" *Criminology* 43 (4): 873–918.

National Council of Juvenile and Family Court Judges. 2016. "Right Kid, Right Time, Right Program." July 26. Available at https://www.ncjfcj.org/right-kid-right-time-right-program.

National Institute on Drug Abuse. 1991. *National Household Survey on Drug Abuse: Population Estimates, 1991.* Rockville, MD: National Institute on Drug Abuse.

Ngwe, J. E., L. C. Liu, B. R. Flay, E. Segawa, and Aban Aya Investigators. 2004. "Violence Prevention among African-American Adolescent Males." *American Journal of Health Behaviors* 28:S24–S37.

Nicholson-Crotty, S., Z. Birchmeier, and D. Valentine. 2009. "Exploring the Impact of School Discipline on Racial Disproportion in the Juvenile Justice System." *Social Science Quarterly* 90 (4): 1003–1018.

Nieman, P., S. Shea, and Canadian Paediatric Society Community Paediatrics Committee. 2004. "Effective Discipline for Children." *Paediatrics and Child Health* 9:37–41.

Nissen, L. 2006. "Bringing Strength-Based Philosophy to Life in Juvenile Justice." *Reclaiming Children and Youth* 15 (1): 40–47.

NRC (National Research Council). 2013. *Reforming Juvenile Justice: A Developmental Approach*, edited by R. J. Bonnie, R. L. Johnson, B. M. Chemers, and J. A. Schuck. Washington, DC: National Academies Press.

Nunner-Winkler, G. 2007. "Development of Moral Motivation from Childhood to Early Adulthood." *Journal of Moral Education* 36:399–414.

Nutt, P. C. 1986. "Tactics of Implementation." *Academy of Management Journal* 29 (2): 230–261.

Nylund, K. L., T. Asparouhov, and B. O. Muthén. 2007. "Deciding on the Number of Classes in Latent Class Analysis and Growth Mixture Modeling: A Monte Carlo Simulation Study." *Structural Equation Modeling* 14 (4): 535–569.

O'Connor, J. M., and L. K. Treat. 1995. "Getting Smart about Getting Tough: Juvenile Justice and the Possibility of Progressive Reform." *American Criminal Law Review* 33:1299–1344.

Office of National Drug Control Policy. 2011. "Above the Influence Fact Sheet." Available at https://obamawhitehouse.archives.gov/ondcp/ondcp-fact-sheets/above-the -influence-ATI.

Ohio Department of Youth Services. 2016. "2016 Recidivism Report." Available at https://www.dys.ohio.gov/Portals/0/PDFs/Home/NewsAndFacts/Statistics/Msc _RecidivismReport_20161103.pdf.

Ohlin, L. E., R. B. Coates, and A. D. Miller. 1975. "Evaluating the Reform of Youth Correction in Massachusetts." *Journal of Research in Crime and Delinquency* 12 (1): 3–16.

OJJDP (Office of Juvenile Justice and Delinquency Prevention). n.d. "Program of Research on the Causes and Correlates of Delinquency." Available at https://www.ojjdp .gov/programs/ProgSummary.asp?pi=19 (accessed May 14, 2019).

———. 1995. *Guide for Implementing the Comprehensive Strategy for Serious, Violent, and Chronic Juvenile Offenders.* Washington, DC: U.S. Department of Justice.

———. 2000. *Second Chances: Giving Kids a Chance to Make a Better Choice.* Washington, DC: Office of Juvenile Justice and Delinquency Prevention.

———. 2017. *OJJDP Statistical Briefing Book.* Washington, DC: U.S. Department of Justice. Available at https://www.ojjdp.gov/ojstatbb.

———. 2019. "Juvenile Justice and Delinquency Prevention Act Reauthorized." Available at https://www.ojjdp.gov/enews/19juvjust/190107.html.

Osgood, D. W. 2005. "Making Sense of Crime and the Life Course." *Annals of the American Academy of Political and Social Science* 602 (1): 196–211.

Osgood, D. W., and A. L. Anderson. 2004. "Unstructured Socializing and Rates of Delinquency." *Criminology* 42 (3): 519–550.

Osgood, D. W., J. K. Wilson, P. M. O'Malley, J. G. Bachman, and L. D. Johnston. 1996. "Routine Activities and Individual Deviant Behavior." *American Sociological Review* 61 (4): 635–655.

Owen, J. W., and A. M. Larson. 2017. *Researcher-Policymaker Partnerships: Strategies for Launching and Sustaining Successful Collaborations.* New York: Routledge.

Paina, L., and D. H. Peters. 2012. "Understanding Pathways for Scaling Up Health Services through the Lens of Complex Adaptive Systems." *Health Policy and Planning* 27:365–373.

Parhar, K. K., J. S. Wormith, D. M. Derkzen, and A. M. Beauregard. 2008. "Offender Coercion in Treatment: A Meta-analysis of Effectiveness." *Criminal Justice and Behavior* 35 (9): 1109–1135.

Parsons, J. T., A. W. Siegel, and J. H. Cousins. 1997. "Late Adolescent Risk-Taking: Effects of Perceived Benefits and Perceived Risks on Behavioral Intentions and Behavioral Change." *Journal of Adolescence* 20 (4): 381–392.

Paternoster, R. 2010. "How Much Do We Really Know about Criminal Deterrence?" *Journal of Criminal Law and Criminology* 100 (3): 765–824.

Paternoster, R., and S. Bushway. 2009. "Desistance and the 'Feared Self': Toward an Identity Theory of Criminal Desistance." *Journal of Criminal Law and Criminology* 99 (4): 1103–1157.

Patterson, G. R., and K. Yoerger. 1993. "Developmental Models for Delinquent Behavior." In *Mental Disorder and Crime*, edited by S. Hodgins, 140–172. Newbury Park, CA: Sage.

Patton, M. Q. 1990. *Qualitative Evaluation Research Methods*. 2nd ed. Thousand Oaks, CA: Sage.

Pawson, R. 2003. "Nothing as Practical as a Good Theory." *Evaluation* 9 (4): 471–490.

Pawson, R., and N. Tilley. 1997. *Realistic Evaluation*. Thousand Oaks, CA: Sage.

Pearson, F. S., D. S. Lipton, C. M. Cleland, and D. S. Yee. 2002. "The Effects of Behavioral/Cognitive-Behavioral Programs on Recidivism." *Crime and Delinquency* 48 (3): 476–496.

Petrosino, A., S. Guckenburg, and C. Turpin-Petrosino. 2010. *Formal System Processing of Juveniles: Effects on Delinquency—a Systematic Review*. Philadelphia, PA: Campbell Collaboration.

Petrosino, A., C. Turpin-Petrosino, M. Hollis-Peel, and J. G. Lavenberg. 2013. *Scared Straight and Other Juvenile Awareness Programs for Preventing Juvenile Delinquency—a Systematic Review*. Philadelphia, PA: Campbell Collaboration.

Pettit, G. S., J. E. Bates, and K. A. Dodge. 1997. "Supportive Parenting, Ecological Context, and Children's Adjustment: A Seven-Year Longitudinal Study." *Child Development* 68 (5): 908–923.

Phillips, D. A., and J. P. Shonkoff. 2000. *From Neurons to Neighborhoods: The Science of Early Childhood Development*. Washington, DC: National Academies Press.

Piquero, A. 2001. "Testing Moffitt's Neuropsychological Variation Hypothesis for the Prediction of Life-Course Persistent Offending." *Psychology, Crime, and Law* 7:193–215.

———. 2004. "Somewhere between Persistence and Desistance: The Intermittency of Criminal Careers." In *After Crime and Punishment: Pathways to Offender Reintegration*, edited by S. Maruna and R. Immarigeon, 102–129. Portland, OR: Willan.

———. 2008a. "Disproportionate Minority Contact." *Future of Children* 18 (2): 59–79.

———. 2008b. "Taking Stock of Developmental Trajectories of Criminal Activity over the Life Course." In *The Long View of Crime: A Synthesis of Longitudinal Research*, edited by A. Liberman, 23–78. New York: Springer.

Piquero, A. R., T. Brezina, and M. G. Turner. 2005. "Testing Moffitt's Account of Delinquency Abstention." *Journal of Research in Crime and Delinquency* 42 (1): 27–54.

Piquero, A. R., J. Fagan, E. P. Mulvey, L. Steinberg, and C. Odgers. 2005. "Developmental Trajectories of Legal Socialization among Serious Adolescent Offenders." *Journal of Criminal Law and Criminology* 96 (1): 267–298.

Piquero, A. R., D. P. Farrington, and A. Blumstein. 2007. *Key Issues in Criminal Career Research: New Analyses of the Cambridge Study in Delinquent Development*. Cambridge: Cambridge University Press.

Piquero, A. R., W. G. Jennings, and D. P. Farrington. 2010. "On the Malleability of Self-Control: Theoretical and Policy Implications regarding a General Theory of Crime." *Justice Quarterly* 27 (6): 803–834.

Piquero, A. R., W. G. Jennings, D. P. Farrington, B. Diamond, and J.M.R. Gonzalez. 2016. "A Meta-analysis Update on the Effectiveness of Early Self-Control

Improvement Programs to Improve Self-Control and Reduce Delinquency." *Journal of Experimental Criminology* 12 (2): 249–264.

Piquero, A. R., K. C. Monahan, C. Glasheen, C. A. Schubert, and E. Mulvey. 2012. "Does Time Matter? Comparing Trajectory Concordance and Covariate Association Using Time-Based and Age-Based Assessments." *Crime and Delinquency* 59 (5): 738–763.

Piquero, A. R., and L. Steinberg. 2010. "Public Preferences for Rehabilitation versus Incarceration of Juvenile Offenders." *Journal of Criminal Justice* 38 (1): 1–6.

Pisciotta, A. W. 1982. "Saving the Children: The Promise and Practice of Parens Patriae, 1838–98." *Crime and Delinquency* 28 (3): 410–425.

Platt, A. 1969. "The Rise of the Child-Saving Movement: A Study in Social Policy and Correctional Reform." *Annals of the American Academy of Political and Social Science* 381 (1): 21–38.

Plomin, R., and D. Daniels. 2011. "Why Are Children in the Same Family So Different from One Another?" *International Journal of Epidemiology* 40:563–582.

Pogrebin, M. R., E. D. Poole, and R. M. Regoli. 1984. "Constructing and Implementing a Model Juvenile Diversion Program." *Youth and Society* 15 (3): 305–324.

Pokhrel, P., T. A. Herzog, D. S. Black, A. Zaman, N. R. Riggs, and S. Sussman. 2013. "Adolescent Neurocognitive Development, Self-Regulation, and School-Based Drug Use Prevention." *Prevention Science* 14 (3): 218–228.

Polk, K. 1984. "Juvenile Diversion: A Look at the Record." *Crime and Delinquency* 30 (4): 648–659.

Pratt, C., and R. Hernandez. 2003. *Building Results: Community Mobilization for Family Well-Being.* Salem: Oregon Commission on Children, Youth, and Families. Available at https://digital.osl.state.or.us/islandora/object/osl%3A6830.

Pratt, T. C., and F. T. Cullen. 2000. "The Empirical Status of Gottfredson and Hirschi's General Theory of Crime: A Meta-analysis." *Criminology* 38 (3): 931–964.

Puzzanchera, C. 2014. "Juvenile Arrests, 2012." *Juvenile Offenders and Victims National Report Series*, December. https://www.ojjdp.gov/pubs/248513.pdf.

Quetelet, A. (1831) 1984. *Research on the Propensity for Crime at Different Ages.* Translated by S. Sylvester. Reprint, Hayez: Brussels.

Raudenbush, S. W. 2005. "How Do We Study 'What Happens Next'?" *Annals of the American Academy of Political and Social Science* 602 (1): 131–144.

Reckless, W. C., S. Dinitz, and E. Murray. 1957. "The 'Good' Boy in a High Delinquency Area." *Journal of Criminal Law, Criminology, and Police Science* 48:18–25.

Regnery, A. S. 1985. "Getting Away with Murder." *Policy Review* 34:65–68.

Reiss, A. J., and D. P. Farrington. 1991. "Advancing Knowledge about Co-offending: Results from a Prospective Longitudinal Survey of London Males." *Journal of Criminal Law and Criminology* 82 (2): 360–395.

Reyna, V. F., and F. Farley. 2006. "Risk and Rationality in Adolescent Decision Making: Implications for Theory, Practice, and Public Policy." *Psychological Science in the Public Interest* 7 (1): 1–44.

Reyna, V. F., and S. E. Rivers. 2008. "Current Theories of Risk and Rational Decision Making." *Developmental Review* 28 (1): 1–11.

Riggs, N. R., M. T. Greenberg, C. A. Kusché, and M. A. Pentz. 2006. "The Mediational Role of Neurocognition in the Behavioral Outcomes of a Social-Emotional Prevention Program in Elementary School Students: Effects of the PATHS Curriculum." *Prevention Science* 7 (1): 91–102.

Robins, L. N. 1978. "Sturdy Childhood Predictors of Adult Antisocial Behaviour: Replications from Longitudinal Studies." *Psychological Medicine* 8:611–622.

Robinson, W. S. 1950. "Ecological Correlations and the Behavior of Individuals." *American Sociological Review* 15 (3): 351–357.

Rodriguez, N. 2007. "Restorative Justice at Work: Examining the Impact of Restorative Justice Resolutions on Juvenile Recidivism." *Crime and Delinquency* 53 (3): 355–379.

———. 2010. "The Cumulative Effect of Race and Ethnicity in Juvenile Court Outcomes and Why Preadjudication Detention Matters." *Journal of Research in Crime and Delinquency* 47 (3): 391–413.

Roest, J., P. van der Helm, and G. Stams. 2016. "The Relation between Therapeutic Alliance and Treatment Motivation in Residential Youth Care: A Cross-Lagged Panel Analysis." *Child and Adolescent Social Work Journal* 33 (5): 455–468.

Rogers, E. M. 1995. *Diffusion of Innovation*. New York: Free Press.

Rogers, J. W., and J. D. Williams. 1994. "The Predisposition Report, Decision-Making, and Juvenile Court Policy." *Juvenile and Family Court Journal* 45 (4): 47–57.

Roper v. Simmons. 2005. 543 U.S. 551.

Rosenblatt, A. 1996. "Bows and Ribbons, Tape and Twine: Wrapping the Wraparound Process for Children with Multi-system Needs." *Journal of Child and Family Studies* 5 (1): 101–116.

Rosenfeld, R. 2016. *Documenting and Explaining the 2015 Homicide Rise: Research Directions*. Washington, DC: National Institute of Justice.

Rothman, D. J. 1980. *Conscience and Convenience: The Asylum and Its Alternatives in Progressive America*. New Brunswick, NJ: Transaction.

Roush, D. W. 1996. *Desktop Guide to Good Juvenile Detention Practice*. Washington, DC: Office of Juvenile Justice and Delinquency Prevention.

Rutter, M. 1989. "Pathways from Childhood to Adult Life." *Journal of Child Psychology and Psychiatry* 30:23–51.

Ryerson, E. 1978. *The Best-Laid Plans: America's Juvenile Court Experiment*. New York: Hill and Wang.

Salekin, R. T., R. Rogers, and K. L. Ustad. 2001. "Juvenile Waiver to Adult Criminal Courts: Prototypes for Dangerousness, Sophistication-Maturity, and Amenability to Treatment." *Psychology, Public Policy, and Law* 7 (2): 381–408.

Sameroff, A. J. 1995. "General Systems Theories and Developmental Psychopathology." In *Theory and Methods*. Vol. 1 of *Developmental Psychopathology*, edited by D. D. Cicchetti and D. J. Cohen, 659–695. Oxford, UK: John Wiley and Sons.

Sampson, R. J. 2006. "How Does Community Context Matter? Social Mechanisms and the Explanation of Crime." In *The Explanation of Crime: Context, Mechanisms, and Development*, edited by P.-O. H. Wikström and R. J. Sampson, 31–60. New York: Cambridge University Press.

Sampson, R., and J. Bartusch. 1998. "Legal Cynicism and (Subcultural?) Tolerance of Deviance: The Neighborhood Context of Racial Differences." *Law and Society Review* 32 (4): 777–804.

Sampson, R. J., and J. H. Laub. 1993. *Crime in the Making: Pathways and Turning Points through Life*. Cambridge, MA: Harvard University Press.

———. 1995. "Understanding Variability in Lives through Time: Contributions of Life-Course Criminology." *Studies on Crime and Crime Prevention* 4:143–158.

———. 2005a. "A General Age-Graded Theory of Crime: Lessons Learned and the Future of Life-Course Criminology." In *Integrated Developmental and Life Course Theories of Offending*, edited by D. Farrington, 165–182. New Brunswick, NJ: Transaction.

———. 2005b. "A Life-Course View of the Development of Crime." *Annals of the American Academy of Political and Social Science* 602:12–45.

———. 2005c. "Seductions of Method: Rejoinder to Nagin and Tremblay's 'Developmental Trajectory Groups: Fact or Fiction?'" *Criminology* 43:905–913.

———. 2016. "Turning Points and the Future of Life-Course Criminology: Reflections on the 1986 Criminal Careers Report." *Journal of Research in Crime and Delinquency* 53:321–335.

Sampson, R. J., J. H. Laub, and C. Wimer. 2006. "Does Marriage Reduce Crime? A Counterfactual Approach to Within-Individual Causal Effects." *Criminology* 44:465–508.

Sanborn, J. B., Jr. 1992. "Pleading Guilty in Juvenile Court: Minimal Ado about Something Very Important to Young Defendants." *Justice Quarterly* 9 (1): 127–150.

Sanders, M. R., and T. G. Mazzucchelli. 2013. "The Promotion of Self-Regulation through Parenting Interventions." *Clinical Child and Family Psychology Review* 16 (1): 1–17.

Savaya, R., S. Spiro, and R. Elran-Barak. 2008. "Sustainability of Social Programs: A Comparative Case Study Analysis." *American Journal of Evaluation* 29 (4): 478–493.

Schall v. Martin. 1984. 467 U.S. 253.

Schneider, A. L. 2009. "Why Do Some Boundary Organizations Result in New Ideas and Practices and Others Only Meet Resistance? Examples from Juvenile Justice." *American Review of Public Administration* 39 (1): 60–79.

Schneider, A. L., and L. Ervin. 1990. "Specific Deterrence, Rational Choice, and Decision Heuristics: Applications in Juvenile Justice." *Social Science Quarterly* 71 (3): 585–601.

Schubert, C. A., E. P. Mulvey, L. Steinberg, E. Cauffman, S. H. Losoya, T. Hecker, and G. P. Knight. 2004. "Operational Lessons from the Pathways to Desistance Project." *Youth Violence and Juvenile Justice* 2:237–255.

Schultz, J. L. 1973. "The Cycle of Juvenile Court History." *Crime and Delinquency* 19 (4): 457–476.

Schur, E. M. 1973. *Radical Nonintervention: Rethinking the Delinquency Problem.* Englewood Cliffs, NJ: Prentice-Hall.

Schwalbe, C. S. 2007. "Risk Assessment for Juvenile Justice: A Meta-analysis." *Law and Human Behavior* 31 (5): 449–462.

———. 2012. "Toward an Integrated Theory of Probation." *Criminal Justice and Behavior* 39 (2): 185–201.

Schwalbe, C. S., M. W. Fraser, S. H. Day, and V. Cooley. 2006. "Classifying Juvenile Offenders According to Risk of Recidivism: Predictive Validity, Race/Ethnicity, and Gender." *Criminal Justice and Behavior* 33 (3): 305–324.

Schwalbe, C. S., R. E. Gearing, M. J. MacKenzie, K. B. Brewer, and R. Ibrahim. 2012. "A Meta-analysis of Experimental Studies of Diversion Programs for Juvenile Offenders." *Clinical Psychology Review* 32 (1): 26–33.

Schwalbe, C. S., and T. Maschi. 2009. "Investigating Probation Strategies with Juvenile Offenders: The Influence of Officers' Attitudes and Youth Characteristics." *Law and Human Behavior* 33:357–367.

Schwartz, J., D. J. Steffensmeier, and B. Feldmeyer. 2009. "Assessing Trends in Women's Violence via Data Triangulation: Arrests, Convictions, Incarcerations, and Victim Reports." *Social Problems* 56 (3): 494–525.

Schwartz, R. G. 2001. "Juvenile Justice and Positive Youth Development." In *Youth Development: Issues, Challenges and Directions*, 231–267. Philadelphia, PA: Public/Private Ventures.

Scott, E. S., N. D. Reppucci, and J. L. Woolard. 1995. "Evaluating Adolescent Decision Making in Legal Contexts." *Law and Human Behavior* 19 (3): 221–244.

Scott, E. S., and L. D. Steinberg. 2008. *Rethinking Juvenile Justice.* Cambridge, MA: Harvard University Press.

Sedlak, A. J., and McPherson, K. 2010. *Survey of Youth in Residential Placement: Youth's Needs and Services.* Rockville, MD: Westat.

Seligman, M.E.P., and M. Csikszentmihalyi. 2014. "Positive Psychology: An Introduction." In *Flow and the Foundations of Positive Psychology: The Collected Works of Mihaly Csikszentmihalyi*, 279–298. Dordrecht: Springer Netherlands.

Senjo, S. R., and L. A. Leip. 2001. "Testing and Developing Theory in Drug Court: A Four-Part Logit Model to Predict Program Completion." *Criminal Justice Policy Review* 12 (1): 66–87.

Sexton, T. L., and J. Alexander. 2000. *Functional Family Therapy.* Washington, DC: Office of Juvenile Justice and Delinquency Prevention.

Shader, M. 2001. *Risk Factors for Delinquency: An Overview.* Washington, DC: Office of Juvenile Justice and Delinquency Prevention.

Sharkey, P., and R. J. Sampson. 2010. "Destination Effects: Residential Mobility and Trajectories of Adolescent Violence in a Stratified Metropolis." *Criminology* 48 (3): 639–681.

Shaw, C. R. (1930) 1966. *The Jack-Roller: A Delinquent Boy's Own Story.* Chicago: University of Chicago Press.

Shelden, R. G. 1999. *Detention Diversion Advocacy: An Evaluation.* Washington, DC: U.S. Department of Justice.

Sherman, L. W., D. C. Gottfredson, D. L. MacKenzie, J. Eck, P. Reuter, and S. D. Bushway. 1998. *Preventing Crime: What Works, What Doesn't, What's Promising; Research in Brief.* Washington, DC: National Institute of Justice.

Sherman, L. W., D. L. MacKenzie, D. P. Farrington, and B. C. Welsh. 2002. *Evidence-Based Crime Prevention.* London: Routledge.

Shlonsky, A., and D. Wagner. 2005. "The Next Step: Integrating Actuarial Risk Assessment and Clinical Judgment into an Evidence-Based Practice Framework in CPS Case Management." *Children and Youth Services Review* 27 (4): 409–427.

Shover, N. 1985. *Aging Criminals.* Beverly Hills, CA: Sage.

Shufelt, J. L., and J. J. Cocozza. 2006. *Youth with Mental Health Disorders in the Juvenile Justice System: Results from a Multi-state Prevalence Study.* Delmar, NY: National Center for Mental Health and Juvenile Justice.

Sickmund, M., and C. Puzzanchera. 2014. *Juvenile Offenders and Victims: 2014 National Report.* Washington, DC: Office of Juvenile Justice and Delinquency Prevention.

Sickmund, M., A. Sladky, and W. Kang. 2017. "Easy Access to Juvenile Court Statistics: 1985–2014." Available at https://www.ojjdp.gov/ojstatbb/ezajcs.

Siennick, S. E., and D. W. Osgood. 2008. "A Review of Research on the Impact on Crime of Transitions to Adult Roles." In *The Long View of Crime: A Synthesis of Longitudinal Research*, edited by A. Liberman, 161–187. New York: Springer.

Silver, E., and L. L. Miller. 2002. "A Cautionary Note on the Use of Actuarial Risk Assessment Tools for Social Control." *Crime and Delinquency* 48 (1): 138–161.

Simon, H. A. 1972. "Theories of Bounded Rationality." *Decision and Organization* 1 (1): 161–176.

Simons, R. L., L. G. Simons, and L. E. Wallace. 2004. *Families, Delinquency, and Crime: Linking Society's Most Basic Institution to Antisocial Behavior.* Los Angeles, CA: Roxbury.

Simpson, D. D. 2002. "A Conceptual Framework for Transferring Research to Practice." *Journal of Substance Abuse Treatment* 22 (4): 171–182.

Singer, S. I. 1996. "Merging and Emerging Systems of Juvenile and Criminal Justice." *Law and Policy* 18 (1–2): 1–15.

———. 1997. *Recriminalizing Delinquency: Violent Juvenile Crime and Juvenile Justice Reform.* New York: Cambridge University Press.

———. 2014. *America's Safest City: Delinquency and Modernity in Suburbia.* New York: New York University Press.

Sisk, C. L., and J. L. Zehr. 2005. "Pubertal Hormones Organize the Adolescent Brain and Behavior." *Frontiers in Neuroendocrinology* 26 (3–4): 163–174.

Skardhamar, T. 2009. "Reconsidering the Theory on Adolescent-Limited and Life-Course Persistent Anti-social Behaviour." *British Journal of Criminology* 49:863–879.

Skeem, J. L., and S. Manchak. 2008. "Back to the Future: From Klockars' Model of Effective Supervision to Evidence-Based Practice in Probation." *Journal of Offender Rehabilitation* 47 (3): 220–247.

Skowyra, K., and J. J. Cocozza. 2006. *A Blueprint for Change: Improving the System Response to Youth with Mental Health Needs Involved with the Juvenile Justice System.* Delmar, NY: National Center for Mental Health and Juvenile Justice.

Slaby, R. G., and N. G. Guerra. 1988. "Cognitive Mediators of Aggression in Adolescent Offenders." *Developmental Psychology* 24 (4): 580–588.

Smetana, J., N. Campione-Barr, and A. Metzger. 2005. "Adolescent Development in Interpersonal and Societal Contexts." *Annual Review of Psychology* 57:255–284.

Smetana, J. G., M. Jambon, and C. Ball. 2014. "The Social Domain Approach to Children's Moral and Social Judgments." In *Handbook of Moral Development,* vol. 2, edited by M. Killen and J. G. Smetana, 23–45. New York: Psychology Press.

Smith, A. R., J. Chein, and L. Steinberg. 2013. "Impact of Socio-emotional Context, Brain Development, and Pubertal Maturation on Adolescent Risk-Taking." *Hormones and Behavior* 64 (2): 323–332.

Snyder, H. N. 1998. "Serious, Violent, and Chronic Juvenile Offenders: An Assessment of the Extent of and Trends in Officially Recognized Serious Criminal Behavior in a Delinquent Population." In *Serious and Violent Juvenile Offenders: Risk Factors and Successful Interventions,* edited by R. Loeber and D. Farrington, 428–444. Thousand Oaks, CA: Sage.

———. 2012. "Juvenile Delinquents and Juvenile Justice Clientele: Trends and Patterns in Crime and Justice System Responses." In *The Oxford Handbook of Juvenile Crime and Juvenile Justice,* edited by B. C. Feld and D. Bishop, 3–30. New York: Oxford University Press.

Snyder, H. N., and C. McCurley. 2008. "Domestic Assaults by Juvenile Offenders." *Juvenile Justice Bulletin,* November. Available at https://www.ncjrs.gov/pdffiles1/ojjdp/219180.pdf.

Snyder, H., and J. Mulako-Wangota. 2017. "Easy Access to FBI Arrest Statistics: 1994–2014." Available at https://www.ojjdp.gov/ojstatbb/ezaucr/asp/ucr_display.asp.

Snyder, H. N., and M. Sickmund. 2006. *Juvenile Offenders and Victims: 2006 National Report*. Washington, DC: Office of Juvenile Justice and Delinquency Prevention.

Snyder, J., L. Schrepferman, J. Oeser, G. Patterson, M. Stoolmiller, K. Johnson, and A. Snyder. 2005. "Deviancy Training and Association with Deviant Peers in Young Children: Occurrence and Contribution to Early-Onset Conduct Problems." *Development and Psychopathology* 17 (2): 397–413.

Spear, L. P. 2000. "The Adolescent Brain and Age-Related Behavioral Manifestations." *Neuroscience and Biobehavioral Reviews* 24 (4): 417–463.

Spoth, R. L., K. A. Kavanagh, and T. J. Dishion. 2002. "Family-Centered Preventive Intervention Science: Toward Benefits to Larger Populations of Children, Youth, and Families." *Prevention Science* 3 (3): 145–152.

Stahlkopf, C., M. Males, and D. Macallair. 2010. "Testing Incapacitation Theory: Youth Crime and Incarceration in California." *Crime and Delinquency* 56 (2): 253–268.

Stanfield, R. 1999. *Overview: The JDAI Story; Building a Better Juvenile Detention System*. Baltimore, MD: Annie E. Casey Foundation.

Steffensmeier, D., and J. Schwartz. 2009. "Trends in Girls' Delinquency and the Gender Gap: Statistical Assessment of Diverse Sources." In *The Delinquent Girl*, edited by M. A. Zahn, 50–83. Philadelphia, PA: Temple University Press.

Steinberg, L. 2005. "Cognitive and Affective Development in Adolescence." *Trends in Cognitive Sciences* 9 (2): 69–74.

———. 2007. "Risk Taking in Adolescence: New Perspectives from Brain and Behavioral Science." *Current Directions in Psychological Science* 16 (2): 55–59.

———. 2008. "A Social Neuroscience Perspective on Adolescent Risk-Taking." *Developmental Review* 28 (1): 78–106.

———. 2010. "A Dual Systems Model of Adolescent Risk-Taking." *Developmental Psychobiology* 52 (3): 216–224.

———. 2014. *Age of Opportunity: Lessons from the New Science of Adolescence*. Boston: Houghton Mifflin Harcourt.

Steinberg, L., D. Albert, E. Cauffman, M. Banich, S. Graham, and J. Woolard. 2008. "Age Differences in Sensation Seeking and Impulsivity as Indexed by Behavior and Self-Report: Evidence for a Dual Systems Model." *Developmental Psychology* 44 (6): 1764–1778.

Steinberg, L., and A. S. Morris. 2001. "Adolescent Development." *Annual Review of Psychology* 2:55–87.

Steinhart, D. J. 1996. "Status Offenses." *Future of Children* 6 (3): 86–99.

———. 2006. *A Practical Guide to Juvenile Detention Risk Assessment*. Baltimore, MD: Annie E. Casey Foundation.

Stinchcomb, J. B., G. Bazemore, and N. Riestenberg. 2006. "Beyond Zero Tolerance: Restoring Justice in Secondary Schools." *Youth Violence and Juvenile Justice* 4 (2): 123–147.

Stolzenberg, L., and S. J. D'Alessio. 2008. "Co-offending and the Age-Crime Curve." *Journal of Research in Crime and Delinquency* 45 (1): 65–86.

Sukhodolsky, D. G., H. Kassinove, and B. S. Gorman. 2004. "Cognitive-Behavioral Therapy for Anger in Children and Adolescents: A Meta-analysis." *Aggression and Violent Behavior* 9 (3): 247–269.

Sullivan, C. J. 2006. "Early Adolescent Delinquency: Assessing the Role of Childhood Problems, Family Environment, and Peer Pressure." *Youth Violence and Juvenile Justice* 4 (4): 291–313.

———. 2013. "Change in Offending across the Life Course." In *The Oxford Handbook of Criminological Theory*, edited by F. Cullen and P. Wilcox, 205–225. Oxford: Oxford University Press.

———. 2014. "Individual, Social, and Neighborhood Influences on the Launch of Adolescent Antisocial Behavior." *Youth Violence and Juvenile Justice* 12:103–120.

Sullivan, C. J., L. Blair, E. Latessa, and C. C. Sullivan. 2016. "Juvenile Drug Courts and Recidivism: Results from a Multisite Outcome Study." *Justice Quarterly* 33 (2): 291–318.

Sullivan, C. J., K. Childs, and S. Gann. 2019. "Peers." In *Oxford Handbook of Developmental and Life-Course Criminology*, edited by D. Farrington, L. Kazemian, and A. Piquero, 404–431. New York: Oxford University Press.

Sullivan, C. J., K. K. Childs, and D. O'Connell. 2009. "Adolescent Risk Behavior Subgroups: An Empirical Assessment." *Journal of Youth and Adolescence* 39 (5): 541–562.

Sullivan, C. J., N. Dollard, B. Sellers, and J. Mayo. 2010. "Rebalancing Response to School-Based Offenses: A Civil Citation Program." *Youth Violence and Juvenile Justice* 8 (4): 279–294.

Sullivan, C. J., and Z. K. Hamilton. 2007. "Exploring Careers in Deviance: A Joint Trajectory Analysis of Criminal Behavior and Substance Use in an Offender Population." *Deviant Behavior* 28 (6): 497–523.

Sullivan, C. J., and P. Hirschfield. 2011. "Problem Behavior in the Middle School Years: An Assessment of the Social Development Model." *Journal of Research in Crime and Delinquency* 48:566–593.

Sullivan, C. J., and D. Jolliffe. 2012. "Peer Influence, Mentoring, and the Prevention of Crime." In *The Oxford Handbook of Crime Prevention*, edited by B. C. Welsh and D. P. Farrington, 207–225. New York: Oxford University Press.

Sullivan, C. J., and E. Latessa. 2011. "The Coproduction of Outcomes: An Integrated Assessment of Youth and Program Effects on Recidivism." *Youth Violence and Juvenile Justice* 9 (3): 191–206.

Sullivan, C. J., E. Latessa, S. Spiegel, S. Gann, D. Mueller, H. McManus, R. Engel, J. Wooldredge, and O. Ilchi. 2016. *Ohio Disproportionate Minority Contact (DMC) Assessment: Final Report*. Columbus, OH: Ohio Department of Youth Services.

Sullivan, C. J., and J. Newsome. 2015. "Psychosocial and Genetic Risk Markers for Longitudinal Trends in Delinquency: An Empirical Assessment and Practical Discussion." *Criminal Justice Studies* 28 (1): 61–83.

Sullivan, C. J., G. C. Ousey, and P. Wilcox. 2016. "Similar Mechanisms? A Comparative Longitudinal Study of Adolescent Violence and Victimization." *Journal of Interpersonal Violence* 31:1367–1392.

Sullivan, C. J., and A. R. Piquero. 2011. "Criminal Career Research: A Statistical and Substantive Comparison of Growth Modeling Approaches." In *Measuring Crime and Criminality*, edited by J. MacDonald, 267–298. New Brunswick, NJ: Transaction.

Sullivan, C. J., A. P. Piquero, and F. T. Cullen. 2012. "Like Before, but Better: The Lessons of Developmental, Life-Course Criminology for Contemporary Juvenile Justice." *Victims and Offenders* 7:450–471.

Sullivan, C. J., B. M. Veysey, Z. K. Hamilton, and M. Grillo. 2007. "Reducing Out-of-Community Placement and Recidivism: Diversion of Delinquent Youth with Mental

Health and Substance Use Problems from the Justice System." *International Journal of Offender Therapy and Comparative Criminology* 51 (5): 555–577.

Sullivan, C. J., B. C. Welsh, and O. S. Ilchi. 2017. "Modeling the Scaling Up of Early Crime Prevention." *Criminology and Public Policy* 16 (2): 457–485.

Sullivan, M. L. 1989. *"Getting Paid": Youth Crime and Work in the Inner City*. Ithaca, NY: Cornell University Press.

———. 2004. "Youth Perspectives on the Experience of Reentry." *Youth Violence and Juvenile Justice* 2 (1): 56–71.

Sweeten, G. 2006. "Who Will Graduate? Disruption of High School Education by Arrest and Court Involvement." *Justice Quarterly* 23 (4): 462–480.

———. 2012. "Scaling Criminal Offending." *Journal of Quantitative Criminology* 28:533–557.

Sweeten, G., and R. Apel. 2007. "Incapacitation: Revisiting an Old Question with a New Method and New Data." *Journal of Quantitative Criminology* 23 (4): 303–326.

Sweeten, G., A. Piquero, and L. Steinberg. 2013. "Age and the Explanation of Crime, Revisited." *Journal of Youth and Adolescence* 42:921–938.

Tanenhaus, D. S. 2004. *Juvenile Justice in the Making*. New York: Oxford University Press.

Taxman, F. S., D. W. Young, B. Wiersema, A. Rhodes, and S. Mitchell 2007. "The National Criminal Justice Treatment Practices Survey: Multilevel Survey Methods and Procedures." *Journal of Substance Abuse Treatment* 32 (3): 225–238.

Teplin, L. A., K. M. Abram, G. M. McClelland, M. K. Dulcan, and A. A. Mericle. 2002. "Psychiatric Disorders in Youth in Juvenile Detention." *Archives of General Psychiatry* 59 (12): 1133–1143.

Texas Attorney General. 2016. *Texas Juvenile Justice Handbook, 2016*. Austin: Office of Texas Attorney General.

Theriot, M. T. 2009. "School Resource Officers and the Criminalization of Student Behavior." *Journal of Criminal Justice* 37 (3): 280–287.

Thoma, S. J., and J. R. Rest. 1999. "The Relationship between Moral Decision Making and Patterns of Consolidation and Transition in Moral Judgment Development." *Developmental Psychology* 35 (2): 323.

Thornberry, T. P. 1987. "Toward an Interactional Theory of Delinquency." *Criminology* 25:863–891.

———. 1997. "Introduction: Some advantages of Developmental and Life-Course Perspectives for the Study of Crime and Delinquency." *Developmental Theories of Crime and Delinquency*, vol. 7, edited by T. P. Thornberry, 1–10. New Brunswick, NJ: Transaction.

Thornberry, T. P., D. Huizinga, and R. Loeber. 2004. "The Causes and Correlates Studies: Findings and Policy Implications." *Juvenile Justice* 9 (1): 3–19.

Thornberry, T. P., and M. D. Krohn. 2000. "The Self-Report Method for Measuring Delinquency and Crime." *Criminal Justice* 4:33–83.

———. 2003. "Comparison of Self-Report and Official Data for Measuring Crime." In *Measurement Problems in Criminal Justice Research: Workshop Summary*, edited by J. V. Pepper and C. V. Petrie, 43–94. Washington, DC: National Academies Press.

———. 2005. "Applying Interactional Theory to the Explanation of Continuity and Change in Antisocial Behavior." In *Integrated Developmental and Life-Course Theories of Offending*, edited by D. P. Farrington, 183–209. New Brunswick, NJ: Transaction.

Thornberry, T. P., M. D. Krohn, A. J. Lizotte, and D. Chard-Wierschem. 1993. "The Role of Juvenile Gangs in Facilitating Delinquent Behavior." *Journal of Research in Crime and Delinquency* 30 (1): 55–87.

Thornberry, T. P., M. Moore, and R. Christenson. 1985. "The Effect of Dropping Out of High School on Subsequent Criminal Behavior." *Criminology* 23:3–18.

Thornberry, T. P., C. A. Smith, C. Rivera, D. Huizinga, and M. Stouthamer-Loeber. 1999. *Family Disruption and Delinquency*. Washington, DC: Office of Juvenile Justice and Delinquency Prevention.

Tisak, M. S., and A. M. Jankowski. 1996. "Societal Rule Evaluations: Adolescent Offenders' Reasoning about Moral, Conventional, and Personal Rules." *Aggressive Behavior* 22 (3): 195–207.

Tisak, M. S., J. Tisak, and S. E. Goldstein. 2006. "Aggression, Delinquency, and Morality: A Social-Cognitive Perspective." In *Handbook of Moral Development*, edited by M. Killen and J. G. Smetana, 611–629. Mahwah, NJ: Lawrence Erlbaum.

Tolan, P. H., and P. Thomas. 1995. "The Implications of Age of Onset for Delinquency Risk II: Longitudinal Data." *Journal of Abnormal Child Psychology* 23:157–181.

Tonry, M. 2006. "Purposes and Functions of Sentencing." *Crime and Justice* 34 (1): 1–53.

———. 2008. "Learning from the Limitations of Deterrence Research." *Crime and Justice* 37 (1): 279–311.

Torbet, P. M. 1996. "Juvenile Probation: The Workhorse of the Juvenile Justice System." *Juvenile Justice Bulletin*, March. Available at https://www.ncjrs.gov/pdffiles/workhors.pdf.

Turiel, E. 2006. "Thought, Emotions, and Social Interactional Processes in Moral Development." In *Handbook of Moral Development*, edited by M. Killen and J. G. Smetana, 7–35. Mahwah, NJ: Lawrence Erlbaum.

Turiel, E. 2014. "Morality: Epistemology, Development, and Social Opposition." In *Handbook of Moral Development*, vol. 2, edited by M. Killen and J. G. Smetana, 3–22. New York: Psychology Press.

Turner, K. M., J. M. Nicholson, and M. R. Sanders. 2011. "The Role of Practitioner Self-Efficacy, Training, Program and Workplace Factors on the Implementation of an Evidence-Based Parenting Intervention in Primary Care." *Journal of Primary Prevention* 32 (2): 95–112.

Turner, R. J., B. G. Frankel, and D. M. Levin. 1983. "Social Support: Conceptualization, Measurement, and Implications for Mental Health." *Research in Community and Mental Health* 3:67–111.

Tyler, T. R., and L. E. Rankin. 2012. "Legal Socialization and Delinquency." In *The Oxford Handbook of Juvenile Crime and Juvenile Justice*, edited by B. C. Feld and D. Bishop, 353–372. New York: Oxford University Press.

Uggen, C., and S. Wakefield. 2005. "Young Adults Reentering the Community from the Criminal Justice System: The Challenge." In *On Your Own Without a Net: The Transition to Adulthood for Vulnerable Populations*, edited by D. W. Osgood, M. Foster, C. Flanagan, and G. R. Ruth, 114–144. Chicago: University of Chicago Press.

U.S. Census Bureau. 2018. "Quick Facts: United States." Available at https://www.census.gov/quickfacts.

U.S. Surgeon General. 2000. *Report of the Surgeon General's Conference on Children's Mental Health: A National Action Agenda*. Washington, DC: Department of Health and Human Services.

U.S. Surgeon General. 2001. *Youth Violence: A Report of the Surgeon General*. Washington, DC: Department of Health and Human Services.

Van Der Laan, A. M., M. Blom, and E. R. Kleemans. 2009. "Exploring Long-Term and Short-Term Risk Factors for Serious Delinquency." *European Journal of Criminology* 6 (5): 419–438.

Van Domburgh, L., R. Loeber, D. Bezemer, R. Stallings, and M. Stouthamer-Loeber. 2009. "Childhood Predictors of Desistance and Level of Persistence in Offending in Early Onset Offenders." *Journal of Abnormal Child Psychology* 37:967–980.

van Mastrigt, S. B., and D. P. Farrington. 2009. "Co-offending, Age, Gender and Crime Type: Implications for Criminal Justice Policy." *British Journal of Criminology* 49 (4): 552–573.

Van Slyke, D. M. 2003. "The Mythology of Privatization in Contracting for Social Services." *Public Administration Review* 63 (3): 296–315.

Vazsonyi, A. T., J. Mikuška, and E. L. Kelley. 2017. "It's Time: A Meta-analysis on the Self-Control-Deviance Link." *Journal of Criminal Justice* 48:48–63.

Vieira, T. A., T. A. Skilling, and M. Peterson-Badali. 2009. "Matching Court-Ordered Services with Treatment Needs: Predicting Treatment Success with Young Offenders." *Criminal Justice and Behavior* 36 (4): 385–401.

Vincent, G. M., L. S. Guy, and T. Grisso. 2012. *Risk Assessment in Juvenile Justice: A Guidebook for Implementation*. Washington, DC: MacArthur Foundation.

Vincent, G. M., and B. Lovins. 2015. "Using a Decision Matrix to Guide Juvenile Dispositions." *Criminology and Public Policy* 14 (1): 51–58.

Virginia Department of Juvenile Justice. 2015. "Data Resource Guide, 2014." Available at http://www.djj.virginia.gov/pdf/about-djj/DRG/FY2014_DRG.pdf.

Von Hirsch, A. 1992. "Proportionality in the Philosophy of Punishment." *Crime and Justice*, vol. 16, edited by M. Tonry, 55–98. Chicago: University of Chicago Press.

Walker, L. J. 2014. "Moral Personality, Motivation, and Identity." In *Handbook of Moral Development*, vol. 2, edited by M. Killen and J. G. Smetana, 497–519. New York: Psychology Press.

Walters, S. T., M. D. Clark, R. Gingerich, and M. L. Meltzer. 2007. *Motivating Offenders to Change: A Guide for Probation and Parole*. Washington, DC: U.S. Department of Justice.

Wandersman, A. 2003. "Community Science: Bridging the Gap between Science and Practice with Community-Centered Models." *American Journal of Community Psychology* 31 (3–4): 227–242.

Wandersman, A., J. Duffy, P. Flaspohler, R. Noonan, K. Lubell, L. Stillman, M. Blachman, R. Dunville, and J. Saul. 2008. "Bridging the Gap between Prevention Research and Practice: The Interactive Systems Framework for Dissemination and Implementation." *American Journal of Community Psychology* 41 (3–4): 171–181.

Ward, G., and A. Kupchik. 2009. "Accountable to What? Professional Orientations towards Accountability-Based Juvenile Justice." *Punishment and Society* 11 (1): 85–109.

———. 2010. "What Drives Juvenile Probation Officers? Relating Organizational Contexts, Status Characteristics, and Personal Convictions to Treatment and Punishment Orientations." *Crime and Delinquency* 56 (1): 35–69.

Ward, T. 2010. "Punishment or Therapy? The Ethics of Sexual Offending Treatment." *Journal of Sexual Aggression* 16 (3): 286–295.

Ward, T., J. Melser, and P. M. Yates. 2007. "Reconstructing the Risk-Need-Responsivity Model: A Theoretical Elaboration and Evaluation." *Aggression and Violent Behavior* 12 (2): 208–228.

Warr, M. 1998. "Life Course Transitions and Desistance from Crime." *Criminology* 36:183–215.

———. 2002. *Companions in Crime: The Social Aspects of Criminal Conduct.* New York: Cambridge University Press.

Washington State Caseload Forecast Council. 2017. *2016 Washington State Juvenile Disposition Guidelines Manual.* Available at https://www.cfc.wa.gov/CriminalJustice _JUV_SEN.htm.

Weerman, F. M. 2003. "Co-offending as Social Exchange. Explaining Characteristics of Co-offending." *British Journal of Criminology* 43 (2): 398–416.

Weisburd, D., N. A. Morris, and E. R. Groff. 2009. "Hot Spots of Juvenile Crime: A Longitudinal Study of Arrest Incidents at Street Segments in Seattle, Washington." *Journal of Quantitative Criminology* 25 (4): 443–467.

Weiss, C. H. 1995. "Nothing as Practical as Good Theory: Exploring Theory-Based Evaluation for Comprehensive Community Initiatives for Children and Families." *New Approaches to Evaluating Community Initiatives: Concepts, Methods, and Contexts* 1:65–92.

Weiss, C. H., and M. J. Bucuvalas. 1980. *Social Science Research and Decision-Making.* New York: Columbia University Press.

Weisz, J. R., B. Weiss, S. S. Han, D. A. Granger, and T. Morton. 1995. "Effects of Psychotherapy with Children and Adolescents Revisited: A Meta-analysis of Treatment Outcome Studies." *Psychological Bulletin* 117 (3): 450–468.

Welsh, B. C., C. J. Sullivan, and D. L. Olds. 2010. "When Early Crime Prevention Goes to Scale: A New Look at the Evidence." *Prevention Science* 11:115–125.

Whitebread, C., and J. Heilman. 1988. "An Overview of the Law of Juvenile Delinquency." *Behavioral Sciences and the Law* 6 (3): 285–305.

White House Office of the Press Secretary. 2016. "Presidential Proclamation: National Youth Justice Month, 2016." September 30. Available at https://obamawhitehouse .archives.gov/the-press-office/2016/09/30/presidential-proclamation-national -youth-justice-awareness-month-2016.

Wikström, P.-O. H. 2005. "The Social Origins of Pathways to Crime: Towards a Developmental Ecological Action Theory of Crime Involvement and Its Changes." In *Integrated Developmental and Life-Course Theories of Offending*, edited by D. P. Farrington, 211–246. New Brunswick, NJ: Transaction.

———. 2006. "Individuals, Settings, and Acts of Crime: Situational Mechanisms and the Explanation of Crime." In *The Explanation of Crime: Context, Mechanisms and Development*, edited by P.-O. H. Wikström and R. J. Sampson, 61–107. New York: Cambridge University Press.

Wikström, P.-O. H., and D. A. Butterworth. 2006. *Adolescent Crime: Individual Differences and Lifestyles.* Devon, UK: Willan.

Wikström, P.-O. H., and R. Loeber. 2000. "Do Disadvantaged Neighborhoods Cause Well-Adjusted Children to Become Adolescent Delinquents? A Study of Male Juvenile Serious Offending, Individual Risk and Protective Factors, and Neighborhood Context." *Criminology* 38:1109–1142.

Wikström, P.-O. H., and R. J. Sampson. 2003. "Social Mechanisms of Community Influences on Crime and Pathways in Criminality." In *The Causes of Conduct Disorder and Serious Juvenile Delinquency*, edited by T. E. Moffitt, B. B. Lahey, and A. Caspi, 118–148. New York: Guilford Press.

Wilcox, P., C. J. Sullivan, S. Jones, and J. L. Van Gelder. 2014. "Personality and Opportunity: An Integrated Approach to Offending and Victimization." *Criminal Justice and Behavior* 41 (7): 880–901.

Williams, J. R., and M. Gold. 1972. "From Delinquent Behavior to Official Delinquency." *Social Problems* 20 (2): 209–229.

Wilson, J. J., and J. C. Howell. 1995. "Comprehensive Strategy for Serious, Violent, and Chronic Juvenile Offenders." In *Serious, Violent, and Chronic Juvenile Offenders: A Sourcebook*, edited by J. C. Howell, B. Krisberg, J. D. Hawkins, and J. J. Wilson, 36–46. Thousand Oaks, CA: Sage.

Winokur-Early, K., G. A. Hand, and J. L. Blankenship. 2012. *Validity and Reliability of the Florida PACT Risk and Needs Assessment Instrument: A Three-Phase Evaluation.* Tallahassee, FL: Justice Research Center.

Wolfgang, M. E., R. M. Figlio, and T. Sellin. 1972. *Delinquency in a Birth Cohort.* Chicago: University of Chicago Press.

Woolard, J. L., M. R. Fondacaro, and C. Slobogin. 2001. "Informing Juvenile Justice Policy: Directions for Behavioral Science Research." *Law and Human Behavior* 25 (1): 13–24.

Wordes, M., and S. M. Jones. 1998. "Trends in Juvenile Detention and Steps toward Reform." *Crime and Delinquency* 44 (4): 544–560.

Yeager, D. S., C. Romero, D. Paunesku, C. S. Hulleman, B. Schneider, C. Hinojosa, H. Y. Lee, J. O'Brien, K. Flint, A. Roberts, J. Trott, D. Greene, G. M. Walton, and C. S. Dweck. 2016. "Using Design Thinking to Improve Psychological Interventions: The Case of the Growth Mindset during the Transition to High School." *Journal of Educational Psychology* 108 (3): 374–391.

Yoshikawa, H. 1994. "Prevention as Cumulative Protection: Effects of Early Family Support and Education on Chronic Delinquency and Its Risks." *Psychological Bulletin* 115 (1): 28–54.

Zahn, M. 2009. *The Delinquent Girl.* Philadelphia, PA: Temple University Press.

Zimmerman, G. M., and S. F. Messner. 2011. "Neighborhood Context and Nonlinear Peer Effects on Adolescent Violent Crime." *Criminology* 49:873–903.

Zimring, F. E. 2005a. *American Juvenile Justice.* New York: Oxford University Press.

———. 2005b. "Minimizing Harm from Minority Disproportion in American Juvenile Justice." In *Our Children, Their Children: Confronting Racial and Ethnic Differences in American Juvenile Justice*, edited by D. F. Hawkins and K. Kempf-Leonard, 413–427. Chicago: University of Chicago Press.

Zimring, F. E., and H. Laqueur. 2015. "Kids, Groups, and Crime: In Defense of Conventional Wisdom." *Journal of Research in Crime and Delinquency* 52 (3): 403–413.

Zimring, F. E., and D. S. Tanenhaus, eds. 2014. *Choosing the Future for American Juvenile Justice.* New York: New York University Press.

Index

Page numbers in italics indicate material in figures or tables.

Christopher J. Sullivan is Professor and Graduate Program Director in the School of Criminal Justice at the University of Cincinnati.